HOMESCHOOL YOUR CHILD FOR FREE

LauraMaery Gold
and
Joan M. Zielinski

HOMESCHOOL YOUR CHILD FOR FREE

More Than 1,200 Smart, Effective,
and Practical Resources for Home
Education on the Internet and Beyond

PRIMA PUBLISHING

3000 Lava Ridge Court • Roseville, California 95661
(800) 632-8676 • www.primalifestyles.com

PRIMA PUBLISHING and colophon are trademarks of Prima Communications Inc., registered with the United States Patent and Trademark Office.

All products mentioned in this book are trademarks of their respective companies. None of the manufacturers of such products have underwritten or in any way sponsored or endorsed this book. Neither the publisher nor the author have any financial interest in the products mentioned in this book.

Efforts have been made to make this book complete and accurate as of the date of publication. In a time of rapid change, however, it is difficult to ensure that all information is entirely up-to-date. Although the publisher and author cannot be liable for any inaccuracies or omissions in this book, they are always grateful for corrections and suggestions for improvement.

Library of Congress Cataloging-in-Publication Data

Gold, LauraMaery.
    Homeschool your child for free : more than 1,200 smart, effective, and practical resources for home education on the Internet and beyond / LauraMaery Gold, Joan M. Zielinksi.
        p.   cm.
    Includes index.
    ISBN 0-7615-2513-0
    1. Home schooling—United States—Computer network resources—Handbooks, manuals, etc. 2. Internet in education—United States—Handbooks, manuals, etc. I. Zielinski, Joan M. II. Title.

LC40.G64 2000
371.04'2—dc21   00-042099
                                                                                                                        CIP

00 01 02 03 BB 10 9 8 7 6 5 4 3 2 1

Printed in the United States of America

How to Order

Single copies may be ordered from Prima Publishing, 3000 Lava Ridge Court, Roseville, CA 95661; telephone (800) 632-8676, ext 4444. Quantity discounts are also available. On your letterhead, include information concerning the intended use of the books and the number of books you wish to purchase.

Visit us online at www.primalifestyles.com

Contents

Foreword

ILIKE MY KIDS. They drive me crazy, but I have to say, I really like them. (I don't feel this way about other people's children, but then, other's people's children have been brought up by other people—and therein, very often, lies the difference.)

When my first child approached the age of five, I realized with a shock that very soon I was going to be expected to pack her off to kindergarten. I'd been to school; I knew what it was like. I looked at that sweet, fresh, intelligent child and felt rebellion welling up in my soul. I didn't feel at all good about shipping my baby away from home. In fact, I knew it was wrong. And the thought of somebody coming along and telling me what to do with my kid really made me angry.

At the time, homeschooling had not gained the grudging acceptance it enjoys today. The most anybody in my state knew about it hinged on a hot news story about a very fringe-y anarchist type who'd gotten in trouble with authorities over some homeschool-like issues. Fortunately, the media balanced that story with another, telling the story of a family that was keeping its kids peacefully and legally at home, educating them in everything from literature and math to auto mechanics. The images of that cheerful family working closely together resonated in my heart and mind, and I started poking around, looking for more information.

What I read was very encouraging. It made sense to me to keep a young child at home where he could feel safe and free to be himself. The more I thought about it, the more I realized that public schooling, a brilliant alternative to ignorance, was no match for a loving private education on any level—intellectual, emotional, or sociological—not when that education is overseen by earnest, excited parents who love life and children and who are still capable of wonder.

If homeschooling your kids seems like a daunting kind of thing, consider this: You once passed whatever grade your "students" are in—the same criteria that qualifies college professors. You knew your stuff then; you still know it. If you fear you've forgotten, the material in this book will jog your memory. And remember that the business of educating a child at home is really the business of shepherding the natural explorations of a born scientist. Because that's what children are—they probe and ask and experiment; they want to know things. Studies show that children learn at an astonishing rate until they are about five years old. Then, for some reason, the rate of learning typically slows between the ages of five and eighteen, at which point the curve mysteriously picks up again.

But in a safe, rich environment—one that allows a child to pursue her fascinations without pressure or competition, without threat of punishment for failing to meet arbitrary standards of performance—there is no reason for the rate of learning to slow. In this situation, it is not only the child's mind that blossoms and expands, but also her spirit, her confidence, her sense of self. Children brought up this way have no trouble carrying on a civilized, intelligent conversation with an adult. I know; I participate in this kind of conversation with my kids all the time.

If you're thinking about homeschooling because you really get a kick out of your kids, and you love learning and talking things over, if what you want for your children is an education that is far more broad and joyful and free than what the public schools can offer, then you are a prime candidate for homeschooling. Notice I say nothing here about credentials. A mind that is fascinated by the world around it qualifies a teacher, degree or no degree.

I warn you, though, of this: A parent who homeschools trades privacy and quiet for constant activity and intellectual stimulation. That parent also trades helpless, clueless children for mature young people who can function independently; a dislocated bunch of strangers who share the same house, for a cohesive, bonded family.

And remember that you can always use the schools as a resource. My kids, old enough to know what they wanted to learn, dipped into the high school curriculum for the classes they thought they'd enjoy.

My oldest child is now a senior at a major university and is the lead alto sax player in the school's world-renowned jazz band. My second child is in his first year of college and has a 3.8 grade point average. My third child, a daughter, is aiming for medical school and can tell you the name of every muscle and bone in your body. My baby knows more about computer graphics than most adults who walk the earth. Not bad for people who never graduated from high school.

My children, pretty much poised to launch themselves into their own lives, will always be my friends. And now, as they head out the door, I never say to myself, "Where did the time go?" I know where it went; I was there.

—Kristen Downey Randle
author and homeschooling mother of four

Kristen Downey Randle *is an author who has won numerous literary awards for her young adult novels* Breaking Rank *and* The Only Alien on the Planet. *She lives with her children, her husband, Guy, and two smiling dogs in a rambling house on the banks of a western river.*

Introduction

CAN YOU REALLY homeschool your child for free? Is it possible to give your children a full education, from preschool through high school, using nothing but free resources?

It's not only possible; it's already being done by lots of home educators.

"We get just about every bit of our curriculum from the Internet," says homeschooling mother Ann Crum, from central Arkansas. She's not alone. When I polled a large group of homeschoolers on one of my homeschool mailing lists, 28 percent described themselves as primarily reliant on free resources, and 46 percent said they relied on a mix of free resources and formal curricula.

Homeschooling from Internet resources takes a bit of effort on your part. What it doesn't require is a master's degree in education.

This book is set up to enable you to develop a solid curriculum—customized for your children—that complies with the legal requirements for your locality.

Once you've decided which subjects you'll be teaching and at which ages, you can gather teaching materials, handouts, texts, lesson plans, and everything else you require from the free resources categorized by subject throughout this book.

You'll also find non-Internet free resources, advice from experts about how to teach academic subjects, and information from homeschooling parents about how they homeschool.

And if that's not enough, owners of the book may also access the *Homeschool Your Child for Free!* Web site (www.hsfree.com) and register to find thousands of additional categorized and rated links. At our Web site, you'll find updates, a discussion forum, facilities for chatting with other homeschoolers, and sign-up information for the Homeschool Resources mailing list and newsletter.

CONVENTIONS

This book makes some assumptions about you and your homeschooled children:

- We assume *you like teaching*. Much of the material in this book will be as educational to you as it is to your child. As you read the resources found here, you'll find your own education expanding, and you'll discover that there's nothing you're not qualified to teach your kids.

- We assume that *you're seeking educational material for all ages*. The material here covers preschool to college. What you don't use this year will come in handy next year; if your youngest child is nearly ready to graduate, put the preschool material on the shelf for your grandchildren.

- We know *you're serious about educating your child*. Even if you are a radical unschooler, you're choosing that path because you believe it builds well-educated human beings. Accordingly, this book describes hundreds of resources, while acknowledging that you are better qualified than anyone else to determine where your child's interests lie and where her education needs to be supplemented.

- While children come in male and female models, English doesn't. In this book, when we speak of a child, in the generic sense, we toss around some pronouns. Dr. Benjamin Spock was the first popular author to employ this model. Sometimes we use *he;* sometimes we use *she*. Except when we refer specifically to males or females, the pronouns are used alternately and interchangeably.

- We assume that because they're homeschooled, *your children are more academically advanced than their peers are*. (Individual attention tends to have that effect on all children.) Therefore, we believe a majority of individually schooled teenagers are capable of learning well from material written at an early college level. Many of the resources in this book are designed for first- and second-year college students. Your intelligent teenager should be presented with this material, with the expectation that even if he doesn't absorb everything in a single sitting, he'll nevertheless broaden his understanding through the exposure.

- We assume that *every child can make academic progress,* no matter what her disability or disorder. Therefore, the material in this book for special education is brief. We believe you're better off working lovingly with your disabled child than knowing everything there is to know about her disorders. In the end, she's not her disorder.

- We assume *you want to cover specific subject matter* when you teach. That's why the resources in this book are grouped by curriculum area, rather than age. When the subject matter isn't clearly directed at a particular age, we designate the target audience by grade level. Sometimes we group several grade levels together using this terminology: *Preschool* is material appropriate for children from birth to age five. Materials designated *primary, younger,* or *elementary* grades are ages 5 to 12. Intermediate, middle, or junior high ages are 12 to 15. *High school, senior,* or *pre-college* ages are 15 to 19. We also use symbols to indicate appropriate age groupings for the various resources in this text. The key to the symbols is located on page xvii.

- We assume *you are capable of monitoring your children's academic progress,* that you don't need day-to-day handholding to ensure that your children are making adequate educational advancement. We invite you to consider the curriculum material both for compliance, if that's an issue in your state, and for reassurance. We also include in the appendix a suggested curriculum scope and sequence to help you get organized. But we don't recommend specific timetables, in the belief that you, your spouse, and your children will make your own decisions about how to incorporate your state's curriculum standards into your own homeschooling philosophy.

- Who learns from the material in this book? We assume that *education is a group effort.* Whether the parent studies the material and teaches the child, or the child learns the material and reports back to the parent, the effort will educate everyone. Therefore, when we say *you,* we generally refer to the parent, while recognizing that in many families, it will be the children who take the lead in deciding how they'll be educated.

CREDITS

The background information for some of the definitions, quotations, and biographies in this text came from the following resources:

Bartleby.com   www.bartleby.com

These include, specifically, the *American Heritage Dictionary of the English Language, Bartlett's Familiar Quotations, Columbia Encyclopedia,* and several others.

Biography.com   www.biography.com

Dictionary.com   www.dictionary.com

Education World Research Center
www.education-world.com/research

Encyclopedia Britannica   www.britannica.com

Funk and Wagnell's Encyclopedia   www.funkandwagnalls.com

Hypertext Webster Gateway
http://work.ucsd.edu:5141/cgi-bin/http_webster?

With access to *Easton's Bible Dictionary.*

Merriam-Webster Online   www.m-w.com

Newbury House Online Dictionary   nhd.heinle.com

Web of Online Dictionaries   www.yourdictionary.com

Several of the people quoted in this text are volunteers at:

AskMe.com   www.askme.com

AllExperts.com   www.allexperts.com

HomeschoolReviews   www.egroups.com/group/0-homeschoolreviews

A number of the site reviews were contributed by members of the Homeschool Reviews list. Among the most prolific contributors were these homeschooling moms: Misty Blagg, Marrenzy Brown, Susie Clawson, Ann Crum, Melody Daisson, Angel Danelle, Ann Glass, Kath Howe, and Robin Tompkins. Many others contributed suggestions and reviews, and I thank all of you for your assistance.

I also thank the good people at Prima Publishing for their commitment to homeschooling and to this project, and specifically Jamie Miller and Tara Mead, for their persistence in getting through the rough spots.

This book was inspired by humble people throughout history who have been taught by their mothers, their fathers, and other angels. By Jamie Miller, who has a vision of how books can change lives. By my parents, who inspired me to my own education. And by Kristen, who inspired me to my children's. With a tip of the hat to *The Education of Henry Adams* (www.bartleby.com/159/1.html).

Dedicated to my husband, who rescues souls and sees to their education. And to an entire houseful of L'il Darlin's who homeschool us every day.

—LauraMaery Gold
Kent, Washington

KEY TO SYMBOLS USED IN THIS TEXT

☆☆☆☆☆	Excellent site: Bookmark it, and return often.
☆☆☆☆	Very good site: Worth revisiting.
☆☆☆	Useful site.
☆☆	Some useful information.
☆	Only a small amount of useful information.

▨ All ages   ▤ Primary ages   ▧ Intermediate ages

▥ Pre-college ages   ▩ Primary & intermediate ages   ▦ Secondary ages

HOMESCHOOL YOUR CHILD FOR FREE

Why We Homeschool

ALL GOOD PARENTS homeschool. Some do it full-time. Some do it part-time. Some supplement their homeschooling with public or private school. Some take on the adventure with support groups. And some parents do it all alone.

Homeschoolers cut across all segments of the population. Although the movement is indisputably largest in the United States (reliable research puts the number of American homeschooled children at 1.5 million, or 1 to 2 percent of school-age children), Canadians, Europeans, and thousands of expatriated North American families in the military, in missionary service, in business, and in the civil service are also embracing homeschooling.

Homeschoolers advocate dozens of educational philosophies, ranging from strict school-at-home programs to militant unschooling. There are parents who have homeschooled from birth, parents who enroll their children in supplemental classes, and parents who embrace public or private school and supplement it with their own after-school and weekend programs.

While the homeschooling movement is often perceived as conservative in nature, a sizable number of homeschoolers are adamantly liberal. Homeschoolers cover the range of human experience. They include self-avowed "hippies," rural farm families, gay couples, single parents, grandparents, stepparents, and kindly aunts.

Some families homeschool in small church or neighborhood "co-ops"; some are affiliated with charter or private schools; and some go it alone. Some homeschooling families are devoutly religious; some have no religious affiliation at all. The homeschooling community includes Pagans, Catholics, Wiccans, Baha'is, Mormons, Jehovah's Witnesses, Protestant Christians, serious atheists, Muslims, and Jews.

Parents homeschool because their children are gifted or learning disabled, behavior disordered or easily overlooked, ADHD or just plain bored. Some parents homeschool because they feel undermined or unsafe. Most parents homeschool for smaller classes, individual attention,

🚶🚶 How We Homeschool

"My husband and I have raised and are still raising four daughters on our family cattle/sheep ranch in the heart of New Mexico. The nearest town is Estancia, and we live about six miles southwest of there. The girls are the fourth generation to live on this land. We're the only homeschoolers."

—**Donna Lee Spruill**, homeschooling mother of four, Estancia, New Mexico

and customized curriculum. And most of all, parents homeschool their kids because they simply want to. Because they're good parents, and they believe it's the best thing for their children.

No matter how—or why—you homeschool, you're welcome here. And congratulations on choosing to teach your children both economically and intelligently.

Intelligently? Absolutely. In choosing this book, you're gaining access to thousands of resources that make up the best and most current information available anywhere. No stodgy 15-year-old out-of-date textbooks for your kids. By choosing to homeschool your child for free, you're also choosing to homeschool your child for *now*. For the world your child lives in today, rather than the world that existed in 1987, when many of her friends' out-of-date social studies and science textbooks were written.

If you use this book properly, you'll also teach your sons and daughters how to find their independent way around modern technology to do the kind of research and study that will make them successful in college and the business world.

By making wise, intelligent, frequent use of the Internet, you're teaching your children two things: one, that there *is* an answer to all their questions, and two, that those answers are within their grasp. You'll teach them how to find information, how to work efficiently, how to avoid time-wasting dead ends, and how to focus on their educational goals.

Do we guarantee that this book will make your child smarter? Sure. Will your child be better off if he's homeschooled? Of course. Is homeschooling the answer to all your problems? Well . . .

🚶‍♂️ *How We Homeschool*

"Eight years ago, I placed my son in a private Waldorf school but just couldn't afford to keep him there. During his second year back in public school, I had to make a change. He was surrounded by drugs and gangs, with no moral code that I could see. I began homeschooling because I knew there had to be a better way. The girl next door—very devoted to church and family—got beat up just for being religious, shy, and quiet. The school did nothing. It happened again, only worse. Her mother took her out of school and began homeschooling. As we talked, I kept saying, 'I can't do that and work a full-time job.' Being a single, divorced parent, I had to work. I prayed about it and knew we had to try, that somehow it would work out. Now we have been homeschooling for four years."

—Joyce Dumire, homeschooling mother of one, Akron, Ohio

Here's how it works. If you haven't yet been on the Internet, it's time to start. Visit your community library, local public school, recreation center, or YMCA, and ask for assistance. In most North American communities, Internet access is available for free. And you can get help from the librarian, the neighborhood computer geek, or a friendly family member. Ask your Designated Tutor to teach you two skills: surfing the Web and using e-mail.

Even if you don't have your own Internet account, you can get free e-mail from any connected computer. There are hundreds of organizations that provide free Web-based e-mail accounts. These sites are my personal favorites; visit one to set up your own free account:

Hotmail www.hotmail.com

It's slow, and all the good names have been taken. Nevertheless, it's indisputably the most popular free e-mail site around. ☆☆☆☆

Iwon www.iwon.com

Free e-mail, and a chance to win $10 million just for signing up. What's not to like? ☆☆☆☆☆

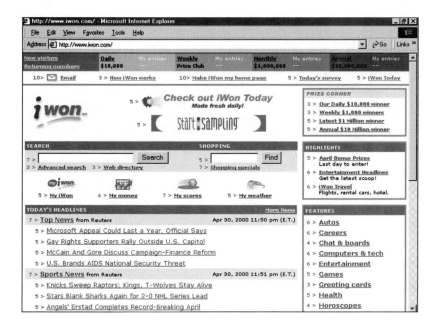

Figure 1.1
_____

Iwon: Free mail,
free cash.

Yahoo   www.yahoo.com

It's a bit of a pain entering all the information that's required to set up your own Yahoo e-mail account, but there are plenty of people who use it! ☆☆☆☆

ZenSearch   www.zensearch.net

I stumbled across this one a few months ago and use it all the time. It's like Hotmail, but it tends to be a bit less congested, and there are plenty of names still available. ☆☆☆☆☆

Once you know what you're doing, save yourself the headache of living at the library, and get online at home. Bet you can do it for free! Here's how: There's someone in your neighborhood, congregation, or family who has an unused computer. (Our own family has to find a home for one of our old computers every year or so, as we upgrade the clunker for something more current.) Put the word out that you're looking for a PC, and offer to barter child care or some other skill in exchange for that computer. To our family, taking the computer off our hands and putting it to good use would be payment enough. Your cost may vary.

How We Homeschool

"My husband first introduced me to homeschooling. Shortly after our first was born, he told me he wanted our children homeschooled. He had children from a prior marriage and had some experience with homeschooling, and was adamant that our children be taught at home. I was opposed at first, but for the sake of peace, I felt compelled to study it more deeply.

"I read several books on the subject at the library, including one by Raymond and Dorothy Moore. My initial response to the books I read was surprise. I was completely surprised that there were parents out there who were homeschooling their children successfully, and their children were growing up well educated and well rounded. I was very impressed.

"So I borrowed some notes from that year's homeschooling convention and read them all. I started to become excited about the prospect of homeschooling. I attended the homeschooling convention the following year, and that sealed it for me. I knew homeschooling was something I had to do!"

—**Mary Batchelor**, homeschooling mother of six, Sandy, Utah

Then get online for free. Visit the library or a neighbor's computer, or use your allotment of free hours on the Prodigy or AOL disks given away at the bank, the local college, or just about anywhere. Once you're online, order the free software for one of the following services:

Free Internet   www.affiliateadvice.com
Reviews of several free dial-up providers. ☆☆☆

FreeInternet   www.freei.net
A newer service, this one provides unlimited access from all over the United States. You'll see an annoying banner advertisement at the top of the page. OK. So nothing's *really* free. ☆☆☆☆

Juno   www.juno.com
The biggest free online service around now allows you only 150 free hours a month and charges $9.95 for anything more. It's still good. ☆☆☆☆

Figure 1.2

Free Internet: If you don't mind the ad, you can't beat the price.

Now you're set to Homeschool Your Child For Free!

This book focuses on four main areas. Chapters 2 and 3 give you the lowdown on homeschooling. In chapter 2, you'll find solutions to all kinds of homeschooling issues. Chapter 3 helps you pull together a full homeschool curriculum, from preschool through pre-college. Chapters 4 through 6 examine the essentials of education: readin', writin', and 'rithmetic. Chapters 7 through 11 provide a full liberal arts education: art, history, music, social studies, and humanities. In the next two chapters you'll find the hard sciences. Finally, we offer graduation guidance: a chapter on college admissions, with an online supplement that discusses careers and independent living/home economics. From cradle to adulthood, your child will be homeschooled for free!

Want more? The following resources are associated with this book, and will supplement and update the material you're holding in your hands. As long as this edition is in print, these resources will be available to you:

Hotlinks

**Homeschool Your
Child for Free!**
www.hsfree.com

Homeschool Reviews
www.egroups.com/group
/0-homeschoolreviews

Why We Homeschool
www.egroups.com/group
/0-WhyWeHomeschool

Figure 1.3

Homeschool Your Child for Free: Stay up to date with new resources.

Homeschool Your Child for Free! www.hsfree.com

The largest homeschool database on the Net. Thousands of sites, reviewed, rated, and updated regularly. As an owner of the most current edition of this book, you can register for access to the site, submit your own resources, search for help, participate in the Homeschool for Free discussion area, and locate additional resources. ☆☆☆☆☆

Homeschool Reviews www.egroups.com/group/0-homeschoolreviews

The mailing list for homeschooling using free curriculum and educational resources. Members who contribute to the list may be eligible to win a free copy of the next edition of *Homeschool Your Child for Free!* ☆☆☆☆☆

Why We Homeschool www.egroups.com/group/0-WhyWeHomeschool

This weekly homeschooling news and commentary column is also distributed on several homeschooling e-mail lists. ☆☆☆☆☆

Homeschool How-To's

THERE ARE TWO kinds of homeschooling families: those who approach it as a right and a duty, and those who come to homeschooling out of necessity or out of frustration with the alternatives.

Because of the great support available through publications, homeschool groups, and, most of all, the Internet, it doesn't take long for those in the second category to convert to the first. And the successes their children experience in homeschool keep them coming back for more.

Joey Easley, a teenager who lives in Gig Harbor, Washington, is an example of the success of homeschooling. Joey was homeschooled for the last nine years of his primary and secondary education and is now attending a local community college. This is Joey's take on the homeschooling experience: "Homeschooling has been great for me. Now that I am going to a community college I have been able to understand better the ups and downs of homeschooling. Probably the biggest plus for me was going at my own pace. Having to sit through sometimes weeks of class learning stuff I already knew was very frustrating. Then again, sometimes the class got going too fast and I got left behind. Another reason I think homeschooling is so great is that it is more focused on just learning, and not on finding out how much you already know.

"The downside, of course, is the social aspect. I have been very blessed because I have so many friends who were homeschooled. If we did our work fast enough, we could get done at noon and play the rest of the day. We also have homeschool sports clubs in which I played soccer and basketball; I also have friends who played varsity sports at the local high school. So I was not lacking at all in my social interactions.

"I think homeschooling gives me the advantage over public-schoolers because I can focus more on the things that I think (actually, my mother usually makes the decisions) would be the most useful in my life, and I get to skip things that might be useful for others but have no relevance to me."

This chapter is your initiation into homeschool. In the next chapter of this book you'll begin building a curriculum and learn about various homeschooling philosophies, and in subsequent chapters, you'll find resources for every academic area you'll encounter as a homeschooler. In this chapter, though, you'll begin your homeschool journey by learning about some of the most important issues facing homeschoolers, and finding supportive answers for your questions and dilemmas.

We start this chapter with a discussion of Internet safety. We then introduce some useful teaching skills, and discuss ways to motivate reluctant homeschoolers. The subsequent sections cover homeschooling difficulties, legal issues, standardized testing, socialization, and three kinds of support: e-mail lists, various sorts of electronic "boards," and real-life support groups.

First, though, an introduction to homeschooling. These resources introduce homeschooling, explain its appeal, and show you how to get started. Bon voyage!

Hotlinks

Homeschool House
www.perkinsfamily.com
/homeschool.html

**Jon's Homeschool
Resource Page**
www.midnightbeach.com/hs

Teen Homeschooler
www.eatbug.com
/homeschool

Topic of the Month Board
www.kaleidoscapes.com
/monthlytopic

Eleven Reasons to Raise Your Own Child
www.alaska.net/~appleb/RaiseYourChild.html

Refrain from institutionalizing your child and choose instead to homeschool, unschool, or nonschool. This site is worth framing. My favorite? Number seven: Let your child learn genuine socialization instead of false and negative socialization and negative coping behaviors. ☆☆☆☆

Famous Homeschoolers   www.core-curriculum.com/page15.html
An interesting list. ☆☆

Famous Homeschoolers
www.geocities.com/Heartland/Estates/6000/famous.htm

Homeschooled writers, judges, scientists, and more. Inspirational. ☆☆☆☆

🚶 How We Homeschool

"I am the mother of a wonderful little boy, almost 21 months, whom I homeschool. Right now, all of life is 'schooling' for Alexander, so I guess that qualifies as 'home-schooling,' for now. Unlike many people, we aren't homeschooling for religious reasons, although I look forward to incorporating the Goddess, the God, and Mother Earth into his education process. We are homeschooling because of the problems in our local educational system, including large classes where individualized instruction is impossible; violence; and drugs in the schools. After my friends' first- and second-grader were assaulted in school (enough to leave marks into the evening and the following day) and nothing was done, I knew I couldn't put my son into that environment."

—vanessa ronsse, homeschooling mother of one, Seattle area

FAQs of Homeschooling
www.geocities.com/Heartland/Shores/1729/freqquest.html

Getting started, information about testing, finding support, and lots more. ☆☆☆☆

From My Personal Files and Experiences
www.geocities.com/Athens/Aegean/3446/personalnotes.html

Coyle's Where in the World site reviews these topical links and describes how to use them in your homeschooling. An excellent resource. ☆☆☆☆

High School Homeschool
www.cis.upenn.edu/~brada/homeschooling.html

If you're homeschooling a teenager, this page will help. Essay on homeschooling teens, learning objectives at the high school level, and much more. ☆☆☆☆

Homeschool Hall of Fame
www.mosquitonet.com/~family/famous.html

Yet another interesting list of people who were homeschooled. ☆☆☆

Homeschool House www.perkinsfamily.com/homeschool.html

The How to Homeschool information is great for beginners, and the Christian-themed unit on American history shouldn't be missed. The remainder of the site is bursting with great homeschooling thoughts, motivations, explanations, and advice. The links page is particularly informative. There's so much original material on this site, it deserves to be on every homeschooler's bookmark list. ☆☆☆☆☆

Homeschool Notes ky-on-line.com/bhe/notes.htm

One family's consideration of various homeschooling issues. Several articles covering many aspects of homeschooling: "Parents as Teachers," "End of Year Checklist," "The Best Way to Test," "Homeschool Difficulties," and more. ☆☆☆☆

Homeschooling www.emtech.net/home_school.htm

Scores of very well chosen resources. ☆☆

Homeschooling: Is It for You?

www.athomemothers.com/infoguides/46a.htm

An information guide from *At Home Mothers* magazine. A good basic introduction, if you're still trying to decide whether to homeschool. ☆☆☆

Jon's Homeschool Resource Page www.midnightbeach.com/hs

The full-service homeschooling resource. Click the Contents link to find connections to support groups, discussion boards, essays, FAQ lists, and much more. Extensive. ☆☆☆☆☆

Should You Teach Your Child at Home? family.go.com/Features
/family_1998_08/hudv/hudv88homeschool/hudv88homeschool.html

This thorough article is one of many at Family.com that explains why homeschooling's popularity is growing. ☆☆☆

Statistics for Educators www.emtech.net/statistics.htm

Scores of very well chosen resources. ☆☆

Teen Homeschooler   www.eatbug.com/homeschool

An online magazine by, for, and about teenage homeschoolers. Articles, humor, and more. The article on the efficacy of a home-schooled education, under the Edification link, is especially well done, but the entire site makes good reading. ☆☆☆☆☆

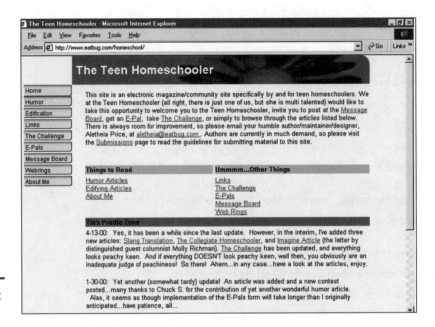

Figure 2.1

Teen Homeschooler: By kids, for kids.

Topic of the Month Board   www.kaleidoscapes.com/monthlytopic

The Kaleidoscape message boards are wonderful: very popular, very helpful. This board tackles a single discussion in-depth. A related board at the same site, the Newbie FAQ board (www.kaleidoscapes .com/newbie/), is for parents who are new to homeschooling! ☆☆☆☆☆

Useful Articles for the Homeschool Teacher
www.alaska.net/~cccandc/artlink.htm

All sorts of advice on curricula, building a library at home, compar-isons with other homeschoolers, and more. ☆☆☆

What Is Homeschooling?
www.accesseric.org/resources/parent/homesch.html

The first of two informational brochures on the legality and philosophies of homeschooling. ☆☆☆

Why I've Chosen to Homeschool

www.mosquitonet.com/~family/choose.html

An insightful discussion from an experienced homeschool mom. Includes links for additional pros and cons. ☆☆☆

Internet Safety

YOU'VE HEARD THE horror stories. And they've probably scared you, right?

You can relax. It really is safe to go back in the cyberwater.

There are lots of good reasons why the Internet is actually a safe place for your children.

First, and foremost, there's the fact that *you* are their parent. As a homeschooler, you already know the importance of being involved in your children's lives. Is there any real chance *your* child has a stash of weapons in the garden shed in preparation for blowing up the neighborhood?

> **Safety:** From the Latin *salvus (safe)*. To be secure from danger, risk, or harm.

The second safety net is related. You *have* taught them right from wrong, right? Many homeschooled parents report that their children are more chary of inappropriate Internet sites than they are themselves.

Cheryl Northrup, a homeschooling mother of seven in Lamar, Colorado, finds that she can trust her children fairly well: "My son did follow a link from a video game site about a year ago that he had been told about by his cousin. He was curious, I guess.

"Anyway, that link wasn't the worst. What happened was that circular links were built into it so he couldn't get out, but kept going to worse and worse places. I inadvertently discovered his trail when checking the history. We had a discussion about it, and he was horrified by what he had seen, as well as the fact that I knew that he had seen it. He has never

Internet Safety

"Our children all share one e-mail address. We look at their in-box together and then, after I see that there are no strange e-mail addresses, they can read the mail alone. They don't go to chat rooms, and they don't go to any new site without me being there with them. They respect what their father and I say very much, so we've never had any problem of them doing anything behind our backs."

—**Kimberley Daly**, homeschooling mother of three, Washington State

been back. I'm a pretty hands-on mom; I know pretty much what they are doing all the time. It's not a 'watching' thing; it's just an awareness."

Cheryl has, of course, had to tutor her kids in Internet safety. "My son is beginning to design a Web page, and we had to caution him not to put too much identifying info on it."

Kathleen Thomas homeschools four daughters in Orange County, California. When one of her daughters accidentally stumbles across porn or other things Kathleen disapproves of, the child has been known to scream and cover up the offending screen! "My younger girls are 11, 8 and 7 and have their own e-mail on AOL with parental controls on. My 18-year-old daughter now has no controls. She stays away from chat rooms but instant-messages many people. Her profile is very carefully filled out. We have taught her to think about what clues she may be giving about herself. We gave her control little by little.

"The younger ones are never on the computer without my husband, daughter, or myself in the room. They cannot instant-message unless we have put the person on their buddy list. They cannot go into chat rooms. AOL also has a message for children that we review with them occasionally for safety. We live in Southern California, so they are aware that there are evil people in this world and that, although God will watch over them, He gave them a mind to use with wisdom and responsibility for safe practices. The accidental bad sites have popped up several times, usually with our oldest daughter. She usually pops back out quickly.

Because of this experience we haven't allowed our younger daughters to surf the Net."

Kathleen makes good use of the third safety net: Internet filtering. Filtering comes in two styles: software you control from your own computer, and filtered Internet service providers, which block offending materials from ever moving down the wire.

In Georgia, Priscilla Pike homeschools one child, and uses a filtered ISP. "We connect just as fast as the other ISP we were on. If I'm unable to view something I might actually want to read, I have a code that I can override. I have not actually tried to go to an XXX site. I think it does catch everything, because on a few e-mails I have had at the bottom 'cannot display image or text.'"

Here's how other homeschooling parents are keeping their kids safe:

Rhonda Brown keeps a close eye on her homeschooler. The Tennessee mother of three uses AOL and has given her kids their own screen names. "But I control *everything*," she says. "I use parental controls to limit their instant messages and send e-mail only to family and a few trusted friends. As for chat rooms, my kids haven't found any yet that they can get to on AOL Kids-Only screen names. They are severely restricted by AOL from visiting sites on the Internet. They mostly play games and talk to family. When they need to work on anything, I take them to my screen name. They have been instructed to call me if they ever receive an instant message while on my name. I'm always in the room but not always watching the screen at those times."

Ann M. Glass has taught her older child to be careful when he surfs. "My seven-year-old is, so far, very responsible and reliable," says the Everson, Washington, mother of two. "I don't allow him to surf the Web or to do a search on his own. If he's looking for something in particular, I search with him. We talk about the undesirable things as they come up. As I come across sites that I deem appropriate and safe for him, I bookmark them. He is allowed to 'browse' the bookmarks to his heart's content."

Ann's house is not without rules regarding the Internet, however. "We do have the rule that he is not allowed to give out any personal information: full name, age, address, e-mail, or phone number. If he wants to do something that requires his name, he has to check with a parent first, and then he may use only his first name. If he inadvertently stumbles on something that is of no relation to the subject matter, seems questionable, or makes him feel uncomfortable, then he is to tell a parent immediately. This kid censors himself on videos, TV, and books, so I trust him with the Internet. However, he is allowed on only when there is a parent in the same room, and we look over his shoulder periodically. Our five-year-old, on the other hand, is not trustworthy and may use the Internet only with a parent."

The following list contains some great tools for teaching your own kids to be safe on the Net. Unfortunately, many of the online resources that purport to care about your child's safety are, in fact, concerned primarily with keeping the Internet "safe" for the unfettered distribution of pornography and other detestable material. If they can persuade parents and legislators that Internet safety is the sole responsibility of parents—the thinking goes—then nobody can attempt to legislate decency.

If you agree with me that protecting children is the responsibility of *every* adult, then beware of that mind-set. Yes, you are responsible for keeping your children safe. At the same time, however, locking up victims so criminals can freely roam the streets is an outrageous way to construct a world. Here's what you need to make your own children wise consumers of the Net:

America Links Up   www.americalinksup.org
Tools and tips for parents and good stuff for kids. This organization encourages parents to participate in their children's Internet activity. ☆☆☆☆

Family Guide Book   www.familyguidebook.com
A worthwhile read for any parent concerned about Internet safety. The Web author writes: "Understanding risks in cyberspace is like using a traffic light. There are times where you can proceed at full speed, and times to stop dead in your tracks." ☆☆☆☆☆

GetNetWise   www.getnetwise.org

Use this online safety guide and tools for reporting trouble to educate yourself and your children about using the Internet safely. ☆☆☆☆

Internet Safety   www.emtech.net/safe.htm

Scores of very well chosen resources. ☆☆

Keeping Kids Safe Online

www.parentsoup.com/edcentral/alu/facts.html

A Parent Soup site. The Web author writes: "Worried about online dangers? Be part of the solution instead of feeling powerless! It's no longer optional for our kids to go online; they need to be there. Even so, as the Net becomes mainstream, we all worry that our kids may find more than they (or we) bargained for out there. We've put together a kind of online safety kit featuring all sorts of good ideas." Very thorough. ☆☆☆☆☆

KidShield   www.kidshield.com

Reviews of parental shielding software, news, safety tips, and some great information on Internet politics. ☆☆☆☆☆

Parent's Guide to the Internet

www.geocities.com/EnchantedForest/Tower/4241

Information on Internet safety, sponsored by a Missouri-based group of Masons. ☆☆☆

SafeKids   www.safekids.com

After your kids sign the Family Contract for Online Safety, you'll know the rules are clear. This is a top-notch source for information on Internet safety. ☆☆☆☆☆

SmartParent   www.smartparent.com

Block the material you don't want in your home, and consider all the tips, news, and links on this very well done site. ☆☆☆☆

Hotlinks

Family Guide Book
www.familyguidebook.com

GetNetWise
www.getnetwise.org

KidShield
www.kidshield.com

SafeKids
www.safekids.com

Figure 2.2

KidShield: Peace
of mind, free.

Teaching Tips

JOYCE DOWLING, A graduated homeschooling mother of two from
Prince George's County, Maryland, has something to say to parents who
are afraid they can't teach their children. "If you can be a good parent,
you can be a good homeschooling parent. After all, what kind of training
did you have for parenting?"

Still worried that it's too hard? Here's a ninth-grader from the
Middle East who's got it all figured out. R. J. Artty's parents are homeschoolers. English is not his first language, but his advice to parents is
brilliant:

1. Always start by explaining.
2. Maintain eye contact to see whether the child is keeping up or not.
3. Head nodding does not necessarily mean that the child has understood. Other signs that the child is not focusing include repeated
   words like "Uh-huh, yeah, go on, I'm listening."
4. Watch out for the glazed-eye expression.

5. Do not bore your child with endless talk.

6. Try making as few mistakes as possible while teaching (i.e., go through what you say before you say it).

7. Never explain anything unless you fully understand it.

8. Do not allow your child to start fidgeting with things.

9. If your child starts to shift position while sitting, this means your child has not understood a word you said, or your child is having a hard time keeping up.

10. To make sure the child is understanding what you are saying, ask them a few questions while explaining what was previously said.

11. Avoid asking "yes" or "no" questions.

12. Keep your explanations as simple as possible and your sentences straightforward.

13. Explain things by rank of difficulty, that is, start with the basics and the easiest stuff.

14. Try to be as creative as possible when explaining or asking questions (this depends on the child's age).

15. Never stay too long on one subject.

Advice:
From the Middle French *avis (opinion)*. Counsel regarding an issue or a course of action.

For parents who are new to the homeschooling game, Luanne, a homeschooling mom in Virginia, has homeschooling down to a science. These are her five tips for a sanity-saving home education:

1. Trust God daily.
2. Take an honest and realistic survey of your life before you begin.
3. Teach the kids to pull their share of the work and responsibility.
4. Be opportunistic.
5. Don't be afraid to try new things.

Robin Tompkins is more philosophical about her homeschooling routines. "The first thing I did was establish a daily routine and schedule," reports the mother of two from Redding, California. "This included teaching the kids to be

On Scheduling

"In studies, whatsoever a man commandeth upon himself, let him set hours for it."
—Francis Bacon, essayist

responsible for getting themselves ready (with some prompting), making their beds, and taking turns feeding our dogs. To encourage them to do this, I made up a job chart. Each morning they got to put on a sticker for each job completed. After about two months they forgot about the stickers, and now they usually fulfill their responsibilities without complaining."

Robin's homeschooling schedule is certainly not set in stone: "We aim to start 'school' at 9:00 A.M. each morning, but if we don't get started until later or are ready earlier, that works. I had to become more flexible so as to make myself easier to live with and make learning a fun experience. I started by writing a weekly lesson plan, which works for us very well. It was especially helpful in the beginning to keep us all on track with the learning goals for the day—though again, I have become more flexible with this and allow the educational interests of the kids to take us away from the plan."

Gina Marie (Wellman) Haugh of Tracy, California, has a practical tip for homeschooling. This is how she deals with homeschoolers who are often "on the road" during school hours: "This is my first year homeschooling. One thing I did was buy each boy a two- or three-inch binder. I cut the bindings from all the workbooks and materials that I don't have to return. Then I three-hole-punched all the pages and inserted them in the binder behind divider tabs. In the front is a tab separator for each day of the week. I go through the materials in the back of each binder and pull out the pages for each day, then put them in each day's tab. If they have a spelling test or something to write, I add blank binder paper so they have everything (except for reading books) right there. We are in the car a lot, and it's hard to carry all their books with them. This way they just have mostly their binder with all the work and the reading books they need."

Ready to try a few homeschooling tricks of your own?

A&E Classroom   www.aande.com/class

The producers of the *Biography* series, *Breakfast with the Arts,* and other educational programs on cable television have developed this

Teaching Freebie

"Family Involvement in Education" supports active participation of parents and family members in children's education. Call Eisenhower National Clearinghouse (800-621-5785).

companion Web site. Register to receive free teaching materials. ☆☆☆

Activity Search www.eduplace.com/search/activity.html

Searchable database of more than 400 original elementary and intermediate classroom activities and lesson plans for teachers and parents. Search for activities by both curriculum area and grade level, or browse activities by theme. ☆☆☆

AtHome Mothers www.athomemothers.com

Whatever it takes to enable you to stay home with your kids, this magazine has it. Transitioning from career to home, financial analysis, home management, college degrees by mail, making money from home, and much, much more. It's about time someone saw the world from *our* point of view! ☆☆☆☆☆

Children's Play and Learning Patterns

www.eplay.com/1999-01-09/company/research.adp

Research on the sources and development of intelligence. Lots of information about stimulating intelligence in children. ☆☆☆

Classroom Management

www.pacificnet.net/~mandel/ClassroomManagement.html

Aimed specifically at large classes, many of these management techniques can be adapted to homeschool. From the Teachers Helping Teachers page. ☆☆☆

Concept Mapping trochim.human.cornell.edu/kb/conmap.htm

How to teach visual learners. Concept mapping is a method of expressing ideas with images so kids can quickly absorb the concepts. ☆☆☆☆

Eclectic Homeschool Downloads www.eho.org/downld.htm

"This excellent site contains all types of materials to use in managing, planning, and teaching your homeschool. It has specific forms that can be used for each subject, as well as chore charts, reading lists,

Hotlinks

AtHome Mothers
www.athomemothers.com

FamilyEducation
www.familyeducation
.com/home

**Homeschool Forms
on the Web**
www.geocities.com
/homeschoolforms

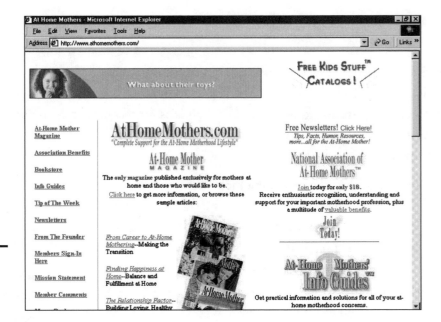

Figure 2.3

AtHome Mothers: Encouragement to stay home with the kids.

attendance record sheets, Bible study scripture forms, and more. It's an organized scheduler's dream." —A.G.☆☆☆☆

Teaching Freebie

ENC Focus: A Magazine for Classroom Innovators covers a variety of innovative teaching techniques. Call Eisenhower National Clearinghouse (800-621-5785).

FamilyEducation   www.familyeducation.com/home/
I love this site! Of particular note is the Expert Advice feature, which includes answers to questions posed to a panel of experts affiliated with homeschool curriculum provider the Calvert School. Ask your homeschool questions here, and talk to other homeschoolers. Also, click on the Ages and Grades link for tons of age-specific information. Most of the site is not specifically homeschool related, but the educational advice is useful nonetheless. ☆☆☆☆

Follow Through: Why Didn't We?
darkwing.uoregon.edu/~adiep/ft/watkins.htm
Fascinating article on why public schools are ignoring research demonstrating that the best way to educate children is to stand there and teach them. ☆☆☆

Full-Text Resources   www.npin.org/library/texts.html

Full texts of parenting-related materials. Hundreds of brochures on teaching math, reading, science, and more to your children at home. Part of the U.S. government's ERIC project. ☆☆☆

Homeschool Forms on the Web

www.geocities.com/homeschoolforms/

This great site was designed by a homeschooling mom who made her own forms, including reading logs, to-do lists, field trip logs, and much, much more. Because they were so much in demand by other moms, she decided to make them available on the Internet. She is hoping to add more forms, some worksheets, and even some unit study ideas." —A.G. ☆☆☆☆

Resources for Homeschoolers

home.att.net/~bandcparker/forms.html

"What can I say? I'm drooling. This site has all kinds of forms and planners, as well as shopping lists and organizers of other types. Impressive!" —A.G. ☆☆☆☆☆

Teaching Resources   www.emtech.net/teachers.htm

Scores of very well chosen resources. See the related sites: Multiple Intelligences (www.emtech.net/mi.htm); Learning Theories (www.emtech.net/learning_theories.htm); and Brain-Based Learning (www.emtech.net/brain_based_learning.html). ☆☆☆

Homeschool Discounts

Barnes & Noble offers discounts to home-schoolers. Bring in proof of homeschooling (a letter from the school district) for a 20 percent discount on educational materials.

Motivators

A SHORT TIME ago, a frustrated homeschooler asked me for advice. "How do you motivate kids who do not wish to learn?" she asked. "My 11- and 14-year-olds act like everything is too hard, when they are very intelligent."

I had a different idea. Kids love to learn, I told her. What they're not fond of is work. That left her two options for teaching her children:

1. Persuade them that they love to work.
2. Modify the work so that it becomes something they love.

My advice to this mom? Do both. Let them learn that work is important and has intrinsic value. That a sense of accomplishment is rewarding. That work is critical to the development of character.

> **Motivate:** From the Late Latin *mōtívus (motion)*. To compel, induce, or incite to action.

At the same time, I said, bribe them. At this age, kids are still motivated by gold stars and points . . . but those gold stars and points must accumulate toward something meaningful. Start small: One day's uncomplaining work results in a new trading card or an hour of computer time. Make their "attitude" a critical component of being rewarded. As you achieve small successes, graduate to long-term successes: Twenty stars earns a family campout.

Another key to success: Look for ways to encourage them to motivate one another. If the 14-year-old teaches the 11-year-old how to convert fractions to decimals by noon, they both get out of doing dishes that night. This way the older child gets the math down cold, and the 11-year-old learns to cooperate. Interdependence builds families.

"Where there is ignorance," wrote Epictetus, "there is also want of learning."

Do your children "want" learning?

Gamesmanship

> "We tried many things, but finally went with games as learning tools for words, parts of speech, and geometry."
> —Joyce Dumire, home-schooling mother of one, Akron, Ohio

Jo-Ann Sturko is preparing to become a teacher in Edmonton, Canada. She has several ideas for motivating reluctant learners: "Children enjoy learning when the topic being taught is relevant to them. If they can see how it can be applied to their lives in a real-world context, they are more likely to find the learning experience engaging and meaningful. When given the opportunity to learn in a 'hands-on' way, information is more easily stored and recalled for future experiences. An example of this is teaching multiple math concepts through visits to the grocery store.

"Hypothetical activity: Give your child a grocery list (a simple one for younger children, a more complex one for older chil-

On Motivation

"If I could put together a packet of books for every new homeschooling parent to read, it would be Raymond and Dorothy Moore's *Better Late Than Early,* Grace Llewellyn's *The Teenage Liberation Handbook,* and Mary Griffith's *The Unschooling Handbook.* Then I would tell them to read anything by John Holt. I would also point them to www.unschooling.com. Maybe after learning about unschooling they would still choose to 'do school at home,' but by then I hope they would do it with greater understanding of how their children learn—which I hope would solve the motivation problems that school-at-homers encounter."

—**Heather Hada**, unschooling mother of three

dren). The child must go through the store, find the items listed, and figure out the final cost, either by estimating or by using a calculator. Be sure to include multiples of items to allow for multiplication. This lesson will also qualify as a reading and language development activity as the child reads labels and chooses the correct products."

Homeschooling mom Gita Schmitz has her own ideas about motivating homeschoolers, especially those who have spent some time in the public school system. "Unmotivated kids?" she says. "That's an interesting one. Parents who decide to homeschool after having their kids in school for a number of years often find their children don't want to do anything, don't care about anything, and are basically do-nothings—for a while. The experience of school squashes the interest they used to have. There are many reasons why this happens, but my point is that it's completely normal, and the common idea is to just let them be. They need to decompress and detoxify themselves from school. After several months or even a year of this, they start asking questions again and showing some interest in life, as they used to. And that means they're ready to homeschool."

Gina Marie Haugh uses games and other activities to get her children enthusiastic about school. The homeschooling mom of four from Tracy, California, says her kids *love* Monopoly, because it teaches them

Teaching Freebie

"Get Involved! How Parents and Families Can Help Their Children Do Better in School" is adaptable to homeschoolers. Call 877-4-ED-PUBS and request the product by name.

On Learning

"Those who are occupied in intellectual work will, I think, agree with me that it is important, not so much to know a thing, as to have known it, and known it thoroughly. If you have once known a thing in this way it is easy to renew your knowledge when you have forgotten it; and when you begin to take the subject up again, it slides back on the familiar grooves with great facility."

—T. H. Huxley, essayist and educator

math, reading, and thinking skills. Gina Marie gets more out of the game than that, however: "My kids also love when I let them roll the dice and they have to add, subtract, multiply, divide, or make fractions of the numbers they roll."

Julia G., a homeschooling mother of three from Niagara Falls, Canada, believes she has found the key to motivating her own kids. "When I make the 'lesson plan,' that's when my daughter's unmotivated. When I let her go her own way, she is *so* unbelievably motivated. I guess we are really unschoolers because we do not follow a curriculum and there is no preset plan. I homeschooled for two years and fought her the whole way. I was introduced to unschooling and thought, 'That sounds nice if only a kid would really choose to learn something.' But after a while, that was the only way to save my sanity. And now—we're in our fifth month of unschooling—she is flying! She is so interested in ancient Egypt that she reads everything she can find about it. Six months ago, she hated to read anything. Now she is attending adult-geared lectures about it, and loving it! She's also pursuing a physics-related interest. I would never have believed my child would do this. This is the same child that would spend three hours writing her list of twenty-five spelling words for the week!"

Hotlinks

Cardboard Cognition: Educational Board Games
edweb.sdsu.edu/courses
/edtec670/Cardboard
/BoardTOC.html

Education 4 Kids
www.edu4kids.com

Virtual Certificate Maker
www.learningoasis.com
/learningoasis
/certificatemaker
/addcert2.qry?function=form

If you're wondering how to get your unmotivated scholar excited about academics, these resources can help:

Articles to Encourage   www.gocin.com/homeschool/week50.htm

Inspiration for Christian homeschoolers. ☆☆

Cardboard Cognition: Educational Board Games

edweb.sdsu.edu/courses/edtec670/Cardboard/BoardTOC.html

Do your kids love board games as much as mine do? This site contains a hundred or more educational board games you make at home. Directions, printable game boards, and everything you need to educate your kids with games. ☆☆☆☆☆

Citizenship Award   www.eduplace.com/ss/citaward.html

Has your daughter been an especially good citizen this week? Has your son been picking up litter around the neighborhood? Print out this award certificate to recognize their good work. ☆☆☆

E-Card Express   www.americangirl.com/ag/features/ecards

Sweet electronic cards to encourage your daughters. An American Girl site. ☆☆☆☆

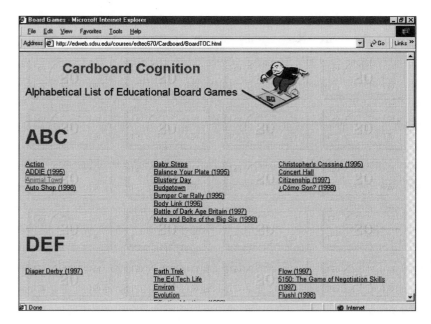

Figure 2.4

Cardboard Cognition: Have fun; get smart.

Education 4 Kids   www.edu4kids.com

Fun, educational, self-administered drills for kids of all ages. Math, social studies, language, and science. It even keeps score! ☆☆☆☆

Kids' Space   www.kids-space.org

Pen-pal search, costumes, and lots more for kids at this award-winning site. ☆☆☆☆

Making Learning Fun   family.go.com/Features/family_1998_05/famf/famf58learnfun/famf58learnfun.html

How to turn learning into a game. This article has fun ideas for math, social studies, science, and English. Worth visiting. ☆☆☆☆

Miscellaneous Items, Other Fun Stuff, and Group Games   www.geocities.com/Athens/Aegean/3446/miscellaneous.html

Coyle's Where in the World site reviews these topical links and describes how to use them in your homeschooling. An excellent resource. ☆☆☆☆

Reviewing the Three R's   family.go.com/Features/family_1998_08/dony/dony88rithmetic/dony88rithmetic.html

Don't let the long address scare you off. Although it's not specifically homeschool-oriented, these tips on motivating children in reading, writing, and math are priceless. ☆☆☆☆

Virtual Certificate Maker   www.learningoasis.com/learningoasis/certificatemaker/addcert2.qry?function=form

Is your child ready to graduate? Make it official. Pierian Spring Software gives you the means to create diplomas, certificates of completion, and certificates of merit, recognition, achievement, and much more. Unfortunately, the resulting certificate prints out as a quarter-sheet document. Diligent graphics users will be able to work around that problem. ☆☆☆☆☆

Dealing with Difficulties

DOES THE THOUGHT of teaching your children at home frighten you? Ever grow weary of the daily grind? Be honest: Do your bickering children sometimes get on your nerves?

Many of the homeschooling parents I've talked with say their biggest discouragement is children who are sometimes sulky, sometimes argumentative, and sometimes cruel to one another.

What works for us? Our children are not permitted to fight. They often debate, and sometimes do so in loud voices, but if they ever get *close* to a fight, I send 'em out to the back porch or the garage or a small bathroom, where they are required to talk together until they arrive at a mutually acceptable solution.

> **Difficult:** From the Latin *difficilis (dis [not] + facile [easy])*. That which requires great effort to overcome.

I perceive that when kids don't learn to get along as children, they'll end up as divorced adults, living alone under a bridge. That's why this problem-solving thing is one of my Parental Articles of Faith. People sometimes express amazement at how well my kids get along with one another, but I assure you, it's not because they're good kids. It's because they've been forced by the evil mommy to resolve their differences. No problem is unresolvable. What's not to get along?

I *never* suggest solutions anymore, mostly because I've learned I don't really know the dynamics of the problem. Nine times out of ten, when I listen in on their back-porch resolutions, it turns out that one or both is actually unhappy over something entirely unrelated to what they were debating in the kitchen. Most of the time, they work out some elaborate "deal" to satisfy one another, the mechanics of which I never fathom.

Our base rule: You don't come back into the family area until you're *both* happy. That way, bullying, name-calling, and criticizing get no truck. Doing so just annoys the sibling, delays the resolution, and causes your feet to get tired! They always return to the house happy and laughing, the problem long forgotten, and excited about whatever new project they've devised.

On Family

"I have had very few problems with others in regards to my decision to home-school. Most people just ask a lot of questions, because they're still stuck on the 'socialization' issue, and the seeming impossibility of doing 'all those subjects' with each of your kids.

"Some people take your homeschooling as an indictment of them sending their kids to government schools, or they are simply stunned that you'd want your kids with you all day.

"My advice to anyone who has problems with other people who don't approve is to just avoid those people and find like-minded homeschoolers. You probably won't change anyone's mind by your words, but when they see what fantastic people you are raising, they might take a second look."

—Gita Schmitz, homeschooling mom

I have three cautions: First, when I suspect my everything's-a-joke-to-me 12-year-old is refusing to solve the problem just so he can force his older brother to stand out on the porch for a long time, I tell him *he* has to participate with his hands on his head. That gets old really fast, and he quickly arrives at a solution.

Second, I've also spent a great amount of energy teaching them how to be active listeners, paraphrasing one another's complaints (so that the other person is satisfied he or she has been heard) before responding or adding their own complaint to the discussion. They don't always use these skills, but when problems seem intractable, it's their final resort.

Finally, I've been doing this since they were toddlers, although I've seen other parents start when their kids were older. When they were young, I simply made them stand in one place and hold hands. My teenagers still fear I'll make 'em hold hands (yuck!) or hug each other (bigger yuck!), so the parentless back porch is considered a real privilege.

Susie Clawson, who homeschools five children in Clearfield, Utah, has a tale for anyone who has had to deal with the common problem of disapproving family members. "About in-laws and other 'interested' people: Being a very opinionated and outspoken person, but hopefully kind and respectful, I've never gotten much grief from in-laws or others. One relative was a public school teacher for years, and at first he'd drill me on things, like 'Are you diagramming sentences?' To which I'd respond. 'Well my oldest is only two, so we probably won't tackle that until he's much older.'

"When I started telling him things I'd read in books by John Holt or the Moores, he'd say, 'Well, I've never heard that before.' But when I offered to let him read the books, he declined and stopped drilling. Now he is thrilled with the progress my children have made and their interest in the world around them. I think he was just feeling a little insecure about his own choices."

Now that your children are learning to settle conflicts appropriately, and you know how to deal with the in-laws and the neighbors, you can move along to being an effective teacher. Here are resources for handling other questions that arise for homeschooling families. We address the dreaded "S" word—socialization—later in this chapter.

Age Segregation in School
learninfreedom.org/age_grading_bad.html
A strong argument for combining children of different ages in the same educational environment. ☆☆☆☆

Bry-Back Manor   **www.geocities.com/Heartland/6459**
Great activities for preschoolers and younger kids. Keep them busy! Some of these pages are more Mac- than PC-oriented. The worksheets for younger kids are printable by any computer. ☆☆☆

Help for Growing Families
www.home-school.com/HELP/HELPTOC.html
Text from a short-lived publication for homeschoolers with large families. The publishers haven't yet put the entire series online. ☆☆

Hotlinks

Homeschool FAQs
www.gocin.com
/homeschool/hs-faqs.htm

Honor Level System
members.aol.com
/churchward/hls

Idea Box
www.theideabox.com

Thoughts on Homeschooling
www.valdosta.peachnet
.edu/~muncyj
/homeschooling
/thoughts.html

Homeschool FAQs   www.gocin.com/homeschool/hs-faqs.htm

Answers to frequently asked questions about homeschooling. Memorize these responses to questions asked by your mother and your neighbor. ☆☆☆☆☆

Homeschool Note   ky-on-line.com/bhe/notes.htm

A collection of short articles on testing, socialization, dealing with problems, and more. Brief and helpful. ☆☆☆☆

Homeschooling: Is It for You?
www.athomemothers.com/infoguides/46a.htm

From *AtHome Mothers* magazine, things to consider when making the decision to homeschool. ☆☆☆

Honor Level System   members.aol.com/churchward/hls

Discipline by design. If you're dealing with discipline issues, this site might change your life. Techniques for classroom control and discipline, including "11 Techniques for Better Classroom Discipline," "Discipline Techniques That Backfire," "Four Stages of Discipline," and "Four Steps for Better Classroom Discipline." ☆☆☆☆☆

Idea Box   www.theideabox.com

Early childhood education and activity resources. The Great Idea for the Day keeps you coming back for more. ☆☆☆☆☆

Thoughts on Homeschooling
www.valdosta.peachnet.edu/~muncyj/homeschooling/thoughts.html

A collection of thoughts on homeschooling by Jim Muncy, including such topics as "Ten Reasons Not to Homeschool." Well considered and worth reading. ☆☆☆☆

What Do I Do to Keep My Toddlers/Preschoolers Occupied During Homeschool?
www.geocities.com/Athens/Aegean/3446/keeplittleones.html

Coyle's Where in the World site reviews these topical links and describes how to use them in your homeschooling. An excellent resource. ☆☆☆☆

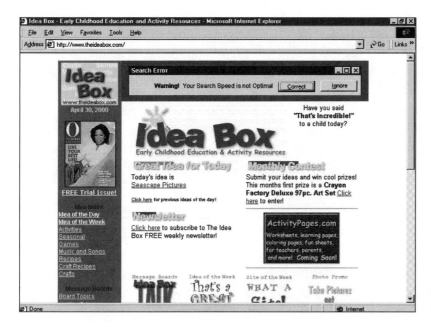

Figure 2.5

Idea Box: Message boards, and lots of educational ideas.

Legal Issues

I'VE HEARD ANY number of horror stories about parents who've had run-ins with local public schools. Sometimes these issues have resolved themselves; sometimes they've been the precipitating factor in a family's decision to homeschool.

The experience of Elizabeth, a Tennessee mother of three, serves as a cautionary tale to parents who get themselves entangled with local educational authorities. Her homeschooling adventure began nine years ago, during spring break. Her daughter, a learning-disabled 13-year-old, was enrolled in special education, and in Elizabeth's opinion, the classes were doing her more harm than good.

After a horrific debate with the school, Elizabeth ended up in court defending her daughter against a school system that, in her opinion, had gone berserk. "We even had a couple of teachers tell us in confidence that my daughter was

> **Legal:** From the Latin *lex (law)*. Rules of conduct established by a governing authority.

John Marshall

One of America's most influential Supreme Court justices, John Marshall, was schooled at home by his parents. Marshall was born in 1755 near Germantown, Virginia, the eldest of 15 children. He spent his childhood on the Virginia frontier, and was taught primarily by his parents and for a short time by an itinerant preacher who lived with the family. He spent only a few months in a formal school setting, but until his death in 1835 he set the direction of the highest judicial body in the United States.

capable of doing more, but that the system would not allow it. One teacher even told us of a lawyer who would take our case on for free." That same teacher now homeschools her children. "This went on for two years; finally the day came for our hearing, and we lost."

Elizabeth and her husband were devastated by the reaction of the school personnel, who openly gloated that they now had free rein with the daughter. "My husband and I cried. The lawyer wanted to take it to the next level in the court system, for free, because he really believed that we had a case. But we told him we would have to pray first and did.

"The next day I was listening to the radio and heard the president of homeschooling for our state. It was a call-in show, so I called in and asked a few questions. He then proceeded to tell me that I could do it and where to call for more information. I did just that. That night we prayed again and put out a fleece to the Lord that if this was the way we should go, that within three days we would hear something. We had never heard of homeschooling before this, so it was all new and a step of faith. Three days later we received a call to take our children out of the school system that day. Homeschooling hasn't always been easy. We've had our bad days, but we do love teaching our children."

While the homeschooling movement is undeniably finding acceptance, there are still parents around the country who have to fight in family courts for their right to homeschool. Others find themselves in

David-and-Goliath battles with truculent educators, some of whom are openly hostile to homeschooling. (As I was doing research for this book, most of the educators I approached for assistance and direction were very helpful. There were half a dozen, though, who responded to my requests with venom, and who refused outright to offer counsel or advice to anyone who would take their children out of public schools to educate them at home.)

The tide seems to be turning, but there's still a lot of fury out there directed at people who buck the system. Here are some sites that will teach you what you need to know to protect yourself.

A to Z Home's Cool

www.gomilpitas.com/homeschooling/regional/Region.htm

"This site includes a page for each of the fifty United States, as well as pages for several other countries. Each page lists annotated links to information about support groups, legal requirements, and resources available. It seems quite comprehensive. I've done some research on my home state, and they've had everything I've needed so far, all in one concise location, with enough info about what's what to let me visit only the relevant areas." —M.B. ☆☆☆☆

Educators Concerned About Homeschooling   family.go.com/Features/family_1999_11/dony/dony119concerns/dony119concerns.html

If you've ever wondered whether your right to homeschool is under fire, here's proof. ☆☆☆

Forced Unionism Is Shutting Down American Education

www.nilrr.org/forced.htm

One of many salvos against those who oppose school choice. ☆☆

Illinois H.O.U.S.E. (Home Oriented Unique Schooling Experience)

www.geocities.com/Athens/Acropolis/7804

Hotlinks

Home School Legal Defense Association
www.hslda.org

National Home Education Network
www.nhen.org

School Choices
www.schoolchoices.org

Sites for National, State, and Local Support
www.geocities.com/Athens/8259/local.html

A network of nonsectarian support groups across Illinois. An information packet with articles on Illinois law and general homeschooling topics can be downloaded right from the site.

Homeschool Compliance Tips   www.kaleidoscapes.com/comply

The Kaleidoscape message boards are wonderful: very popular, very helpful. Turn to this board for answers to questions regarding state laws and complying with homeschool regulations. ☆☆☆☆☆

Home School Legal Defense Association   www.hslda.org

This organization has been embroiled in some controversy, but all your inquiries about the legality of homeschooling should begin here. ☆☆☆☆☆

Homeschool Watch   www.homeschoolwatch.com

An Idaho organization that monitors legislatures. Quick and effective information, support network, and more. A good model for other states. ☆☆

Homeschooling Is for All Kinds of Folks!
www.expage.com/page/folcfolks

An organization that objects, strenuously, to the exclusivity of the Home School Legal Defense Association (HSLDA). Seems to me like a lot of hue and cry, but you can make your own decision. ☆☆☆☆

Laws and Regulations
www.home-ed-press.com/HSRSC/hsrsc_lws.rgs.html

Helen Hegener's article "On Jumping Through Hoops" is interesting, but the section on state laws is invaluable. ☆☆☆☆

Letter of Intent   www.geocities.com/Heartland/Estates/6000/letter.htm
Sample letter of intent to homeschool. ☆☆

Milton and Rose D. Friedman Foundation   www.friedmanfoundation.org
Milt Friedman has always been inspired about economics; he's even more inspired about school choice. His foundation supports the prin-

ciple of educational freedom and suggests ways to become politically active in the cause. ☆☆☆☆

National Home Education Network   www.nhen.org

A more broad-based, inclusive organization than the HSLDA, but not nearly so influential. ☆☆☆☆☆

School Choices   www.schoolchoices.org

Here's the research demonstrating that school choice works, and that private education is more effective than public. Lots of articles, essays, and information on getting politically active in protecting your right to homeschool. ☆☆☆☆☆

Sites for National, State, and Local Support
www.geocities.com/Athens/8259/local.html

How to start homeschooling, plus links to information about local law, compliance, and support groups. ☆☆☆☆☆

State by State   www.inspirit.com.au/unschooling/states/states.html

State-by-state resources and laws for homeschoolers. ☆☆☆☆☆

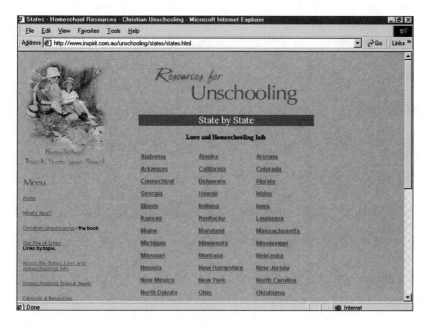

Figure 2.6

State by State: Laws and home-schooling informa-tion for your state.

Assessment Testing

TO COMPLY WITH the education law in your state, you may be required to do annual assessment testing. But even if it's not required, you might wish to assess your children's academic progress with standardized tests, in-home assessments, or some other form of performance evaluation.

Testing may be the single most incendiary issue among homeschoolers. Those who test are viewed by some as traitorous; those who don't are viewed by others as dangerously defiant. Among those who must, there's only grudging compliance. The tests are usually administered in an environment that's unfamiliar to the homeschooled student, and there's a strong belief among homeschoolers that unless they "teach to the test"—that is, spend valuable educational time training children to parrot meaningless test-oriented trivia—the scores will imply that homeschooled children are poorly educated.

On top of everything else, there is evidence that some test administrators have cheated in reporting scores or administering the tests.

In Colorado, assessment testing has been a mixed bag for homeschooler Shari Setter. "We are required to test in grades 3, 5, 7, 9, and 11," she says. "The first year my special-needs son tested, he was in the first percentile, but he was not held to task. He would answer one or two questions, then watch everyone else in the room! The next year he went up to the 13th percentile mark (I was happy)." Shari's daughter has scored consistently above average, and well into college levels for non-core subjects. Testing has caused Shari to have what she calls "hang-ups" about getting her children through the exams, although she's trying to ease up a bit.

> **Assessment:**
> From the Medieval Latin *assessus (assist)*. An appraisal.

Another mother, whose child has been diagnosed with attention deficit/hyperactivity disorder (ADHD), explains how standardized testing fails to account for the benefits of homeschooling. "I'm a homeschooling mom with seven kids. I don't know whether my 17-year-old will do tremendously well on his ACT and SAT tests, but because I rescued him in time, he will at least be *taking* those exams. Before I started homeschooling, he had been kicked out of his junior high school for disruptive behavior and was in an alternative school, where he was socializing with drug addicts and criminals, and building birdhouses. Now he's being taught at home by Mom, studying for his GED (just passed the math and science sections at 94 and 87 percent, respectively), planning to attend community college this spring, and earning money so that he can go on a church mission when he turns 19.

"What the standardized tests don't account for is the high incidence of children who are *saved* from a future of drugs, crime, and unemployment by coming home to the loving, full-time attention of their parents."

Homeschooler Gita Schmitz has several reasons for not testing: "First, in my opinion, tests measure only the facts you've retained at that particular time (and if you're a lousy tester like I was, they don't even do that). I don't care whether my kids know the population of China, or what battle happened in what year. I'm much more interested in the political and historical 'big picture' of the world: why things happened, and what the effect was of those things, and whether they see similarities between those things and what's going on in this country today.

"I want them to understand issues such as how a country like ours, that started out with such a liberty-loving, independent people who wanted government out of their lives, has been transformed to today's people who appear to want government to take care of them, and who are appearing to embrace socialism while thinking they're 'free.' Government-written school tests are never going to ask the questions and demand the thinking that I would like."

Whether you embrace standardized testing, revile it, or are simply forced into it by local law, the following resources will help you stay the

Hotlinks

Assessment Information
www.awesomelibrary.org
/Office/Teacher/Assessment
_Information/Assessment
_Information.html

Exercises in Math Readiness
math.usask.ca/readin
/menu.html

FairTest
www.fairtest.org

Quiz Lab
www.funbrain.com/quiz

course. You'll find related sections on placement testing in chapter 3 and college testing in chapter 14.

Assessment   www.emtech.net/assess.htm

Scores of very well chosen resources. ☆☆

Assessment Information   www.awesomelibrary.org/Office/Teacher /Assessment_Information/Assessment_Information.html

A tremendous collection of information on student assessments. Not specifically homeschool-oriented, but by the time you work through this information, you'll have some strong opinions on the subject. Collections of links don't usually earn a high rating, but this set is exceptional. ☆☆☆☆☆

Best Way to Test   ky-on-line.com/bhe/notes.htm#TEST2

Testing advice for homeschooling parents. ☆☆☆

Exercises in Math Readiness   math.usask.ca/readin/menu.html

From basic addition to advanced theory components, here's everything anyone needs to prepare for advanced college math. Each section has a brief overview, followed by introductory, moderate, and advanced exercises. Do the exercises online, and see your instant score. ☆☆☆☆☆

FairTest   www.fairtest.org

The National Center for Fair and Open Testing advocates for reform in assessment testing. Every homeschooler should be knowledgeable about this site, whether or not you are currently required to do assessment testing of your children. ☆☆☆☆☆

Homeschool Achievement Tests   www.thurbers.net/teatests.html

This site sells achievement tests and provides good background information on achievement testing for homeschooling. ☆☆☆

Homeschool Headlines
www.homeschoolheadlines.com/pastnewsletter.htm

This newsletter has lost its steam, but the slow-downloading collection of articles on testing is well worth the wait. A dozen other articles on homeschooling make this a "settle down for an hour to read" site. ☆☆☆

InteractiveTest   www.interactivetest.com

Make your own interactive multiple-choice tests, and put them online for free. You can also make tests and exams over the Internet and get comprehensive statistics on the fly. An eclectic collection that makes fun use of technology but that doesn't provide the background materials necessary to make the tests really useful. ☆☆

National Center on Educational Outcomes
www.coled.umn.edu/NCEO

Home of the controversial "outcome-based education" philosophy. Their research is worth understanding. ☆☆☆

Quiz Lab   www.funbrain.com/quiz

A tremendous site from FunBrain. Use any of the hundreds of ready-made nonstandardized tests on dozens of subjects, or make your own tests. Kids log on separately from parent/teachers to take their exams, or you can simply print out your tests and distribute them the

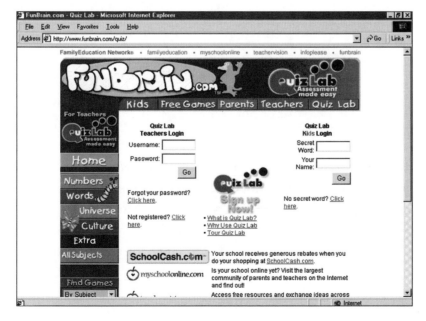

Figure 2.7

Quiz Lab: Build 'em yourself.

old-fashioned way. A grade book keeps track of scores, a calendar tracks dates, and a links page lets you generate your own "textbook" so your children can bone up on a subject you designate. This site is, well, perfect! ☆☆☆☆☆

S.O.S. Math: CyberExam   **www.sosmath.com/cyberexam/cyber.html**
Mathematics exams that will help you assess the progress of your older children. ☆☆☆☆

Standardized Testing for Homeschoolers   **testtaker.homestead.com**
A list of standardized achievement tests approved by the State of Washington for homeschoolers. ☆☆☆

Why Standardized Tests Don't Measure Educational Quality
www.familyeducation.com/article/0,1120,1-6219,00.html
Why the yardstick is wrong. ☆☆☆☆

Why Test Homeschoolers?
www.geocities.com/Heartland/Shores/1729/articles.html#Why
Part of a great homeschooling newsletter, this article explains the argument against standardized testing. ☆☆☆☆

That "Socialization" Question

AT SOME POINT, every single homeschooling family has to answer this outrageous question from disapproving family and friends: "What about socialization?"

The "socialization" that goes on in schools is, for many homeschoolers, precisely the thing they hope to avoid by homeschooling. It's more than the peer expectations of drugs, sex, alcohol, and foul language. It's more than the relentless pressure to be thinner, stronger, wealthier, and more clever. It is, for many homeschoolers, the not-so-subtle undermining of values taught in the home. Homeschoolers argue that far from being a place where children meet people who are different from themselves, school is a place where children learn instead to gravitate to those most like themselves, and to create stereotypes about those who are different. They learn that adults are the "enemy," that younger people are to be mocked, and that older people are dangerous.

Robin Tompkins explains some of the concerns she had about putting her two young children in public school. "I am constantly confirmed in my belief that we are doing the best for our children," says the Redding, California, homeschooler. "Among many other reasons, we were concerned

> ## Socialization:
> From the Latin *socialis* (*companionship*). Participation in communities.

with the vulnerability of our children's character, and desired to keep them under our protective influence until they are able to stand firm against peer pressure. Our oldest has already enjoyed learning and we have always enjoyed teaching her, so once I found out what public schools were teaching, I realized that she would not be very challenged academically."

Homeschooler Barbara Ritter suspects that it's only the "10 percent who had 90 percent of the fun" in high school who worry about socialization.

She may have a point, but I have a different perspective. I'm one of that 10 percent, and I probably had 98 percent of the fun. I was involved in every social group, academic group, and activity I could squeeze in. My friends were the focus of my high school world, and I was sure they were the most important people in the universe.

Who are my best friends today? The ones I've kept throughout my life? They are my parents, my two sisters, and my brother. I spent far too little time with my three precious siblings while I was busy getting "socialized" in public school, and they now mean everything in the world to me. Homeschooling creates strong family bonds and builds a permanent social structure. The family is the "society" you keep, and it's the only one that, ultimately, makes any real difference.

That's not to say friends aren't important too. They certainly are, and homeschoolers aren't shy about finding appropriate opportunities

Socialization

"Social resources were the most difficult, but when I didn't find a homeschool support group in my neighborhood that was tolerant of people of a variety of religious beliefs, I started one myself, advertising in the Pennysaver and putting fliers in the libraries, holding the meetings at my church. I also started an e-mail list that was more specific to my needs when I didn't find just what I wanted. Now we're participating in a wide variety of activities during regular 'after-school hours.' Sports, hobbies, and dances are also avenues of socializing."

—Joyce Dowling, graduated homeschooling mother of two,
Prince George's County, Maryland

to be social. Recent research from the National Home Education Research Institute[1] suggests that homeschoolers are anything but anti-social. A study of more than 3,500 homeschooled children found that 87 percent regularly play with friends, 84 percent participate in field trips, and more than three-quarters attend youth classes at church. Nearly half are involved in organized sports, and the same number take music classes. More than a third are involved in Bible clubs, a third in some sort of ministry program, and a third in volunteer work. A significant number are also involved in 4-H, dance classes, and Scouts, and one quarter are involved in other unnamed social activities.

Cindy, a mother of two homeschooled boys in the Chicago area, exemplifies how "socialized" homeschoolers really are. "We are involved in a lot of activities: Boy Scouts, 4-H, band, bowling, soccer, and a great homeschool group. I still work as though I have to get a full curriculum done to be good at this! I am easing up a little, but still not enough not to be stressed!"

1. National Home Education Research Institute, 1990 and 1996 studies, as quoted in Nanette Asimov, Teaching the Kids at Home, *San Francisco Chronicle*, January 29, 1999, www.sfgate .com/cgi-bin/article.cgi?file=/chronicle/archive/1999/01/29/MN87634.DTL.

Philosopher and educator John Dewey made an observation that ought to put grandparents' and neighbors' minds at ease. "Education *is* a social process," he wrote. "Education is growth . . . Education is not a preparation for life; Education is life itself."

Are your kids ready to make friends? Here's help. (See related information on resolving other homeschooling issues earlier in this chapter.)

Alternative Views on Socialization and Homeschooling
www.geocities.com/Athens/Forum/2780/social.html

The Homeschooler Defender collects and describes links specifically related to responses to "The Question." ☆☆☆☆

Homeschooling and Socialization of Children
www.indiana.edu/~eric_rec/ieo/digests/d94.html

Real research! It concludes, in part: "[A]s self-concept is a reflector of socialization, it would appear that few homeschooled children are socially deprived, and that there may be sufficient evidence to indicate that some homeschooled children have a higher self-concept than conventionally schooled children." Hang on to this one. ☆☆☆☆☆

Missing the Mark
www.gocin.com/homeschool/week8.htm

A Christian focus on the socialization question. ☆☆☆☆

Neighborhood Organizing
family.go.com/Features/family_0103_02/famf/famf010302_neighbor /famf010302_neighbor.html

A great idea for meeting all the kids in your extended neighborhood. ☆☆☆☆

Online Class Projects   www.emtech.net/Online_Class_Projects.htm
Scores of very well chosen resources. ☆☆

Hotlinks

Homeschooling and Socialization of Children
www.indiana.edu /~eric_rec/ieo /digests/d94.html

Neighborhood Organizing
family.go.com/Features /family_0103_02/famf /famf010302_neighbor /famf010302_neighbor.html

What About Socialization?
www.gocin.com /homeschool /hs-faqs.htm#faq-2

Figure 2.8

Neighborhood
Organizing: Turn
your neighbors
into friends.

"S" Word: Socialization   ky-on-line.com/bhe/notes.htm#SOCIAL

Brief responses to questions about socialization. ☆☆☆

Socialization Issues and Concerns   core-curriculum.com/page12.html

A lengthy treatise on the fallacy of socialization as an educational goal.
☆☆☆☆☆

Student Online Publishing   www.emtech.net/student_publishing.htm

Lots of very well chosen resources. ☆☆

**Truth About Homeschooling and Socialization   www.nhen.org/emfiles
/The%20Truth%20About%20Homeschooling%20And%20Socialization.txt**

An interesting article by Lucinda H. Kennaley, who says, "It's time for
homeschoolers to tell the truth about 'socialization.'" ☆☆☆

**What About Socialization?   www.gocin.com/homeschool/hs-faqs
.htm#faq-2**

One of a suite of answers to frequently asked questions. Memorize
this list. ☆☆☆☆☆

E-Mail Lists

THE FASTEST WAY to get up and running with your homeschooling is to sign up for an e-mail list. An e-mail list, sometimes called a loop or a group, is simply a group of people who converse via e-mail.

There are two kinds of e-mail lists. The first is a read-only list, to which only the list owner or owners contribute, and subscribers are anonymous. These lists tend to take the form of newsletters, announcements, and bulletins.

The second type is participatory. Members are invited to contribute information relevant to the subject matter of the list, and everyone who participates reads all the mail that is exchanged within the group. These lists are sometimes moderated, and depending on the nature of the group, traffic can range from one or two messages a month to hundreds of messages a day.

You "subscribe" to a list (it's always free), and—if it's a participatory list—after reading the mail for a while and introducing yourself to the group, you simply send e-mail messages to a single address, and the mail is automatically routed to the entire list.

When I asked homeschoolers about their favorite e-mail lists, the suggestions came flying. So many were offered, in fact, that I couldn't begin to include them all in this book. It was Misty Blagg, a homeschooler from Alexandria, Louisiana, who made the most cogent observation. She told me about a favorite list that supports her spiritual beliefs and has a nonjudgmental quality, but observed, "It likely doesn't stand out as the 'best support mailing list anywhere, ever,' but it is a good one. And support lists have to be centered around the needs of so specific a segment of the population to work properly, that I'm not sure there *could* be a 'best ever,' anyway."

She's absolutely right. In researching this book, I spent several weeks monitoring nearly every homeschooling and

> **Mail:** From the Middle English *male* (*bag, wallet*). Written messages conveyed from sender to receiver.

Homeschool Your Child for Free!

There's a very active mailing list associated with this book. Sign up at www.egroups .com/group/0 -homeschoolreviews.

My Favorite Lists

"I like Homeschooling Older Kids (www.egroups.com/group/HSOK) very much. There is plenty of good information and support. I also like Virginia Knowles's Web site and e-mail list (www.homestead.com/hopechest/welcome.html)."

—**Ann Crum**, homeschooling mother of two, central Arkansas

Hotlinks

0-WhyWeHomeschool
www.egroups.com/group
/0-WhyWeHomeschool

**Homeschooling E-mail
Interest Groups**
www.geocities.com/Athens
/8259/e-mail.html

Homeschoolzone
www.egroups.com/group
/homeschoolzone

Hope Chest
www.egroups.com
/group/HopeChest

educational mailing list that was open to me. There are lists to support every homeschooling philosophy you can imagine. Classical LDS Homeschool (www.egroups.com/group/Classical-LDS-hs) is an example of how narrowly focused an e-mail list can be. The list is specifically for Mormon homeschoolers who use the classical approach to education. The list www.egroups.com/group/00-Homeschooling, on the other hand, is open to anyone, anywhere, who has ever considered homeschooling, or whoever might do so at any time in the future. This high-volume list is the *New York Times* of homeschool lists. In a single month, list members exchanged nearly 400 messages.

Homeschooling mom Cheryl, a mother of two in the metro Atlanta area, likes homeschool lists because she can get the help she needs, when she needs it.

"I really enjoy the homeschool lists because I can read them at my leisure, in my home, and delete the threads that don't interest me. I've also had people reply to me privately with suggestions when I had just started and had many questions.

"I also enjoy the links and have more than I could ever use, but I still keep bookmarking more. The other thing I like about the lists is occasionally I'm able to help someone else. The Internet rules!"

It really does. Below are some of the most popular e-mail lists on the Internet, along with a few interesting pages on joining lists. Some lists are announcement only; others are very participatory. Something here will help you on your way.

00-Homeschooling   www.egroups.com/group/00-Homeschooling

If you homeschool your children, or are considering doing so in the future, you are invited to join this chatty list with some 300 members. Discuss any aspect of homeschooling. ☆☆☆☆

0-WhyWeHomeschool   www.egroups.com/group/0-WhyWeHomeschool

This weekly homeschool news column is distributed on a number of mailing lists, or you can sign up here for direct delivery. If you sense some self-interest here, you're right; it's my own list. ☆☆☆☆☆

123Ahomeschoolforme
www.egroups.com/community/123ahomeschoolforme

A list for homeschooled kids and parents. Exchange ideas, provide support for each other, find links for school materials, or chat about scriptures, God, church, parents, kids, home. About 250 members. ☆☆☆☆

ABC_Homeschoolcurric
www.egroups.com/group/abc_homeschoolcurric

Like the TUAC list (below), this list is dedicated to the resale of quality used homeschool curriculum and supplies. About 300 members. ☆☆☆☆

Christianfocus   www.egroups.com/group/christianfocus

This moderated list provides an area for Christian homeschoolers to gather. It's sponsored by the Homeschool Zone and features articles and a place for fellowship. Nearly 300 members. ☆☆☆☆

Eclectichomeschool   www.egroups.com/group/eclectichomeschool

This announcement-only list has more than 900 members. *Eclectic Homeschool Online* is a magazine for creative homeschoolers. The newsletter contains updates on the latest articles, resources, and support group information added to the Web site. It's distributed about twice a month. ☆☆☆☆☆

E-mail Tips   www.emtech.net/email_tips.htm
Dozens of very well chosen resources. ☆☆

Homeschooling E-Mail Interest Groups
www.geocities.com/Athens/8259/e-mail.html

A very thorough compilation of general, children's, Christian, other religious, unschooling, Australian, Canadian, U.S., and other e-mail lists. Includes information on starting your own. ☆☆☆☆☆

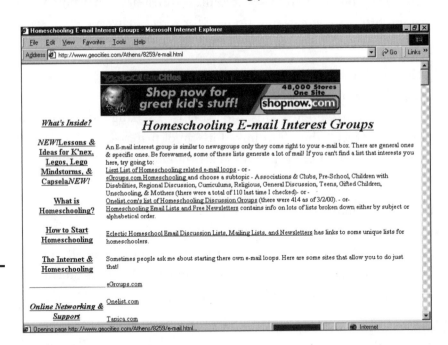

Figure 2.9

Homeschooling E-Mail Groups: Lists of interest to homeschoolers.

Homeschooling Lists
www.geocities.com/Athens/4663/listinfo.html#hslist

Small collection of homeschool e-mail lists. ☆☆

Homeschoolzone   www.egroups.com/group/homeschoolzone
This list is fully moderated and contains suggestions for being a better teacher, whether you're a parent who homeschools full time or one

who just wants to help out with homework at the end of the day. Teachers are welcome as well. With more than 1,500 members, this may be the largest nonsecular list on the Internet. ☆☆☆☆☆

Hope Chest   www.egroups.com/group/HopeChest
Perhaps the largest homeschooling e-mail list around, *Hope Chest* is a free monthly e-mail homeschool magazine offering ideas, information, and inspiration from a Christian perspective. Each issue has a general theme, such as language arts or world geography, and also includes contributions from a few of the more than 1,500 readers. Back issues are archived. ☆☆☆☆☆

PA_Exchange   www.egroups.com/group/PA_Exchange
Some 600 Pennsylvanians participate in this restricted list dedicated to helping families homeschool "in knowledge and confidence rather than ignorance and fear."

Tipz Times' Boards   www.onelist.com/group/0-TipzTime
Another announcement list. This describes updates to the Tipz Time site at www.tipztime.com. Includes household tips, frugal tips, free stuff, chore charts, and homeschool charts. ☆☆☆☆☆

TUAC-Curric-Swap   www.egroups.com/group/TUAC-Curric-Swap
The 720 members of this list buy and sell used curricula. You can also place "wanted" ads. A great way to save money. ☆☆☆☆☆

The Boards

AKIN TO E-MAIL lists, these newsgroups, chat rooms, and boards (which now incorporate discussion forums and BBSes) all provide different kinds of online support.

Personally, I find each of them somewhat less useful than the e-mail lists above. To participate in newsgroups, you must either open the newsgroup reader of your browser—a not very intuitive process—or access the groups through a Web site such as Deja.com (www.deja.com/usenet).

Anything said on a newsgroup is both public and permanent. (E-mail lists, on the other hand, tend to be of no interest to anyone outside the group, and it's unlikely that anyone has the time, disk space, or energy to maintain a permanent searchable public archive.)

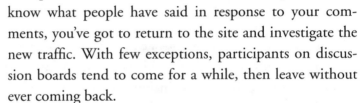

Board: From the Middle English *bord (plank)*. Table at which a council meets.

Web chats and other chat mechanisms tend to be, well, chatty. They're an odd alternative to actual human friends; I've yet to find a chat that was genuinely helpful. I rate chatting as the leading time waster on the Internet. Nevertheless, there are more than a few people who think Internet chatting is the best thing going.

Discussion boards, forums, and electronic bulletin boards (BBSes) require a special trip to the Web site or other resource. If you want to know what people have said in response to your comments, you've got to return to the site and investigate the new traffic. With few exceptions, participants on discussion boards tend to come for a while, then leave without ever coming back.

Nevertheless, your Internet experience isn't complete until you've experienced the entire spectrum . . . and who knows? You might actually enjoy it. Here are some of the top newsgroups, chat areas, and forums for homeschoolers.

Hotlinks

Homeschool Talk and Swap!
www.vegsource.com
/homeschool

Kaleidoscapes
www.kaleidoscapes
.com/wwwboard

ParentPatch
www.parentpatch.com

Deja.com's Usenet Discussion Service
x29.deja.com/usenet
Enter "home-school" in the search engine. This newsgroup has no religious or other tight charter and is very active. ☆☆☆☆

Finding Homeschool Support on the IRC Channels
www.geocities.com/Athens/8259/IRCchat.html
Chat up a storm. Here's everything you need to know about using Internet Relay Chat, including instructions for IRC chats and a list of regular homeschool IRC channels. ☆☆☆☆

Holden Homeschool Message Board

www.bravenet.com/forum/show.asp?userid=cc18245

Nice board, but it's not the most active place on the Web. ☆☆☆

Homeschooling Chats on the Web

www.geocities.com/Athens/8259/webchats.html

Looking for someone to talk to? This fine collection of chat areas for homeschoolers is sure to get you hooked up with someone who wants to talk. See a related link for Homeschooling Message Boards at www.geocities.com/Athens/8259/message.html. ☆☆☆

Homeschool Talk and Swap!   www.vegsource.com/homeschool

This is one of the most popular homeschooling sites on the Net: Sixteen well-populated discussion boards addressing every aspect of homeschooling, along with a large number of boards for buying and selling homeschooling materials. ☆☆☆☆☆

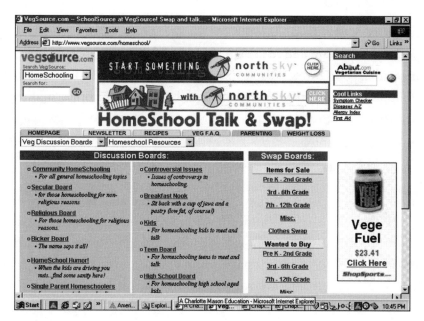

Figure 2.10

Homeschool Talk and Swap! Talk about virtually anything!

ICQ Chat   www.emtech.net/icqchat

Everything you'd ever want to know about setting yourself up on the ICQ chat system. ☆☆

Kaleidoscapes Discussion Board for Home Educators
www.kaleidoscapes.com/wwwboard

The Kaleidoscape message boards are wonderful: very popular, very helpful. This board—the main discussion area for homeschoolers and unschoolers—offers tremendous support, up-to-date discussions, tips and suggestions, and the like by home educators from all walks of life. A related, but chattier, board is at www.kaleidoscapes.com/sidetracks. ☆☆☆☆☆

Parent Patch   **www.parentpatch.com**

An entire collection of homeschooling- and special needs-related discussion boards. You'll also find boards for specific educational interests. ☆☆☆☆☆

Support Groups

THE BEST KIND of support of all: friends. Make friends with a local support group, and find sustenance for your decision to homeschool, along with a good source of socialization and activities for your children.

Support groups are rather a mixed bag for the homeschoolers I talked to while researching this book. Some support groups are helpful and interesting; some are silly and unsupportive; and some simply weren't a good fit for a particular homeschooling family.

Support: From the Latin *supportare* (sub + porte [to carry]). To encourage a person or cause.

"I have had both good and bad experiences with homeschool groups," says Susan Burton, a homeschooling mother of two from Somerdale, Ohio. "I have found that the ones that keep it to an educational goal are by far easier to handle." She said one of the support groups she was in degenerated into a gossipy play group. "Although having fun was important, as Mom, Teacher, Wife, and every other job I do, it really needed to be worth the time away."

👥 *How We Homeschool*

"I attended a local homeschool group skate day, and although I did make a friend there, it wasn't what I'd call 'helpful.' I do intend to go again, though, because I enjoy talking to other people and hearing how they go about their day, and because of the potential of making more friends."

—**Cheryl**, homeschooling mother of two, metro Atlanta area

When Cheryl Northrup was a new homeschooler, support groups were very important to her. "I needed feedback and constant support." The mother of seven lived in Denver then. "There was a group that shared my LDS faith, which made it nicer, but I had to drive a long way to them. The other group was eclectic, and I still really appreciated it.

"My daughter met one of her best friends at one of the first meetings we went to. We did lots of activities, field trips, and moms' nights out. As I have gotten more secure in homeschool, my need for the group comes and goes."

Ann Glass is a homeschooler in a remote area of Washington State. A few years ago she was involved with a moms' group that would meet at a private home one evening a month to talk, share, and ask questions. One day a month, all the participants and their kids would get together for a play day. "Sometimes that would be free play," she said. "Sometimes we moms would plan a special activity. I enjoyed the moms-only evenings, and at times I miss that. The play day, however, seemed to be just one more thing to do on my list. My boys didn't need the play day for socialization; they had friends, cousins, and church. This type of support group was nice, but not something I felt really met me where I was at or what I needed. As a result, I've tended to stay away from 'organized' support groups."

That's not to say Ann doesn't find support, though. "What I have found has worked the best for me, and given me the most satisfaction, has been developing friendships with two other moms and their families.

🚶 *How We Homeschool*

"I am in a homeschool support group. I find it very helpful and I am glad I joined. We have P.E. each week and arts and crafts every other week. Once a month we go roller-skating, ice skating, and on a field trip. We have coffee once a month for the mothers (where we get together and discuss what we're doing, and upcoming events). The kids have math bees, state and capital bees, and geography bees. If I have a problem, I know I can ask one of the other moms what she would do if she had that problem. Last year my family struggled because we didn't have any support."

—**Priscilla Pike**, homeschooling mother of one, Georgia

I've found that while the moms may connect, the kids might not, and worse, the dads might not care for each other. It's important that every member of a family 'jives' with every member of the other family. We three families share the same faith, the same basic homeschooling philosophy (although our methods may differ), and the same value system (with some variance). In other words, we all like each other and feel comfortable with each other. We've become an extended family. The kids call all the adults aunt and uncle.

"We meet once a month at the local McDonald's first thing in the morning to talk, and share ideas and newfound materials. The seven kids have the play area all to themselves. Once every other month we rotate the host mom, and she plans a teaching day focused on one theme. The three all-day events coming up are Pioneer Days, Japan, and Mexico. We start at 9:00 A.M. and end at 1:00 P.M. I also teach music (folk, Sunday school, ethnic, and patriotic songs) one morning a week to all the kids. The rest of the time we teach our own kids, but when each mom comes up against a problem in her weak subjects, she calls the mom who is strong in that subject for help. All in all, this arrangement seems to work the best for me and is the most fulfilling."

In Estancia, New Mexico, homeschooling mother of four Donna Lee Spruill has found support groups to be somewhat unhelpful, in large measure because she's grown out of her need for them. "Several years ago a support group formed about twenty miles away (that's close for us). Most of the parents were *much* younger than we, their children were all under 12 years, and the majority had been homeschooling only a short time. We were the people who had spread out our kids over decades and had been doing this for quite some time. I was actually bored and so were the two still at home: one too old, the other too young.

"After trying several times to get involved, we came to the conclusion that we really didn't need this activity. We had been our own 'support group' for too long."

But Orange County, California, homeschooler Kathleen Thomas had the opposite experience: "I homeschooled for six years without a support group," says the mother of four, "and have homeschooled since January with a group. The group has been very nice; I have a comfortable feeling with them, even though I didn't know any of them before January. They have been so kind and are there for me without any critical attitudes, even though we all homeschool our own way. If someone has a question, there are suggestions available. I have seen other groups that are not like this, but I am very happy with this support group."

Bottom line? If your local group isn't meeting your needs and you can't seem to resolve the issues, don't hesitate to look around for a better fit. You're homeschooling, after all, for your kids. Don't let a bad support group experience throw you off track when there are so many good groups available.

The following links will get you connected with a good homeschooling support group, either online or in the real world:

California Homeschool Network   www.cahomeschoolnet.org

This is one of the best, most complete homeschooling support sites on the Net. You don't have to be homeschooling in California to find

Hotlinks

California Homeschool Network
www.cahomeschoolnet.org/

Homeschooling Sites by States
members.aol.com/stretrat/homeschool/states.html

Sites for National, State, and Local Support
www.geocities.com/Athens/8259/local.html

value in the California Homeschool Network's Web site—though it certainly wouldn't hurt. Legal stuff, politics, tips, FAQs, and much more. The recommended reading list is a great place for beginning homeschoolers to start. ☆☆☆☆☆

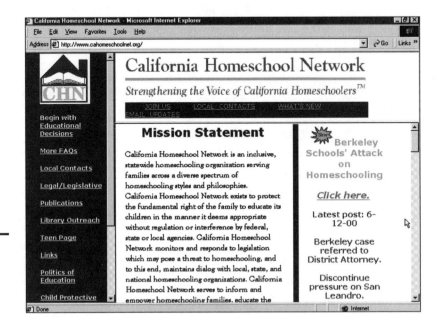

Figure 2.11

California Homeschool Network: Homeschool fun in the sun.

Christian Homeschool Fellowship   www.chfweb.com

Prayer groups, encouragement, message boards, and much more for Christian homeschoolers. ☆☆☆☆☆

Christian Homeschool Forum   www.gocin.com/homeschool

Discussion groups, advice, and much more. Great support for Christian homeschoolers. ☆☆☆☆

Collaborative Learning   www.indiana.edu/~iweb/collabo.html

Collaborate on projects with students at other schools, or with other homeschoolers. ☆☆☆☆

Contact People and Support Groups for Homeschooling
www.geocities.com/Athens/4663/contacts.html

A small list organized by state or province. ☆☆

Homeschool Organizations and Associations

www.books4homeschool.com/HS-assoc.htm

Links to several national homeschooling organizations. ☆☆☆

Homeschooling Sites by States

members.aol.com/stretrat/homeschool/states.html

Homeschooling organizations for every state, and lots of countries. A very comprehensive list. ☆☆☆☆☆

Islamic Educational and Muslim Home School Resources

home.ici.net/~taadah/Homeschool/muslim.html

Good information for Muslim teachers seeking educational material on Islam, as well as resources for the Muslim homeschooling family. Lots of material on an attractive site. ☆☆☆☆

Jewish Home Educator's Network   www.snj.com/jhen

FAQs on homeschooling from a Jewish perspective, plus a quarterly national newsletter. ☆☆☆☆

LDS Homeschooling Page   home1.gte.net/shannon2

Support for homeschooling members of The Church of Jesus Christ of Latter-day Saints. Owner Karen Rafferty includes several articles and links of interest to Mormons. ☆☆☆☆

Sites for National, State, and Local Support

www.geocities.com/Athens/8259/local.html

This is how I first found my own state homeschooling contacts. Includes Canadian and other national contacts. ☆☆☆☆☆

Support Groups   www.home-ed-magazine.com/groups/orgs.html

A very good collection of information on homeschooling support groups. You're sure to find a group to your liking. ☆☆☆☆

Curriculum Core: Scope and Sequence

THE FIRST TASK for a homeschooling family is deciding what and how to teach. Eventually, every homeschooling family chooses its own path. That's not much reassurance, though, to families who are just starting out.

Initially, our family's homeschooling experience overseas was more a matter of necessity than of choice. I had a special-needs child who was becoming increasingly disruptive in class, and it eventually became necessary to bring him home to ensure that he got an education at all.

I knew many homeschoolers overseas, but didn't realize the growing size of the movement in North America until we returned to the States and started meeting homeschoolers everywhere we went. The movement fascinated me, and I felt a strong desire to continue homeschooling. But the homeschooling curriculum materials I was reading were unimpressive, and I had difficulty imagining how I would incorporate them into a program for our family.

When we eventually decided to go ahead and homeschool in the United States, we were required by the local school district to submit a curriculum plan. I had been reading lots of homeschooling resources and realized that many, many families were choosing to avoid formal curricula altogether, in favor of an eclectic approach. I had been conditioned, though, to think in more formal terms, so I had a bit of a dilemma.

On Education

"It is possible to store the mind with a million facts and still be entirely uneducated."
—Alec Bourne,
A Doctor's Creed

I continued to research. Eventually I found lots of curriculum resources, including the educational outcome goals for our own school district, available online. As I read through the district's curriculum, I realized that everything there was available to me without purchasing a full-scale set of curriculum materials from a professional developer. It was a go.

Curriculum development needn't be as difficult for you as it was for me. You have, essentially, three choices: use prepackaged curriculum ma-

How We Homeschool

"I have said for a long time that we aren't raising children, we are raising adults. I believe it is not our job to make or force our children to do anything, but to help teach them guidelines for making wise choices, and help them learn from the consequences of their choices. That includes making, understanding, and obeying rules and laws, but it also means they learn how to think for themselves."

—**Cheri Christensen**, homeschooling mother of four, Salem, Utah

terials, build your own curriculum, or take the eclectic approach, doing a little bit of both. The prepackaged route has traditionally been the most popular, but there are many ways to do it for free—or nearly so.

Two studies from National Home Education Research Institute (NHERI) indicate that 71 percent of homeschooling programs are designed by parents. Just less than a quarter are complete, off-the-shelf curriculum packages. Ten percent of parents use a combination or some other method. The NHERI surveyed 1,657 families with 5,402 children.[1]

Homeschooler Gita Schmitz advises parents to do a bit of planning before spending anything on pricey curriculum materials. "Parents need to first figure out what their teaching style will be, and the best way their kids learn."

To save money, Luanne, a homeschooling mom from Virginia, organized a consortium of homeschoolers who exchange curriculum materials. Here's how she did it:

"Shortly after starting homeschooling, I became keenly aware of my inability to get the books and other resources that I wanted for teaching with my very limited budget. I also learned that there were families homeschooling in our area, part of our group, who had used books and things packed away in boxes and sitting collecting dust on shelves. These

Self-Determination

"Only the educated are free."
—Epictetus,
A.D. C. 50–c. 138

1. *San Francisco Chronicle,* January 29, 1999, www.sfgate.com/cgi-bin/article.cgi?file=/chronicle/archive/1999/01/29/MN87634.DTL.

Curriculum Tips

"How do I handle scheduling and curriculum? It depends on the age and family situation. When my children were young, I would have a time for outdoor activities, theme and craft activities, and reading every day, but other things were flexible and occurred according to their interests. I didn't purchase expensive curricula; mostly I used library books, the Internet, some software, and lots of field trips."

—Joyce Dowling, homeschooling mother of one teenage boy, Akron, Ohio

could be sold at used book sales or conventions, but the profit was small for the sellers; and for me, the opportunity didn't come very often to make it to these events to buy. Also, even that much money was hard to come by at times.

"On the other hand, I had collected quite a few nice books at the high school level—teacher's manuals and assorted books that had been given to me by family members. We could use these later, but at that time my son was in the first grade.

"Sounds like bad timing, but it isn't if other homeschoolers are willing to put their collections together for common use. This we did, and it has grown into a marvelous organization. Our library is small; we call it the Home Education Consortium because it is a place for us to share our common resources. It has grown in many ways other than just the sharing of used curricula and other books.

"Now our group does the *Weekly Reader* program and earns free books, which go into the consortium for all to use. When we want to honor one of our members, we donate to the consortium a book that is meaningful to that member. We keep this collection at the church where we are so graciously allowed to have our weekly meetings and activities, so all members can use its resources freely."

Buying curriculum materials is a practical matter for Debbie Hostetler, a homeschooling mother of three in Newport Beach, California. She attends every local used-curriculum fair she can find, and buys used books for her family's curriculum. "When we're finished using the curriculum, we pay anywhere from one to five dollars for a space at the next used-curriculum fair, and sell the items we're finished with. By careful shopping, I have always come out even . . . even after paying for the space. I just increase the price of the item by five to ten cents. We end up selling about three half-days per year, but are able to have a rich and varied curriculum at no cost!" She also recommends the fairs as a great place to preview curricula, "so you don't waste money in the first place."

For homeschooling mom Susie Clawson, buying curriculum materials has been nothing but a waste of money. She has several tips for dealing with the expensive curriculum materials that you've already purchased:

- Put the curriculum on the shelf.
- Sell it.
- Adapt it to suit the needs of your kids.
- Skip the boring stuff.
- Supplement with fun library books and videos.
- Add lots of field trips, even if they don't relate to what you're learning.
- Use the Scouting and 4-H projects as their curriculum.
- Use a unit study approach.
- Allow each child to pick a project, and help the child find materials to learn.

The Clearfield, Utah, mother of five says her family used this last system to do a science fair project one year. She and her children read the library books together, and each child worked individually on his or her displays.

The problem with using set curricula is their inflexibility, as Shari Setter has discovered. "Our first year we used Christian Liberty Academy Satellite School program," says the Peyton, Colorado, mother of five. "It was good for getting started. It forced us to do school daily and be accountable. But it left me feeling like I was pushing my kids through, just to get through. It didn't matter if they understood; we had a deadline!

"We joined ATIA [a Christian educational organization], and the first year of that was great, but then it got so complicated with so many different ages to teach. Right now we are using Alpha Omega Life Pacs for my two boys (grades 5 and 2), and my daughter (grade 9) is doing the BOLA online program through Alpha Omega."

Donna Lee Spruill, a homeschooling mother of four in Estancia, New Mexico, has taken the eclectic approach in an effort to get around the flexibility issues. "We've used curriculums from noted entities, such as Calvert, International Institute, Bob Jones University, and Abeka. And we've designed our own and combined ideas and books. This has been a labor of love for us . . . all of us. And we wouldn't have done anything differently."

Another eclectic philosophy, of sorts, is that of an Englishwoman named Charlotte Mason. She lived in the early 1900s and advocated a gentle form of teaching that involved nature walks, journals, and reading classic literature. Christine Blair, a homeschooling mother of two in Massachusetts, has taken Charlotte Mason to heart. "I have started homeschooling the Charlotte Mason way, using the book *The Gentle Art of Learning*. We are enjoying school immensely, and I feel like my life is also being enriched."

Susan Clawson has also embraced the Charlotte Mason approach. "We use *some* Charlotte Mason ideals in our schooling, but we're very eclectic and approach unschooling. We get totally engrossed in various projects and spend the entire day working on something like a notebook. 'Whatever works' is our motto!" She has also used what she calls a Scout curriculum. "For a while, the only way I could motivate my oldest was to make her studies part of a badge or belt loop award for Scouts. I'm my daughter's Brownie leader as well, and her sash is covered with her Try Its. Our troop used to be mostly homeschooled girls, but now it is open to the girls at the private school where we meet. The homeschoolers usually end up with more badges simply because they work on things with their family and friends as part of their learning. Many mothers told us in advance that they wouldn't be involved except to bring their girls to the meetings. Sad but true."

On Success

"Success is the sum of small efforts— repeated day in and day out."
—Robert Collier, author

On Curriculum

"An understanding heart is everything in a teacher, and cannot be esteemed highly enough. One looks back with appreciation to the brilliant teachers, but with gratitude to those who touched our human feeling. The curriculum is so much necessary raw material, but warmth is the vital element for the growing plant and for the soul of the child."

—Carl Gustav Jung, Swiss psychiatrist

Another Scout curriculum user is Susan Amiot, a homeschooling mom of five in Orlando, Florida. "I used some of the Scout badges for 'homeschool' stuff. My daughter didn't think of it as school. This is a great way to do homeschool, at least a part of it, very cheaply without buying all the books on the market."

Annie Glass, on the other hand, has figured out how to do everything for free, using nothing but the resources of the Internet as her curriculum. Annie lives near the Canadian border in Everson, Washington, where she teaches music lessons and homeschools her two boys. Her story may inspire you to follow her lead:

"I've been using the Internet as my curriculum for about a year now. Finances are tight, of course, and I've been able to save hundreds of dollars by printing exactly what I need. I stick with the sites that are specifically for teachers, where I find detailed lesson plans for every subject and grade.

"Obviously, in homeschooling, one's pace is varied and flexible, depending on the child and the activities of each family member. However, I do try to loosely plan a couple of years ahead. Math, reading, spelling, and grammar are dependent on learning skills systematically, so I look for fun, relevant practice tools.

"In subjects that are more flexible, such as science, social studies, history, or the fine arts, I try to sketch out a general outline of the order and age at which each will be covered. For example, in science I am covering the six days of creation:

On Education

"I have never let my schooling interfere with my education."
—Mark Twain, author

1. light, energy, and matter; 2. water and the atmosphere; 3. land and plants; 4. sun, moon, and stars; 5. birds and sea life; and 6. land animals and humans.

"This material could be covered in a year, but we tend to become immersed in a topic for several weeks. We have covered only days one and two this year. Weather will be carried over, and we'll probably cover only day three next year.

"I have a notebook that I've organized into sections with Web addresses: Web field trips, best sites for lesson plans, and sites to check out, as well as sections on the specific subjects. When I reach a site I like, I print out the lesson plans, worksheets, or activities. If it's a site that is best used online (such as an interactive one or an Internet field trip), I print out the home page so I can see exactly what it's about. I put all the printed material in manila folders in inexpensive cardboard boxes and file it by subject and the potential year I plan on using it. For example, this coming year is all in green and my social studies folders are as follows: map skills, U.S. Constitution, Louisiana Purchase, War of 1812, and the Civil War. We will spend a week or two learning about farms. We also do a country study each year.

"I think homeschoolers are becoming much pickier as they gain confidence in what they are doing. Most of us are living on a single income, many with large families to support. We want the best for our children, but can't afford to spend much in dollar amounts. That's why I think this book is much needed and will be welcomed by the homeschooling community."

This chapter introduces everything you need to build a curriculum of your own, whether you're trying to supplement a set curriculum or devise one of your own from scratch. Whether you're a devout "school at home-er" or a committed unschooler or something in between, this is where you get started.

We begin with a section on placement testing, so you'll be able to evaluate your child's current educational level. Then we locate some great resources for lesson plans and for worksheets. The next section discusses unit studies, an alternate educational philosophy in which multi-

On Teaching

"The best teacher is the one who suggests, rather than dogmatizes, and inspires his listener with the wish to teach himself."
—Edward Bulwer-Lytton, English author

disciplinary units rather than single subjects are taught. After that come sections on field trips, preschool, special education, and, finally, unschooling, a philosophy of child-led learning. We've got you covered.

First, though, are a few of the best curriculum links on the Internet. Use these resources to build a traditional curriculum that parallels the public school system, or build your curriculum around any mixture of alternative philosophies that fit your family's learning style. In the appendix at the end of this book, you'll also find a suggested Scope and Sequence that may help you in devising your own curriculum. Additional curriculum requirements, by state, are found in the resources in chapter 2 under the Legal Issues heading.

A Charlotte Mason Education Will Benefit Your Children
members.aol.com/beeme1

This tremendously influential woman advocated short lessons, classic literature, nature walks, and journal keeping as the basis of a lasting education. This page brings it all together. If you haven't found something that works for your family, Charlotte Mason is worth considering. I've not yet met a homeschooling parent who used the CM method and disliked it. ☆☆☆☆☆

Classical Homeschooling
www.classicalhomeschooling.org

Many home educators are returning to classical education to teach art, languages, rhetoric, and more. ☆☆☆☆☆

Copernicus Curriculum Matrix
www.copernicus-matrix.com

This is a thorough curriculum program, organized by subject and grade level. You'll find a combination of lesson plans, content standards, assessment tests, and learning activities for a variety of subject areas. ☆☆☆☆☆

Core Knowledge   www.coreknowledge.org

Educator E. D. Hirsch Jr. caused quite a stir among educators, parents, and homeschoolers with his Core

Hotlinks

Developing Educational Standards
putwest.boces.org
/Standards.html

Faithful Servant's Books
www.geocities.com
/Heartland/Pointe/1249

Home2School
www.home2school.com

MeritBadge
www.meritbadge.com

Curriculum

Curriculum

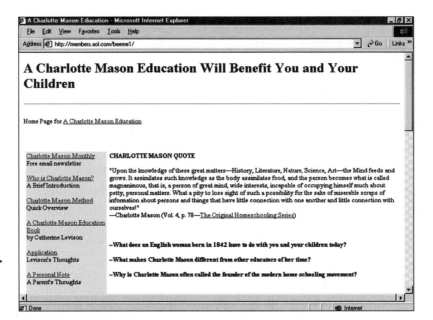

Figure 3.1

Charlotte Mason:
Long walks and
good books.

Knowledge Series. Grade by grade and subject by subject, Hirsch outlines what your child needs to know and offers lesson plans and a complete sequence for elementary education in language arts, history and geography, visual arts, music, science, and math. Unfortunately, you'll still have to buy the books to use this site effectively, but the site has plenty of useful links. ☆☆

Curricula Discussion and Tips Board
www.kaleidoscapes.com/curricula

The Kaleidoscape message boards are wonderful: very popular, very helpful. Meet other homeschoolers to discuss and evaluate curricula. ☆☆☆☆☆

Curriculum Guides and Resources   www.emtech.net/curr.htm
Scores of very well chosen resources. ☆☆☆

Developing Educational Standards   putwest.boces.org/Standards.html
Curriculum standards by state, by subject area, and by nation; U.S. government standards; state departments of education standards; and

much more on this site developed by a group of New Yorkers building a new high school. ☆☆☆☆

Faithful Servant's Books   www.geocities.com/Heartland/Pointe/1249

Free books. Well, almost free; you pay shipping, but this is a Christian ministry to homeschooling families. ☆☆☆☆☆

Home2School   www.home2school.com

This site builds a custom curriculum for your child based on his or her age and geographic location. As your child learns each skill or principle, you check it off the list and begin teaching another concept. Enter the names of several children, and Home2School accommodates them all. The site has hundreds of essential learning objectives correlated to each of the fifty states' academic requirements. Includes parent tutorials for you to refresh your memory as you teach. ☆☆☆☆☆

MeritBadge   www.meritbadge.com

If you want to design your own curriculum, you really should consider the Scouting program as a model. This site has a listing of all the BSA merit badges, along with the requirements and resources for earning them. This site will—the author promises—soon be as useful for female scouts as it presently is for males. Nevertheless, homeschooled kids of either gender will find plenty here worth learning. ☆☆☆☆☆

Plan the Syllabus Tutorial   www.syllabus.umn.edu/tutorial

A tutorial that teaches you how to build your own syllabus. ☆☆☆☆

Scout School   www.cis.net/~cmmeyer/ScoutSchool

"This lady centers a lot of her homeschool program around Scouting requirements. I like this site a lot." —M.H. ☆☆☆

The Well-Trained Mind   www.welltrainedmind.com

This is the book that is inspiring a hugely popular homeschooling movement toward classical education. Tons of resources. I've seen the material discussed on almost every major homeschooling list. ☆☆☆☆☆

Typical Course of Study   www.worldbook.com/ptrc/html/curr.htm

"Curriculum, arranged by subject, for all age levels. Helps parents who are designing their own curriculums in math, reading, language arts, social studies, and more. Good starting point for beginners, but not very specific." —M.D. ☆☆☆

Typical School Curriculum Guide from Anywhere, U.S.A.

www.graceland.edu/~jackg/curr_guide/contents.html

Actual curriculum guide from a school district somewhere in the Midwest. Includes curricula for art, drug education, guidance and counseling, health, language arts, library and media, mathematics, music, reading, science, and social studies. Appropriate for all age levels. ☆☆☆☆

Placement Testing

PLACEMENT TESTING HELPS you get a handle on your child's educational level in reading, math, science, and other subjects.

For our purposes, placement testing is a specific procedure that new homeschoolers can use to determine their children's academic strengths or educational gaps. It's also for parents making decisions about formal homeschooling for their kindergarten-age children.

Level: From the Latin *libella (libra: balance).* The line at which everything is everywhere parallel.

Placement testing is different from the assessment testing required by some states (see the assessment testing section of chapter 2 for more information on assessment testing). For homeschoolers, placement testing is strictly for your own information and so can be as formal or as informal as you wish.

Homeschooling mom Joyce Dumire in Akron, Ohio, explains how placement testing worked for her and her son: "We started late with homeschooling. My son was already a teenager. He was the one that really wanted to do the homeschooling. I wanted to, but having a full-time job, it just didn't seem possible. He really wanted this to work, because if it didn't, he went back to public school.

"When we started, I tested him in all subjects with a test purchased from a commercial supplier called Alpha Omega. The results were not pretty. He had a lot of catching up to do. But I just went to that grade level and started from there. He whizzed through it at first, but it slowly (and sometimes rapidly) got harder. He'd walk away, but come back—maybe in a few minutes, maybe in a few days. If he didn't, I'd put that aside and go back a bit.

"Today he proudly will announce, 'I love math, I've always been good at math.' He's right, it's always been a successful subject for him."

The placement testing material in the following list isn't as formal as the prepackaged set Joyce used. It will, nevertheless, give you good information about your young child's school readiness, and your older child's comprehension of basic academic subjects.

Assessment of the Highly Gifted
www.hollingworth.org/assess.html

> A good framework for determining the intellectual capacity of intelligent children. ☆☆☆

Calculus Page   math.uc.edu/calculus

> Computer-graded Web version of a university calculus placement test. Try it! The scores are recorded, so take it under some other name if you want to make sure they stay anonymous! Twenty or more correct responses is considered good. Detailed solutions are available after the test is scored. ☆☆☆☆

COMPASS Sample Items
www.csi.edu/ip/ADC/testing/compass.htm

> Sample test items designed to illustrate the form of the questions in the COMPASS battery of tests. Includes pre-algebra, algebra, trigonometry, and reading and writing skills. ☆☆☆

Hotlinks

EuroPlus+ Reward
www.reward-net.com
/placement.htm

Free Tests
www.brain.com/tests

Nation's Report Card
nces.ed.gov
/nationsreportcard
/itmrls/intro.shtml

Saxon Math
www.saxonmath.com
/placement_tests.htm

Early Childhood Education Internet Resources
www.kidsinc.com/Homepages/links.html

Is your five-year-old developmentally ready to be schooled? These resources are organized by area of social-emotional development, by an organization that does testing for kindergarten readiness. ☆☆☆

EuroPlus+ Reward   **www.reward-net.com/placement.htm**

An English-language placement test. Take the test online, and see the score immediately. The "Euro" part of the name means the test is administered in British English. ☆☆☆☆

Free Tests   **www.brain.com/tests**

Timed tests on intelligence, mental performance, memory, emotional state, and more. The whole site is helpful in understanding the mind, but these free tests alone are worth the visit. ☆☆☆☆☆

Kindergarten Readiness Checklist
www.pcsb.k12.fl.us/prek/readiness.htm

A seven-part checklist for school readiness. Each part covers a different developmental area and includes helpful advice for parents who are preparing their young children for academia. ☆☆☆☆

Math and English Assessment   **www.lapc.cc.ca.us/usr/assess/test.html**

Sample placement tests, with free downloadable answers. These exams test skills in English and several levels of math. Appropriate for upper-level students. ☆☆☆

Mathematics Placement Examinations   **www.math.niu.edu/placement**

Free online placement exams from Northern Illinois University. Find your middle or high school–aged child's appropriate math level. ☆☆☆☆

Nation's Report Card   **nces.ed.gov/nationsreportcard/itmrls/intro.shtml**

A tremendous testing tool. Extensive online tests in reading, math, writing, civics, arts, sciences, U.S. history, and geography. Can be customized for fourth-, eighth-, and twelfth-grade levels. ☆☆☆☆☆

Saxon Math   www.saxonmath.com/placement_tests.htm

Publishers of the well-known Saxon math series post these placement tests online. Parents can administer and score the test. ☆☆☆☆☆

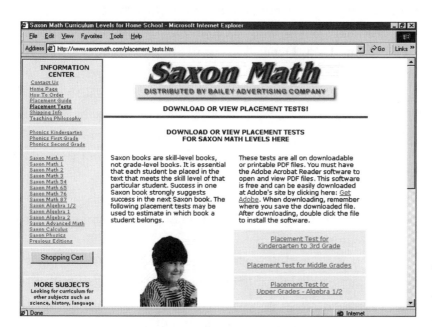

Figure 3.2

Saxon Math: Test your child's math placement level.

Stanford Achievement Test   www.tampareads.com/sat

Sample test questions for young students. ☆☆

Test Your English   englishtest.berlitz.com

For nonnative speakers, an English-language placement test in 19 different languages. Because the test is administered in a non-English language, you can, practically speaking, test yourself in reverse, as well. ☆☆☆☆

Testing in the Real World
www.nhen.org/emfiles/Testing%20In%20The%20Real%20World.txt

An article in which the author writes: "Tests come in many shapes and sizes, they're given for many reasons, and the way a person perceives testing is shaped by his experience with tests. Our children have never been tested in the traditional sense for one simple reason: we trust them to learn what they need to know." ☆☆☆

Lesson Plans

NOW THAT YOU know your children's academic levels and have developed your curriculum program, it's time to start teaching.

What you want is to avoid getting into the situation experienced by Sherrie Rosenau of Van Dyne, Wisconsin. Sherrie, a mother of six, is in her first year of homeschooling. She says that with her set curriculum, she's spending more time making agendas and corrections than teaching.

Melody Daisson, an Orem, Utah, mother of three, has a similar struggle. "I guess my biggest frustration is that I never feel on top of things. I started out wanting to plan lessons for three months; now I'm just happy to have it for a week at a time!"

Throughout this book we focus on specific curriculum areas and provide a comprehensive, focused selection of research resources, lesson plans, and teaching tips.

Lesson: From the Latin *lection (reading)*. Exercises or readings given as part of a course of instruction.

The following collection of lesson plans is slightly different. Here we look at several broad-based sites that combine multiple curriculum areas in a high-quality library of lesson plans.

These lessons tend, for the most part, to be either fairly interactive, meaning that the parent becomes highly involved in the teaching process, or fairly independent, meaning that focused students will be given rough guidelines, a start-up list of resources, and time to absorb the material. With either approach, your burden as a teaching parent goes from agenda-focused to education-focused. Dive in!

Academy Curriculum Exchange
www.ofcn.org/cyber.serv/academy/ace

"This site offers an exchange of lessons for students of any age. I think it was originally intended for public school teachers but has been adapted for homeschoolers. Subjects cover math, language, social studies, and science, as well as miscellaneous material. The ideas are very good and the lessons are very detailed and concise, but they

On Teaching

"Students in some schools are still 'spoon fed' for examination purposes. They are given frequent tests and set daily tasks. The teachers dictate copious notes, explain even minor matters in detail, and provide elaborate lists of points for examination answers. Such highly directed teaching is a poor preparation for higher courses which assume that the students can not only organize their own times of work but also decide for themselves what is important and what is not."

—Harry Madux, *How to Study*

Curriculum

require a lot of sifting through pages. Some material looks too hard for primary-aged students." —M.D. ☆☆☆

Across Subjects   www.awesomelibrary.org/Library
/Materials_Search/Lesson_Plans/Across_Subjects.html

Lesson plans from Awesome Library. A very thorough collection. ☆☆☆

Activity Search   www.eduplace.com/search/activity.html

Hougton Mifflin's Education Place is a searchable database of more than 400 original classroom activities and lesson plans for grades young students. Search the activity database by grade level and subject. ☆☆☆☆

Collaborative Lesson Archive (CLA)
faldo.atmos.uiuc.edu/CLA/

Teachers post a lesson to the archive, and others comment on how they used it. Lessons are searchable by age level and subject. ☆☆☆☆

Discovery Channel School Lesson Plans
school.discovery.com/lessonplans

The Discovery Channel School presents half a gazillion lesson plans covering history, science, health, and literature, divided into upper and lower grades. Some of the lessons attempt to sell you Discovery Channel videos, but, hey, you can be strong. ☆☆☆☆

Hotlinks

**Collaborative
Lesson Archive (CLA)**
faldo.atmos.uiuc.edu/CLA/

**Discovery Channel School
Lesson Plans**
school.discovery.com
/lessonplans

**Lesson Plans and
Reproducibles**
teacher.scholastic.com
/lessonrepro

Teacher Lesson Plans
www.education-world
.com/a_tsl

Lesson Links   www3.sympatico.ca/ray.saitz/links.htm

From the Outta Ray's Head collection of library, writing, and literature lessons: links to lesson plans or lesson ideas. To qualify for this list, material must be free, of reasonably high quality, and aimed at an intermediate or senior level. ☆☆☆

Lesson Plans and Teaching Strategies
www.csun.edu/~hcedu013/plans.html

"Lots of information here, but don't feel you need to follow the lesson plans to the letter. Part of the fun of homeschool is the flexibility we can enjoy." —S.C. ☆☆☆

Lesson Plans and Reproducibles   teacher.scholastic.com/lessonrepro

The entire Scholastic site is a treasure hunter's dream, but this subpage of lesson plans and reproducibles is the most valuable: hundreds of lesson plans for elementary and intermediate ages, in about 100 categories. Search by grade and subject. When you've exhausted this page, click the links at the top to find helpful information that will keep you busy for days. ☆☆☆☆☆

Lesson Plans   www.lessonplanspage.com
"Tons of lessons for all ages." —S.C. ☆☆☆

Marc Sheehan's Lesson Plans
www.halcyon.com/marcs/lessons.html

Very small collection. Includes a theme unit, four plans, and links to lesson plan sites. ☆☆☆

Matrix of Examples   edweb.sdsu.edu/webquest/matrix.html

Some 200 lesson units covering every major academic area, arranged by age and listed by academic categories. Great illustrated units on subjects as diverse as the Great Depression and the World of Pigs. ☆☆☆☆

On Education

"Education is an ornament in prosperity and a refuge in adversity."
—Diogenes Laërtius, 412–323 B.C.

MiniThemes   www.eagle.ca/~matink/mini.html

Everything you want to know about a small number of interesting, eclectic topics: bats, dragons, origami, genealogy, science fairs, and

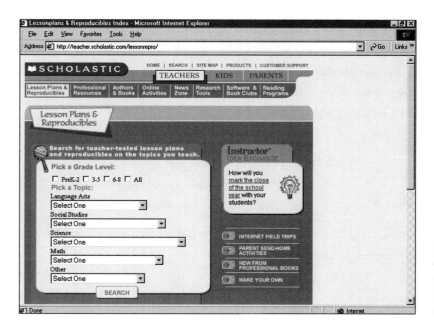

Figure 3.3

Lesson Plans and Reproducibles: Pick a topic; pick a level.

more. It's primarily a collection of links, with little original content. ☆☆

Miscellaneous Lesson Plans

www.uen.org/cgi-bin/websql/utahlink/lessonbook.hts?book_id=115

Dozens of lesson plans, with text documents to support the lessons. Sponsored by UtahLink. ☆☆

Teacher Lesson Plans   www.education-world.com/a_tsl

Diversity is good, right? If you agree, you'll enjoy the diversity of the lessons found here. Teacher Lesson Plans is an ever-changing, eclectic collection of lesson plans submitted by educators. The entire site is a great place, so spend a few hours. ☆☆☆☆☆

Teacher's Room Lesson Plan Wizard

www.globefearon.com/teachers/wizard.html

This site for teachers lets you search for lesson plans by interest (grade) level or by content area. Use the existing database, or add your own lessons. For all ages. ☆☆☆☆

Zoom School   www.zoomschool.com/school/Schoolhome.shtml

"This place has many wonderful resources on various subjects. When we did dinosaurs and space, we used this site a great deal. It includes coloring sheets that the little ones enjoyed and useful information for my older children." —S.C. ☆☆☆

Worksheets

IT'S REAL SCHOOLWORK. It's how you reinforce learning and test understanding. It's the dreaded worksheet!

Work: From the Ancient Iranian *varəzem* *(activity)*. Specific task or assignment that is part of some larger project.

Actually, when Mom and Dad tailor the learning, worksheets needn't be the boring make-work you experienced when you were in school. Homeschooling mom Barbara Jermstad from Hampton, Virginia, says her oldest son *loves* worksheets! And workbooks were the very successful foundation of Joyce Dumire's homeschooling. When the Ohio mom took her teenaged son out of public school, "the school let me keep the books that were assigned to him for that school year— until the end of the year. We worked on them and finished out his school year with what he had been using. My son loved the workbook method for math and hated it for everything else. That's when we started mixing it up to make it more fun for both of us."

The worksheet resources in this section cover almost every academic subject, as well as a lot of subjects that are fun but probably only marginally educational. Some even allow you to create your own worksheets, so you're covered from every angle.

On Excellence

"We are what we repeatedly do. Excellence then is not an act but a habit." —Aristotle, 384–322 B.C.

ABCTeach   www.abcteach.com

"There are lots of helpful free printables: research cards, reading charts, activity sheets, bookmarks, and more! Cute designs that kids will really like—even a coloring page and some mazes to print out." —A.C. ✰✰✰✰

Autumn's Free Activity Page for Kids

www.geocities.com/EnchantedForest/Dell/5232

Fun, colorful worksheets on an eclectic variety of topics. For younger students. ✰✰✰✰

Buck Babies   www.geocities.com/EnchantedForest/Glade/7399

"This is an enormous site chock-full of links to printables of all types: everything from custom calendars to certificates, play money to paper dolls (Civil War or Elvis, anyone?), worksheets to story creations, games to coloring books, kids' family tree to shopping lists." —A.G. ✰✰✰✰✰

Dositey Educational Site   www.dositey.com

Lots of free elementary-level worksheets for reading and math. Workbook-type interactive exercises and mini-lessons. I couldn't locate answer sheets. If you know the stuff or can find the answers, this is a really, really well done site. The worksheets look great. ✰✰

Free Worksheets   www.freeworksheets.com

This site claims to have some 7,000 worksheets available. That number seems inflated, but the hundreds of worksheets that are on the site are well done. Arranged by subject, some with answer keys. Aimed primarily at primary school-aged students. ✰✰✰✰

Free Worksheets for Whole Number Arithmetic

www.sssoftware.com/freeworksheets

Worksheets for whole-number operations that parents of elementary school-aged children can print and recopy. An answer sheet accompanies each worksheet. You can also generate your own worksheets. ✰✰✰✰

Hotlinks

Autumn's Free Activity Page for Kids
www.geocities.com/Enchanted Forest/Dell/5232

Buck Babies
www.geocities.com/Enchanted Forest/Glade/7399

Tutorial World
www.tut-world.com

Young Minds
www.geocities.com/doyo1 /forms.htm

Curriculum

Homeschool Is Cool   www.geocities.com/Athens/Academy/8238

"This site offers free, printable worksheets for early primary grades. Also offers lesson plans, links to lesson plans listed by subject matter (i.e., Valentine's Day, U.S. presidents, dinosaurs), a message board, and much more! There is also an addendum site at www.50megs .com/phdmom, with many more worksheets." —M.D. ★★★★☆

Investigating Worksheets Around the Net
my.ohio.voyager.net/~baugust/worksheets.htm

Links to dozens of pages of worksheet creators, categorized by subject. Includes links to miscellaneous forms, charts, and reports. You could spend days here. ★★★

M-Tech Worksheet Generator   www.mtech.on.ca

A free online worksheet generator. You enter the words or paragraphs, the generator makes the worksheet in seconds, and you print it from your browser. Easy to use. There's also an extensive archive of worksheets. ★★★★

Lessons Plans and Reproducibles
teacher.scholastic.com/lessonrepro

"Worksheets from Scholastic Books, for primary and intermediate levels. Offers online issue of *Scholastic News*. These worksheets may be incorporated into the accompanying lesson plans." —M.D. ★★★

RHL School   www.rhlschool.com

Zillions of ready-to-use worksheets: English, math, reading comprehension, reference skills. Includes answer keys. Quite a bit of additional information on this page, but the worksheets alone are worth coming back for. ★★★★★

Tutorial World   www.tut-world.com

Tutorial World is a Singapore-based company (hence the British English) that provides a collection of free worksheets to complement the math, English, and science curriculum. It's an ugly site, but the worksheets are very well done. ★★★★

On Work

"Man hath his daily work of body or mind Appointed."
—John Milton

Figure 3.4

RHL School:
Questions and
answers.

Worksheets www.awesomelibrary.org/Library/Materials_Search
/Lesson_Plans/Worksheets.html

Lesson plans from Awesome Library. A very thorough collection. ☆☆☆

Worksheets Unlimited rozalski.tripod.com/WorksheetsUnlimited.html

Hundreds of worksheets and flash cards for early readers. The author
recommends laminating the flash cards and keeping them together
with a metal ring. The subjects include letters, numbers, colors, states,
and much, much more. ☆☆☆☆

Young Minds www.geocities.com/doyo1/forms.htm

Aimed specifically at homeschoolers. Handwriting charts, stargazing,
and other fun, useful information that will remind you why you're
homeschooling. ☆☆☆☆☆

Unit Studies

MANY HOMESCHOOLERS TAKE an entirely new approach to education: rather than teach a subject, they teach a unit. Unit studies is an

Unit: From the Latin *unitas (one).* A group of items combined as a single entity.

Hotlinks

Amanda Bennett's Unit Study Adventures
www.unitstudy.com

Gander Academy's Complete List of Theme Pages
www.stemnet.nf.ca/CITE /complete.htm

Third Millennium Classroom
www.millennaire.com/pbl.html

Unit Lessons
www.thsresources.com /lessons.htm

Unit Studies Forum
www.kaleidoscapes.com /unitstudies

educational philosophy that uses a single topic—seeds, for example, or the Civil War—to teach multiple curriculum areas.

Ann Crum's homeschooled daughter understands the principle behind unit studies. Ann says: "The other day my 12-year-old daughter said, 'Mom, you know what I really like about homeschool? The fact that if I want to I can breeze through a subject as fast as I need to. But if something stumps me, I know you are there to help me through it, to learn it, and I can take what time I need to really learn it without a class leaving me behind.'" That, says Ann, is exactly the point of homeschooling.

These popular unit studies resources will engage your children's attention, and will probably teach them something as well!

Amanda Bennett's Unit Study Adventures
www.unitstudy.com
What's *not* on this site? There must be something, but I don't know what it would be. A full-blown education. ☆☆☆☆☆

Browse by Theme
www.eduplace.com/search/frames
A small collection of themes. They're only slightly better than average, but the subjects are interesting. ☆☆☆

Free Online Unit Studies
www.alaska.net/~cccandc/free.htm
More than 300 online unit studies can be found on this award-winning site. Frogs, geography, humor, Japan, Macbeth, Mother Goose. . . . These units run the gamut and are well worth repeat visits. ☆☆☆☆☆

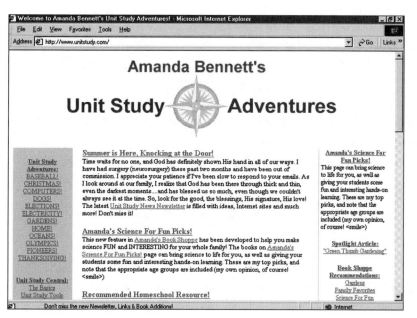

Figure 3.5

Amanda Bennett:
Endless unit studies.

Gander Academy's Complete List of Theme Pages
www.stemnet.nf.ca/CITE/complete.htm

Mammals, Amelia Earhart, origami, and volcanoes are some of the approximately 100 themes on this page, each of them very well done. The Theme Page button at the top links to dozens more. ☆☆☆☆☆

Homeschool in the Woods   home.rochester.rr.com/inwoods

A homeschooling family explains how it incorporates unit studies into its homeschooling. Good, inspiring thoughts. ☆☆☆☆☆

KiddyHouse: Thematic Lessons and Activities
www.kiddyhouse.com/Themes

"This site has all kinds of unit studies for learning about frogs, holidays, rain forests, and Native American Indians. The Teachers Corner has lesson plans, worksheets, and lots more." —K.H. ☆☆☆

Marcia's Lesson Links   members.aol.com/MGoudie

Marcia creates theme units for elementary grades. Covers money, colors, winter, and more. ☆☆☆

Michelle's Thematic Units for Teachers
www.wwa.com/~jstankev/teacher

More than a dozen well-done themes on topics such as friendship, women's history, and dental hygiene. ☆☆☆

Multidisciplinary   www.awesomelibrary.org/Library/Materials_Search /Lesson_Plans/Multidisciplinary.html

Lesson plans from Awesome Library. A very thorough collection. ☆☆☆

Online Activities   www.csun.edu/~hcedu013/onlineactivities.html

Approximately 200 unit studies, with commentary and reviews. ☆☆☆☆

Special Theme Center   www.education-world.com/a_special

Great collection, frequently updated, with an archive worth bookmarking. Eclectic, fun, and educational. ☆☆☆☆☆

Thematic Unit Ideas
www.geocities.com/Athens/Thebes/9673/teachers.htm#thematic

Good themes, organized by month, with lots of additional links. Not a very large collection. ☆☆☆

Third Millennium Classroom   www.millennaire.com/pbl.html

Project-based learning gets a workout here. Terrific, top-quality projects for all grade levels. ☆☆☆☆☆

Unit Lessons   www.thsresources.com/lessons.htm

Dozens of really fun themes. Everything is covered here. ☆☆☆☆

Unit Studies   www.geocities.com/Athens/8259/unitstud.html

Unit studies, reviewed and linked, along with lots of other good homeschooling information. ☆☆☆☆

Unit Studies Forum   www.kaleidoscapes.com/unitstudies

A very popular, very active bulletin board from Kaleidoscapes for homeschoolers and unschoolers wanting to discuss unit studies. The cohosts are experts in creating unit studies. ☆☆☆☆☆

On Success

"The only place success comes before work is in the dictionary."
—Vince Lombardi

Unit Studies and Mini-Lessons on the Web

pages.ivillage.com/ps/crossroads16/unitlinks.html

Links to individual unit lessons across the Web. Blinding colors, but the collection is great. ☆☆☆

Unit Study Pages on the Web

www.geocities.com/Athens/4663/units.html

Links and a few groupings that together make up their own unit studies (Lindbergh, Christmas, entomology, and more). ☆☆

Unit Study Planner   www.mosquitonet.com/~family/usplanner.html

This planner sets out everything you need to do to create a study unit. Includes a form you can complete for distributing unit information to your kids. ☆☆☆☆

Field Trips

SOMETIMES THE ZOO, sometimes a museum, sometimes online . . . but always educational. How do *you* handle field trips?

Ann Crum, a homeschooling mother of two in central Arkansas, is careful to make her family's field trips educational. "On field trips where we have listened to a guide person or watched a film, I ask questions afterward that tell me how much my kids were listening," she says. "I also quiz them on whatever the sermon at church happens to be about. I may also ask for an oral review of a film, program, or lecture."

Robin Tompkins recently had a tremendous field trip for her two young children. During a unit study of homes and neighborhoods, the Redding, California, mom covered fire safety. She explained to her children the importance of developing and practicing a fire escape plan, and had each child practice opening windows, removing screens, jumping to the ground, and meeting at the designated location. She followed up with a field trip

> **Field:** From the Germanic *feld (field)*. A setting for practical learning outside one's usual place of education or work.

Recommendation

"For a *great* field trip or holiday, the Winona Farm in Minnesota is excellent! You can find out about them at members.xoom.com/winfarm. We visited there for a month in 1998 and it was fantastic! The people are nice, and the experience was something each of my children will remember their whole lives—even my then-two-year-old still talks about it. Winona Farm touts itself as being for unschoolers, but welcomes homeschoolers as well."

—Julia G., homeschooling mother of three, Niagara Falls, Canada

to a fire station, where the kids were told how the firefighters lived at the station. They also saw the tools of the trade and watched one of the firefighters get dressed in gear, including full mask and oxygen, which prepared the children not to be afraid should they ever need to be rescued.

To make the trip more enjoyable, Robin invited other homeschool families to join in. "There were seven families with a total of about fourteen kids in attendance, with many good questions to be asked," she says.

Some homeschooling parents are overwhelmed by the notion of trying to teach their children about the arts. If you've considered making your field trips more cultural, more focused on the arts, you may have dealt with the same concern. Michael Brownlee, a professional actor and playwright living and working in Chicago, offers suggestions for homeschoolers visiting the theater or a concert for the first time: "I think the first thing to remember when approaching the subject of seeing a play or a concert is to make it fun," Michael says. "Try to incorporate the play or music into the lesson plan. If it's a play, then have the children act out some of the scenes."

Michael says living the play is the best way to teach kids to appreciate the drama. "I remember reading *Romeo and Juliet* in high school and being bored to tears because that's all we did—read it. Get them on their feet and into the play. I think you learn a lot about a play if you are suddenly one of the people in it. It doesn't have to be Broadway worthy; just

👪 *How We Homeschool*

"I live in Orlando, Florida, and have three kids in my homeschool group. We just got back from Venice Beach, where we searched for sharks' teeth and found quite a few. We recently got a pass for Sea World that works for the rest of the year, so we'll be going there a lot and work on some badges too."

—Susan Amiot, homeschooling mother of five, Orlando, Florida

have fun. The same thing goes for attending a concert or visiting a museum: Find some way to make them a part of it, not just spectators. Ask what their favorite songs are and what it is they like about those songs. Then put it all in context with what they are going to see. Bach was the Bon Jovi of his time."

Stephanie Coomer, an unschooling mother of four in Michigan, is a committed field tripper. She and her husband Ron, whom she says is as much into homeschooling as she is, love to take the family camping. Her husband is home a great deal of the time, which means the family can go camping anytime they want. "This is great bonding time, and we can look for berries, flowers, types of rocks, animal tracks, and fossils."

Ron and Stephanie have made virtually everything an education for their family. "We go to museums, zoos . . . we even went to Kansas to buy a home and to see places along the way in all the different states. We have been camping with other homeschool families, gone to Home Depot to build items (for free, by the way), and have seen *The Wonders of Egypt* at our tiny local museum."

Stephanie operates a local homeschooling support group, which has gone on many field trips together. Stephanie's group operates a mailing list to discuss field trips a few months in advance, and one person actually does the organizing. "The one originating the visit sets up a time, a date, and a price. Four to six weeks before the trip, that person sends out a memo and starts posting the

Field Trip Freebie

"Informal Education" highlights educational programs and materials related to parks, zoos, aquariums, and museums. Call ENC at 800-621-5785.

Curriculum

names of those who have confirmed. Someone makes the nametags and works with the originator. A week ahead, they remind those who have not paid, confirm new people, send out a map and directions, name a meeting place, and send out reminders about all the little details. We all meet, pass out nametags, and *enjoy*!"

The unschooling experience means anything is possible. As an unschooling family, Stephanie says, they try to make every field trip fun but educational. "Our life is a learning experience, and that's how we make it fun for the children. It's not unusual to find one of the children talking about the different colors in the clouds, or why the water is different today than yesterday." She and her husband make it easy for all questions to have answers, she says, "and if that means looking up a word before answering a question, we do it."

Dena Anderson is in her second year as the field trip coordinator for her Alabama support group of more than 150 homeschooling families. Dena has found that the best field trips are the *free* ones. "They're available in all shapes and sizes, if you just look," she says. Factory tours tend to be free of charge, for example; Dena's group has visited factories making Bud's cookies and Goldenflake chips. "All sorts of that stuff is available, from pizza to donuts." State parks often offer naturalist tours for free. "We have gone to two of those. One was a killer hike *up*hill to an indoor wild animal rescue and rehabilitation facility. The other was a watershed tour where they took us to a creek and we had a hands-on look at creek life. Both were wonderfully done."

Susie Clawson has been homeschooling her five children from the beginning. She belongs to a local homeschool support group that is very active with field trips. "For us, they aren't 'extracurricular' but a part of our learning. We have a very relaxed approach to learning, and we do it as a family. When we visit a place, we usually review proper behavior while en route, and sometimes we'll read a book or watch a video in preparation or in review."

Field Trip Freebie

"Museums and Learning: A Guide for Family Visits" offers suggestions on how museums can inspire and inform. Call 877-4-ED-PUBS and request product number MIS 98-6506.

👪 *How We Homeschool*

"When we take field trips, we like to look up information about the subject ahead of time on the computer. We use a variety of methods: either searching the Internet or using our Microsoft Encarta encyclopedia. The kids really get excited when they have some tangible information to connect to what they are seeing. Sometimes we just go and explore on our field trips. Exploring and discovering are wonderful ways of finding out our children's interests.

"Sometimes we will go to the library ahead of time and research our subject, checking out books that correspond to what we are going to be seeing. It helps the kids retain so much more of what they learn when they can read about it, look at pictures, and then be able to experience it firsthand!"

—**Nancy J. Rose**, homeschooling mother of two, West Palm Beach, Florida

She tries to keep up her children's enthusiasm. "I try to not ruin the fun with too much preparation. I try not to force their focus, as I've seen done in public-school field trips. I allow the kids to explore on their own at times and we explore together at times, depending on the place we visit. I don't press them to move on before they've had their fill of a display or gallery or project. Being blessed with no time constraints (as opposed to a public school field trip), we have this luxury.

"Our family's philosophy of life and learning is that they're interconnected. You can compartmentalize learning, but why would you want to? Everything in the world is educational in one way or another, and the joy of learning is to find that and use it to enrich your own life. I see my children learning to do this. They glean and grow from their experiences."

Many of the following Internet resources will help you prepare for field trips. Others will serve as field trips of another sort, by taking your children on an online trip to places far, far away.

CultureFinder   **www.culturefinder.com**

Everything cultural, everywhere. A city-by-city listing of arts and culture in more than 1,300 locations, plus culture guides that explain music, opera, and everything else you really ought to know. ☆☆☆☆☆

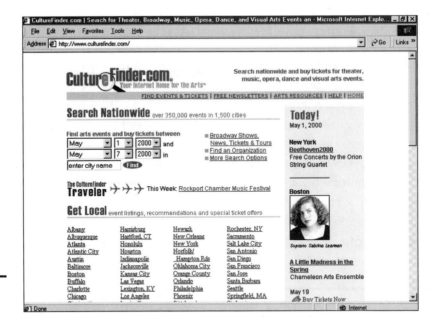

Figure 3.6

CultureFinder: It's what's for fun.

Hotlinks

CultureFinder
www.culturefinder.com

Our Museum, Zoo, and Historical Site Recommendations
www.spiritone
.com/~andersen
/museum.html

WebMuseums
sunsite.unc.edu/wm

World Wide Art Resources
www.wwar.com

Electronic Field Trips Tips and Techniques

commtechlab .msu.edu/sites/letsnet/frames/bigideas/b1 /b1tips.html

Good advice for taking the kids "out" on the Internet to find their favorite zoo or museum. ☆☆☆

Field Trips   www.eduplace.com/links/gen/field_trips.html

Online field trips to museums and collections, from Houghton Mifflin's list of social studies education sites. ☆☆☆

Going to a Museum?   curry.edschool.virginia.edu/curry /class/Museums/Teacher_Guide

A teacher's guide for kids of every age. Includes a museum field trip planning guide, sample museum lesson plans written by teachers, and Internet resources. You'll also find science lesson plans that provide many classroom activities and practical ideas related to museum field trips. ☆☆☆☆

Internet Field Trips   teacher.scholastic.com/fieldtrp/index.htm

Guided tours to the best of classroom-appropriate Web sites. Each field trip provides quick suggestions for using targeted Web sites to teach a specific topic. Includes a teacher's guide for using the Internet for field trips. ☆☆☆☆

Musee   www.musee-online.org

A spotlight museum of the day opens this site. The remainder is an outstanding, searchable collection of every sort of museum—art, science, history, zoos, archaeology, aquariums, and more. ☆☆☆☆

Museum Loan Network   loanet.mit.edu/CSWN/vi_exhibit.html

How about a museum tour this afternoon? With a few clicks—and a free piece of software you can download directly from this site—you can visit a Japanese sculpture garden in Mobile, African art in Brooklyn, or Egyptian art in Los Angeles. And it's all in three dimensions. ☆☆☆☆

Museums   www.emtech.net/museums.htm

Scores of very well chosen resources. ☆☆

Museums   www.sciam.com/bookmarks/editselect.html#k

From the editors of *Scientific American,* a list of favorite resources, along with evaluations. ☆☆☆

NASA for Kids   www.nasa.gov/kids.html

Go on a virtual space mission. This site answers questions and lets kids see an actual space launch, online. ☆☆☆☆

100+ Field Trip Ideas   www.kaleidoscapes.com/100fieldtripideas.html

This will keep you busy! It's Florida oriented, but adaptable to your own locale. ☆☆☆☆

Our Museum, Zoo, and Historical Site Recommendations
www.spiritone.com/~andersen/museum.html

Unschooler John Andersen describes great museums in the United States and Europe that he and his family have visited. Great read! ☆☆☆☆☆

Playroom   www.4kids.com/Playroom/koffline.html

Stuff to do, activities to participate in, and more than a hundred other fun ideas for keeping your kids engaged when offline. ☆☆☆☆

Walking Tours   www.altavista.com

This isn't a "site," per se. It's an instruction. In the Search box enter the words "walking tour" (in quotations) plus the name of your city or town to find everything there is to do in your town that's free. Have fun! ☆☆☆☆

WebMuseums   sunsite.unc.edu/wm

Go on a virtual field trip. This very popular site is a "must see." Special exhibitions (Paul Cézanne was a recent feature) and tons of museum resources of interest to kids of any age . . . and their children. ☆☆☆☆☆

World Wide Art Resources   www.wwar.com

The new Your Local Arts link at www.wwar.com/towns is a real treasure. No matter where you live or travel in the United States, this link will have some local artistic resource worth visiting. The site is stuffed with information about museums, artists, art history, galleries, and dozens of other topics. ☆☆☆☆☆

Preschool

THE WHOLE "BABY" thing was behind me: The baby clothes were long gone, I was planning a tenth birthday celebration for my youngest, and my only concern was getting my kids into college.

So why was I pregnant?

Now that we have a baby again, and our home is filled with blocks and duckies and Dr. Seuss, I'm finding that the Internet is even more fun than I'd thought. And homeschooling a one-year-old is an entirely different experience than teaching her older siblings.

Early: From the Old English *ær* (*before*). An initial stage of development.

For one thing, she has a whole house full of "teachers."

Seattle-area mom vanessa ronsse, a committed homeschooler with a preschool-aged son, says that over the past few months, she has changed the way she homeschools her toddler. "I used to think, 'I have to read to him X hours every day. I can't ever let him watch TV. I have to spend time every day on alphabet and numbers.'"

No more. "Now that he is old enough to be interested," she says, "I just let him lead the way. Some days he reads books all afternoon and never plays with a block. Other days he wants to color and play with the cats and couldn't care less if I read a story to him or not. And some days all he can talk about is hockey, hockey, *hockey*, so we read Dad's hockey books and magazines or watch one of the old taped games for a bit."

She expects to continue letting her son direct his own education, "perhaps directing him now and then when interest lags or becomes too lopsided. But, as we are just getting started, I know everything will change at least 1,500 times before he finishes his education at home . . . if we ever finish."

Melody Daisson's preschool is more formal. "I have set up a preschool for my kids teaching religion, self-care, manners, music, reading, math readiness, social studies, and science," she says. "My theme this year is 'Learning together is fun.' I teach the subjects according to ability and interest."

This year, Melody's goal is to determine each child's learning style. "I am in the 'this works, that doesn't work' stage," she says. "Our mistakes are definitely learning experiences. For example, I started out teaching five days a week. We were all overwhelmed! So now we cut down to three days of formal school and just enjoy playing together the rest of the week. I think what I want to accomplish by homeschooling is to teach them that we love them and we are their parents and their best friends."

Teresa Cavender from Tennessee is homeschooling her 18-month-old son. "I know you may think I'm crazy for saying that I homeschool," she says, "but it's a way of life for us. And since his life began eighteen months ago, we've been homeschooling."

Preschool Freebie

The "Smart from the Start: Strengthening Early Learning, from Infants to Preschoolers" video focuses on strengthening early learning. Call 877-4-ED-PUBS and request Satellite Town Meeting #66.

How We Homeschool

"What we are doing right now is basically learning about the world. We are working on ABCs, numbers, colors, and animals. I have a few TV shows I let him watch from time to time, including *Bear in the Big Blue House*, *Blue's Clues* (his favorite), and *Sesame Street*.

"Other than that, we spend lots of time building things with blocks, reading books (his favorite activity), coloring, and playing with our five cats. He just *loves* to give them 'hugs and kisses,' whether they like it or not! Every night we take a walk as a family. It gives us 'family time' without TV, telephone, or computers. We usually end up at our local mall, which is quite close, and always have to go to the pet store for him to pet the birds and small animals."

—vanessa ronsse, homeschooling mother of one, Seattle area

Hotlinks

All About Farm Animals
www.kiddyhouse.com/Farm

Coloring
www.ravenna.com/coloring

Free Worksheets: Ages 3 to 6
www.freeworksheets.com
/sub_cat1Ages3to6.asp?
cat=Ages3to6

Perpetual Preschool
www.perpetualpreschool
.com

Teresa also runs a very small educational child care program from her home, where she teaches a three-year-old girl and a set of five-year-old twins. Her experiences are instructive to any parent of a preschooler:

"We recently read 'The Little Hero of Holland' out of the book *The Children's Book of Virtues*, edited by William Bennett. I explained a couple of words I thought they might not know (such as 'dike') before we began the story, and asked them if they knew where Holland was located. Of course they said no, so I told them we would look it up after we read the story. After a couple of pages, they wanted to narrate (I guess they realized their little brains were filling up), so we stopped and they narrated and then we continued. When we finished the story and narration (very short story), they jumped up and said, 'Okay, let's look up where Holland is.' We went to the big map I have mounted on the wall. We looked and looked and looked and couldn't find the country called Holland. So we went to the computer to see what we could find. I allowed them to use the mouse, type, and browse the Web. We found that another name for Holland is the Netherlands. We went back to the map and looked for the name *Netherlands*, and we found it. I must sheepishly admit that I didn't know that they were one and the same. I, of course, didn't let on anything of the kind and made it seem as though that was part of the lesson! It does remind me that I will be learning as much as the children will, though.

"My son was in the thick of the whole lesson. He wanted to 'play' on the computer, run back and forth with us from computer to map, and sat a little bit through the story. It was great fun and a great experience watching the children get so excited about learning."

Ready to homeschool your own preschoolers? Here are the best resources for getting started.

All About Farm Animals   www.kiddyhouse.com/Farm

Great illustrations, songs, crafts, activities, and worksheets for younger children, all about ducks, sheep, cows, and other farm animals. So cute, you'll laugh. ☆☆☆☆

Coloring   www.coloring.com

Every one of my kids—even the 17-year-old—loves this darling little page. We use it to entertain the baby. ☆☆☆☆☆

Early Childhood   www.emtech.net/early_childhood.htm

Scores of very well chosen resources. ☆☆

Early Childhood Center   www.education-world.com/early_childhood

Teaching a preschooler demands a lot of attention. Isn't it nice to know there's a place out there that does some of the mundane preparation for you so you can spend more time with Junior? This center is a community at Education World, offering preschool discussions, resources, and dozens of related links. Not quite as great as other parts of Education World, but well worth a visit. ☆☆☆☆

Free Worksheets: Ages 3 to 6
www.freeworksheet.com/sub_cat1Ages3to6.asp?cat=Ages3to6

Colors, following directions, numbers, reading activities, and lots more to get your little ones onto the academic track. ☆☆☆☆☆

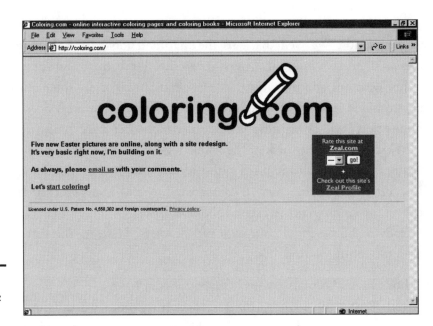

Figure 3.7

Coloring: Reds, greens, and a whole lot more.

Kids' Fonts   kidsfonts.mivox.com/

"This site has downloadable fonts that allow students to trace their alphabet and numbers. Create your own worksheets! It also has a font for crayons to color in." —v.r. ☆☆☆

Little Explorers   www.LittleExplorers.com

Click a letter and hear it pronounced in a child's voice. Click a picture and listen to the name of the penguin or peacock or any other entry in this wonderful children's picture dictionary. The illustrated links make it usable, even by pre-readers. The dictionary is also available in English-to-French, German, Spanish, or Portuguese. ☆☆☆

Montessori Homeschooling   www.montessori.edu/homeschooling.html

A site for parents who would like to use a Montessori curriculum at home for their preschoolers. Lots of help. ☆☆☆☆

Nuttin' but Kids   www.nuttinbutkids.com

"Offers unit lessons for preschoolers on various subjects, including holidays, gardening, fire safety, and health care. It's aimed at helping day-care providers, but it's easy to adapt to homeschool. Lots of fin-gerplays, songs, and art projects. Mainly for preschoolers, but some material is suitable for kindergarten age." —M.D. ☆☆☆☆

Parenthood   www.parenthoodweb.com

"The Web site for the "Slow and Steady, Get Me Ready" program. It has so many activities. Really good for unit studies or just playing. I love it." —A.D. ☆☆

Parent and Teacher Guide to Early Childhood Education
tlc.ai.org/techiidx.htm#LP

Reading, coloring, numbers, nursery rhymes, and more than 100 other subjects. Great links collection. ☆☆☆

Perpetual Preschool   www.perpetualpreschool.com

Woodworking, art, blocks, and so much more. Tons of lessons for the little ones. ☆☆☆☆☆

Preschool   www.geocities.com/Heartland/Shores/1369/preschool.html

You'll love this Letter of the Week program that uses the alphabet as a preschool curriculum format. ☆☆☆☆

Preschool and Kindergarten Skills Links
www.geocities.com/Athens/Aegean/3446/preschool.html

Coyle's Where in the World site reviews these topical links and de-scribes how to use them in your homeschooling. An excellent re-source. ☆☆☆☆

Teacher Guide to Early Childhood Education   tlc.ai.org/techiidx.htm

The Access Indiana Teaching & Learning Center contains lessons, re-sources, and more. A good foundation. ☆☆☆

Year Round Preschool and Bible Themes
www.geocities.com/Heartland/Valley/8004/preschool.html

"Great unit studies!" —T.C. ☆☆☆☆☆

Special Education

I'M THE MOTHER of an entire houseful of "special needs" children. Some of them are "special needs" because of attention or behavior disorders; one has a slight learning disability; one was classified as "special needs" by the local government because she was two years old when she was adopted; some are "special needs" because they're gifted; another is "special needs" because she's an entire decade younger than anyone else in the house and believes the world rotates around her whims. (She's right, of course. It's a handicap, being exceptionally cute and spoiled rotten.)

> **Special:** From the Latin *species (kind)*. Surpassing the common or usual.

Whether you're dealing with learning disabilities, behavior disorders, physical or mental disabilities, gifted children, or a combination of "exceptional" educational issues, your homeschooling takes on a different cast from the norm.

Some of the most difficult children to homeschool are those with behavior disorders. Dr. K. Ross is a Texas psychologist who specializes in classroom management and working with the "problem child." Dr. Ross was hired by the Dallas Independent School District to run a high school–level alternative education program after they lost control of their "problem kids."

Dr. Ross offers some advice to parents who are homeschooling children with behavior disorders: "You don't need to reinvent the wheel. I have observed, and made a lot of mistakes working with, kids. The following is what I have found (through observation, education and experience) that works, even with the toughest kids.

"Kids seek pride from adults they respect. They want us to be proud of them. Sometimes I see well-intentioned teachers and parents with big hearts make the biggest mistakes. If you love your children, *make them mind*. Expect proper behavior,

Special Needs Freebie

At Our Own Pace is Jean Kulczyk's bimonthly newsletter about homeschooling special needs children. Send an e-mail request to <Yukko5@aol.com> with your mailing address.

On Gifted Education

"I'm homeschooling my 11-year-old gifted son after a disastrous first semester in seventh grade. I had homeschooled him in second grade, and he rejoined the class the week before standardized testing. The teachers were worried he would bring down the average, since he did not have the 'benefit' of two months of worksheets similar to the test. Well, he scored in the 99th percentile! And that was on a diet of *Goosebumps* books.

"I basically unschooled, although I didn't know the term for it. I was newly divorced, severely underemployed, and depressed. I made it a priority to rise out of my funk to be present fully and answer any question he asked about anything in adult terms. If he still wasn't satisfied, we went to the library (the Internet had not yet hit the masses)."

—**Cathy Babis**, homeschooling mother of two, St. Louis, Missouri

acknowledge and appreciate them when you see it, and when you see willful disregard and disobedience, take swift action. Set clear rules and expect them to follow them. Inappropriate behavior *will not* stop without consistent consequences. The rule for consequences is consistent, *non*-hostile action that immediately follows any willful disobedience to the rule.

"This is easier said than done. However, one of the worst things parent-teachers do is threaten with no action. All you do is reinforce their behavior and wear yourself out 'til you're angry and have some unhealthy resentments. The worst thing teachers do is lose their temper. Do not ever lose your temper, or you will lose all respect and ability to manage your students. This is particularly true the older they get.

"The important thing to remember is to take some action, even if it is small. Talk is not action. Kids are used to the 'lectures' and usually stop for only a short time. Other kids don't even wait for the lecture to end. Remember: Kids learn from experience, and if they don't receive a consequence, they didn't learn not to repeat their

Tip

Get a free copy of "Achieving in Spite Of," a booklet on learning disabilities, by calling 800-323-7938.

mistake. They will cease the inappropriate behavior when it is easier to choose to comply.

"If you have shown them you will do these things and follow through, they really do begin to understand that you care. Your words begin (in time) to have real value to them so when you do say, 'Great job, Johnny,' it means something. It means you're proud of them; and kids, like the rest of us, tend to take care of things they are proud of."

Massachusetts mother Christine Blair is dealing with a problem even more severe. "I am homeschooling two boys, ages nine and six, both with autism. This is my second year of homeschool, and we now just love what we are doing.

"I started out homeschooling because I believed my boys need individualized educations. I wanted to meet them where they were and move forward from there. I wanted the freedom to move through areas quickly if they 'got it' right away, but stop and sit on a subject if they needed more time. I bought a packaged curriculum and they were going to keep the records and grades. I quickly found out that this was not the way for us. You would have thought some form of medieval torture was going on at our house during school hours. I forced my older son to do every problem because that was what was required from the school. We did this for more than half of the school year until I finally gave up in frustration. I bought a unit study and a few other things and finished out the rest of the year that way.

On Giftedness

"What is called genius is the abundance of life and health."
—Henry David Thoreau

"I started to learn about the Charlotte Mason way of teaching: short lessons, little or no workbooks, narration as a way of checking comprehension, nature walks and nature journals, and good books. We have been doing this for the last few months, and my boys are thriving and absolutely loving school. We are still doing our Abeka math, although I pick and choose from the page what I want them to do. I will be getting *Making Math Meaningful* soon, which is more hands-on with manipulatives. We are reading great books like *Robinson Crusoe* and biographies of people like Corrie Ten Boom."

Ann Glass has discovered lots of tricks for making homeschool work for her "squirrely" five- and seven-year-old sons: "First, we have rules and

How We Homeschool

"We are in our second year of homeschooling. I have a son in second grade who was diagnosed with attention deficit disorder (ADD) a year ago. Staying patient with my son has been my biggest challenge in homeschooling. He doesn't have extreme behavior problems like so many ADD kids do, but he is extremely distractible.

"My son focuses very well on TV and computer screens. Most of the time I need to stay nearby, though, doing something, so that I can keep an eye on him.

"Being organized helps him too. The first thing that helped was that I made a schedule for his school day, so he knows what to expect next on most days. That seems to help him to stay with the task that he is on at the moment. He does like it when I change it occasionally, but if I do it two days in a row, we have a difficult time getting back into the groove of learning again.

"The doctors wanted to put him on Ritalin last year. We just weren't comfortable with that. In January, after a particularly bad day, I was looking at one of the e-mail lists I'm on for ADHD and read about some parents giving their kids Mountain Dew. So I tried it the next day. It has been unbelievable. His school time is cut by a third to a half. I bought the diet version because I am convinced sugar makes him lose focus too.

"I find structure is very important; I try to start the school day at the same time and keep it as much the same each day as possible. I find the more distracted I am (working on other things in another part of the house), the more distracted he is. If I stay 'available' in the same room, he does much better."

—**Connie Horn**, homeschooling mother of two, Milford, Pennsylvania

expectations in the area of listening, just as we have rules and expectations in all the other areas of family life. My firm belief is that learning cannot take place if there is no discipline—and I don't necessarily mean punishment, but rather training.

"We intersperse 'seat work' with more active, hands-on learning. When I am actively teaching or reading aloud, I ask questions, and the boys offer their suggestions and speculations. Often they really do know the answer. I keep my explanations short. I also have them repeat back to me any instructions that I've given.

"If they're really stumped, I step in and help them think through it. It all comes back to listening. The boys have found that it pays to listen carefully the first time and ask questions at that time to clarify it, rather than to be without a clue later and left to struggle for a while.

"We also insist that they listen in church. We've had wonderful discussions on the way home. We've asked our pastor to let us know his scripture and the topic of his sermon beforehand, so the boys are somewhat prepared. They listen eagerly to see what Pastor has to say, since they've already formed their own opinions on the topic. We're also fortunate that our pastor has the ability to preach about profound things in simple terms."

No matter what the needs of your exceptional child, the following resources will contain *something* useful. Give them a try!

Attention Deficit Disorders
www.emtech.net/add.htm
Scores of very well chosen resources. ☆☆

Davidson Foundation   www.davidsonfoundation.org
Funds programs for gifted children. Of particular note is the link to questions and answers about gifted children. The organization advocates homeschooling for gifted children as the best alternative for meeting their educational needs. ☆☆☆☆☆

ERIC Clearinghouse on Disabilities and Gifted Education   ericec.org
This government-affiliated organization provides support for exceptional children. The Digests link has hundreds of articles as well as FAQs on every type of special education. Defines giftedness and offers some insight into what parents can do to act as their child's best advocate throughout the school years. ☆☆☆☆☆

Hotlinks

Davidson Foundation
www.davidsonfoundation.org

**Hoagies' Gifted
Education Page**
www.hoagiesgifted.org

**Homeschooling the
ADHD/ADD Child**
www.mosquitonet.com
/~family/adhd.html

**Resources for
Unschooling:
Special Needs
Children**
www.inspirit.com.au
/unschooling/resources
/hsspecialneeds.html

50 Tips on the Classroom Management of Attention Deficit Disorder
www.chadd.org/50class.htm

This site is oriented to the public school classroom, but the advice on creating order is useful for homeschoolers as well. ☆☆☆☆

Gifted Resources   www.eskimo.com/~user/kids.html

Dozens of resources for evaluating and teaching gifted students. ☆☆☆

Hoagies' Gifted Education Page   www.hoagiesgifted.org

No one is more exhilarating, or more frustrating, than the gifted child, asserts this site. Hoagies' is one of the best gifted and talented resources around, and it doesn't skip the homeschooling focus. The articles on this page are brilliant. ☆☆☆☆☆

Hollingworth Center for Highly Gifted Children
www.hollingworth.org

Of particular interest is the link to homeschooling the gifted, but there are dozens of other links that will assist in setting up a strong educational program for your gifted child. ☆☆☆☆☆

Homeschooling the ADHD/ADD Child
www.mosquitonet.com/~family/adhd.html

Lots of advice, and a mailing list support group, for homeschooling ADHD/ADD kids. ☆☆☆☆☆

Homeschooling Children with Special Needs
www.geocities.com/Athens/8259/special.html

A very nicely done, homeschool-oriented collection of links for families dealing with blindness, dyslexia, learning disabilities, ADD, autism, Down's syndrome, Tourette's syndrome, and more. ☆☆☆

NACD   www.nacd.org/resources.html

The National Academy for Child Development provides numerous articles and special education packets via its Web site. Lots of interesting research and motivational information. ☆☆☆☆

National Association for Gifted Children   **www.nagc.org**

The counseling link contains some interesting research on gifted education, and the parenting link contains a good argument for providing special educational challenges to gifted children. You'll also find a link for other resources that connects to gifted organizations in most states. ☆☆☆☆

Resources for Unschooling: Special Needs Children

www.inspirit.com.au/unschooling/resources/hsspecialneeds.html

This site is affiliated with an unschooling page, but no matter what your homeschooling philosophy, these very well organized resources will be useful. Gifted, learning disabled, speech and language disorders, and lots of other special-needs categories are addressed. ☆☆☆☆☆

Special Education   **www.awesomelibrary.org/Library/Special_Education /Special_Education.html**

For teachers of children with any of the following special education needs: assistive technology, ADD, blind and visually impaired, deaf and hearing impaired, developmental disabilities, gifted, homeschooling, individualized education plans, learning disabilities, mental health, mental retardation, physically challenged, severe or chronic illness. Lesson plans, educational materials, and more. Not specifically homeschool oriented, but much of what's here can be adapted to your classroom at home. ☆☆☆☆☆

Special Education   **www.emtech.net/sped.htm**

Scores of very well chosen resources. ☆☆

Special Education   **www.pacificnet.net/~mandel/SpecialEducation.html**

Lesson plans from the Teachers Helping Teachers page. These lessons are submitted by teachers and include grade-level designations. Unfortunately, they're not subdivided by topic. ☆☆☆

Special Education Center   **www.education-world.com/special_ed**

An entire community of resources relating to gifted and talented children, disabilities, developmental delays, parents' rights, mild-severe challenges, individualized education plans, and much, much more. This entire site is a great place, so spend a few hours. ☆☆☆☆☆

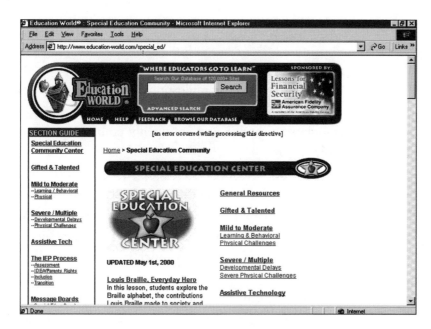

Figure 3.8

Special Education Center: For every kind of gifted and disabled student.

Special Needs Education: Parent and Teacher Resources
tlc.ai.org/tspedidx.htm

The Access Indiana Teaching and Learning Center contains lessons, resources, and more. A good foundation. ☆☆☆

Special Needs Message Board   **www.kaleidoscapes.com/special**

The Kaleidoscape message boards are wonderful: very popular, very helpful. For parents who are homeschooling special-needs kids. ☆☆☆☆

Wrightslaw   **www.wrightslaw.com**

Looking for support in your effort to homeschool your special needs child? Parents, advocates, educators, and attorneys come to Wrights-law for accurate, up-to-date information about effective advocacy for children with disabilities. The site has hundreds of articles, cases, newsletters, and other information about special education law and advocacy in the Wrightslaw Libraries. This important site tracks legislation and court decisions that affect your ability to get assistance for special needs kids. ☆☆☆☆☆

Unschooling

I'M NOT AN unschooler. Not for any philosophical reasons, mind you; I simply lack the courage.

Other homeschoolers are braver and are openly embracing the unschooling movement.

Lillian Haas is one. Unschooling is practically an article of faith for this unschooling mom of two in Audubon, New Jersey. "My husband and I unschool our eight-year-old and almost-three-year-old sons. We are complete unschoolers. . . . My son learns from life, just as he has since birth. We are constantly amazed at how much he learns from living in the world day after day.

"We're way out on the radical fringe of unschooling, in that we don't consciously 'teach' anything. Alex reads constantly, and we make sure he's exposed to as much of the world as possible. When he asks questions, or when we see or read something we think would interest him, we explain as best we can.

Un-: From the Greek *an- (not)*. Prefix meaning to reverse or undo an action.

"His latest project is making models of weapons through history, and he's putting together a museum in his bedroom. It wouldn't be my subject of choice, but he's doing research and hands-on crafts and creating signs on the computer. It's wonderful."

Unschooling mom Gita Schmitz explains how she evolved into unschooling: "Actually, there are hundreds of ways people homeschool, from structured, like school, to unstructured and spontaneous," she says. "Most people start homeschooling by 'doing school at home.' They quickly realize whether that particular way is right for them. In my own case, it took about three months to realize that neither my son nor I liked it. The whole situation was stiff and awkward and was killing his whole

Mark Twain

Samuel Clemens was four years old when his family moved to Hannibal, Missouri, on the bank of the Mississippi River. He spent his childhood playing alongside the river, fascinated by the romance of steamboats, keelboats, and the river life all around him. Hannibal's wooded hills, fishing, and nearby island fired the imagination of the man who grew up to call himself Mark Twain, in honor of the river that so influenced his childhood.

When he was 13, Samuel was apprenticed to a local printer, and when his older brother Orion established a newspaper, the *Hannibal Journal,* Samuel became a compositor—the beginning of his professional life as a newspaperman and author.

interest in learning, period. So we evolved into unschooling. He reads everything in sight and we pursue whatever grabs him. I know it sounds like nothing, but kids do eventually get around to most things, at the time that the 'fire is hot.'"

Lauren Frazer, an unschooler from New Jersey, has plenty of advice for new unschoolers. "I think one thing I have had to do is remember that this is homeschool; you can do it your way. Homeschooling parents sometimes get caught up in grading and following a curriculum. As long as my son learns what is required by the end of the year, it doesn't matter how I do it."

Heather Hada, an unschooling mother of three, is an advocate of unschooling, and believes it's the best way to teach children. "Many homeschooling families are geared toward 'school at home'," she says. "We are unschoolers, so we don't have problems with curriculum, testing, or motivation. In fact, one of the first things I tell parents who are considering homeschooling is to not buy a curriculum right away.

"Unschooling is hard to explain. I know this because a few years ago I would have thought these ideas crazy. But now what I don't understand is why schools still operate as they do, and why they totally ignore child education research. Learning is a natural process and can't be forced."

🚶🚶🚶 *How We Homeschool*

"With unschooling, sticking to a schedule is not a problem; the only schedule we have to adhere to is the free-swim time at the Y and programs on the Discovery Channel. *So much less stress!*"

—Julia G., homeschooling mother of three, Niagara Falls, Canada

Heather didn't start out unschooling. "When I first started homeschooling I bought a book full of worksheets that was supposed to cover every subject for first grade. I figured that that would do until I could find a suitable curriculum. My son hated it. It was like pulling teeth to make him do the worksheets. I found out about deschooling, so I figured I'd let him recover for a while. He had a bad experience with his first-grade teacher which is why I chose to take him out of school."

Heather's approach illustrates the difference between homeschooling and unschooling. "Most unschoolers don't do school at home, unless that's what their child wants to do. There is a lot of open communication between the parent and the child. The parent acts more as a facilitator. We do a lot of field trips. We also explore the Internet together; my husband buys lots of educational software, and I buy a lot of hands-on stuff such as science kits and models.

"I don't look at my son as an empty vessel whom I have to fill with knowledge, but rather as a growing plant that just needs love and care. Everything that children do is educational."

Thinking about unschooling for your own family? These resources provide a good foundation for making the decision:

Amy Bell's Natural Learning Page   home.rmci.net/abell

Natural learning, or unschooling, is a philosophy of child-led learning. Among the other resources offered on her site, author Amy Bell has a growing list of reasons to unschool your own children. ☆☆☆☆

ePlay Learning Center   www.eplay.com/home.adp

This site advocates play as a form of education. A bit silly, but your kids might enjoy the Bug Libs. There's a grammar lesson in there somewhere. ☆☆

Family Unschoolers Network   www.unschooling.org

Resources and info for unschooling, homeschooling, and self-learning. Helpful information on the site includes homeschooling FAQs and an events listing. Site is mirrored at members.aol.com /FUNNews. ☆☆☆☆

Home Schooling: One Mother's Story   family.go.com/Features /family_1997_02/minn/minn199702_school/minn199702_school.html

A very well researched, very long introduction to and explanation of unschooling. ☆☆☆☆☆

Reasources for Unschooling

www.inspirit.com.au/unschooling

Good resources for homeschoolers and unschoolers. Very informative. ☆☆☆☆

Seven Things to Do This Week to Help Your Pupil Make the Grade   family.go.com/Features /family_1998_03/lapt/lapt38study/lapt38study.html

This is not an unschooling page per se, but the writer is advocating unschooling nevertheless. Projects are both fun and educational. ☆☆☆

Unschooling   www.unschooling.com

Everything to support the unschooler: FAQs, essays, editorials, support, and resources. ☆☆☆☆☆

Unschooling

www.suite101.com/welcome.cfm/unschooling

Author Teri Brown is an advocate of unschooling and does a great job encouraging the movement on this page of articles, reviews, and discussions. ☆☆☆☆☆

Curriculum

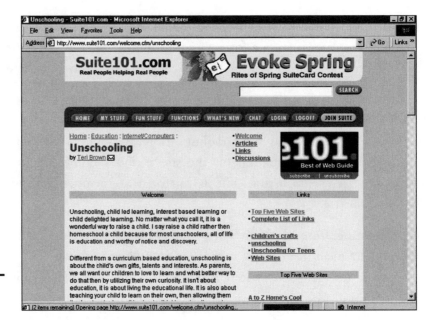

Figure 3.9

Unschooling: An
online advocacy.

Unschooling Articles   www.midnightbeach.com/hs/FAQ's.other.f.html
Unschooling articles and links to online unschooling resources. From
the FAQ link, click Unschooling. This site is part of Jon's Homeschool
Resource Page. ☆☆☆☆

Education Essentials

FOR MANY YEARS we lived on a small island off Hong Kong, where my children were enrolled in the local public school. It was an interesting experience for them. There was a small, two-room schoolhouse buried in a jungle of trees. During the day, island children would sit quietly under the drone of fans, dressed in their uniforms of shorts and short-sleeved shirts. My children—the only blondes in their class—would chant along with their Chinese classmates the lessons they learned each day. Then they would sit for hours and work through their daily routine of writing Chinese characters with brush strokes, answering math problems, and reading their reading books. Their social studies lessons and English lessons and science lessons were brief and to the point, because the main purpose of school for the Chinese is: Reading. Writing. Arithmetic. And these tiny children would come home from school at lunchtime, backpacks loaded down with books, and be ready to start their afternoon of homework.

They were getting a first-class education.

Then we moved back to the States.

Imagine my dismay when my kids came home from public school with stories about what they had learned that day in their drug abuse class, or in their AIDS-prevention discussion in health class. Or about the horrible things that took place on the playgrounds during recess. Or the pep rally they had attended that day. Or any of the hundreds of time fillers assigned by overburdened teachers who were spending time dealing with discipline problems in the classroom. What I came to realize was that public school for my kids meant they were doing anything but learning to read or write or do arithmetic.

When I finally got the courage to homeschool, guess what my first priority was? You got it. Reading. Writing. Arithmetic.

In this chapter and the following two chapters, you'll be introduced to everything you need to get your kids through the essentials of education. This chapter covers the basic educational skills that will make your

👪 *How We Homeschool*

"For me, homeschooling started as an exciting opportunity to really explore life and bond with my children. In order to work through my initial insecurities about teaching my children by myself and doing a good enough job at it, I bought an entire first-grade commercial curriculum and started working through it with my little three-year-old. The phonics didn't work for me, so I ended up experimenting with other phonics programs until I settled on one that worked. I was very focused at that time about keeping my children one grade level above where they would have been had they gone to public school, so that I could be reassured that they were not falling behind their peers. It helped give me confidence in the beginning. I don't do that anymore."

—**Mary Batchelor**, homeschooling mother of six, Sandy, Utah

children lifelong learners; chapter 5 covers language literacy; and chapter 6 presents the entire spectrum of mathematics.

We start this chapter with tools for teaching the most essential skill of all: the value of service. Then we locate resources for teaching library and media skills, listening skills, and logic and critical thinking. We list some great sites for reference materials, then look at tools for teaching research and reporting skills, study skills, and values, standards, and ethics.

Community Involvement and Public Service

HOMESCHOOLING FAMILIES ARE amazing. Far from being the recluses they're sometimes portrayed as, homeschooling families are out working in and serving their communities in a multitude of ways. "I have organized and run a food pantry at our church," reports Georgia homeschooling mom Priscilla Pike. "My daughter goes with me and helps me work in it each week. She helps give out food, stocks shelves, and is learning to help people in need." Priscilla is also planning to take

Community:

From the Latin *communitas (common)*. A group having common interests; society as a whole; the public.

her daughter to a larger food bank to help sort food. "I know this isn't much, but it is something."

Priscilla is one of thousands. Other homeschoolers get involved in political groups and in community organizations, such as Scouting and 4-H. Cheryl Northrup, a Colorado homeschooler, describes some of the many ways her family gets connected: "Our sons have always been involved in Scouts, and for rank advancement they are required to do much service," Cheryl says. "We now live in an area where there are few members of our church, with lots of move-ins and move-outs, so again, my sons get much opportunity to serve." Her daughters get involved in their church community by cleaning, babysitting, and providing meals for shut-ins.

Volunteering also has a religious theme for the central Arkansas family of Ann Crum, a homeschooling mother of two: "Our children are heavily involved in several aspects of our church's ministry, including visiting nursing homes, assisting with church services or singing, taking food to less fortunate members of the community, caring for the church grounds, and helping during church camps. We feel that these activities take our children's minds off themselves and make them aware of others around them in a real way. They volunteer to help with cleanup in the kitchen at church, to decorate for special occasions, to visit folks in the community. Helpfulness has become such a habit that they readily open doors for others and even help folks inside when it's raining by taking an umbrella out to them—without being told."

Donna Lee Spruill's Estancia, New Mexico, family gets politically connected: "Our family has been involved in the political process for years. We take our children to rallies and attend our political party's meetings; they have always gone with us to vote in elections and learned the process. After the voting time limit, we meet at the courthouse to check the winners and losers." Donna Lee says that when she serves on jury duty, her daughters sometimes tag along to observe the court process.

Shea Wilkinson's young children are already learning about the importance of taking a political stand. "My children are still very young, so civic involvement hasn't really been an issue," she says. "But we are talking to our four-year-old son about what elections mean. We have been very clear to him that we vote and that we think voting is a great privilege. We are hoping that our boys will grow up with the desire to vote and participate in elections on all levels."

The Huntington, Virginia, mother of two also participates with her children in service functions at their church. "We have served dinner to families following funerals and visited shut-ins at nursing homes. We want them to realize that all people are important, not just the ones in our immediate or even our church family."

Tracy Jenkins is a homeschooling mother of two in Hagerstown, Maryland. She is a member of a local homeschool support group, and she and another member of the group lead a girls club that does acts of service within the community. "We go to a nursing home twice a year, and we take homemade gifts and serve a snack and sing songs. The residents love it! We also brought in gently used toys and cleaned them up and sent them to Romanian orphanages and the Dominican Republic. In addition, the girls also made Valentine's Day cards to send to the VA hospitals this year. We also participated in the American Heart Association's Jump Rope for Heart and raised $1,366.80!"

Joyce Dumire from Akron, Ohio, has had her homeschooled son volunteer to teach younger kids. "Teaching something is the best way to really learn," she says.

North Carolina's Tracee Stewart takes her family out to do some hands-on service. "We clean up our streets and roadsides, and go to the town square to help clean it. My son is involved with the Scouts, so he does a lot of community service. My daughter and I are involved with our church group that provides services to the elderly and handicapped. We help out where we are needed and meet all kinds of people."

Jennie Littrell, who homeschools two children in Michigan, says service doesn't always have to be planned out. "We were out on a walk tonight. It has been a windy day, and my seven-year-old observed that there was a lot of garbage blowing around. She asked if we could go

Free Videos

Libraries and Blockbuster Video outlets around the United States offer free rentals of community service videos.

Education Essentials

How We Homeschool

"We've just begun homeschooling, but my plans are to ask a nearby nursing home/residential facility to allow my 11-year-old son to teach basic computer skills and Internet/e-mail to the residents.

"Also, on holidays we volunteer at a local church (they require that we cook the food, slice it, and participate in serving it). Finally, we're helping a friend who is involved with spinal-cord-injury fundraising."

—**Cathy Babis**, homeschooling mother of two, St. Louis

around the neighborhood with a garbage bag and pick it up. So that's what we are doing in the morning."

Annie Glass, a homeschooling mother of two from Everson, Washington, looks for innovative ways to involve her children in service. "We live in a small community, about 1,800 people. There are two senior centers where we regularly sing. I play the guitar and love the old folk, band, and vaudeville songs. We're the only group with young children that sings the songs the older people like, and so they request us often. We sing about twice a month for them. We're certainly not professional, but we can carry a tune, sort of. Our reward is the joy and delight on these people's faces.

"When the gal who had usually put together our church's weekly bulletin had to quit, our boys (five and seven) were asked if they would like to take over the job as a way to serve the church. The congregation has been very understanding when bulletins aren't folded as straight as they should be or inserts are missing from some. Over the past few months the boys' work has much improved and they feel thrilled to be 'needed.'"

Kim Eckles' daughter Heather, who is in her freshman year, "is on the committee for the century celebration for our community, where she gathers information about the schools and meets with people who have lived here all their lives. Heather is also a junior docent at the Neville House, the historical home of General John Neville, where she gives tours and participates in fundraisers."

Franklin D. Roosevelt

One of the best-loved and most powerful presidents in United States history was homeschooled. Franklin Delano Roosevelt was an only child, born into a wealthy family that traveled frequently between Europe and New York. Roosevelt, reared to be a gentleman and to be responsible to those who were less fortunate, was taught at home until he was 14, at which time he entered a private school in Groton, Massachusetts. In his late thirties he was struck with a crippling case of polio and through sheer force of will regained partial use of his legs. He eventually led the United States out of the Great Depression and through World War II, and in so doing became the only president to be elected to four terms in office.

Whether your service is simple or large, there's no doubt that working together as a family to serve your community is educational. Here are some great Internet resources to get you pointed in the right direction:

CASA   **www.casanet.org/nuts**
This site helps potential volunteers learn about service opportunities and news concerning child abuse and neglect projects. ☆☆☆

Cyber Activism Tutorial
members.tripod.com/~ElizBrunner/Activism/StepOne.html
This tutorial doesn't take a stand on what you should be involved in; it just suggests, step by step, how to get involved. ☆☆☆☆☆

earthhope
earthhopenetwork.net/how_to_go_in_to_online _environme.htm
An environmental action site. If you want your family involved in environmental activism, this is a good place to get started. ☆☆☆☆

Hotlinks

Cyber Activism Tutorial
members.tripod.com
/~ElizBrunner/Activism
/StepOne.html

earthhope
earthhopenetwork.net
/how_to_go_in_to_online
_environme.htm

Education Essentials

Education Essentials

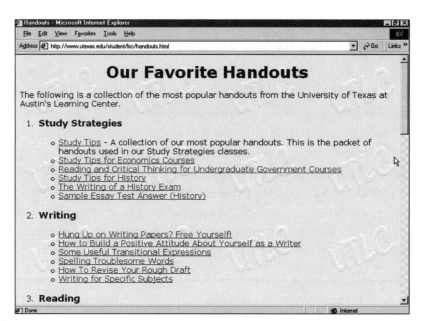

Figure 4.1

earthhope: A bit of service to the world.

Energize: Volunteer Management Library   www.energizeinc.com/art.html

Lots and lots of articles, book excerpts, and links on volunteerism. ☆☆☆

Food for the Poor   www.foodforthepoor.com

This organization provides food, drinking water, medical care, and emergency aid to countries around the world. See how you can get involved. ☆☆☆

Helpful Hints for Volunteering   www.volunteerinfo.org/volhints.htm

A list of things to consider when volunteering. ☆☆☆

National Charities Information Bureau   www.give.org

Be sure that your donation dollars are used appropriately with this free service that rates charities. ☆☆☆☆

Library and Media Skills

ANOTHER MARK OF a well-educated person is the ability to use all the resources of the library. Homeschooling mom Tracee Stewart, who raises two children in North Carolina, says her family is at the library a lot! "We go at least once a week, if not more!" She has taught her children how to look for and locate books and other library resources. "The most important tool that helps them is the card catalog, now that it's on the computer. They type in what they need; the computer tells them the number of the book; they go to the aisle and find it. Simple to them. I've taught them the Dewey decimal system." Tracee's church also has an expansive library that her family uses often.

> **Library:** From the Latin *librarius (of books)*. A collection of literary and artistic materials.

Tracee's involvement with local libraries doesn't stop there. "We attend free seminars and library programs in my area. We have a science-works place here in town that offers monthly programs and lessons for homeschoolers, and our community also has book fairs and such."

The library complements lessons at home for homeschooler Colleen Lee in Maine. "The library has tons of great books to supplement my curriculum, and also we make use of free educational videos to complement a concept or to introduce a new idea.

Lillian Haas, who homeschools two children in Audubon, New Jersey, takes her kids to the library at least two or three times a week. "My kids can take out as many books as they can take care of," she says. "I never taught my older son (he's eight) to use the library; he just figured out the computer system when he wanted to find specific books. He had a bit more trouble learning to find the books on the shelves, but he can do that now too."

For the Bridgeville, Pennsylvania, Eckles family, the library is a weekly destination. Mom Kim says her five children really enjoy their library experience. In the early days, though, teaching them to use the library meant getting their hands a little dirty: "I taught the girls to use the card catalog (shows my age), but now we use the computer for information. The computer was a big tool in our learning and still is."

Kim's family is getting an eclectic education from their library experience: "We borrow the classics as well as fun books to read about crafts, vacation spots, languages (using the free audiotapes), history, and more.

Small Library

"I don't use the local library at all! The one here in town is very small, and the staff isn't that helpful. We are planning to move soon, and I am looking forward to being in a city with a *real* library!"

—vanessa ronsse, homeschooling mother of one, Seattle area

The video collections are great, particularly eyewitness movies like *Schindler's List.*"

But that's only the beginning. "Our library also gives tours to tell us about the number system. We have used the reference books to find college money and to look into the colleges before we call for information. Many libraries offer storytelling or reading programs (ours does). There are contests to see who can read the most books. I can't even list all of the things we do because there are so many."

Kim has a great suggestion for making good use of the library: "After we read a classic, we check to see if there is a movie version of it, and we critique the movie compared to the book! It's lots of fun to see what the director of the movie did in comparison to the original book."

Michigan's Jennie Littrell has lots to do with her two young children. "I had the librarian give my daughter a tour of the library. She showed her everything." Jennie lets her daughter check out free movies for fun. "We watch fairy tales a lot, because they get her imagination flowing. She usually writes something about each movie for composition or draws a picture of her favorite scene."

Ready to make the library a big part of your homeschooling experience? Here's what the experts say.

Dewpoint   ivory.lm.com/~mundie/DDHC/DDH.html

The Dewey decimal system is looking a little dated after all these years, but it's an interesting categorization of human knowledge. ☆☆☆

Information Literacy Tutorial

www.mctc.mnscu.edu/academicAffairs/library/tutorials/infolit/index.html

This self-paced tutorial helps students preparing to take the MCTC information literacy competency examination, but anyone learning about how libraries work would benefit. The pre-test is designed to test your knowledge before you begin. Each module also includes a quiz that allows you to test your understanding of the information presented in the module. ☆☆☆☆☆

Dame Agatha Christie

Author Agatha Christie turned her homeschooling experience into a life of mystery. She was educated at home by her mother, and began writing detective stories while she was a World War I nurse. She published her first novel, *The Mysterious Affair at Styles,* at age 29, and over the course of her life published some 75 novels. Her books have sold more than 100 million copies and have been translated into more than 100 languages.

Just Think Foundation   www.justthink.org
A media literacy organization that seeks to educate children about the role and influence of the media. Lessons, projects, resources. ☆☆☆

Let's Use the Library!   www.ed.gov/pubs/parents/LearnPtnrs/library.html
How to use the library. Ideas for getting kids involved. ☆☆☆

Library Lessons   www3.sympatico.ca/ray.saitz/library.htm
From the Outta Ray's Head collection of lesson plans. This site by Ray Saitz and many contributors provides handouts and ideas. All of the lessons have been used and refined in the classroom. ☆☆☆☆

Library Science   www.educationindex.com/libsci
Reviews of dozens of library-related sites. Learn about the Library in the Sky project, and more. ☆☆☆

Library Services   www.npin.org/library/pre1998/n00273/libserv.htm
"Encourage your kids to participate in summer reading programs," advises this government-sponsored site. Information for preschoolers, children, and teenagers on how to make good use of the library. ☆☆☆☆☆

Media Literacy   www.emtech.net/media_literacy.html
Scores of very well chosen resources. ☆☆

Hotlinks

Information Literacy Tutorial
www.mctc.mnscu
.edu/academicAffairs
/library/tutorials/infolit
/index.html

Library Lessons
www3.sympatico.ca
/ray.saitz/library.htm

Library Services
www.npin.org/library
/pre1998/n00273
/libserv.htm

Education Essentials

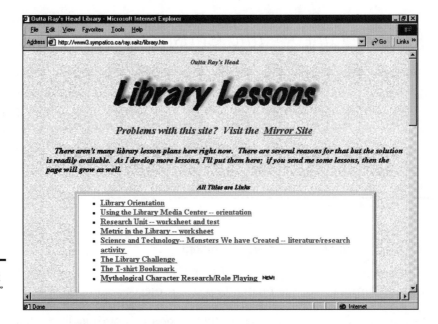

Figure 4.2

Library Lessons: Get your daily "Ssshhh!" here.

Working With Libraries

www.nhen.org/emfiles/Working%20With%20Libraries.txt

A collection of homeschoolers' personal experiences and advice on working with libraries. ☆☆☆

Listening Skills

"SSSHHHH! LISTEN!"

"You're not listening. . . ."

"Be quiet and listen to me!"

It's the universal call of the parent and the teacher. Whether you're the kind of parent who commands order and attention, or the sort who spends time on your knees talking eye to eye with the short people in your home, you've probably been frustrated by your kids' inability to follow instructions and absorb meaning from what they hear. So why is it that kids all over the planet aren't listening to their parents? Perhaps they just haven't been taught.

> **Listen:** From the Sanskrit *srosati (he hears)*. To give consideration and thoughtful attention.

To teach her own children the skill of listening, Cheryl Northrup, a Colorado homeschooler, took inspiration from a motivational speaker. "We have tried, with varying success, to use inspirational speaker John Bytheway's idea of a 'church journal,' to teach the kids to take notes as a speaker speaks and learn to outline on the spot." She's been a bit more pragmatic about day-to-day interaction with her older boys. "When faced with teenaged boys who would act as if they were listening to me, then completely forget what I told them to do, I found that having them repeat the instructions back to me helped a great deal. A 'narration' approach, I guess!"

For Tracee Stewart, the skill of listening is a more formal lesson. The North Carolina homeschooler of two says her family uses books as their listening resource. Tracee reads, and her children answer her questions at the end of each chapter. She also uses chapters of books or paragraphs. "I read them the paragraph in a set time, and they write answers to questions that I make up," she says. "Mostly I give them three minutes. This helps them listen well, because they don't ever know what I'm going to ask." When they were younger, she says, she did the same thing using colors and shapes. "I might say (and only one time), 'Color the square blue. Draw a circle in red.' This helped them learn their colors and shapes as well. It's great to know they're learning two or three things at once!"

Storytelling also plays a large role in Kim Eckles' lessons in listening. Her five daughters range from five years old to college age. She's repeating tried-and-true skills with her youngest daughter: "I have found that reading them a story, then having them retell it at a later time, helps with the listening and comprehension skills. If we come across a word that I feel my youngest may not understand, we talk about what it might mean. At the upper levels, we tear apart the sentence to find the meaning."

For Seattle-area mom vanessa ronsse, teaching her toddler to listen involves simply not talking too much. "The best thing I can do to help my son to hear and follow directions is to KISS—Keep It Simple, Stupid. The other thing is to not raise my voice—a difficult thing when he is doing the same thing for the fifteenth time

On Listening

"Let a fool hold his tongue and he will pass for a sage."
—Publilius Syrus, C. 45 B.C.

Just Listen

"My kids learn to listen the same way they learn to talk."
—Lillian Haas, homeschooling mother of two, Audubon, New Jersey

Education Essentials

🚶 *How We Homeschool*

"When it comes to trying to find what works for teaching your kids, I don't think you can ever stop searching for new ways to teach. The 'stage' of 'This works; that doesn't work' never really ends. As your children grow, their interests and talents will manifest themselves. You will discover that some things work well for one child, yet not for another. You may have to modify your approach, your routines, your teaching style, on an ongoing basis. This may sound challenging, but I have come to discover that this is what raising children is all about. Embrace the challenge! Don't be afraid to try new things, even when you think you've found the 'right' one or the 'right' way. That right book or method might be perfect for the moment, the month, the year, or that particular child, but not forever!"

—Mary Batchelor, homeschooling mother of six, Sandy, Utah

in a row! But I hate hearing my own voice raised, and it just seems to shut him down."

Ready to do some listening of your own? Here's what the experts want you to hear:

How Can Parents Model Good Listening Skills?
www.accesseric.org/resources/parent/listenin.html

A great lesson in learning to communicate, from the U.S. government's ERIC project. Well worth reading and teaching. ☆☆☆

Language Arts: Listening
ericir.syr.edu/Virtual/Lessons/Lang_arts/Listening

A very small collection of lesson plans from the U.S. Department of Education's AskERIC project. ☆☆

Language Arts: Listening Comprehension   thegateway.syr.edu
/index2/languageartslisteningcomprehension.html

Young kids learn to rhyme; older kids describe an image while their partners draw what they hear. A very large collection of lesson plans from the U.S. Department of Education's Gateway to Educational Materials. ☆☆☆☆☆

On Repetition

"Attention and repetition help much to fix ideas in the memory."
—John Locke

Education Essentials

Listening Skills   www.kidsource.com/kidsource/content2/How_Can_Parents_Model.html

Teach your kids to become better listeners and better communicators. KidSource OnLine provides lots of suggestions to improve listening skills. ☆☆☆☆

Speaking and Listening Activities

www.sasked.gov.sk.ca/docs/mla/listen.html

These activities in phone skills, meetings, introductions, and general conversation are aimed at classroom teachers but will be invaluable to any student. You'll have to move partway down the page to find the listening segment. ☆☆

Storytelling in the Classroom

www.storyarts.org/classroom/usestories

How to assess your children's listening skills through storytelling. Part of the fantastic Story Arts site (www.storyarts.org), where you can find inspiration to read to your kids, whatever their age! ☆☆☆☆☆

Hotlinks

Language Arts: Listening Comprehension

thegateway.syr.edu/index2/languageartslistening comprehension.html

Storytelling in the Classroom

www.storyarts.org/classroom/usestories

Education Essentials

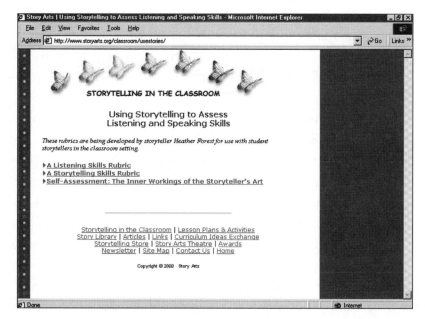

Figure 4.3

Storytelling in the Classroom: Become a great storyteller!

Logic and Critical Thinking

IF YOUR FIRST duty as a parent is to teach your children to be ethical, then your first duty as their teacher is to teach them to evaluate. If you accomplish nothing else as an educator, you must, of course, teach them to think. "It is not enough," said French philosopher René Descartes, "to have a good mind. The main thing is to use it well."

The skill of critical evaluation arises in part from simply being part of a family. Whether your only child learns to debate social issues with her parents, or your seventh son learns to solve problems with his younger brother, logic, evaluation, and critical thinking are essential life skills.

Greeley, Colorado, computer programmer Bryan Smith, who earned his degree in philosophy, explains the importance of understanding the principles of logic in the real world: "Logic is a unique skill in that it almost never is directly or consciously invoked in common everyday interactions, but it is, in fact, one of the most important skills one can have in those interactions.

"An intimate knowledge of logic so changes the thought process that, once a person has acquired it, it is applied constantly with little or no knowledge of the fact that it is being applied. Very few people ever, in everyday conversation, construct Aristotelian syllogisms out of what other people say in order to fully understand them. However, after acquiring the skill of constructing such valid argument forms, you find things that are invalid strike very discordantly with you. Hence you are much less likely to be fooled by trickery and scams.

"A professor I once had would hand out arguments from advertisements to the students and ask them if there was, based on the evidence given, a reason to believe the conclusion (or what the ad was trying to make you believe). He proved every time that people not schooled in logic will often say that there is good reason to believe things in support of which there is absolutely no evidence.

Logic: From the Greek *logos (reason).* The science of reasoning through a sequence or relationship of facts to arrive at a conclusion.

Education Essentials

On Logic

"Histories make men wise; poets, witty; the mathematics, subtle; natural philosophy, deep; morality, grave; logic and rhetoric, able to contend."
—Francis Bacon

👪 How We Homeschool

"We've been homeschooling for over nine years. When we started we were very rigid and 'school-like' in our approach. I felt that [my children] had to sit and write their ABCs to perfection, that only bookwork was school, and so on. I felt that I needed a curriculum or text for everything. If I didn't know something, I felt I'd have to learn about it before teaching it to my children.

"Unfortunately, we met with resistance. My son was very young and I was really pushing him. It wasn't fun and he didn't want to do it. At first I considered this a failure, but in later years I saw that I was just learning how to be a homeschool mom to this particular kid and to find an approach that worked for our family. We've lightened up a great deal and had fun.

"There's been no need to gain cooperation from my kids since then, as they're more than happy to learn. I find that when they don't want to do something, it is either a meaningless 'school-like' activity and they see through it, or they don't understand. My five- and three-year-olds love playing with educational computer games, the ABC magnets, workbooks and coloring books, cutting and pasting with colored paper, and so on. My older children eagerly practice piano, explore math, do science experiments, and more. They aren't as thrilled to clean their rooms.

"I don't consider myself an extremely organized person. I don't do lesson plans; just a brief sketch of what we hope to accomplish. My homeschool closet is total chaos, filled with books and materials that looked great in the catalog but turned into busywork and not fun. Our bookshelves are overstocked with interesting materials that were once organized by topic (science, history, and so on). These books are used continuously.

"We do chores as part of our day. My kids are rather independent, relying on their imagination and a wide variety of resource materials to fuel their exploration and projects. This really frees me up to explore my own passions. Even my two youngest children will grab some pens and paper and tell me they're doing school stuff and practice writing and making numbers and shapes on their own."

—**Susan D. Clawson,** homeschooling mother of five, Clearfield, Utah

An ingrained knowledge of logic often spawns the desire for more *proof* in everyday life. After taking even an intro class, I have had students tell me that they no longer find it possible to accept things they hear with no supporting evidence.

Hotlinks

Categorized Index of Fallacies
www.aros.net/~wenglund/logic101a.htm

Critical Thinking
www.sjsu.edu/depts/itl/007

Critical Thinking Community
www.criticalthinking.org

Thinking Skills
www.parenttime.com/ParentTime/behavior/archive/thinking/

"Sadly, most people (those not schooled in logic) *will* accept something as true with no proof or very faulty 'proof.' With most people, learning logic creates a deep desire to seek truth in everyday life; they will beg for reasons when told something and point out contradictions in beliefs held by others. So, logic is a unique skill. It's not like carpentry, which you use only while building stuff, or computer programming, which you use only while programming computers. It's a skill that permeates and infects your very life and being."

Logic and critical thinking skills will carry your children through college and life. These resources will help them get started. (Find related information in the section on public speaking in chapter 5.)

Academic Subjects: Critical Thinking
www.wannalearn.com/Academic_Subjects/Critical_Thinking
Tutorials, instructional materials, and more from the WannaLearn site. ☆☆☆

Categorized Index of Fallacies   www.aros.net/~wenglund/logic101a.htm
The most thorough index I've ever seen. The author defines hundreds of fallacies based on faulty logic, irrelevant information, issue avoidance, distractions, the absence of information, misleading or errant information, faulty conceptualizing, and insufficient or ambiguous information. He also provides links to other Web sites dealing with fallacies, informal logic, and critical thinking. ☆☆☆☆☆

Critical Thinking   www.sjsu.edu/depts/itl/007
I got immediately engrossed in the online lessons here. This interactive online course in critical thinking, deductive and inductive arguments, and fallacies is very usable. Readers immediately test their understanding online as they complete each small section. Beautiful. Um, that's an "evaluative" statement. ☆☆☆☆☆

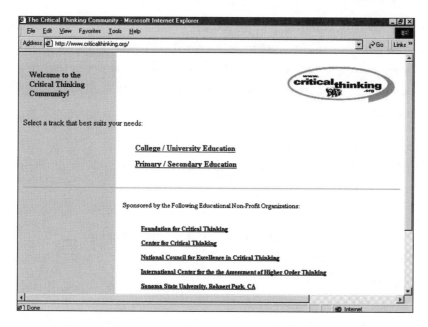

Figure 4.4

Critical Thinking:
Select a track to bet-
ter thinking skills.

Critical Thinking Community   www.criticalthinking.org

Helping teachers develop their own critical thinking skills and those of their students. Articles, curriculum guidelines, and lesson plans. ☆☆☆☆

Game Theory: An Introductory Sketch

williamking.www.drexel.edu/top/eco/game/game.html

Got a game lover in the house? Make his or her obsession an educational experience. This site examines the logic of some famous philosophical puzzles. ☆☆☆☆

Group Summarizing   www.owu.edu/~mggrote/pp/child_lit/c_group.html

Developing group summaries helps children review and remember information, which in turn helps them understand it better. This page contains directions for helping young children develop summaries. ☆☆☆

Logic, Reasoning, and Problem Solving

education.indiana.edu/cas/ttforum/lesson.html#logic

Three lessons in logic. ☆☆☆

Make Your Kids Smarter   family.go.com/Features/family_1998_04/dony
/dony48homelearning/dony48homelearning.html

Don't let the very long address throw you off. These seven lessons that parents can teach at home will help turn everyday activities into educational opportunities. ☆☆☆☆

Peirce's Logic   plato.stanford.edu/entries/peirce-logic

For your older children: logical theory that will influence the way they think. ☆☆☆

Thinking Skills

www.parenttime.com/ParentTime/behavior/archive/thinking/

A collection of articles on developing thinking skills, from *ParentTime* magazine. ☆☆☆☆

Reference Materials

ISN'T TECHNOLOGY GREAT? What took you and me hours and hours—and a trip to the library—to look up in our childhood is now available to your children with no more effort than typing a few words and clicking in the right places.

Over the past two years, there has been an amazing improvement in the research material available on the Internet. Just a short time ago the best on-line encyclopedia, *Britannica*, charged a subscription fee, and all the other general research sites were hardly worth the energy it took to look at them.

No more.

There are now hundreds of great reference sites on the Internet. Dictionaries, thesauri, encyclopedias, translators, atlases, almanacs, and much more are all available, free, on the Net.

> **Reference:** From the Latin re- + *ferre (to carry back).* A source of information containing useful facts.

Before they start doing research, your kids will probably want to know where they can go to find the information they need. Whether they want to know how to spell *rutabaga,* find a synonym for *earthy*, or learn about cetaceans, the following resources are the places to start.

AllExperts   www.allexperts.com

Communicate with experts on every imaginable subject. This is the pioneer "free experts" site, staffed by volunteers willing to share their expertise for free. See a similar site at www.askme.com. ☆☆☆☆☆

American Memory   memory.loc.gov

Want to read Abraham Lincoln's papers? George Washington's? They're here. More than seventy collections of primary documents. ☆☆☆☆

APA Style Resources

www.psywww.com/resource/apacrib.htm

More than a dozen links to style guides using the house style of the American Psychological Association. ☆☆☆

Bartleby: Great Books Online   www.bartleby.com

In one place: a searchable database of *Columbia Encyclopedia, American Heritage Dictionary, Roget's New Thesaurus, American Heritage Book of English Usage, Simpson's Contemporary Quotations, Bartlett's Quotations,* a book of verse, and the works of dozens of great writers, including Shakespeare. What a collection! ☆☆☆☆☆

Britannica   www.britannica.com

The entire contents of the *Encyclopædia Britannica,* searchable and free! And more. The site includes a search tool that brings up related current events, as well as relevant information from around the Net. ☆☆☆☆☆

Dictionaries/Thesauri

home.earthlink.net/~ruthpett/safari/megalist.htm#Jump1

A great collection of stuff. And nearly all of it is useful! ☆☆☆☆

Dictionary   www.dictionary.com

Lots of fascinating material here for word lovers. Search the dictionary or thesaurus, do Web queries, and much more. ☆☆☆☆

Hotlinks

AllExperts
www.allexperts.com

Bartleby: Great Books Online
www.bartleby.com

Britannica
www.britannica.com

VoyCabulary
www.voycabulary.com

Education Essentials

Encyclopedia   www.encyclopedia.com
Search the *Columbia Encyclopedia*. It's no *Britannica,* but with 14,000 articles online, it's worth knowing about. ☆☆☆☆

Funk and Wagnalls   www.funkandwagnalls.com
The quickest way to "look it up in your Funk and Wagnalls." Requires registration, which brings its rating way, way down. Except for that irritation, it's competitive with its English counterpart. ☆☆☆

General References   www.emtech.net/genref.htm
Scores of very well chosen resources. ☆☆

Household Cyclopedia   members.xoom.com/mspong/contents.html
What happens if all humankind were suddenly to lose all its accumulated knowledge? This online book attempts to collect the useful experience, observations, and discoveries of mankind during the past ages of the world. Interesting, anachronistic stuff. ☆☆☆☆

Internet FAQ Archives   www.faqs.org
The collected knowledge of the Usenet. This huge array of frequently asked questions covers topics as diverse as fractals, Kuwait, and Tiny Tim. Click the By Category link to browse hundreds of them. ☆☆☆☆

Links to Reference and Study Guide Materials
www.geocities.com/Athens/Aegean/3446/reference.html
Coyle's Where in the World site reviews topical links and describes how to use them in your homeschooling. An excellent resource. ☆☆☆☆

Martindale's Reference Desk   www.sci.lib.uci.edu/HSG/Ref.html
Online calculators, science tables, language translation, math reference materials, and much, much more. Encyclopedic. ☆☆☆☆☆

OneLook Dictionaries   www.onelook.com
Searches some 600 specialized dictionaries at once. ☆☆☆☆☆

Reference Sites   www.emtech.net/reference_sites.htm

Scores of very well chosen resources. ☆☆

Research Center   www.education-world.com/research

From one site, access four encyclopedias, seven almanacs, and dozens of calculators, calendars, converters, museums, news sites, dictionaries, thesauri, and much more. ☆☆☆☆☆

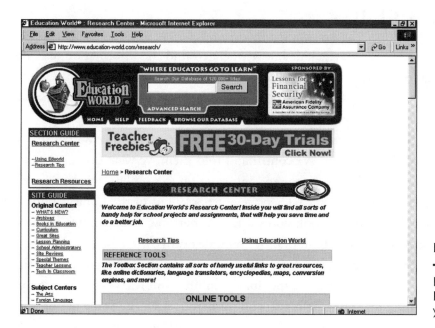

Figure 4.5

Research Center: Reference library at your fingertips.

S.O.S. Math: Tables and Formulas

www.sosmath.com/tables/tables.html

All the math stuff you'll ever need: prime numbers, factorization, logarithms, conversions, derivatives . . . and then some *really* advanced math. ☆☆☆☆

VoyCabulary   www.voycabulary.com

Type in the URL of a Web site, or just write or copy words into the form. Then decide whether you want to translate to another language, define it, locate synonyms, or conduct any of several other investigations. You'll love this one. ☆☆☆☆☆

Web of On-line Dictionaries   www.yourdictionary.com
Find links to some 800 dictionaries in 160 languages, on a wide range of subjects. Scroll down to view your options. The opening screen links to *Merriam-Webster;* below it are links to more than 1,000 other sources, arranged by topic. I use this one a lot. ☆☆☆☆

Research Skills

NOW THAT YOUR kids know where to find the information, can they figure out what to do with it? Kim Eckles's kids can. The mother of five teaches her children to write research papers—lots of them—from about the fourth grade on.

"One research project I remember doing was about Wisconsin. We called the capital of Wisconsin and told them we were doing a research paper, and asked them to send information to us. (This was before computers or the Internet.) Then we got books out of the library about the state. We read and took notes. I taught her how to take notes and compile them in some kind of order on index cards.

"Since the Internet, we have used computer programs, Web sites, the Library of Congress, the library on line, and real books. We compile information and write reports on numerous subjects. Some of our topics in the past have been abortion, teen suicide, Generation X, states, Y2K, and various diseases. My children have grown greatly by doing the research, and it is essential if they are going to attend college. My daughters in college do on the average of four research papers a term!"

Research: From the Middle French *recerche (to search)*. To investigate thoroughly.

Nancy J. Rose, a homeschooling mother in West Palm Beach, Florida, turned a business trip into an educational experience for the family by researching the history of the place they had visited. Nancy homeschools two children, ages ten and eight. "A few months ago, my husband had some meetings near Daytona," she said. "We were able to visit a historic battleground, and then we came home and looked up the site we had visited on the computer encyclopedia. It made it so much more tangible, and helped us relate to the event by being able to see where it took place."

Research is the basis of Ann Crum's homeschooling method. "Yes! We do research!" she says. "Researching a topic draws out details that might otherwise be left out. I try to do a bit of pre-research to ensure that what I have assigned them is truly able to be found. But I merely suggest to them where to look or what to type into a search engine."

As a result of their research, the central Arkansas family has gained a broader vision. Ann says her two kids "have learned so much about people around the world and can now view them not as statistics, but as real people—just like themselves. They have learned the histories of different countries and how it is that a country lives by a certain philosophy or what their cultural base is. Sometimes they will come to me and say, 'Did you know thus and such?! Wow, I never knew that before!' They really get excited. Writing the research paper is another step in getting it embedded in their brains. So reading, writing, and telling all help to reinforce what they are learning."

Even though her six children are very young, Mary Batchelor of Sandy, Utah, is already getting started on teaching them the basics of research and helping them get familiar with the resources in the library. "I have shown the kids how to find authors and names of specific books on the library computers," she says, "and they have helped me locate the books on the shelves."

Mary says her children are still very young for in-depth research projects, "but we go to the library regularly, sometimes every week. I let them pick out several books each, and they are responsible for their particular books. I steer them toward books at or above their reading level so that they can be challenged but not disheartened, and for every educational book they choose (for reading time or for studying), they can pick out one noneducational book for fun."

On Knowledge

"It is only the ignorant who despise education."
—Publilius Syrus, c. 45 B.C.

Education Essentials

፨ How We Homeschool

"We are in our second year of homeschooling. When we started, my husband was not really for the idea. I felt very strongly about not wanting them to go to public school. I did not want someone teaching our children things that we don't believe in. I didn't want someone pushing their beliefs about morality on our children, or teaching them their own beliefs about sex, and so on. I kept after my husband and asked him to let me try, and said that if he was not satisfied with the results, we could put our daughter in school.

"He agreed, and within a few weeks' time he saw how much the girls were learning and has supported me all the way."

—**Kath Howe**, homeschooling mother of two, Tulsa, Oklahoma

Whether your children are young or old, they'll benefit from the great research guides below. Related information, including style guides and basic research resources, are located in the Reference Materials section, above, and in the Writing section of chapter 5.

Hotlinks

Research and Writing Step by Step
www.ipl.org/teen/aplus/stepfirst.htm

Researchpaper
www.researchpaper.com

Writing Research Papers
www.simpson.edu/academics/Hawley/Research.html

Digital Classroom
www.nara.gov/education/classrm.html
The government's National Archives and Records Administration produces help, research materials, and original documents online. Tremendous lesson plans and other educational resources. ☆☆☆☆

Research and Writing Step by Step
www.ipl.org/teen/aplus/stepfirst.htm
Writing the paper is only the final step in research. This illustrated guide teaches students how to research information online for college and university papers. It covers how to get started, discovering and choosing a topic, looking for and forming a focus, gathering information, preparing to write, and writing the paper. Very readable; your high school students will enjoy this site. ☆☆☆☆☆

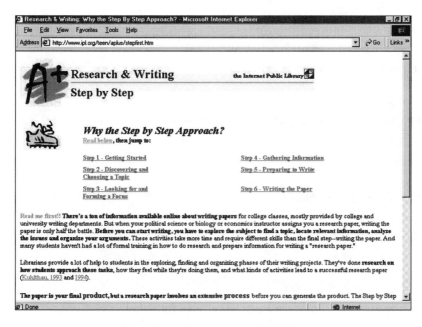

Figure 4.6

Research and Writing: A step-by-step approach.

Education Essentials

Researchpaper   www.researchpaper.com

Research, research, research: more than 100 categories and thousands of research topics. This may be the Web's largest collection of topics, ideas, and assistance for school-related research projects. ☆☆☆☆☆

Research Skills Tutorial   www.umuc.edu/library/tutor

This site's first and second modules on the research process and plagiarism are particularly well done, but the entire site is worth visiting. Written for a college level, but very useful for the high school level. ☆☆☆☆

Research Tools   memory.loc.gov/ammem/ndlpedu/research.html

Citing electronic resources, copyright law, answers to questions about research, and more. ☆☆☆☆

Student Research Online   www.emtech.net/student_research.htm

Not exactly a "how to research" site, but you'll be inspired by all the research posted online by other students and teachers. Scores of very well chosen resources. ☆☆

Writing a Research Paper

owl.english.purdue.edu/Files/132/5a-resource.html

How to handle various kinds of materials while researching. ☆☆☆

Writing and Research

www.pbs.org/teachersource/recommended/rec_links_art&lit.shtm#9

A collection of recommended Web sites from PBS TeacherSource. ☆☆☆☆

Writing Research Papers   www.mcrel.org/resources/plus/research.asp

Good information on quoting, paraphrasing, summarizing, and other tricks of the research writer's trade. Includes lesson plans, activities, and teachers' guides. ☆☆☆☆

Writing Research Papers

www.simpson.edu/academics/Hawley/Research.html

All about the research writing process, style guides, plagiarism, and more. Includes good commentary on the difference between research papers and documented essays. ☆☆☆☆☆

Study Skills

ONE OF THE most challenging parts of homeschooling may be the part where you teach your children how to study. The casual atmosphere makes it difficult for many parents who want to establish some structured study.

If you think your children's education could be better served with a little more structure, this is the section for you.

Whether you do "school at home" or are simply preparing your older children for college, there comes a time when everyone, even the most unschooled child, needs to learn basic study skills.

> **Study:** From the Latin *studium (to apply oneself)*. Careful consideration of a subject in order to acquire knowledge.

The following sites contain scores of handouts, articles, tests, and lessons on improving study skills. As your children work through these re-

👪 How We Homeschool

"The greater the mix, the more my son learns. At first I used videos from the library, educational programs on TV, and field trips, and followed a main study book. This worked, but we are now much more flexible.

"He's in high school, so there are certain topics I feel we must cover to give him the basics for college. This week he sat in on his first computer class for Microsoft Systems Engineer. This was for observation only, to see if he would like it. He came home so excited, gave me a big kiss on the forehead, and said, 'Mom, I love you. It was great!' He was never this excited in public school.

"He will most likely start computer classes for his postsecondary training, paid for by the state. It's this type of flexibility that makes homeschooling great for the kids. They can test lots of different things and pick their direction with their parents' guidance. They are learning and never realize it."

—Joyce Dumire, homeschooling mother of one, Akron, Ohio

sources, they will learn the essential skills of note taking, exam preparation, outlining, sticking to task, and many other critical educational skills.

So pull out a pencil. It's time to learn.

Electric Desk   www.pinkmonkey.com

Register at PinkMonkey, and click the Electric Desk link for a really well done guide to developing study skills. There are 24 lessons and a self-test that explain test taking, home study, note taking, reading, memory improvement, and more. ☆☆☆☆

Helping Your Child Succeed in School
www.ed.gov/pubs/parents/Succeed

An excellent publication from the U.S. government that shows parents how to teach their children basic educational skills. Addresses organization, listening, task completion, and much more. ☆☆☆☆

Helping Your Child with Homework
www.ed.gov/pubs/parents/Homework

A government-sponsored site that attempts to get parents and teachers together. (Isn't that what we call homeschooling?) Includes

Hotlinks

Looney Bin
www.geocities.com/Athens
/3843

Our Favorite Handouts
www.utexas.edu/student/lsc
/handouts.html

Study Guides and Strategies
www.iss.stthomas.edu
/studyguides

On Study

"If you think education
is expensive, try
ignorance."
—**Derek Bok**, former president, Harvard University

practical ideas for helping children complete homework assignments successfully. Some of the ideas on this site may also be helpful for high school students. ☆☆☆☆

Let's Do Homework!
www.ed.gov/pubs/parents/LearnPtnrs/home.html
Aimed at parents of public-school students, this page has good advice for homeschooling parents as well. Tips for getting organized, providing guidance, creating a good workspace, and more. ☆☆☆

Let's Succeed in School!
www.ed.gov/pubs/parents/LearnPtnrs/succeed.html
Tips for parents on helping their children succeed in school. These activities and lessons are equally useful for homeschooled students. From the U.S. Department of Education. ☆☆☆

Looney Bin   www.geocities.com/Athens/3843
A darling little site full of tips on how to study, including information on passing exams and tests, note taking, report writing, and more. Cute. ☆☆☆☆

Our Favorite Handouts
www.utexas.edu/student/lsc/handouts.html
Handouts on study strategies, reading faster, how to study in math and science, overcoming procrastination, and dozens of other topics. Includes subject-specific study tips, how to build a positive attitude about yourself as a writer, spelling troublesome words, writing for specific subjects, brief suggestions for increasing speed and effectiveness of reading, and more. ☆☆☆☆☆

Study Guides and Strategies   www.iss.stthomas.edu/studyguides
Written for college students, but easily adapted to younger ages or to prepare your high school students for the future. Produced by the

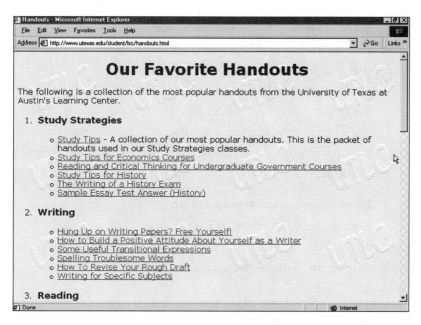

Figure 4.7

Our Favorite Handouts: A how-to-study handbook.

University of St. Thomas in St. Paul, Minnesota, these guides cover goal-setting, managing stress, paying attention, memorization techniques, and more. ☆☆☆☆

Values, Standards, and Ethics

THE FINAL AND most critical area of education essentials: Teaching your children to be good human beings.

Teaching ethics may be the best argument for homeschooling. Public schools have their hands tied when it comes to teaching values.

Fifty years ago, there was a good likelihood that parents and teachers shared the same values, and so parents felt safe sending their kids to school, confident that the values they taught at home were being reinforced in the classroom. Now, though, whether your family has strong religious values or is a devout believer in secularism, there's a good chance that your position won't find support in the

Ethics: From the Greek *ēthikos (character)*. A system of moral values and standards.

On Virtue

"The very spring and root of honesty and virtue lie in the felicity of lighting on good education."

—Plutarch, A.D. 46–100

public schools. In many—if not most—school districts, teachers are discouraged from taking a position on any ethical issue that is not part of the approved curriculum.

Fortunately, you have no such problem: You have boundless opportunity to teach your kids right and wrong.

The Internet has some terrific resources for parents looking for a framework for teaching moral behavior. Here's where you can start:

Breakpoint   www.breakpoint.org

Love him or hate him, Chuck Colson will definitely get you and your kids talking. Click the Free Stuff! link to order a free copy of booklets such as William Bennett's "Does Honor Have a Future?" ☆☆☆

Character Counts!   www.charactercounts.org

The essays and the quotes are of particular interest to homeschoolers, but throughout the site you'll find great information on teaching character and integrity. ☆☆☆☆

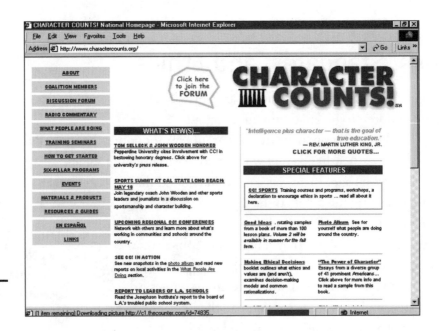

Figure 4.8

Character Counts! And how!

George Washington

George Washington, the first president of the United States, grew up on a Virginia farm on the Rappahannock River. From age seven to fifteen he attended school sporadically, but appears to have spent a large part of his childhood learning on his own. At the age of fourteen he transcribed in his copybook a set of moral precepts, called *Rules of Civility and Decent Behaviour in Company and Conversation*. During these years he became conversant in practical math and enough trigonometry to become a qualified surveyor. In addition, he learned a little Latin and geography, and read some of the classics. Some of his best training came through his outdoor vocations, tobacco growing and stock raising. By his early teens he had already begun surveying, which served as the beginning of his distinguished career as a farmer, military leader, politician, and statesman.

Character Education Links

www.emtech.net/character_education.htm

Scores of very well chosen resources. See a related site, Ethics, at www.emtech.net/ethics.htm. ☆☆

Lone Scout Plan

www.scouting.org/factsheets/02-515.html

If your sons aren't able to participate in an established Scout troop, consider enrolling them in the Lone Scout program of the Boy Scouts of America. The program is designed to accommodate homeschooled students, as well as students with disabilities or other situations that prevent them from participating in an established troop. ☆☆☆☆

Social Ethics and Political Morality

www.indiana.edu/~eric_rec/bks/at13ex.html

Using Tom and Huck to Develop Moral Reasoning. Demonstrates how to use dilemma situations in

Hotlinks

Character Counts!
www.charactercounts.org

Lone Scout Plan
www.scouting.org
/factsheets/02-515.html

Teach with Movies
www.teachwithmovies.org

literature to develop adolescent moral reasoning. Dilemmas involve questions of responsibility, fairness, rightness and wrongness, empathy and caring, and motive or intention. Sample activities focus on *The Adventures of Huckleberry Finn* but can be adapted to any piece of literature that involves making value decisions. ☆☆

Teach with Movies   www.teachwithmovies.org

These guides provide information that helps parents use movies to teach the consequences of bad associations *(West Side Story)*, cheating *(Quiz Show)*, and crime *(Oliver Twist)*, and the importance of compassion *(A Christmas Carol)*, courage *(Old Yeller)*, duty *(The Pirates of Penzance)*, and dozens of other values. Click the Character Development link to find movies arranged by values. ☆☆☆☆

Education Essentials

Chapter 5

Language Literacy

© PHOTODISC

Language

W HEN I WAS twelve years old, I decided I'd grow up to become a writer. A book called *Harriet the Spy*, by Louise Fitzhugh, had inspired me. The book's title character is an adolescent girl determined to be a famous writer when she grows up, and in preparation she maintains a notebook of candid observations of her friends, family, and neighbors. The book set the course for my entire life.

Harriet was a rather unattractive, frumpy little girl, and even though her wealthy East Coast private-schooled life was completely different from my middle-class West Coast upbringing, Harriet was someone I could identify with. She couldn't fathom people who didn't decide early on what they were going to do with the rest of their lives; each of her friends had a career in mind, and that struck me as a very reasonable thing to do. In preparation for her career, Harriet carried around a book and made notes about the people on her daily "spy route."

I recently did an Internet search on *Harriet the Spy* and was astounded to find that *lots* of people had decided on a career while in the sixth grade because they'd been inspired by the book (c.f., *Harriet the Spy*, www.pleiades-net.com/choice/books/HS.1.html).

"You cannot teach a man anything," said Galileo. "You can only help him find it within himself." It was literature that taught me to find the potential within myself.

This chapter introduces two of the three R's ('Rithmetic is covered in chapter 6).

Here you'll find everything you might ever need to teach English to your kids. We begin with a discussion of etymology: the origin of words. The second section covers grammar, usage, and punctuation. The subsequent sections cover literature, reading skills, speaking, spelling, vocabulary, and written expression.

To get you started, here are some of the most helpful sites on the Internet for pulling together a general English curriculum.

👪 *How We Homeschool*

"We always knew we would homeschool. My oldest started to read on his own and learned math through grocery shopping and other activities.

"One thing we did right was always putting the Lord first in our school. We have let the kids lead us through things they like to do and have used many workbooks that were just that—a lot of work, with no learning.

"A schedule for us was really great. We would homeschool in the morning and rest and relax from 1:00 to 3:00 every day. We still do this, and my oldest still loves this relaxation time. Every Wednesday is social studies and science day. It breaks up the week, and my husband works with the kids. It is great. I have always taken time for myself in the morning, and it works. It gets me ready for the day with four children, all boys."

—**Angel Danelle**, Kendall, New York

Academic Subjects: English

www.wannalearn.com/Academic_Subjects/English

Tutorials, instructional materials, and more from the WannaLearn site. ☆☆☆

BBC Online: English

db.bbc.co.uk/education-webguide/pkg_main.p_results?in_cat=548

A veddy British education, from the BBC's Education Web Guide. It's English by age group, plus separate sections on lesson plans and Shakespeare. Subject specialists describe how to integrate each site into your teaching. ☆☆☆☆☆

English, Literature, Language Arts, Spelling, Vocabulary Links

www.geocities.com/Athens/Aegean/3446/english.html

This site from Coyle's Where in the World reviews these topical links and describes how to use them in your homeschooling. An excellent resource. ☆☆☆

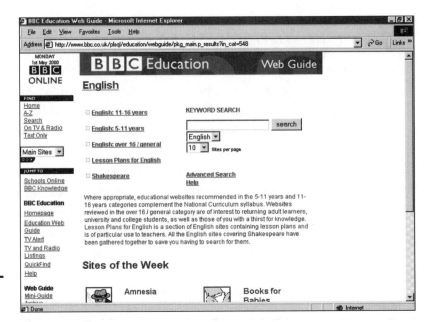

Figure 5.1

BBC Online: English
from the English.

English Pages   www.awlonline.com/englishpages/

Everything on this site is great, but most unusually useful is the Basic Skills link, with lots of tremendously well-considered reading passages that have related writing exercises, research suggestions, and more. The site has some commercial affiliation, but the free stuff is tremendous. ☆☆☆☆☆

Experts in English Grammar and Punctuation
www.askme.com/cat/showcategory_805_xp_1.htm

Want to talk directly with an expert who has volunteered to answer questions about English? AskMe.com is one of several expert sites on the Internet. See a related link at allexperts.com. ☆☆☆☆

Language Arts   teacher.scholastic.com/fieldtrp/index.htm#language

Internet Field Trips are guided tours to the best of classroom-appropriate Web sites. Each field trip provides quick suggestions for using targeted Web sites to teach a specific topic. ☆☆☆

Language Arts   www.csun.edu/~vceed009/languagearts.html

Hundreds of links to lesson plans, references, activities, literature, and much more. A great collection. ☆☆☆☆

Language Arts   www.emtech.net/language_arts.htm

Scores of very well chosen resources. ☆☆

Language Arts

www.pacificnet.net/~mandel/LanguageArts.html

Lesson plans from the Teachers Helping Teachers page. These lessons are submitted by teachers and include grade-level designations. Unfortunately, they're not organized by topic. ☆☆☆

Language Arts Lesson Plans

www.col-ed.org/cur/lang.html

Lesson plans sorted by grade level. Not a very attractive page, but the information is useful. ☆☆☆☆

Lesson Plans: Language Arts

educate.si.edu/resources/lessons/langlist2.html#start

Lesson plans by the Smithsonian. ☆☆☆

Teacher Guide to Language Arts   tlc.ai.org/tlaindex.htm

The Access Indiana Teaching & Learning Center contains lessons, resources, and more. A good foundation. ☆☆☆

Hotlinks

BBC Online:
English
db.bbc.co.uk/education
-webguide/pkg_main
.p_results?in_cat=548

English Pages
www.awlonline.com
/englishpages

Language Arts
www.csun.edu/~vceed009
/languagearts.html

Etymology and Linguistics

IT'S ONE OF the newer sciences.

Rather than learn a lot of languages (which is what polyglots do), linguists learn a lot *about* languages. They study word origins and language acquisition, the structure of language, and its usage.

One of the most interesting branches of linguistics is etymology. (No, not the bug science—that's entomology.) Etymologists trace the history and origin of words.

Why is the origin and construction of language worth studying? I have found this to be true: The more my children learn about the origin

Language

Etymology: From the Greek *etymon* *(word)*. The branch of linguistics that deals with word origins.

of words, the better they become at spelling, vocabulary, grammar, and all the other elements that go into making them good writers.

Want another reason? It's just plain fun. Discovering the etymological relationship between words such as *hippopotamus* and *feather* (www .facstaff.bucknell.edu/rbeard/hippo.html) is as much fun as solving any Arthur Conan Doyle mystery.

Some of the subcategories of linguistics—other than etymology—include phonology (the study of sounds), syntax (the study of sentence structure), morphology (the study of word parts), and semantics (the study of meaning).

If you'd like to turn your own kids into expert word sleuths, investigate these fun Web sites:

Hotlinks

Take Our Word for It
www.takeourword.com

Web of Linguistic Fun
www.yourdictionary.com
/fun.html

Word with You
www.wordwithyou.com

About Some Words and Their Origins
members.aol.com/rlongman1/genlangu.html
An interesting list of unusual words, traced to their origins. ☆☆

Brief Look at the History of English
www.m-w.com/about/look.htm
Merriam-Webster explains how English came to be. This is necessary knowledge. ☆☆☆☆

Etymologic!   www.intuitive.com/cgi-local/etymologic.cgi
May actually be what it claims: the toughest word game on the Web. Pick the correct definition from a list of likely possibilities. ☆☆☆☆

Lexical FreeNet   www.raisch.com/lexfn
Discover the connections between words. Some of these are pretty obscure, but the search is a lot of fun. ☆☆☆☆

Origin of Phrases   members.aol.com/MorelandC/Phrases.htm
The origin of "dead ringer" and scores of other phrases. A fun, easy-to-use site. ☆☆☆☆

On School

"School days, I believe, are the unhappiest in the whole span of human existence. They are full of dull, unintelligible tasks, new and unpleasant ordinances, brutal violations of common sense and common decency."

—H. L. Mencken, *journalist, 1880–1956*

Phrase Finder   **www.shu.ac.uk/web-admin/phrases/search.html**

Meanings and/or origins of 6,000 phrases. Also fun is the Misheard Lyrics link. ☆☆☆☆

Take Our Word for It   **www.takeourword.com**

Can you distinguish between *may* and *can*? The curmudgeons at Take Our Word for It explain that and more in a weekly newsletter. ☆☆☆☆☆

Figure 5.2

Take Our Word for It: The low-down on linguistics.

Web of Linguistic Fun   **www.yourdictionary.com/fun.html**

The Phantom Linguist introduces a plethora of information on how words and language came to be. "Mama teached me talk?" and

"Can colorless green ideas sleep furiously?" are two of my favorites. You'll enjoy the rest. ☆☆☆☆☆

Where Do Expressions Come From?
www.cam.org/~jennyb/origins.html
About 100 phrases and their origins. ☆☆☆

Word with You   www.wordwithyou.com
A fun site, worth reading every day. Daily columns on word histories, a regularly updated hangman game, and much more. ☆☆☆☆☆

Grammar, Usage, and Punctuation

WE MOVE FROM the simple origin and history of language to modern English usage. If you had to endure sentence diagramming in school, this is probably the stuff you once hated.

Despite the tedium of watching a sentence being diagrammed, however, grammar really does have important real-world applications. Brent Ayers, a copy editor and sports writer in Greensboro, North Carolina, explains: "Grammar is extremely important in my field. Because no one is perfect, my job is to correct problems with grammar, among other things, when reporters send stories to me.

Grammar: From the Greek *grammatikos (of letters)*. The art of using language with propriety and correctness.

"As a reader, I see things in a document that others may not. Grammar and style are two of the most important things in a newspaper. They give it consistency, clarity, and power to inform.

"I am very qualified to address how to prepare for this job in high school because that's exactly what I did. First, I had a teacher who was a stickler for grammar. Then I began working for my high school newspaper, writing as much as possible. You may be embarrassed to have others read your writing, but that's something you'll have to get over sooner or later.

♜♜♜♜ How We Homeschool

"I have made the Bible part of homeschooling just as important, if not more important, than the reading, writing, and math. We spend just as much time on Bible study, praying and memorizing, as we do on phonics, writing, math, and reading.

"I am not being as structured with time as I thought I would be. I am a very structured, organized person, but I am teaching myself to be more flexible with schooling times."

—Melissa Critz, homeschooling mother of three (so far!), Round Rock, Texas

"To prepare for this field of work, find a small local newspaper—preferably a weekly, but a daily would work too. Find a way to be around the office as much as possible. If you can get a paying job doing something, great. If not, volunteer for an internship; it may turn into a paying job."

Samuel J. Sackett, Ph.D, a career counselor in Oklahoma City, says grammar can make all the difference when it comes to getting a well-paid job. "As a career counselor, I help my clients prepare their resumes and other documentation that supports their efforts to get jobs. Since nothing makes a worse impression on a prospective employer than a resume with grammatical errors, my work frequently involves correcting these documents and explaining to my clients just why what they wrote is wrong—hoping that they won't make the same mistakes again."

Here are some great grammar, usage, and punctuation sites. Rest assured, they're considerably more fun than watching Mrs. Grumpy's backside as she diagrammed sentences on a squeaky chalkboard!

Banned for Life   www.sevenquestions.com/banned.htm

▊ Journalists' pet peeves. Once you start reading, you'll be tempted to submit a few of your own. ☆☆☆☆☆

Chaucer's Pronunciation, Grammar, and Vocabulary
www.courses.fas.harvard.edu/~chaucer/lang_ling.html

▊ Learn to read Middle English and Chaucer. The audio files suggest how Middle English might have sounded originally. ☆☆☆☆

Language

Common Errors in English   www.wsu.edu/~brians/errors

▦ Is it *forego* or *forgo*? What does it mean, to *beg the question*? Hundreds of interesting insights on English usage from a university professor. ☆☆☆☆

Hotlinks

Banned for Life
www.sevenquestions.com
/banned.htm

Elements of Style
www.bartleby.com/141
/index.html

Grammar Rock
genxtvland.simplenet.com
/SchoolHouseRock
/grammar.hts?hi

Language Corner
www.cjr.org/resources/lc

The Elements of Style

www.bartleby.com/141/index.html

▦ If you haven't read this 1918 treatise from Strunk and White, you're not yet educated. Blunt enough? ☆☆☆☆☆

English Department   www.gcse.com/recep.htm

▦ Who better to teach your kids English than, well, the English? This is what the Brits want their students to know about grammatical structure and English lit. Let your kids buzz through the tutorials on this colorful page, and they'll be smarter by the time they're done, guaranteed. Designed to tutor British students for the national GCSE examination, which is comparable to the American GED, this tutorial is a great fundamental overview of grammar and literature (pronounced, of course, "lit-ra-tewer"). ☆☆☆☆

Grammar Rock   genxtvland.simplenet.com
/SchoolHouseRock/grammar.hts?hi

▦ Remember Grammar Rock from when you were a kid? "Conjunction Junction" may be the best kiddie song ever. Use music to teach your kids about pronouns, interjections, verbs, nouns, and much more. ☆☆☆☆☆

Guide to Grammar and Style

andromeda.rutgers.edu/~jlynch/Writing

▦ Rutgers University professor Jack Lynch has compiled an extensive directory of topics related to usage. He explains the rules in plain and friendly language. Click the Contents link to get directly to the list. ☆☆☆☆

Language

Figure 5.3

Grammar Rock: Sing along from the '70s.

Guide to Grammar and Writing

webster.commnet.edu/HP/pages/darling/original.htm

"Grammar at sentence level; writing at paragraph level and essay level. An entire Web site for writers in English composition courses, featuring handouts on getting started, structure, tone, transitions, editing, logic, formats, rhetorical patterns, argumentative essays, research papers, and more, accompanied by an abundance of successful sample essays." —M.M. ☆☆☆☆

Language Corner   **www.cjr.org/resources/lc**

Columbia Journalism Review discusses contemporary language uses and abuses. Excellent. ☆☆☆☆

Parts of Speech

aix1.uottawa.ca/academic/arts/writcent/hypergrammar/partsp.html

An easy-to-read explanation of the eight parts of speech. ☆☆☆☆

Preliminary Grammar Book   **www.englishinstitute.co.uk/intro.html**

Lots of lesson plans on grammar, by the English Institute. ☆☆☆

Language

Literature

IN THIS SECTION on literature—which could easily be expanded to a book of its own—we locate resources for teaching children to comprehend and appreciate literature.

If you have a grudging reader, it might help him or her to understand how a thorough knowledge of literature is important to gaining a complete education.

"I believe that the study of literature serves several purposes in the 'real world,'" says the very literate P. Timothy Ervin, a professor of English at Yasuda Women's University in Hiroshima, Japan. "In no hierarchical order, I view literature in the following ways: First, literature provides a basic background to human cultures, both past and present (Emily Dickinson's 'There is no frigate like a book / To take us lands away'); second, literature provides a basic education, a language with which to communicate (the 'traverse even the poorest take / Without oppress of toll'); and, third, literature gives us a deeper understanding of human nature ('How frugal is the chariot / That bears the human soul')."

Linda Clay, who teaches English at a technical college near Atlanta, suggests that literature would solve the lack of thinking skills among high school graduates: "One of the biggest stumbling blocks I encounter in students at the college level is the paucity of critical thinking skills. In the 'real world,' we must apply logic and use good, solid reasoning daily, whether to solve the plethora of problems that arise or to make sound decisions.

"The study of literature finely tunes our ability to think logically and critically, because when we analyze literature, we are analyzing and critically evaluating a wide variety of people and life situations. Although these situations and people are fictitious, they mirror life and what we encounter in life.

"I like to compare literary analysis to my two dogs, Todd and Tara, playing together. Research shows us that Todd and Tara are doing far more than playing. They are, through these mock 'fights' that they enjoy

👪 How We Homeschool

"Between my sister and myself, we could probably start a small library. Having been raised with books in the home, we both love them and collect them like mad. We never run short of reading materials, research sources, or educational materials. What I don't have, my sister does.

"We also haunt the yard sales and flea markets for books, books, books. Where my sister lives, the library has a huge rack and table of books to give away. They also have an annual sale, which she attends."

—**Ann Crum**, homeschooling mother of two, central Arkansas

so much, practicing for real-life situations in which they might have to defend themselves against an attack. All animals do this when they play, even though they don't realize it. When we analyze literature, we are exercising our brains in much the same way so that our minds will be well suited to make sound decisions in our daily lives.

"In reading and analyzing literature, we also open our minds to a world of diverse people, places, circumstances, beliefs, cultures, ideas, value systems. We learn vital life skills such as tolerance and understanding. We learn to appreciate and understand people different from us and ideas different from our own. Thereby we increase our knowledge and our ability to think critically."

Practically speaking, familiarity with literature *is* the mark of an educated person. For that reason, I asked Carl M. Sharpe, an English teacher from Westborough, Massachusetts, to recommend five books that every high school student should have read. These, he said, are the five books, in no particular order, most critical to becoming a well-rounded, fully educated human being:

> **Literature:** From the Latin *litteratus (lettered)*. The study of written works with a high and lasting artistic value.

- *Hamlet*
- *To Kill a Mockingbird*

Language

- *The Norton Anthology of Poetry*
- *Lord of the Flies*
- *All Quiet on the Western Front*

My viewpoint is that those books represent the darker side of the human experience. I prefer that my children learn optimism and joy, and so I would substitute, for Hamlet, Shakespeare's *The Tempest*. Amy Tan's *Joy Luck Club* is an accurate, beautifully written portrayal of the minority experience of Asians in a Western world. My children learned to love poetry by reading Shel Silverstein's *Light in the Attic*. For a more realistic, and more loving, vision of adolescent angst and the pain of being outcast, there is no better book than *Harriet the Spy*. And Steinbeck's *The Moon Is Down* portrays the ascendancy of the human spirit in time of war better than any book ever has.

If you've come to this section looking for William Shakespeare, prepare for disappointment. You'll find one good Shakespeare site on this list; Shakespeare's works are covered in much more depth in the Drama section of chapter 11. Nor will you find material on basic reading skills; that's covered in the following section.

What you will find here is a good selection of books and literature resources available online. These materials will help you teach your children to love literature.

American Literature

www.pbs.org/teachersource/recommended/rec_links_art&lit.shtm#5
A collection of recommended Web sites from PBS TeacherSource. See World Literature, a related Web site, at www.pbs.org/teacher source/recommended/rec_links_art&lit.shtm#4. ☆☆☆☆

Books Every Child Should Read

homearts.com/depts/relat/bookintr.htm
Authors and others describe their favorite children's books. ☆☆☆☆

Twain Says

"Training is everything. The peach was once a bitter almond; cauliflower is nothing but cabbage with a college education."
—Mark Twain,
Pudd'nhead Wilson

Language

Children's Literature

teacher.scholastic.com/fieldtrp/index.htm#child

Internet Field Trips are guided tours to the best of classroom-appropriate Web sites. Each field trip provides quick suggestions for using targeted Web sites to teach a specific topic. ☆☆☆

Classics Archive   **classics.mit.edu**

Some 500 classical works by 59 authors, including Homer, Aristotle, and Plato. And it's searchable. ☆☆☆☆☆

English Literature

www.pinkmonkey.com/coreconcepts/subjects/english-lit.htm

A list of research resources, organized by subject. Register for free at PinkMonkey (www.pinkmonkey.com). ☆☆☆

Glossary of Literary Terms   **www.sccu.edu/faculty/R_Harris/litterms.htm**

If your kids learn the material on this page, they'll be well prepared for college lit. Too bad it lacks an index. ☆☆☆

Greek and Roman Mythology   **www.cybercomm.net/~grandpa**

Mythology from around the world. Argus, Chichevache, Hippocampus, and other strange mythical creatures. ☆☆☆

Handbook of Terms for Discussing Poetry

www.cc.emory.edu/ENGLISH/classes/Handbook/Handbook.html

Very basic introduction to poetry. Covers figurative language, rhythm and meter, and related topics. ☆☆☆

Literature Resources

members.tripod.com/~JBrennan/academic/literature.html

One homeschooling family's database of information. ☆☆

Literature Lessons   **www3.sympatico.ca/ray.saitz/litera1.htm**

From the Outta Ray's Head collection of lesson plans, with handouts and ideas, by Ray Saitz and many contributors. All of the lessons

Hotlinks

Classics Archive
classics.mit.edu

Luminarium
www.luminarium.org
/lumina.htm

Online Books
digital.library.upenn.edu
/books

Project Gutenberg
www.promo.net/pg

Language

have been used and refined in the classroom. See a related poetry site at www3.sympatico.ca/ray.saitz/poetry.htm. ✮✮✮☆

Luminarium   www.luminarium.org/lumina.htm

An illustrated collection of medieval and Renaissance literature. Nicely presented. ☆☆☆☆

Mr. William Shakespeare and the Internet
daphne.palomar.edu/shakespeare

Complete annotated guide to the scholarly Shakespeare resources available on the Internet. Includes Charles and Mary Lamb's wonderful *Tales from Shakespeare,* indisputably the premier work for introducing Shakespeare to children. ☆☆☆☆☆

Mythology   www1.askme.com/showcategory.asp?cid=978

Want to talk directly with an expert who has volunteered to answer questions about this subject? AskMe.com is one of several expert sites on the Internet. ☆☆☆☆

Online Books Page   digital.library.upenn.edu/books

Thousands of books on this site, plus a well-maintained list of links to books online at other sites. ☆☆☆☆☆

PinkMonkey   www.pinkmonkey.com

My favorite college textbook was the *Riverside Shakespeare.* The annotated notes made all the difference when it came to understanding jokes in Elizabethan English. Your kids deserve the same kind of background, and here it is. This amazing site contains study notes on more than 250 novels, as well as links to more than 2,000 works of literature, online textbooks, study skills lessons, and much more. How is it possible to make all this stuff free? ☆☆☆☆☆

Project Gutenberg   www.promo.net/pg

The original Internet text-collection project. Project Gutenberg gets about 750,000 visitors (not just hits!) per month, most of whom are looking for books by a particular author. ☆☆☆☆☆

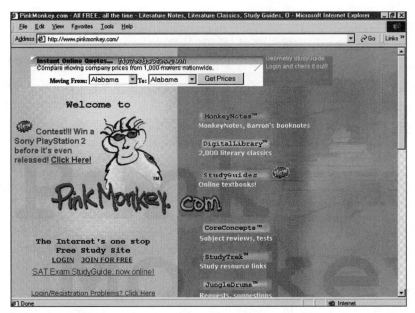

Figure 5.4

PinkMonkey:
Sonnets and more,
for the gorilla
your dreams.

Scholastic Resource Finder: Literature

teacher.scholastic.com/ilp/index.asp#3

Literary materials in a wide array of categories: everything from author studies to survival and adventure. Great stuff on topics as diverse as an interview with R. L. Stine and a pantomime play on the weather.
☆☆☆☆☆

Reading Skills

A FEW DAYS ago I exchanged letters with a mom who was worried that her kids weren't "keeping up with the Joneses" when it came to learning to read.

I advised her to do what my mother did to get me reading by the time I was four. The three components of my mother's very successful 1960s early reading program were letters, words, and stories. Oh, and there was also a fourth component: sibling competition. (I was the oldest child and, as such, had to show up my little sister, who was picking this stuff up as fast I was; she started reading at three.)

Language

Reading: From the Old English *ræden (to advise).* To examine and grasp the meaning of printed or written characters.

This is how my mother got her daughters reading almost before they were out of diapers: She put capital letters on flash cards, and hooked them together with a metal ring so they never got scattered. Then she made a competition out of learning those letters and their sounds. Whichever kid shouted the sound out first would win.

To teach words, she would place the names of household objects in block capital letters on strips of paper, and tape each strip to the appropriate object. For the longest time, I thought the thing our family calls a couch was a sofa, because that's the word my mom taped to the couch. Over the few months we learned to read, our entire house was labeled; to this day, though, I remember going around the house "reading" the word strips. Every once in a while my mom would change them around to see whether she could catch us out, but eventually we got to where we could spot the changed words. That's how it happened that the first English word I learned to read was "refrigerator." I always knew when the *long* word got moved!

Finally, stories. The first one I learned to read was a Dr. Seuss–like story called *Nose Is Not Toes.* It was clipped together with a metal ring and had about twenty-five words written in all capital letters. Now I make up my own silly stories for my own kids. I use simple rhyming words to get them reading: "The cat is fat. The bat is not fat. The cat is not the bat. The bat is not the cat. The bat sat on the cat. The cat sat on the bat. Fat cat! The bat ran away from the fat cat. What's that? Uh-oh! Flat cat. The bat saves the cat. The cat is not flat. Happy bat. Happy cat." Get the kids to sit on your lap and read homemade stories with you over and over until they recognize all the words. Then repeat the flashcard system, this time with all the story words clipped together, until they recognize them. Presto! You've got successful readers!

If you still have trouble motivating your kids to tackle reading, Maureen Supple, a distributor of literacy materials

Reading Freebie

"Simple Things You Can Do to Help All Children Read Well and Independently by the End of Third Grade" includes a general outline for starting a literacy program. Call 877-4-ED-PUBS and request product number ARC 97-4500.

and the mother of two young sons in Indian Head, Maryland, says she has a proven strategy for helping children develop a love of reading from the very start. "My major strategy for motivating children to read is to find reading material that *they* are interested in. I think it's important to follow the child's interest as much as possible, particularly for homeschoolers. Parents, with their broader knowledge of the world, can then steer the child to information that will broaden his or her horizons.

"For example, if a child is interested in martial arts, find a how-to book first. That could be followed by fiction that features martial arts as part of the story. Then the exploration could follow several paths: history of China or Japan, Oriental cooking (using recipes to support math lessons), travel guides to place the development of martial arts geographically, and so on.

"Many times, providing reluctant readers with material of interest to them will help them to develop a greater love of (or tolerance for) reading."

Mary Batchelor, a homeschooling mother of six in Sandy, Utah, has had some reading successes of her own. She says: "I've taught every one of my children to read (the last two are still coming up). I *love* learning with them when we study something that I may not have known or studied. I love them to see my own excitement when I learn something, and I love to see their excitement when they learn something."

Mary has found a great way to get her children excited about reading. "I signed all the kids (except my two tiniest) up for the library reading program last summer. For every two hours of reading (with or without me, but recorded and supervised by me), the kids were rewarded with a prize. Upon reaching the final goal, they were given a book and a coupon for a kid's meal at a local fast-food restaurant. Their dad took all four of them out for their kid's meals, as a special treat. During that program, we probably made two or more trips to the library each week, because the kids were eager to get their prizes.

"I want to experience the first time they really start reading, and see the thrill on their little faces when they realize they've cracked the code

Reading Freebie

America Reads Challenge is a kit with tips for instructors on how to administer reading and writing activities. Call 877-4-ED-PUBS and request product number EA 0082P.

Language

How We Homeschool

"When I started homeschooling, my son was in the ninth grade. I took it very seriously. We had sit-down study for specific amounts of time, and he had to get the workbooks or units done on time. That was the first year. Now I mix and match. We might do one subject all day or all week. We incorporate other activities into the learning. We are more flexible. ("I am more flexible" might be more like it.) I use workbooks, study guides, the Internet, volunteer work, anything, as an opportunity to learn. When we started, all subjects were from one source only, and we followed the courses very closely. I had to learn to unschool myself before we could really begin to learn and enjoy homeschooling."

—Joyce Dumire, homeschooling mother of one, Akron, Ohio

to language! Why would that be less important or less exciting than being there for my child's first step? First smile? First spoken word? On the contrary, it is equally important, and I don't feel I should be deprived of the experience, any more than my children should be deprived of sharing it with me!"

The following resources will help you teach your babies to read. They cover topics such as phonics, word attack, and comprehension. The literature section, which covers teaching kids *what* to read, is located earlier in this chapter.

ABCTeach   www.abcteach.com

"Free educational printables, and lots of them: research cards, reading charts, activity sheets, bookmarks, and more! Cute designs that kids will really like. Even a coloring page and some mazes to print out." —A.C. ☆☆☆☆

Chateau Meddybemps   www.meddybemps.com/9.601.html

"This is kind of fun: little words with little pictures." —S.C. ☆☆☆☆

4 Blocks Literacy Chat Board   www.teachers.net/mentors/4blocks

Curriculum materials for a classroom literacy program. May be effective for large families. ☆☆☆

International School of Foundational Phonics

members.tripod.com/~BillJanaeCooksey/Classes.html

An acclaimed reading program, and it's all online and free. This phonics-based program incorporates lesson plans, activities, games, and songs. ☆☆☆☆☆

Internet Public Library Story Hour

www.ipl.org/youth/StoryHour

Lots of early-childhood stories for reading aloud or reading together. A great way to introduce small children to reading. ☆☆☆☆

MomSoft Early Reader

www.momsoftco.com/earlyread.htm

"This is technically not free; it is US$35 shareware. However, a functional demo for Windows NT and Windows 95 is available. The program is very simple. You use an intuitively navigable interface, your keyboard, and your microphone to record a list of words. Then you activate the program and the words appear, in random order, each accompanied by a recording of your voice. You can adapt the color of the background, the color and font of the text, and the length of time for which each word is displayed. The demo allows only fifteen words in the database at a time, but you can change what they are at will. My son adores this program. (Part of the reason may be that his daddy recorded the words for him, so he can listen to it while Dad's at work.)" —M.B.

Reading Better and Faster   english.glendale.cc.ca.us/speed1.html

Want to improve your reading skills? This site has great tips for older students and adults. ☆☆☆

Reading Is Fundamental   www.rif.org

Click the icon to find links to research and resources. This U.S. Department of Education–affiliated site includes tips and more, but doesn't live up to its potential. ☆☆

Hotlinks

International School of Foundational Phonics
members.tripod.com
/~BillJanaeCooksey
/Classes.html

Seussville
www.randomhouse.com
/seussville

Tampa Reads
www.tampareads.com

Language

READY*SET*READ

www.npin.org/library/pre1998/n00238/n00238.html

 Early childhood language activities for children from birth through age five. A U.S. Department of Education project. ✩✩

Seussville   www.randomhouse.com/seussville

 I'm a big Seuss fan, so I don't even mind the obvious commercialism of the site. Click through the brilliant illustrations and links to find the reading section . . . but the whole thing's a fun read, so don't stop there. ✩✩✩✩

Figure 5.5

Seussville: The Cat comes back!

Tampa Reads   www.tampareads.com

 Reading-support activities and worksheets for primary- and elementary-aged children. This is a fantastic site with vocabulary, reading, writing practice, and more, all integrated to build young reading skills. The link to phonics research is particularly noteworthy, if you're teaching basic reading. ✩✩✩✩

Teacher Guide to Literature Reading   tlc.ai.org/tlitread.htm

 The Access Indiana Teaching & Learning Center contains lessons, resources, and more. A good foundation. ✩✩✩

Public Speaking

IF YOUR CHILDREN ever take you seriously when you tell them they can grow up to be president or prime minister, you'd better get them ready to become public speakers!

I love the observation of English philosopher John Stuart Mill, who said of his taciturn countrymen, "Among the ordinary English . . . the habit of not speaking to others, nor much even to themselves, about the things in which they do feel interest, causes both their feelings and their intellectual faculties to remain undeveloped, reducing them, considered as spiritual beings, to a kind of negative existence."

Homeschooled children have a unique challenge when it comes to learning the skills of effective public communication. Without a handy public forum, opportunities for public speaking have to be determinedly arranged. At the same time, though, those who are raised in larger families also have a unique opportunity to practice their intrapersonal communication skills nearly every waking moment. Fortunately, there actually are opportunities for even young children to take a deep breath and stand up in public to speak:

> **Forensics:** From the Latin *forensis (public forum)*. The study of formal debate; argumentation.

- *Field trips.* You might require your children to ask a certain number of intelligent questions of their guide.
- *Public meetings.* Your civic-minded children can be encouraged to go before a town council to request consideration of a particular issue.
- *Auditions.* Your children might be interested in auditioning for a part in a local play or a church choir or other performing group.
- *Service organizations.* Your Scout or Camp Fire Girl or 4-H'er can find a multitude of opportunities to organize an activity or event that requires him or her to stand before a group and speak.
- *Church.* If your congregation doesn't encourage youngsters to address either the youth organization or the entire congregation,

Abraham Lincoln

The best-loved president in U.S. history had very little formal education. As a boy, he is reported to have said, he had attended school 'by littles': a little now, a little then. In all, the future attorney and politician had no more than a year's formal education, but he was known for his willingness to walk for miles to borrow a book. And by the time he was an adult—despite having been raised by parents who were barely literate themselves—he was able to read, write, and multiply a bit. The few books Lincoln did read, he absorbed thoroughly.

Hotlinks

Debate Central
debate.uvm.edu

Excel in Public Speaking
www.ronkurtus.com
/speaking.htm

Workbook
www.la.psu.edu/speech
/100a/workbook/wrkbk.htm

perhaps it's time you had a word with your priest, rabbi, or minister. How better to understand their faith than for youngsters to prepare to teach someone else what they've learned?

This section covers effective oral communication, speech and debate. The following online resources will have your children up and speaking publicly in short order. See related information in the section on logic and critical thinking in chapter 4.

Allyn & Bacon Public Speaking
www.abacon.com/pubspeak/
Investigate these illustrated interactive modules to learn about the process of public speaking. Teaches students how to prepare speeches and how to assess their speechmaking. Learn to analyze an audience, research a topic, organize and write a speech, and deliver a presentation. ☆☆☆☆

Debate Central   **debate.uvm.edu**
Everything about debates and debating. Learn the skill of holding your own in public discourse, and how to use logic to influence and persuade others. Lots and lots of well-written information. ☆☆☆☆☆

Language

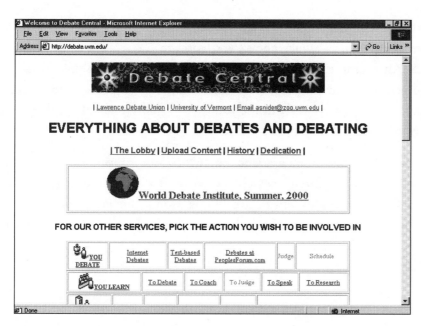

Figure 5.6

Debate Central:
Like your teenager
doesn't argue
enough!

Excel in Public Speaking   **www.ronkurtus.com/speaking.htm**

A very well written online course that teaches students how to effectively communicate verbally with individuals or groups. After completing the lessons in this course, your children should be able to speak effectively to groups, write speeches, and give presentations. The site also addresses how to overcome the fear of speaking to a group. ☆☆☆☆☆

Language Arts: Debate

thegateway.syr.edu/index2/languageartsdebate.html

Lesson plans from the U.S. Department of Education's Gateway to Educational Materials projects. Includes lessons on effective speaking in a debate, free speech, and issues worth debating. Provides resources for elementary- through high school-aged children. ☆☆☆☆

Speeches   **speeches.com/open.asp**

Write a speech online, or search for a speech by speaker's last name or topic. ☆☆☆

Language

Virtual Presentation Assistant

www.ukans.edu/cwis/units/coms2/vpa/vpa.htm

An online tutorial for improving public speaking skills. Learn to determine your purpose, select and research your topic, analyze your audience, support and outline your points, use visual aids, and present your speech. Nicely done. ☆☆☆☆

Workbook   **www.la.psu.edu/speech/100a/workbook/wrkbk.htm**

Can your children research and write a speech? Here's a great place to learn how. This online workbook from The Pennsylvania State University teaches students how to develop and deliver a public speech. ☆☆☆☆☆

Spelling

I LEARNED TO spell when I was a copy editor for a daily newspaper. It was learn or lose a job, so I learned. I sat there with one hand on a dictionary and the other at the ready, and looked up every single word that caused me any doubt at all.

When I realized I was looking up the same words rather often, I began making marginal notes in the dictionary. Once I'd looked up the same word three times, I would manually copy and re-copy the word during my breaks until I had it memorized.

Retired high school and college teacher Harry Livermore, from Valdosta, Georgia, describes the importance of learning to spell: "Have you ever noticed, after having dinner with friends at a nice restaurant, that you had a tiny piece of green spinach right smack in the middle of your front tooth, and you knew that everyone at the table saw it? Have you ever been listening to a choir at church sing the most beautiful music you have ever heard, and the organist hit a wrong note, loudly? Have you

> **Spell:** From the Middle French *espeller* *(to spell)*. To write or speak the letters that make up a word in their correct order.

Language

ever seen the most beautiful girl in the world or the most handsome guy in the world, but when she or he opened her or his mouth, there was a deep black gap where two front teeth should be?

"If any of these strike a chord with you, you know what misspelled words do to a person with a reasonably good eye for our language. Misspelled words are a sign of either ignorance or carelessness. Frankly, as a teacher, I would rather work with ignorance than with carelessness. Ignorance can be corrected. Carelessness seems to be a congenital disease that affects us all, to some degree, but affects some more than others. I do not want anyone who may be careless to handle anything that is critical to me.

"I'm not talking about the misspelled word that shows up in a quick note you dash off to a friend or to yourself as a reminder. I'm talking about misspelled words that show up in business letters, job applications, accident insurance reports, formal and informal essays, and school reports.

"If you have a few words that you *always* misspell, sit yourself down and memorize their spelling. Don't let your poor spelling cast a shadow over your character and personality."

The following resources are already helping to change my bad spellers into—if nothing else—adequate spellers.

Acronyms and Abbreviations   www.ucc.ie/info/net/acronyms/acro.html
It's not indexed—a shame, because once you start looking up acronyms, it becomes addictive. ☆☆☆

Language Arts: Spelling   ericir.syr.edu/Virtual/Lessons/Lang_arts/Spelling
Take a break from the usual system of rote memorization. Take a look at this small but well-written collection of spelling lesson plans from the U.S. Department of Education's AskERIC project. ☆☆☆☆

Hotlinks

Semantic Rhyming Dictionary
bobo.link.cs.cmu.edu
/cgi-bin/dougb/rhyme.cgi

SpellingB
spellingb.homestead.com

Why Direct Spelling Instruction Is Important
teacher.scholastic.com
/professional/teachstrat
/foorman.htm

Language

Scripps Howard National Spelling Bee   www.spellingbee.com

Learn how your children can participate in the National Spelling Bee, then follow the tips in Carolyn's Corner to help them improve their spelling. ☆☆☆☆

Semantic Rhyming Dictionary
bobo.link.cs.cmu.edu/cgi-bin/dougb/rhyme.cgi

Not only can you find rhymes with most English words, but this site will even locate rhymes with various numbers of syllables. Includes a thesaurus and other tools for finding whatever you need to write poetry that actually rhymes. ☆☆☆☆☆

SpellingB   spellingb.homestead.com

Hundreds of frequently misspelled words. Pick ten and create a spelling test. This is my own creation: words I've had trouble spelling and eventually forced myself to memorize. ☆☆☆☆

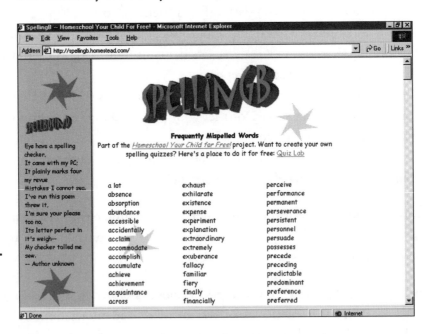

Figure 5.7

SpellingB: For the next generation of homeschooled spelling champs!

Spelling Test   www.sentex.net/~mmcadams/spelling.html

Take it online, and repeat it every week until you get them all right! ☆☆☆

Spelling and Vocabulary www.eduplace.com/rdg/hmsv

This integrated program for elementary and intermediate children includes lots of activities and projects to teach spelling. Part of Houghton Mifflin's Eduplace site. ☆☆☆☆

SpellWeb www.spellweb.com

Use a lifeline to ask the audience. Enter two choices, and SpellWeb polls the Web. I *love* this site! It's great for trivia and for unusual words that aren't in traditional dictionaries. ☆☆☆☆

Why Direct Spelling Instruction Is Important
teacher.scholastic.com/professional/teachstrat/foorman.htm

An argument for teaching spelling as a separate subject. Includes sections on phonology and orthography; how patterns, principles, and rules help organize instruction; and what should be taught in a spelling program. ☆☆☆☆☆

Vocabulary

> **Vocabulary:** From the Medieval Latin *vocabularium (verbal)*. The sum of the words an individual is able to use.

WHEN I WAS a little girl, I loved to go to my grandparents' house. The food was OK and my grandpa told funny stories, but mostly, I'm afraid, I liked to go because they kept a stash of *Reader's Digest*s that went back for decades.

Any time I could get away from the notice of my keepers, I would sneak away with a handful of *Reader's Digest*s to hide in a corner and read.

The anecdotes and stories were great, but one of my favorite sections in the entire magazine was "Improve Your Word Power," the monthly vocabulary test. Each issue I'd pit myself against the experts, and come away determined to earn a perfect score the next time.

I don't know that all the test taking helped me improve my score much—the words never seemed to repeat—but I do know that the experience had a beneficial effect on my own Word Power.

On Vocabulary

"The *Oxford English Dictionary* contains about half a million words. The average college student can recognize about 150,000 words. But the number of words he actually uses in speech or writing is, of course, much smaller. In telephone conversations, only about 5,000 different words are used, and about half of colloquial speech is made up of cliches and ready-made phrases such as 'How are you?' 'Raining again!' and 'What's on the telly?'

". . . The popular press and the organs of mass entertainment deliberately confine themselves to familiar words and to hackneyed phrases. So if you wish to develop a more adequate vocabulary you will have to read more widely and converse more deeply than the general run of people."

—Harry Madux, *How to Study*

Following are some of the best resources anywhere for developing and expanding your kids' word knowledge—including, of course, a link to the *Reader's Digest* site, where your own kids can play games to improve their Word Power.

Hotlinks

Things Useful to the Educated Reader
www.naciente.com /reader.htm

Vocabulary Workshop
www.southampton.liunet .edu/academic/pau/course /webesl.htm

Word Safari
home.earthlink.net /~ruthpett/safari

Dillon's Online Vocabulary
home.ici.net/~dillon /vocabulary.html
Find interactive quizzes with definitions and etymologies. Includes twenty-six intermediate-level quizzes and three at the "master's" level, plus lots of helpful links and a new quiz based on words from other languages. ☆☆☆☆

Grade 4 Reading Vocabulary Support   **www .readingkey.com/vocabulary/4thgrade/bothgrade4.htm**
These vocabulary lists are arranged in categories and organized into weekly lists for a four-period school year. Be sure your youngster knows all these words on sight. ☆☆☆☆

Notorious Confusables

webster.commnet.edu/HP/pages/darling/grammar/notorious.htm

Useful mnemonics for words that are, well, notoriously confused. *Except* or *accept*? *Bad* or *badly*? Lots more. ☆☆☆☆

Reader's Digest   **www.readersdigest.com**

Click the Word Power link in the left column to access three levels of vocabulary games. ☆☆☆☆☆

Figure 5.8

Reader's Digest: There's power in words.

Sheppard Software   **www.sheppardsoftware.com/vocabulary.htm**

Vocabulary quizzes at many levels. Take a quiz, maybe even win a hundred bucks! ☆☆☆

Things Useful to the Educated Reader   **www.naciente.com/reader.htm**

Sometimes the mark of an educated person is simply being able to pull out useful information at appropriate moments. This site can help; it's full of a lot of stuff your children really ought to know: confusing word pairs, conversational French phrases, manuscript Latin, and more. ☆☆☆☆☆

Language

Vocabulary

home.earthlink.net/~ruthpett/safari/megalist.htm#Jump5

▊ Visit a few of the Word of the Day sites each day, and you'll soon be a vocabulary master. Lots of links to useful resources. ☆☆☆

Vocabulary Workshop

www.southampton.liunet.edu/academic/pau/course/webesl.htm

▊ Meanings of prefixes and suffixes with a list of vocabulary words. The more your children know about the parts of words, the easier it will be for them to expand their vocabularies. ☆☆☆☆

Word Fun   dent.edmonds.wednet.edu/IMD/wordfun.html

▊ Dozens and dozens of resources for teaching your kids how to add new words to their vocabulary. They'll enjoy these games. ☆☆☆☆

Word Safari   home.earthlink.net/~ruthpett/safari

▊ Expand your word knowledge while surfing the Web. A playful approach to sharpening your academic vocabulary. Enjoyed this site a lot! ☆☆☆☆

Written Expression

AT THE BEGINNING of my senior year in high school, I fancied myself quite a writer. I was, after all, on the staff of our school newspaper and was even writing a column for the city paper.

I suspect I walked with quite a swagger.

One of the required courses for graduation was a senior-level composition class. I wasn't the least bit worried; I had, after all, gotten easy A's in every writing class I'd ever taken.

So as Mrs. Kelleher, the toughest English teacher in the western United States, explained how to write a composition, I sat back and contemplated my fingernails. I tossed together my first

Sophocles

The ancient playwright Sophocles was raised by parents of modest means. It appears that, unlike the wealthy Greeks with whom he associated as an adult, Sophocles was raised by a father who was either a carpenter or a bronze worker. Despite his humble beginnings, Sophocles grew to become perhaps the most influential playwright in all of history, as well as an important politician.

essay on its due date, on the bus, on the way to school. And a couple of days later, Mrs. Kelleher returned my essay to me, marked with a big fat D–.

I'm still embarrassed. I got the courage to talk to her after class and asked for an explanation.

"That's not a composition," she told me. "That's a bunch of garbage you probably threw together on the bus, on the way to school!"

She had my number.

She gave me permission to try it again, and this time, she said, she planned to grade me harder than she'd graded anyone else. If I wanted to make the grade, I had to figure out how to write.

That was some pretty serious motivation.

I buckled down and worked my tail off. I learned the structure of an essay, learned how to do research, and figured out how to use transition statements, cobble together a strong thesis statement, and build supporting arguments.

I think I actually earned the "A" I got out of that class. And more importantly, I learned how to write.

English teacher Carl M. Sharpe of Westborough, Massahusetts, says the skills learned in composition are useful in all walks of life. "I would say that a knowledge of composition is useful virtually every day, even outside of the academic environment," he says. "Right now, for example,

Writing Freebie

"Checkpoints for Progress in Reading and Writing for Families and Communities" provides developmental milestones for children of all ages. Call 877-4-ED-PUBS and request product number ARC 97-4502.

Language

as I write these thoughts, I do not believe that electronic communication or modern technology will ever replace or change the need for clear written communication.

"I use my writing abilities on a day-to-day basis in everything from memo writing to press releases. I have written for a newspaper, and I do a lot of writing and editing for people who seek my assistance."

This section describes the best resources for teaching expository, fictional, and critical writing. For those in need of additional resources, see the section on grammar, earlier in this chapter, which discusses usage and style guides; the section on literature, also earlier in this chapter, which covers literary analysis and various genres of literature; and the research section of chapter 4, which covers writing research papers.

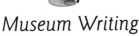

Museum Writing

"Collecting Their Thoughts: Using Museums as Sources for Student Writing" is a Smithsonian pamphlet that suggests ways to use museums to teach writing. Smithsonian Institution, OESE, Arts and Industries Bldg., Room 1163, MRC 402, Washington, DC 20560; 202-357-2425.

BYU Writing Center
humanities.byu.edu/writingctr/Handouts/indexb.htm

Handouts on the writing process, elements of writing, punctuation, grammar, vocabulary, research, literary theory, literary analysis, preprofessional information, and more. It's university level, but very adaptable to high school. ☆☆☆☆

CoreConcepts: Writing
www.pinkmonkey.com/coreconcepts/subjects/writing.htm

A list of research resources, arranged by subject. Register at the pinkmonkey.com Web site. ☆☆☆

Free Things for Your Students or Classroom
www.nea.org/grants/free.html

Your kids can work on their writing skills by writing to request one of these free educational products. This list of dozens of free resources for classrooms and teachers, compiled by the National Education Association, includes both Internet links and items worth writing away for. ☆☆☆☆

Guide to Writing Basic Essays   members.tripod.com/~lklivingston/essay

Very clear, well-written, easy-on-the-eyes explanation of essay writing. ☆☆☆☆☆

Language Arts

www.uen.org/cgi-bin/websql/lessons/query_lp.hts?corearea=1103&area=2

Complete lesson plans on writing for elementary children. See a related site for Secondary Curriculum Units at www.uen.org/cgi-bin/web sql/lessons/query_lp.hts?corearea=1&area=2. Very thorough. ☆☆☆☆☆

Online Journals, Zines, and Newsletters

www.emtech.net/online_journals.htm

Scores of very well chosen resources. ☆☆

Principles of Composition

webster.commnet.edu/hp/pages/darling /grammar/composition/composition.html-ssi

In the Overcoming Writer's Block segment, one of the dozens of practical articles on this site, students learn how to overcome thoughts like this: "I am XX years old and I have done nothing, discovered nothing, been nothing, and there are absolutely no thoughts in my head that anyone would ever want to read about." One of the best sites for writing resources, lessons, and ideas. The guide is very thorough, covering all areas of composition in an organized and easily digested manner. ☆☆☆☆☆

Rememory   www.rememory.com

I don't remember things as I used to. I don't remember things as I used to. Good thing I signed up for Rememory, where I can chronicle my childhood and enter daily writing contests. If your kids enjoy telling stories, they'll enjoy this site. ☆☆☆☆☆

Writing Assignments: Writing from Literature

www.indiana.edu/~eric_rec/bks/teachnsa.html

Several activities to be carried out in conjunction with the study of a single assigned book, or to take the place of the traditional book report. Each topic can be modified to "fit" different pieces of literature

Hotlinks

Guide to Writing Basic Essays
members.tripod.com /~lklivingston/essay

Language Arts
www.uen.org/cgi-bin /websql/lessons/query_lp .hts?corearea=1103&area=2

Principles of Composition
webster.commnet.edu/hp /pages/darling/grammar /composition/composition .html-ssi

Rememory
www.rememory.com

Language

Figure 5.9

Rememory: A regular reminder to write.

or to accommodate students of greater or lesser sophistication. A good program to get your kids thinking about literature. ☆☆

Writing, Grammar, and Vocabulary Resources
members.tripod.com/~JBrennan/academic/writing.html

One homeschooling family's database of information. ☆☆

Writing Lessons   www3.sympatico.ca/ray.saitz/writing.htm

From the Outta Ray's Head, by Ray Saitz and many contributors. Provides a collection of lesson plans, with handouts and ideas, that have been used and refined in the classroom. ☆☆☆

Writing to Learn: Journal-Writing Activities
www.indiana.edu/~eric_rec/bks/ctr&wex.html

Using journals to increase writing fluency, stimulate cognitive growth, reinforce learning, and foster problem-solving skills. A program to teach critical thinking skills. ☆☆

Language

Chapter 6

Mathematics Mastery

© EYEWIRE

I CONFESS: I was a mathematical idiot. Oh, I managed—somehow—to get through the usual high-school mathematics courses. But when I took my college entrance exams, it certainly wasn't the math that got me admitted.

That's why during my first year at university, I was required to take the dummies' math class; it turned out to be one of the smartest things I ever did. Here's how the class worked: The first day, the teacher told an auditorium full of my fellow math dummies, "Get this packet. When you finish, take the test. Dismissed." You can imagine the shock. There I was, a proven idiot, and this teacher expected me to learn math without anybody holding my hand . . . and he expected me to learn based on a book that didn't even have a cover!

That packet of math papers changed my life. I went home and got to work. The packet started at 1 + 1 and worked straight through to trigonometry, in a systematic fashion that made everything completely clear. Fractions, decimals, polynomials, factoring . . . by the time I finished the packet, math made sense. And that's how a math dummy ended up studying finance in college.

Math—more than any other subject addressed in this text—would seem to require the formalized, disciplined use of a book. Don't let that slow you down. Here's how you can still teach math—and teach it well—for free. First, borrow a math book. It might come from a cooperative local school district, or you might check one out from the library. Math hasn't changed dramatically over the past century, so any age-appropriate book you choose will suit our purposes. When you've got your book, put it on a shelf and leave it there for one reason: as a backup to the great Internet resources found in this chapter. Use your borrowed book to double-check your progress and to ensure that you're covering all the material. Let it be a backup when you find your own explanations inadequate. In any event, even if you're as

Mathematics

weak at math as I once was, you'll rest easy knowing that your kids are on track.

In this chapter, you'll find resources for teaching your children basic math, pre-algebra, algebra, geometry, computer math (including calculator math), trigonometry, calculus, and statistics. We begin with resources and tools for teaching the entire spectrum of mathematics. Use them as your primary text or as a supplement to that borrowed book. Either way, with these interactive, well-written materials, your kids will learn to love numbers:

Convert It   www.microimg.com/science

"This site has conversion tables to 'convert just about anything to anything'! I think this site is meant for students, but boy, can we parents use it too!" —A.G. ☆☆☆

Education World: Math Center

www.education-world.com/math

From a single terrific site, access lesson plans, tools, themes, and curriculum standards for every level of math. There's so much good stuff here it just has to be seen. ☆☆☆☆

Explorer   explorer.scrtec.org/explorer

Click the mathematics curriculum link to find a full set of lesson plans, from basic math to algebra and statistics. It might take some hunting to find the most useful plans, but they're well organized. ☆☆

Harcourt Animated Math Glossary

www.harcourtschool.com/glossary/math

"From addition to zero properties, this site defines every mathematical term students may encounter. Best of all, the definitions are animated to explain concepts in a fun way. Students will enjoy using this reference tool while learning math." —K.H. ☆☆☆☆☆

Hotlinks

Harcourt Animated Math Glossary
www.harcourtschool.com/glossary/math

Math Forum
forum.swarthmore.edu

Mrs. Glosser's Math Goodies
www.mathgoodies.com

WebMath
www.webmath.com

Helping Your Child Learn Math   www.ed.gov/pubs/parents/Math

A government publication that tells, step by step, how to introduce math to your children through activities such as taking them to the grocery store. ☆☆☆☆

Internet Field Trips: Math
teacher.scholastic.com/fieldtrp/index.htm#math

Scholastic sponsors these Internet field trips—guided tours to the best educational Web sites. The math field trips cover such topics as math history, activities, measurement, problem solving, geometry, and more. ☆☆☆

Math   www.pacificnet.net/~mandel/Math.html

Lesson plans from the Teachers Helping Teachers page. These lessons are submitted by teachers and include grade-level designations. Unfortunately, they're not subdivided by topic. ☆☆☆

Mathematics History   score.kings.k12.ca.us/math.history.html

A collection of lesson plans for California math students. See Mathematical Reasoning, a related site, at score.kings.k12.ca.us/reasoning.html. ☆☆☆

Mathematics Lessons That Are Fun, Fun, Fun
math.rice.edu/~lanius/Lessons

This collection of fifteen mathematics lessons ranges from math puzzles to algebra and geometry. Lessons include Calendar Fun, in which students use a simple algebraic formula to determine which four days add up to a given sum, and The Hot Tub, where students interpret data from a graph to tell a story. The site includes a description of each lesson. ☆☆☆☆

Math Forum   forum.swarthmore.edu

This great site from Swarthmore College has it all. Ask Dr. Math is incredible, but there is also a nearly infinite number of math resources by subject, math education, key issues in math, and, best of all, problems of the week for different levels and math subjects. ☆☆☆☆☆

Math Words and Some Other Words of Interest
www.geocities.com/Paris/Rue/1861/etyindex.html

Fascinating collection of math-related words and their histories. Use it as a motivator for your language-oriented math-phobic students. ☆☆☆

Mrs. Glosser's Math Goodies   **www.mathgoodies.com**

Interactive math lessons that really engage students. Innovative math lessons work both online and offline in your Web browser. These lessons cover probability, integers, percentages, number theory, and geometry topics. ☆☆☆☆☆

Saxon Math   **www.saxonmath.com/placement_tests.htm**

The publisher of the well-known Saxon math series posts Saxon placement tests online. Parents can administer and score the tests. ☆☆☆☆☆

Scientific American: Ask the Experts
www.sciam.com/askexpert/index.cfm?subject=math

Ask your math-related questions, or read the interesting answers to previous math questions. Responds to queries such as "What is pi, and how did it originate?" ☆☆☆☆☆

SMILE Program Mathematics Index
www.iit.edu/~smile/mathinde.html

Want to teach memorable lessons about geometry and measurement, patterns and logic, probability and statistics, recreational and creative math, practical and applied math, arithmetic, graphs and visuals, algebra and trigonometry, and more? Choose from this collection of almost two hundred single-concept lessons. Very well done. ☆☆☆☆

WebMath   **www.webmath.com**

Instant answers to dozens of kinds of basic and advanced math problems. Find your category, type in your problem, and let WebMath calculate the answer. This is a great way to let kids test themselves or check their own work. Covers every level of basic and

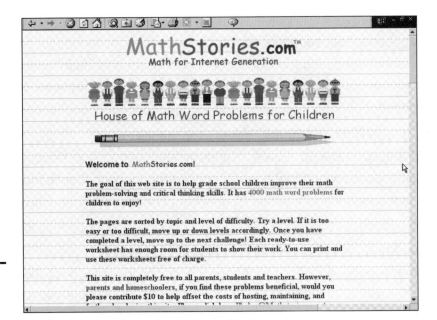

Figure 6.1

SMILE Program:
Lessons, lessons,
and more lessons.

secondary math, including calculus, physics, and trigonometry.
☆☆☆☆☆

Basic Math

IT'S ARITHMETIC TIME! Teaching math to younger children requires a lot of interaction. Keeping them motivated can be a challenge. One homeschooling mother, Mary Batchelor from Sandy, Utah, says she motivates her young math students by using a variety of materials: "I have all kinds of manipulatives, such as pattern blocks, interlocking cubes, links, dominoes, and geo boards. I have mostly used the cubes, blocks, and boards when teaching primary ages. We purchased a very nice clock with a descriptive face, but you can easily use your own clock right off the wall. It is especially good if you have one with a second hand.

Arithmetic: From the Greek *arithmein (to count)*. Adding, subtracting, multiplying, and dividing positive real numbers.

"I generally teach telling time in stages, at the same time that I teach the calendar. First I explain that the day is divided into A.M. and P.M., then that the day is divided into 24 hours, and that some hours are A.M. and some are P.M. I teach to the hour and to the half hour for a while, then I teach to the five-minute increments, then to the minute. Throughout this process, the kids learn to count by twos, fives, or tens, so when I tell them that numbers on a clock represent counting by fives, they fully understand.

"I use manipulatives to show my kids what they need to learn in math. We also work regularly with worksheets and with educational software. I do not require them to do all the problems on their worksheets. I usually pick and choose what I want them to do ahead of time, and then, as we progress through that day's work, I might cut or add some problems. From time to time, I also let the kids negotiate what they want to learn or practice."

Ready to extend your kids' learning? Use this information to teach your elementary- and middle school–aged children basic mathematical operators, multiplication tables, fractions, decimals, and percentages, so they'll be well prepared to learn more advanced math.

AllMath   www.allmath.com

Want to make a math lover out of Junior? This site features flash cards, metric tools, biographies of mathematicians, and more! ☆☆☆☆

Brain Teasers   www.eduplace.com/math/brain

Each week new brainteasers appear on this site, organized by age of test-taker. It's frequently updated, so stop by again and again. ☆☆☆☆

Math Activities for Grades K–4

daniel.calpoly.edu/~dfrc/Robin/elem.html

All together now: flap your wings! Each of these lesson plans uses an aircraft theme to teach unit conversions, estimating, basic

Hotlinks

MathStories
www.mathstories.com

Multiplication Rock
genxtvland.simplenet.com
/SchoolHouseRock
/multiplication.hts?hi

Multiplication Table Applet
www.netrover.com
/~kingskid/MulTab
/Applet.html

Rick's Math Web
users.black-hole.com
/users/rsch/indexnew.html

geometry, graphing, subtraction, symmetry, and writing about math.
☆☆☆☆

Mathematics Problem Solving   www.rhlschool.com/math.htm
A new worksheet every week. Riddles, puzzles, illustrated worksheets. The answer key arrives by e-mail. ☆☆☆

Mathematics Worksheet Factory Lite
www.worksheetfactory.com/mathlite.html
Download this free software package that lets you easily create your own basic math worksheets for the practice of arithmetic facts.
☆☆☆☆

MathStories   www.mathstories.com
Remember how much you hated word problems as a kid? They still served a useful function, though, didn't they? If your youngster hasn't mastered the fine art of pulling correct information out of a real-life problem, here's help. More than 4,000 math word problems indexed by grade level. And it's free. ☆☆☆☆

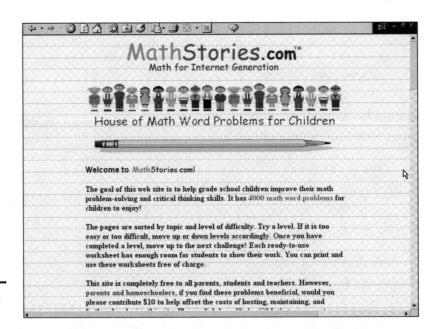

Figure 6.2

MathStories: You've got story problems!

Multiplication Rock

genxtvland.simplenet.com/SchoolHouseRock/multiplication.hts?hi

It's the times tables set to music. Can you think of a better way to memorize them? You'll love this Schoolhouse Rock site. ☆☆☆☆☆

Multiplication Table Applet

www.netrover.com/~kingskid/MulTab/Applet.html

"Here's an interesting online, interactive table. Very cool. I like that it actually shows the math instead of just the answer. If you do four times four, you get four rows of four blocks." —S.C. ☆☆☆☆☆

Number Sense   score.kings.k12.ca.us/number.sense.html

Creating lesson plans is time consuming. Why not just build onto the lessons that someone else has already developed? This site has a substantial collection of lesson plans for California math students. ☆☆☆

PBS TeacherSource: Math

www.pbs.org/teachersource/recommended/rec_links_math.shtm

Tap, tap, tap. Computer-oriented kids will get a lot out of this site: basic computation, computers in math, geometry and shapes, interdisciplinary math, measurement and statistics, problem solving and online games, reference and tutorials. A collection of recommended Web sites from PBS TeacherSource. ☆☆☆

Rick's Math Web   users.black-hole.com/users/rsch/indexnew.html

Educator Rick Schauer has developed thousands of basic and less basic math problems, along with teaching tips for helping your children understand these fundamental mathematical concepts. Includes word problems, fractions, and all the usual operators. ☆☆☆☆

Pre-Algebra

WHEN SHOULD YOU start teaching algebraic concepts? Early, say the experts. "The concepts of algebra, most specifically the concepts of variables, should be introduced as early as possible, even before junior high school. This helps prepare the student for being able to start a regular algebra curriculum by the time he or she reaches seventh or eighth grade," writes Gary McMurrin, a high school math teacher from Valencia, California. "But very clearly, the foundation must be established in the grade schools with the skills of the four basic operations and an understanding of variables."

Pre-algebra:
Introduction to formulas and measurements.

Why learn algebra? For one thing, it's the basis of all higher math. Retired thermodynamics and heat transfer engineer Jim Taylor, who lives in southeastern Pennsylvania, tells homeschoolers about some real-life applications for algebra: "Being an engineer, mathematics has always played an important role in my work. Early in my career, I specialized in thermodynamics and heat transfer, and a great deal of algebra was involved with calculating heat flow in designing such things as heat exchangers. I also worked on our country's missile programs in the early days and found a great need for math in the design of missile nose cones, which are subjected to terrific heating upon re-entry into the atmosphere. And of course, everyone is familiar with the Apollo program and landing on the moon; I used a lot of mathematics on all sorts of design and operational problems that had to be solved when I worked on that program. Much of this was advanced mathematics, but algebra was more or less the building block from which all other forms flowed."

Starting Young

"Some students don't seem ready for algebra because there is a lack of good instruction at the earlier stages of schooling."
—**Gary McMurrin**, high school math teacher, Valencia, California

Gary McMurrin worries that teenagers don't appreciate the need to learn mathematics: "I started teaching at age 48 after many years in a few different careers, so I have had some real-world experience and can appreciate the need for mathematics in the workplace. In my previous careers in financial services as a stockbroker and life insurance agent, I used math skills every day to analyze various investments and life insurance policies for clients. Without the analytical skills learned in high school and college, I would never have been able to perform my job duties."

Real-World Algebra

"I use algebra every day in my classroom, my kitchen, my car, my study, and on my computer. Algebra (and all math concepts) allows us to function in the real world. I travel on occasion, and, being a teacher, I cannot afford to waste money or time on the road. I use the formula for distance ($d = rt$) to make sure I use the most efficient means of transportation.

"I love to cook, and math concepts and theories are often incorporated in my menus. I often surprise store clerks when I can give them the price of my purchases before their cash register can. Math is all around us everywhere we go; without it we could not buy things, we would not have computers, Nintendo would not be a household word, and athletic teams could not score points."

—Will Person, eighth-grade algebra and pre-algebra teacher, Dripping Springs, Texas

This section presents a collection of resources for teaching pre-algebra to your middle school-aged children. When they're well grounded in the basics, they'll be ready to move to the next section.

Algebra and Functions

score.kings.k12.ca.us/algebra.functions.html

This collection of early algebra lesson plans was developed for California math students. Your kids will benefit, with or without the nearby beach. ☆☆☆

Algebra I   score.kings.k12.ca.us/algebra.html

A related collection of lesson plans developed for California math students. ☆☆☆

Factoring Whole Numbers Tricks

users.black-hole.com/users/rsch/factor.html

This site provides a good review of the basics of factoring, prime numbers, and more. Part of Rick's Math Web, it's a site with thousands of math problems devised by an educator and at-home dad. ☆☆☆

Hotlinks

FunBrain Math
www.funbrain.com/math

Math Activities for Grades 5–8
daniel.calpoly.edu/~dfrc
/Robin/midd.html

New Zealand Maths
www.nzmaths.co.nz

FunBrain Math   www.funbrain.com/math

This online math game takes students from easy to much harder. It is a very good start for algebra. ☆☆☆☆

Math Activities for Grades 5–8
daniel.calpoly.edu/~dfrc/Robin/midd.html

There's a little bit of everything on this site, and it all incorporates an aircraft theme. Algebra, measuring angles, area and volume, unit conversions, estimation, graphing, the Pythagorean theorem, rational numbers, and writing about math. ☆☆☆☆

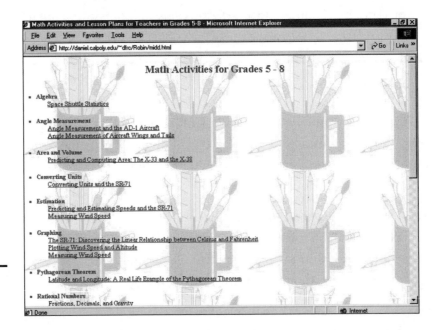

Figure 6.3

Math Activities: Fly through intermediate math.

Math Concepts Strand Overview
www.ups.edu/community/tofu/lev1f/conframe.htm

The University of Puget Sound developed this selection of intermediate math lessons. The math concepts include spreadsheet basics, calculator activities, fractions, geometry, functions, and other common pre-algebra topics. The site also offers journaling lesson plans that encourage writing about math. ☆☆☆

Mathematics/Algebraic Ideas   explorer.scrtec.org/explorer/explorer-db /browse/dynamic/Mathematics/folder/b19.html

Pardon our URL. It's a long address, but it's worth the visit. An introduction to the principles of algebra. Ugly layout; fun lessons. ☆☆☆☆

Mathematics Glossary—Middle Years

mathcentral.uregina.ca/RR/glossary/middle

Can't remember whether −2 is an integer? How many parallel sides to a trapezoid? This alphabetized glossary will help. ☆☆☆

New Zealand Maths   www.nzmaths.co.nz

The New Zealand Ministry of Education developed these lessons, which cover the basics of statistics, measurement, and problem solving. Each lesson includes a statement describing the problem, objectives, teaching sequence, specific learning outcomes, extension tips, the solution, and a printable student worksheet. ☆☆☆☆☆

Seventh Grade Mathematics

www.rialto.k12.ca.us/frisbie/coyote/math/math.html

Here's the standard: By the times kids reach their early teens, they should be able to handle the measurement of angles, basic probability, area, perimeters, and the rest of the material found in this collection of interactive math lessons. Each lesson includes a student activity page with classroom activities and printable handouts. ☆☆☆☆

Algebra

MOVING FROM THE rote memorization of basic math into the philosophical concepts of advanced math can be a tough leap. A high school math teacher, Eugene Karel Pilouw of Harlingen, Texas, told me that even when algebra seems difficult, it's important not to give up. Mr. Pilouw spent three years touring Alaska, Japan, Korea, and West Germany "as a guest of the U.S. Army" and has taught secondary

Algebra: From the Arabic *al-jabr (reduction)*. The branch of mathematics in which symbols are used to represent all numbers in a set.

English and math since 1968. This is what he says about the importance of learning algebra: "*Algebra*—a word that strikes fear into the hearts of the bravest of the brave. The truth of the matter, however, is that we all use algebra every day in our lives without calling it by that distasteful name. (Remember what Shakespeare had to say about names.)

"Did you ever:

- budget your spending for the week or month?
- plan which bills will be paid out of this week's paycheck and which will be paid from next week's?
- determine the area of the walls in a house so you could buy the right amount of paint?
- decide which size of a certain product in a store was the better buy?
- calculate how much herbicide, pesticide, or fertilizer you would need to treat your yard, a flower bed, or a field on a farm?
- figure out, at a theater or game, which candies or drinks you could afford after you had paid for the tickets?
- purchase a certain amount of material to make an article of clothing and base the amount on the dress size you wear and the money in your budget?
- place a bet on an event (a legal event and a legal bet, of course) after you had carefully weighed the odds?
- plan how much you could place on layaway for a gift according to the amount of disposable income you had left in your household budget or allowance?
- arrived at a solution after using numbers in any way?

"If you said yes to any of these or to similar situations, then you have used algebra in the real world. The actual study of algebra formalizes these procedures and puts them in a logical sequence. Sometimes we have difficulty with the rigor involved, but don't let it frighten you into quitting before you begin. Sometimes algebra, or any subject, can seem

On Studying Algebra

"I have a rather nontraditional explanation of Algebra. Students often question me about when they will ever use a particular skill. Honestly, they may never ever use that skill, so why learn it?

"Algebra is a brain tool. It is a series of skills that increases one's ability to reason and to think logically.

"For example, a carpenter uses a hammer and a screwdriver. Someone taught him how to use those tools, the basics behind how they work, and what they do. Of course, it wouldn't be very hard for a carpenter to learn to use a hydraulic hammer or a power screwdriver. By applying the concepts of the simple tools, the carpenter can use the advanced tools. And a carpenter who uses power tools surely is more efficient than the one who is limited to hand tools.

"Arithmetic is your hand tool. Applying the rules of arithmetic to abstract ideas is the learning of algebra. Algebra would be more like the power tools . . . an advanced way to use numbers."

—Jerilynn Trice, high school math teacher, Houston, Texas

---

to be a frustrating ordeal, but that is usually true of anything we preconceive as insurmountable. Whatever you do, don't quit!"

Sometimes it helps to understand how algebra is useful in the here and now. An algebra-loving student, Chhoeun Sann from Fall River, Massachusetts, explains how algebra is useful to teenagers: "I do algebra just for fun. I love to develop my own video games," says the junior at Massachusetts Institute of Technology. "I design my characters using 3D transformations, using my knowledge of geometry, algebra, and some calculus. I program my keyboard to correspond to the actions of each figure with complex mathematical formulas. This way I can move the figures easily without any further programming. When I add intense graphics, I use even more complex geometric figures. It really takes patience to do this, but that's what I like to do.

"I also use the basic I = PRT formula to budget and to find the status of my investments. I use algebra for shopping, when I use the ratio and proportion to determine which item is cheapest. There are many other ways to apply algebra. It can actually save you thousands of dollars a year if you use it right, maybe even more. I'm glad there's algebra."

Would you like your own kids to be "glad there's algebra"? Here's how you start.

Algebra   www.physics.uoguelph.ca/tutorials/algebra
This tutorial from the University of Guelph physics department is easy to understand. A basic review of algebra for physics students. ☆☆☆☆

Hotlinks

Algebra Text
www.pinkmonkey.com

QuickMath
www.quickmath.com

S.O.S. Mathematics: Algebra
www.sosmath.com
/algebra/algebra.html

Stressed Out
math.rice.edu/~lanius
/Algebra/stress.html

Algebra Activities
daniel.calpoly.edu/~dfrc/Robin/algebra.html
Teach distance calculations, graphing, logarithms, the Pythagorean theorem, and solving for one unknown with these algebra lesson plans, all created using an aircraft theme. ☆☆☆☆

Algebra Online   www.algebra-online.com
Talk algebra with students, teachers, and parents throughout the world. The site offers free private tutoring, a message board, and live chat. ☆☆☆☆

Algebra Text   www.pinkmonkey.com
The full textbook, online. Register at the tremendous Pink Monkey site (it's free), then click on the Study Guides link to access the text. ☆☆☆☆

Algebra II   score.kings.k12.ca.us/algebra2.html
A collection of lesson plans for California math students. ☆☆☆

CoreConcepts: Algebra
www.pinkmonkey.com/coreconcepts/subjects/algebra.htm
A list of research resources, divided by subject. Register at the PinkMonkey Web site (www.pinkmonkey.com). See also the related site, Algebra II, at www.pinkmonkey.com/coreconcepts/subjects /algebra2.htm. ☆☆☆

Easy Start Algebra   www.gcse.com/Maths/algmen.htm

This British site prepares students to pass the national GCSE exam, which is comparable to the American GED. Use these Easy Starts to review algebra basics; then move along to the heavy-duty stuff. ☆☆☆☆

Interactive Algebra

www.accessone.com/bbunge/Algebra/Algebra.html

Fourteen interactive algebra lessons give pre-college students practice on equations, factoring, and graphing skills, with multiple levels in each topic. The site generates random problems, which students work on paper. They can check their answers when they're ready. Hints are also provided. ☆☆☆☆☆

Math Activities for Grades 9–12

daniel.calpoly.edu/~dfrc/Robin/high.html

Distance formulas, graphing, logarithms, and the Pythagorean theorem, all via lesson plans using an aircraft theme. ☆☆☆☆

QuickMath   www.quickmath.com

When you submit a question to QuickMath, it is processed by Mathematica, the largest and most powerful computer algebra package available. The answer is then sent back to you and displayed right there on your browser, usually within a couple of seconds. And it's free! Solve algebra problems, equations, inequations, calculus, and matrices in seconds! ☆☆☆☆☆

S.O.S. Mathematics: Algebra   www.sosmath.com/algebra/algebra.html

The whole durned book, right there online. Step-by-step instructions, beginning with fractions. Great stuff! Also of interest is the companion section on matrix algebra at www.sosmath.com/matrix /matrix.html. ☆☆☆☆☆

Stressed Out   math.rice.edu/~lanius/Algebra/stress.html

How do slopes apply to real life? This primer explains slopes and rates of change in a way any intermediate- or higher-level student will understand. ☆☆☆☆☆

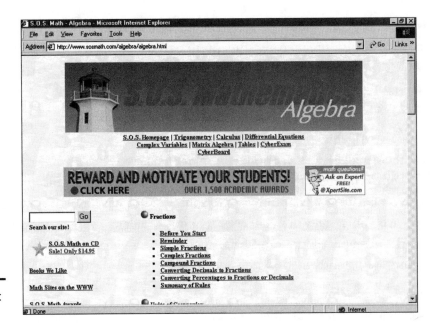

Figure 6.4

S.O.S. Mathematics:
Virtual textbook.

Geometry

GEOMETRY MAY BE the most practical of all the maths. Mathematics and chemistry teacher Kari Farrell Matthews from Rossville, Illinois, explains how before she became a teacher, she worked for a large agricultural company. A large part of her job involved training farmers and other agricultural professionals to use satellite receivers to track the exact global position of tractors and other farm implements in their fields. "This technology is being used in many industries, including cartography, trucking/shipping, aeronautics, and real estate." She says, "Understanding how to use the satellite receivers was contingent on a solid knowledge of geometry. I used the geometry skills I learned in high school every day!

"In my personal life, I find that geometry comes in handy regularly. For instance, my husband has built some of our furniture, and he remodeled the kitchen. If you ever want to tackle

Geometry: From the Greek *geometrein* *(to measure land)*. The study of the properties of points, lines, angles, planes, and objects.

furniture and remodeling projects on your own, geometry knowledge would be indispensable! We used geometry to determine how to get our new countertop into the house and between two walls. Our calculations were perfect, and the time we spent doing the calculations saved us a lot of hassle in the end. These are just a few of the ways that I use geometry in everyday life. Geometry concepts really do permeate our lives."

When your own kids are ready to take the geometry challenge, here's where they should start:

Conjectures in Geometry

www.geom.umn.edu/~dwiggins/mainpage.html

This online project features twenty conjectures found in typical geometry texts. Included in each conjecture are definitions, sketches, and explanations. You may need to download some software—a demo version of which is linked from the page—to use the lessons. ☆☆☆☆☆

Gallery of Interactive Geometry

www.geom.umn.edu/apps/gallery.html

Investigate the geometry of rainbows, roses, pinball, tiles, and more. The interactivity makes this a real hands-on course. It'll challenge your smarter kids. ☆☆☆☆

Geometry   score.kings.k12.ca.us/geometry.html

A collection of lesson plans for California math students. Also of interest is the section on measurement and geometry, at score.kings.k12.ca.us/meas .geometry.html. ☆☆☆

Geometry and the Imagination

www.geom.umn.edu/docs/education/institute91

For smart kids only. Here are notes and handouts for a remarkable geometry course developed at Princeton University. Approaches geometry from a whole other, um, plane. ☆☆☆☆

Hotlinks

Conjectures in Geometry
www.geom.umn.edu /~dwiggins/mainpage.html

Gallery of Interactive Geometry
www.geom.umn.edu/apps /gallery.html

Geometry and the Imagination
www.geom.umn.edu/docs /education/institute91

Math 129 Home Page
www.math.csusb.edu /courses/m129home.html

Mathematics

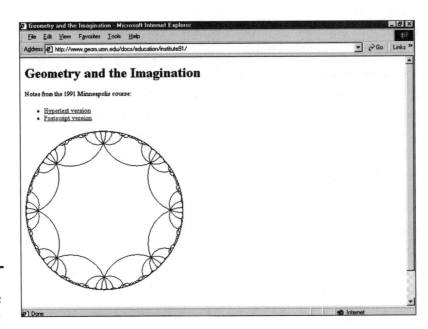

Figure 6.5

Geometry and the
Imagination: Explore
the fun of geometry.

Geometry Junkyard   www.ics.uci.edu/~eppstein/junkyard

A massive collection of links, papers, thoughts, and more, all related to geometry. Collected by a math professor at the University of California, Irvine. ☆☆

Geometry of the Sphere   math.rice.edu/~pcmi/sphere

Great site for serious students of geometry. Learn all there is to know about sphere geometry. This site builds on what your child will have learned in plane geometry. ☆☆☆☆

Graph Paper Printer   perso.easynet.fr/~philimar/graphpapeng.htm

An online application that allows you to print out graph paper. Yep, the stuff with the blue lines. You choose from a variety of options for making graph paper: polar, logarithmic, and more. Highly configurable and free! ☆☆☆☆

Math 129 Home Page   www.math.csusb.edu/courses/m129home.html

A work in progress, but the geometry lessons are ready for use. Topics include constructions with straightedge and compass, polygons (including tessellations) and polyhedra, symmetry and transformational geometry, coordinate geometry and measurement, and perspective drawing. ☆☆☆☆

Mathematics/Geometry   explorer.scrtec.org/explorer/explorer-db /browse/dynamic/Mathematics/folder/b14.html

All sorts of fun geometry lessons, compiled on a really ugly page. ☆☆☆☆

PBS TeacherSource: Geometry and Shapes

www.pbs.org/teachersource/recommended/rec_links_math.shtm#4

A collection of recommended Web sites from PBS TeacherSource. ☆☆☆

Sample Zome Lesson Plans

www.zometool.com/planet/teacherslounge/lessons

It's a commercial site, but the free resources make great lessons. The site features hands-on geometry explorations. ☆☆☆

Computer Math

IF YOUR KIDS are going to be competitive in the adult workplace, they'll need to know how to handle the technology. And that includes understanding the principles of computer math.

In colleges today, five-dollar calculators are as much an anachronism as slide rules and abacuses are. Your children need to know how to handle scientific or business calculators with some dexterity. They also need to know how to operate computers, of course. But of equal importance is their ability to understand the basic principles of mathematical operations as those operations relate to computers.

Here's how the work world looks for people who understand computer math: "In the nine years that I've been with my present employer, I've moved up the ladder higher than many of my peers who have two or

> **Computer math:** From the Latin *putare (to consider)*. Binary and hexadecimal systems, calculator math, and other math processes that integrate technology.

On Information Processing

"Maybe 'computer logic' is a good description of information processing. The two main mathematics that are used are the binary system (base 2), for representing information, and Boolean logic, which is used to reason in base 2. All our math is 'discrete,' since we do not reason about infinity or infinitesimals. If we think about computers and information at a higher level, then this might be called 'information sciences.'"

—Professor Robert Levinson, Department of Computer and Information Sciences, University of California at Santa Cruz

three times more experience," writes Scott "Warlock" Windhorn, a systems control technician in New Ulm, Minnesota.

"Many people with experience in electronics say, 'You don't need to know any of those equations.' That's only true if you just want to get a job, never move up, be the first in line for layoffs, do the same thing every day, and basically have a boring life. The best service technicians are those who understand the machines they're servicing. To truly understand a machine, you must know the electronics, mechanics, and mathematics that make it work."

Your math-literate offspring will have a great time at the following sites. Don't have a graphing calculator? Don't worry. There are loaner programs available from major manufacturers (see the following links), and there are plenty of online calculators on the Internet.

Casio Classroom   education.casio.com
Great calculator activities from Casio, a top calculator manufacturer. There's a link here to an interesting loaner program, but what you should look for is the activities/lessons link. ☆☆☆☆☆

Computers and Maths Teaching   users.interact.net.au/~phob
This Australian site explains spreadsheets, functions from linear algebra to calculus, modeling, and much more. Your older students will appreciate the perspective. ☆☆☆☆

Fuzzy Systems—A Tutorial   life.csu.edu.au/complex/tutorials/fuzzy.html

A college-level tutorial on artificial intelligence and fuzzy logic, by James F. Brule. It's actually an easy read. For college-bound kids who have a good grasp of English. ☆☆☆☆

Graphing Calculator Guide

cesme.utm.edu/resources/math/grcalc/toc.html

Teachers attending a summer workshop developed this collection of lessons that integrate graphing calculators into the math curriculum. Topics include basic calculator concepts, transforming graphs, solving linear inequalities, using statistical data, investigating slope, and constructing trigonometric concepts. ☆☆☆☆

hpcalc   www.hpcalc.org

Amazingly, this site is not affiliated with Hewlett-Packard. But a better friend they'll never have. Everything you could ever want to know about using, buying, and programming an HP calculator. ☆☆☆☆☆

Hotlinks

Casio Classroom
education.casio.com

hpcalc.org
www.hpcalc.org

Mathematics

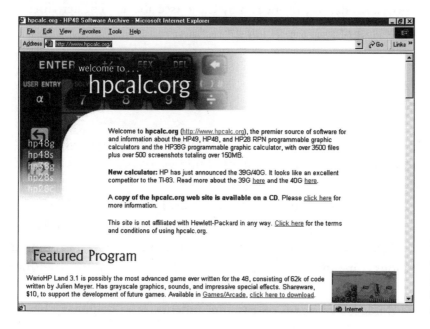

Figure 6.6

hpcalc: Computing answers to tough math problems.

Introduction to Binary and Hexadecimal
www.geocities.com/SiliconValley/Lakes/7139/atrtut01.html

A heady tutorial on all the different ways you can count from zero to ten. Geeky, but interesting. ☆☆☆

PBS TeacherSource: Computers in Math
www.pbs.org/teachersource/recommended/rec_links_math.shtm#3

A collection of recommended Web sites from PBS TeacherSource. ☆☆☆

Technology for the Math Classroom   lonestar.utsa.edu/efox/lesson.htm

Sample lessons for integrating technology, computers, and the Internet in secondary classrooms. I'm not in favor of teaching kids how to play the lottery, but the other lessons in probability and statistics do a good job of integrating math and technology. ☆☆☆

TI Calculators and Educational Solutions
www.ti.com/calc/docs/cacontnt.htm

If you own a Texas Instruments calculator, you'll enjoy the resources available from this site. TI operates a loaner program for schools, similar to the one run by Casio (see above). The activities link is where most of the action is. ☆☆☆☆

Trigonometry

THE REALLY FUN stuff! Do your children know interesting words like *sine, cosine, tangent, cotangent, secant,* and *cosecant*? No? Then it's time to learn some trig.

Trigonometry is important stuff. Really. John Reed, an electrical engineer in Oak Ridge, Tennessee, explains why: "I actually use much more algebra and trigonometry than calculus. Vector algebra and matrix inversions come up pretty often. In control systems, Laplace transforms and Z transforms are very important.

"I think the emphasis on rushing students into calculus is a big mistake. A lot of math that needs to be absorbed is omitted. They learn the quadratic equation, but how many 'advanced placement' students can solve a cubic or quartic equation? How many understand where the roots of a quadratic equation have gone when a parabola doesn't cross the x-axis? Can they calculate the volume of an irregular tetrahedron knowing only the edges?

"They do simple trig problems with shadows and trees, but how many could take an aerial photograph and determine the time of day and the day of the year when it was made? How many understand spherical coordinates well enough to have navigated a ship back in the eighteenth century? How many could operate a theodolite or understand the geometry involved in aligning the front wheels of a car?

"None of this involves any calculus, and it represents a huge gap in understanding engineering problems. I suspect that a lot of students today fail in engineering not because they weren't given a head start in calculus, but because they were shortchanged in other areas. A little exposure to calculus is OK, but don't skip the other stuff."

> ### Trigonometry:
> From the Greek *trigonon* *(triangle)*. The study of triangles and angles and their functions.

Wanita Talbot is a homeschooling mother in St. Louis. She is studying to be an electronics engineer technician, and she uses trig every day for such things as figuring out the phase angle of current and voltage to troubleshoot circuits. "The phase angle is theta, and to find it, you have to solve for a right triangle," she said. "It's not difficult, nor is it too challenging, but it is a process that technicians have to do. You have to know every aspect of circuitry to find and fix the problem."

Persuaded yet? Let's hit the books.

AITLC Student Guide to Calculus   tlc.ai.org/calculus.htm#PRE
▤ Despite the name, this is a substantial collection of trigonometry resources from Access Indiana. ☆☆☆

CoreConcepts: Trigonometry
www.pinkmonkey.com/coreconcepts/subjects/trig.htm
▤ A list of research resources, divided by subject. Register at the PinkMonkey Web site (www.pinkmonkey.com). ☆☆☆

Frequently Asked Questions About Trigonometry

www.catcode.com/trig

A great overview of trig. Simple explanations, great diagrams. This is the ideal starting point. ☆☆☆☆

Hotlinks

Frequently Asked Questions About Trigonometry
www.catcode.com/trig

Introduction to Trigonometry
www.ping.be/~ping1339 /gonio.htm

Pascal's Triangle
forum.swarthmore.edu /workshops/usi/pascal

S.O.S. Mathematics: Trigonometry
www.sosmath.com/trig /trig.html

Introduction to Trigonometry

www.ping.be/~ping1339/gonio.htm

Pretty much the whole textbook, online. It assumes you already know big words like *orthogonal* and *radians*. ☆☆☆☆

Mathematics Tutorials: Trigonometry 1

www.gcse.com/Maths/teach/trig1.htm

What the Brits want their students to know about basic trigonometry problems. Designed to tutor British students for the national GCSE examination (similar to the American GED), this tutorial is a great fundamental overview of trig. ☆☆☆☆☆

Name Project: Trigonometry

www.acts.tinet.ie/trigonometry_645.html

A simple online trig course. Your intelligent kids will appreciate the explanations; your less advanced kids will have a difficult time with the language. Still, it's very thorough. ☆☆☆☆

Pascal's Triangle   **forum.swarthmore.edu/workshops/usi/pascal**

Students of every age will learn from these lessons, links, and standards related to Pascal's Triangle. Lesson plans feature questions, answers, discussion, and printable student worksheets on this famous triangle. The site includes background information for the teacher and links to other resources. ☆☆☆☆☆

S.O.S Mathematics: Trigonometry   **www.sosmath.com/trig/trig.html**

The most important results, techniques, and formulas in college and pre-college mathematics. An excellent study course. ☆☆☆☆

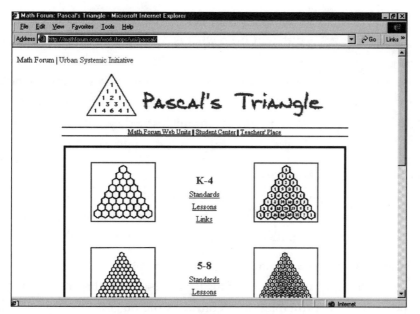

Figure 6.7

Pascal's Triangle:
The ins and outs of
triangular math.

Trigonometry   score.kings.k12.ca.us/trigonometry.html
A collection of lesson plans for California math students. ☆☆☆

Trigonometry   www.physics.uoguelph.ca/tutorials/trig/trigonom.html
This tutorial from the University of Guelph physics department is
easy to understand. A basic review of trig for the benefit of physics
students. ☆☆☆☆

Calculus

AND NOW, THE *really* advanced stuff. If you get your child through
calculus, you'll have a well-grounded college applicant on your hands.

Calculus is most useful to students who plan to enter the hard sciences, technology, or mathematics fields. Engineer John Reed explains the
real-world application of calculus principles: "Calculus is important for
understanding relationships involved in engineering. A competent engineer will want to understand why and under what circumstances an equation is valid, not just plug in the numbers and crank out an answer. If the
student aspires to a career in development, then in-depth knowledge is

Calculus: From the Latin word for stone. A mathematical field that involves calculations using logical notation.

essential." Sometimes you face a situation that is different from what is covered by a handbook equation. Then you have to have the mathematical competence to analyze the problem or you can't handle it." Your pre-college students will be more competent to analyze problems if they take advantage of these resources:

Calculus   www.pinkmonkey.com

Full text, online. Register at the PinkMonkey site, then click Study Guides to find this book. The book covers functions, limits, continuity, derivatives, integration, and definite integrals. ☆☆☆☆☆

Calculus   www.ies.co.jp/math/java/calcjava.html

After looking at these forty-plus Japanese-designed applets, I finally understood the principles of calculus. It's the biggest "aha!" your kids may ever experience in mathematics. ☆☆☆☆☆

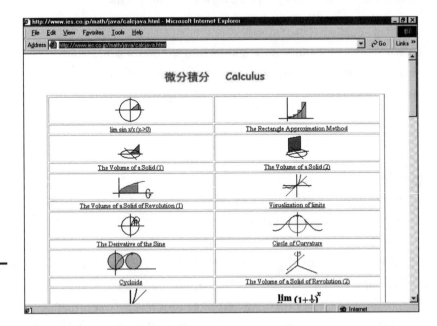

Figure 6.8

Calculus: The Pokémonization of higher math.

calculus@internet   www.calculus.net

This lab is designed to get beginning college students through a course of calculus. Your own kids can benefit, too. It's a bit of

Mathematics

 *Honda Soichiro*

Japanese auto executive Honda Soichiro was a self-taught engineer. The some-time mechanic and racecar driver founded his renowned motorcycle company in the 1940s and began producing cars in the 1950s. He started a revolution with his clean-burning CVCC engine, which won Honda cars a prominent place in the U.S. automotive market.

a mishmash, but the answers to most questions can be located. ☆☆☆☆

Calculus Survival   www.calculussurvival.com

How to survive your first year in calculus class. ☆☆☆

CoreConcepts: Calculus

www.pinkmonkey.com/coreconcepts/subjects/calc.htm

A list of research resources, arranged by subject. Register at PinkMonkey (www.pinkmonkey.com). ☆☆☆

Java-Powered Calculus   www.usm.maine.edu/~flagg/jpc

Function grapher and a scientific calculator. ☆☆☆

SimCalc   tango.mth.umassd.edu

An interesting extracurricular diversion for your calculus student. It won't teach her calculus, but it might persuade her it's worth learning. The University of Massachusetts at Dartmouth sponsors this project to build and test a series of software simulations and curriculum materials designed to support learning of the underlying ideas of calculus. ☆☆☆

S.O.S Mathematics: Calculus

www.sosmath.com/calculus/calculus.html

What your kids need to be ready for college math. Also of interest may be the section on differential equations at www.sosmath.com

Hotlinks

Calculus
www.ies.co.jp/math/java
/calcjava.html

**University of Cincinnati
Calculus Page**
math.uc.edu/calculus

Visual Calculus
archives.math.utk.edu
/visual.calculus

Mathematics

/diffeq/diffeq.html or the unit on complex variables at www.sosmath .com/complex/complex.html. An excellent study course. ☆☆☆☆

Trigonometric Integrals   php.indiana.edu/~dhart/calculus/m216_7
How to integrate trigonometric functions using calculus equations. Developed by David Hart at Indiana University. ☆☆☆

University of Cincinnati Calculus Page   math.uc.edu/calculus
Computer-graded Web version of a university calculus placement test. Try it! The scores are recorded, so take it under some other name if you want to make sure they stay anonymous! A score of 20 or more is considered good. ☆☆☆☆

University of Minnesota Calculus Initiative
www.geom.umn.edu/education/calc-init/
Calculus labs that teach how calculus properties apply to real life. ☆☆☆☆

Visual Calculus   archives.math.utk.edu/visual.calculus
This cool site from the University of Tennessee at Knoxville steps students through the solutions to calculus problems. ☆☆☆☆

World Web Math   web.mit.edu/wwmath/main.html
Enough trig to prepare you for the calculus portion of this hyper-text book, sponsored by the Massachusetts Institute of Technology. Sections on calculus and vector calculus are available. It's college-level stuff for smart upper level students. ☆☆☆☆

Statistics

STATISTICS LITERACY GETS far, far too little attention in most edu-cational curricula. And it may be one of the most critical literacies of all. For one thing, the media are rife with misused statistics. Unless your kids are knowledgeable about what they're reading, they're liable to get sucked into foolish agendas and social "problems" that aren't prob-lems at all.

A good understanding of statistics will also help your kids in their personal lives. Barry Richardson, a senior lecturer in psychology at Monash University in Australia, says statistical analysis played a very important role in a major decision in his life. "While living in England a few years ago, I was unemployed and found that at 50 years of age, nobody wanted to hire me. I noticed that many newspaper job ads had age limits (e.g., 'You will be between 26 and 35'), but I needed to quantify this and compare the frequency of such ads between publications and countries. Using the chi square statistic and others, I was able to show that Britain showed significantly more age discrimination in employment than the United States, Australia, and Canada. In 1990 I founded an organization called IMMPACT to help older people start their own businesses."

For Luis Enrique Demestre, a university professor and a psychologist with a master's degree in organizational development, a working knowledge of statistics is critical. Luis teaches statistics at the Catholic University Andrés Bello in Venezuela. "I find statistics quite useful in carrying out my three jobs: father, teacher, and social scientist," he says. "When my children were small, I used statistics to understand their grades in school. Our grading scale is from 1 to 20. I used to take down their grades in each subject, and then I obtained the arithmetic mean and the standard deviation of all their grades and the same statistics for each of them. Then I compared the grades between them to determine whether the differences were significant. For example, Patricia (the oldest one) had a mean of 16.12, which was not too bad, but Debora (the second oldest) got 17. Then I would ask myself whether these differences were important. Could they be attributed to Debora's greater effort, or was it just chance? If Debora's 17 was because she had studied really hard, she deserved a reward.

Statistics: From the New Latin *statisticus (statecraft)*. The study of population samples.

"I also used to record all the 'good things' they were doing, such as keeping their room clean and tidy, helping their mother in the kitchen, or avoiding fighting. Every Saturday we would gather together to count all the good things. If there was a statistically significant increase in the number of the good things, they would obtain some privileges or rewards.

"Of course, my wife and I were quite flexible, which is why the system never worked properly, but still, we had a great time and lots of fun. There were many family situations where I could apply numbers and statistics, always keeping in mind that the important thing was the knowledge my wife and I got from them, and that we could find ways to help our kids to grow up and become good persons."

Statistics as a character builder? Why not? Here's how to make your own wise statistical analyses.

Hotlinks

Adventures in Statistics
forum.swarthmore.edu
/trscavo/statistics.html

Data Analysis Learning Units
www.nsa.gov/programs
/mepp/esdata.html

**Mathematics Tutorials:
Probability**
www.gcse.com/Maths
/tprob1.htm

Adventures in Statistics
forum.swarthmore.edu/trscavo/statistics.html
A math project involving the area of classrooms. Students develop a hypothesis, then use measurement, graphing, computation, and data analysis to present results. ☆☆☆☆☆

Chance and Data in the News
www.ni.com.au/mercury/mathguys/mercindx.htm
This Australian site encourages the use of newspapers in the study of statistical methods. ☆☆☆

Data Analysis Learning Units
www.nsa.gov/programs/mepp/esdata.html
A collection of statistical analysis lessons using candy bars, pennies, and other items that will help younger students understand principles of statistics. ☆☆☆☆

Data Surfing on the World Wide Web
it.stlawu.edu/~rlock/datasurf.html
Data analysis for students of high school age and older. ☆☆☆☆

K–12 Statistics   www.mste.uiuc.edu/stat/stat.html
Despite the name, I don't expect that your five-year-old will be spending a lot of time on this page, but your college-bound 16-year-

old will find much worth knowing. This is a sort of tossed-together statistics manual that includes lots of diagrams to clarify the lessons. ☆☆☆

Math and Statistics Links   www.emtech.net/math2.htm
Scores of very well chosen resources. ☆☆

Mathematics Tutorials: Probability   www.gcse.com/Maths/tprob1.htm
Increases the probability of improving your grade, but not of winning the lottery! This is what the Brits want their students to know about basic statistical problems. Designed to tutor British students through the national GCSE examination (comparable to the American GED), this tutorial is a great fundamental overview of stats. ☆☆☆☆

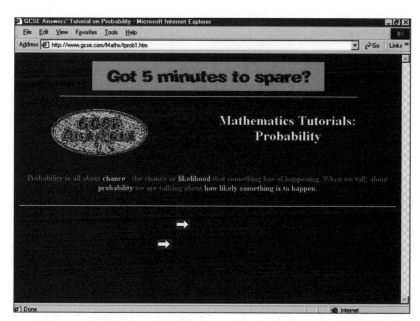

Figure 6.9

Mathematics Tutorials: All math all the time.

PBS TeacherSource: Measurement
www.pbs.org/teachersource/recommended/rec_links_math.shtm#m
A collection of recommended Web sites teaching statistical measurement and probability, from PBS TeacherSource. ☆☆☆

Mathematics

Mathematics

Probability and Statistics   score.kings.k12.ca.us/prob.and.stat.html
A collection of lesson plans for California math students. ☆☆☆

Statistics for Educators   www.emtech.net/statistics.htm
Lots of educational research, combined with dozens of resources for teaching statistics. ☆☆

Art Appreciation

I GREW UP in a house of artists. My mother majored in art before becoming an art educator in the public schools. My brother attended an arts college on full scholarship and is now working as an architect. Both of my sisters surround themselves with beauty. Their homes, their clothes, their dinner parties are all exquisite. Even my husband, the painter, has astonishingly good taste.

Me? It seems I took after my father—the Boeing engineer who believes green plaid slacks look swell with a red plaid tie. In June. At a wedding.

That's why I was so pleased to find a treasure trove of art resources online.

As my kids and I have considered these resources and discussed art and artists, I've noticed a swelling sense of . . . well, if not taste and culture, at least a dislike of polyester and plaid.

I've also come to see the very real benefits of teaching children about art. Oh, not the kind of "art" that I learned in school—not the kind where we became really, really good at coloring inside the lines.

As our family has considered various artists and discussed what constitutes "art," I've seen in my growing children a sense of the visual and an appreciation for good taste.

Here's Joan Zielinski, an artist, a retired art instructor in the public schools—and my own mother—on the benefit of having your children learn about art: "Teaching the arts—and visual arts in particular—reaches and uses intelligences that traditional pencil/paper activities, which form the bulk of most school activities, don't reach. Teaching the arts gives success to many who otherwise don't do as well in school. Students who are schooled in the arts score much higher on college admissions tests than those who have not been schooled in this important field. One reason is that we teach the whole child in this way, not just one small part of the child. The child is able to develop more of his or her brain by being trained in the arts."

👫👫 *How We Homeschool*

"I have a twin sister who has kids much older than mine (she was married seven years before I was!), and she homeschooled. It looked like so much fun that I was intrigued. Then when my son came along, he was a 'December boy.' That meant he would have been going to kindergarten with kids who had turned five the January before. He was physically very small, and since he was only four, that was my deciding factor. If he had been eager to learn, my life might be different now, but it was the right choice for us. And now with three kids, I'm even happier with my decision! It would have been just way too hard sending my baby off to somebody else to see all those milestones!"

—**Holly Cameron**, homeschooling mother of three, Canada

How should parents teach their children the arts? "It doesn't mean that at Thanksgiving time we teach the child how to cut out paper turkeys and that at Christmas we make green and red paper chains . . . though there is a place for these activities.

"To do a complete curriculum, it's important to study the great masters, both past and present. Both parents and children should learn how to analyze great works of art. Become familiar with the vocabulary of the visual arts so that its usage becomes a part of your kids' vocabulary as much as any other part of their speech. Such concepts as texture, line, contrast, color, and space are necessary for understanding art.

"By studying great works of art, the child will be learning about great artists as well as about the periods of time and place in which the artists created their work."

My mother is also keen on incorporating art into other curriculum areas. "There are many wonderful resources for finding out about the stories of artists' lives. Sometimes these ideas will fit well into a social studies curriculum so that everything dovetails together and a large unit of writing, history, geography, reading, and art can be coordinated."

It's not just the artistically inclined who will benefit from the following resources. Even the art-impaired can learn to find beauty through an understanding of artistic principles.

The Benefits of Arts Education

"Arts education benefits the student because it cultivates the whole child, gradually building many kinds of literacy while developing intuition, reasoning, imagination, and dexterity into unique forms of expression and communication. This process requires not merely an active mind but a trained one. An education in the arts benefits *society* because students of the arts gain powerful tools for understanding human experiences, both past and present. They learn to respect the often very different ways others have of thinking, working, and expressing themselves. They learn to make decisions in situations where there are no standard answers. By studying the arts, students stimulate their natural creativity and learn to develop it to meet the needs of a complex and competitive society. And as study and competence in the arts reinforce one other, the joy of learning becomes real, tangible, and powerful."

—**"What Students Should Know and Be Able to Do in the Arts,"** from the introductory statement of the National Standards for Arts Education (www.menc.org/publication/books/summary.html)

In this chapter, you'll be introduced to art history and appreciation, crafts, design, drawing, painting, sculpture and ceramics, and visual arts.

You'll find related humanities resources for dance, drama, and other performing arts in chapter 11. We start here with general tools for teaching and understanding art.

Art Projects   www.bway.net/~starlite/projects.htm
Art projects for older elementary and middle school-aged students. ☆☆☆

Arts
www.awesomelibrary.org/Library/Materials_Search/Lesson_Plans/Arts.html
Lesson plans from Awesome Library. A very thorough collection. ☆☆☆

Arts   www.pacificnet.net/~mandel/TheArts.html
Lesson plans from the Teachers Helping Teachers page. These lessons are submitted by teachers and include grade-level designations. Unfortunately, they're not subdivided by topic. ☆☆☆

Beyond the Frame

educate.si.edu/resources/lessons/currkits/beyond/artkit.html

▣ Using Art as a Basis for Interdisciplinary Learning. A lesson plan from the Smithsonian. ☆☆☆☆

Floral Radiographs: The Secret Garden

www-personal.umich.edu/~agrxray

▣ Dozens of links to serious art sites. No reviews, but it's a great collection. ☆☆

KinderArt   www.kinderart.com

▣ Ever consider covering a table with finger paint and letting the little ones go nuts? Then this is the site for you. Crafts, drama, folk art, painting, sculpture, print-making, and dozens of other topics, each with its own lesson plans and instructions. ☆☆☆☆☆

Hotlinks

Beyond the Frame
educate.si.edu/resources
/lessons/currkits/beyond
/artkit.html

KinderArt
www.kinderart.com

World Wide Art Resources
www.wwar.com

Figure 7.1

KinderArt: Finger-paint your tables and other fun projects.

KnowledgeHound: Art

www.knowledgehound.com/topics/art.htm

▣ Links to a handful of really great lesson plans. ☆☆☆

Art Appreciation

Let's Do Art!   www.ed.gov/pubs/parents/LearnPtnrs/art.html

▤ How to encourage young children in art. ☆☆☆

PBS TeacherSource: Arts and Literature

www.pbs.org/teachersource/recommended/rec_links_art&lit.shtm#8

▤ A collection of recommended Web sites from PBS TeacherSource. ☆☆☆☆

Teacher Guide to Fine Arts   tlc.ai.org/tfineart.htm

▤ The Access Indiana Teaching and Learning Center contains lessons, resources, and more. A good foundation. ☆☆☆

Virtual Curriculum: Elementary Art Education

www.dhc.net/~artgeek

▤ I love the lessons on this site. The lessons are categorized by art principles, elements, and geography. Good information for budding artists of all ages. ☆☆☆☆

World Wide Art Resources   www.wwar.com

▤ The new Your Local Arts link is a real treasure. No matter where you live or travel in the United States, this page will have some local artistic resources worth visiting. The site is flush with information about museums, artists, art history, galleries, and dozens of other topics. ☆☆☆☆☆

Art History and Appreciation

FOR THOSE WITHOUT any particular inclination to *create* art, this is the fun part: learning to *appreciate* it.

Studying great artists—learning about the symbolism and the milieu and the techniques of a work of art—brings about those great aha! moments that we enjoy so much as parents and teachers.

One of the best things to do when you are teaching art is to take your little ones down to the public library when it's quiet and pull out some of the oversized art books that contain colored plates of beautiful artwork.

Leonardo da Vinci

Born to an unmarried peasant woman, young Leonardo was taken into his father's house in Florence and raised as a legitimate son. There he learned reading, writing, and arithmetic, although he didn't become a serious student of Latin for many years. It appears that he was a talented artist from a young age, inasmuch as he was apprenticed to a Florentine artist at the age of 15. During his apprenticeship he learned painting, sculpting, and the technical and mechanical arts. By the age of 20 he had joined the local painters' guild, but he continued studying in his master's workshop for five more years.

My mother, again: "Of course, my favorite activity is studying artists first and then taking kids to a local art museum where they can be surrounded with the works of that artist. They can drink in the atmosphere there.

"In addition, most art museums have terrific educational programs where groups of students can work with docents and produce their own works of art at the museum. You can be put on the mailing lists of all the museums in your area to keep up on what's happening in the field of art.

"Working to make art an integral part of the curriculum you teach, not just one hour every Friday, will help your children develop to their best potential."

Ann M. Glass, from Everson, Washington, is a homeschooling mother of two. She has made Friday her family's art day. "We take most of the morning, since we have dropped other subjects for the day. We study an artist and a composer. For the artist, we learn about his life and what he was known for, talk about his paintings (ideally, we've been able to find pictures at the library or off the Net), and then try our hand at that style of art. For the composer, again, we learn about his life and listen to and discuss his music. We also learn about different kinds of instruments

> **Art:** From the Greek *artios (fitting, even).* Created works of aesthetic value.

Art Appreciation

On Vision

"Vision: the art of see-
ing things invisible."
—Jonathan Swift

and styles of music. Some of our favorite art sites are metalab
.unc.edu/louvre/paint/auth, a Web museum artist index; www
.virtualfreesites.com/museums.interest.html, which has tons of
links to virtual museums all over; and www.nmaa.si.edu, the
Smithsonian American Art Museum."

As you prepare to introduce your own children to art appreciation, consider the following resources. Some are games;
some are visual; all are educational.

A. Pintura, Art Detective   www.eduweb.com/pintura

What a great way to teach art appreciation to younger students:
an art lesson wrapped in a mystery. This site deserves the awards and
recognition it's won. ☆☆☆☆☆

Figure 7.2

A. Pintura: An on-
line adventure in art.

Adventure in Art History   www.eduweb.com/insideart

By the time your kids work through this adventure story, they'll
have a much greater appreciation of such artists as Monet and van
Gogh. Beautifully done. ☆☆☆☆☆

Arts: Art History   ericir.syr.edu/Virtual/Lessons/Arts/Art_History
A small collection of lesson plans from the people at AskERIC Lesson Plans. ☆☆☆☆

Art Images for College Teaching
www.mcad.edu/AICT
Images from five periods: ancient, medieval, Renaissance and baroque, eighteenth to twentieth century, and non-Western. Not much explanation, however. ☆☆☆

Arts and Culture
metalab.unc.edu/collection/artsandculture.html
Art relating to Judaism, Kurt Vonnegut, North Carolina, and more. A few dozen art exhibits, of an eclectic nature. ☆☆☆☆

Eyes on Art   www.kn.pacbell.com/wired/art2
This art appreciation resource requires parental leadership. A list of questions suggests ways a parent can urge a child to view art in new ways. Beautiful artwork illustrates the lessons on color, lines, and other elements of the fine arts. ☆☆☆☆☆

Fine Arts and Art History Resources
members.tripod.com/~JBrennan/academic/art.html
One homeschooling family's database of information. ☆☆

LouvreW3   www.louvre.fr/louvrea.htm
Well, it is, after all, the Louvre. Where else will you find the *Mona Lisa*? An award-winning site with lots of artwork and commentary. ☆☆☆☆☆

Transforming Ideas for Teaching and Learning the Arts
www.ed.gov/pubs/StateArt/Arts
Really helpful suggestions for teaching art to students of all ages. Includes curriculum suggestions. ☆☆☆☆

Hotlinks

A. Pintura, Art Detective
www.eduweb.com/pintura

**An Adventure in
Art History**
www.eduweb.com/insideart

Eyes on Art
www.kn.pacbell.com
/wired/art2

**Fine Arts and Art History
Resources**
members.tripod.com
/~JBrennan/academic
/art.html

Art Appreciation

Vision and Art   krantzj.hanover.edu/Krantz/art/

▥ How various elements combine to create art, along with a history lesson in how those elements came to be used in fine art. ☆☆☆

Crafts

I DO TWO crafts, and I do them very well. I sew. It's no longer economical to sew, so I don't do it often, but I know how to sew. And I make scrapbooks and cards. I use rubber stamps, colored pens, fancy scissors, and all sorts of other little doodads that allow me to build memory albums for my family.

I've just about gotten my entire extended family hooked as well. On the first Sunday of each month, we have a family gathering and drag out my "stamping" boxes. Photos and cutters and rubber stamps and inkpads and interesting paper I've collected burst from boxes. We clear a long table and go to work.

Craft: From the Old English *cræft (strength)*. Artistic creation requiring manual dexterity or skill.

What started as a moms' activity, though, is turning into a kids' activity, as our little ones clamor for access to the paper goods. Now if I could just get them to neatly label my four thousand unlabeled photos. . . .

Crafting draws families together. Whether your crafts decorate your home or just give you an excuse to sit with the kids and poke clay buttons with a fork, crafting builds creativity in a happy, lighthearted way that all kids enjoy. Here are some resources to get you started.

Art and Craft Project Links
www.geocities.com/Athens/Aegean/3446/art.html

▥ An excellent resource. Includes several dozen reviews, along with suggestions about how to use these resources in your homeschooling. ☆☆☆☆

Arts and Crafts   www.awesomelibrary.org/Classroom/Arts
/Arts_and_Crafts/Arts_and_Crafts.html

▥ Two dozen projects, plus lesson plans and more. ☆☆☆☆

Art Appreciation

♙♙♙ *How We Homeschool*

"I teach math by using pattern blocks, links (chains that can be linked together for multicolored necklaces to create patterns or for counting), interlocking cubes, geo boards, beads and laces (my kids make enormous necklaces out of these, and I'm expected to wear them!), and dominoes—all examples of manipulatives. You can purchase these or make them yourself by collecting necessary materials (if you're crafty enough!)."

—**Mary Batchelor**, homeschooling mother of six, Sandy, Utah

Christmas Crafts   www.geocities.com/Athens/4663/chriscraf.html
Instructions for dozens of handcraft projects. ☆☆☆

Crafts and Hobbies   www.wannalearn.com/Crafts_and_Hobbies
Pull out the crochet hook! This site offers free online lessons for anyone taking up a new craft or hobby: crocheting, knitting, sewing, toy making, needlework, woodworking, origami, bookbinding, quill making, and more. ☆☆☆☆☆

Figure 7.3

Crafts and Hobbies: Pick your needle!

Hotlinks

Crafts and Hobbies
www.wannalearn.com
/Crafts_and_Hobbies

Hobby World
www.hobbyworld.com

Homemade Art Supplies
www.crafterscommunity.com
/articles/artsupplies.html

World Wide Quilting Page
mail.kosmickitty.com
/MainQuiltingPageS.html

Art Appreciation

Hobby World   www.hobbyworld.com

A touch of down home, with helpful articles on dyeing, journal keeping, cider pressing, bread making, and great weekend hobbies. ☆☆☆☆☆

Home and Workshop Online

members.aol.com/jonpress2/97-2/brdhou-1.htm

A birdhouse the kids can make! Complete plans and easy directions for building a wooden birdhouse. Nicely illustrated. ☆☆☆

Homemade Art Supplies

www.crafterscommunity.com/articles/artsupplies.html

How to make your own paste, finger paint, water colors, sticking gum, sidewalk chalk, play dough, and cookie crayons. What a great means to a good end. ☆☆☆☆☆

Knowledge Hound: Hobbies and Crafts

www.knowledgehound.com/topics/hobbiesc.htm

Links to everything from antique guides to wristwatch building. Includes lessons on dolls, CB/ham radio, sewing and needlecraft, costumes, stamp collecting, and more. ☆☆☆

PBS TeacherSource: Arts and Crafts

www.pbs.org/teachersource/recommended/rec_links_art&lit.shtm#1

A collection of recommended Web sites from PBS TeacherSource. ☆☆☆☆

World Wide Quilting Page   www.ttsw.com/MainQuiltingPage.html

Claiming to be the oldest and largest quilting site on the Net (I haven't seen a real contender), this site is affiliated with a quilt-block contest and provides scores of resources for quilters. The quilt-block links are particularly helpful to newcomers. You'll also enjoy the children's projects found on the miscellaneous quilting topics page (the link is near the bottom of the main page). ☆☆☆☆☆

Design

AS A CONCEPT, design incorporates everything from the composition of a photograph to the structure of *la cathédrale de Notre Dame*. It involves the principles I used in college to lay out newspaper and magazine pages and the concepts Martha Stewart uses to arrange a tray of cookies.

Fundamentally, design involves a principle called the Fibonacci sequence—the "golden mean" observed by the Greeks and explained by a fellow named Fibonacci. All of these people observed a natural phenomenon that demonstrates that beauty can be quantified. The resources in this section explain not only Fibonacci, but also other composition and design principles as they're used in art, architecture, and interior design.

> **Design:** From the Middle French *designer (to designate)*. To create or construct according to plan.

Arts: Architecture
ericir.syr.edu/Virtual/Lessons/Arts/Architecture
Small collection of lesson plans from the U.S. Department of Education's AskERIC project. ☆☆

Bad Human Factor Design   www.baddesigns.com
Do you go nuts trying to remember which side of the car your gas tank is on? Then you'll appreciate this site, and so will your kids. It's design gone bad! ☆☆☆☆

Building Connections, Architecture for Kids
www.burgoyne.com/pages/bldgconn/a.htm
Interesting information about a particular home style, and links to good architecture sites. ☆☆☆☆

Decorating Your Home
www.decorating-your-home.com/contents.html
Principles involved in home design. This is a full online course in home decorating, complete with

Hotlinks

Decorating Your Home
www.decorating-your-home.com/contents.html

Design Awareness Is the Magic of Creativity
www.watercolor-online.com/WaterWest/NewsLetter/spring/Page4.html

Spaces and Places
www.artsednet.getty.edu/ArtsEdNet/Resources/Sampler/b.html

Art Appreciation

👪 How We Homeschool

"We will discuss our trip to a museum before we plan to even take it. I try to plan the trips so that the museum is directly related to what my kids are studying at the time. We also frequently visit historic sites and learn the who, what, and when of them. Generally after a museum or site visit, we have a long discussion that tells me what new things they learned and what they were most impressed with.

"We incorporate art into several subjects. I require on our field trips that they not only take notes, but also make sketches of things they see. Even in our microscope work, I require them to draw what they have seen."

—Ann Crum, homeschooling mother of two, central Arkansas

images and video files. Lessons cover all areas of the house, color schemes, focal points, centerpieces, and more. ☆☆☆☆☆

Design Awareness Is the Magic of Creativity
www.watercolor-online.com/WaterWest/NewsLetter/spring/Page4.html

The fundamentals of design theory. Includes an instructional article on basic visual design elements, color impact, shape size, edge quality, open and closed composition, and more. ☆☆☆☆

Phi Nest   evolutionoftruth.com/goldensection

Proof that it's possible to take any good idea way too far, this interesting site goes over the top in explaining the principle behind the Fibonacci sequence, the design rule that determines aesthetically pleasing proportions. ☆☆☆☆

Quick and Easy Decorating   www.bhglive.com/househome/decorate

A *Better Homes & Gardens* page full of short instructional guides on decorating a home. ☆☆☆

Spaces and Places
www.artsednet.getty.edu/ArtsEdNet/Resources/Sampler/b.html

An elementary-level unit on architecture. Begins with a study of building spaces; moves to a study of what architects do and how they

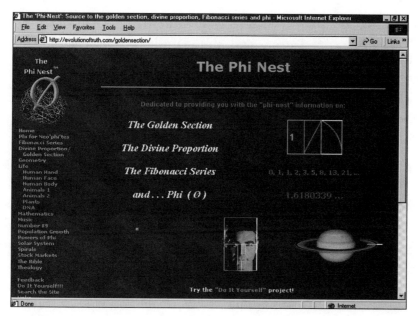

Figure 7.4

Phi Nest: No mistaking the Fibonacci sequence.

go about their discipline; and then introduces the famous American architect, Frank Lloyd Wright. Children interpret the expressive qualities of architectural spaces, collect and display photographs that depict types of buildings, draw floor plans, study the influences of geography and environment on architects' plans, and construct their own model buildings with paper forms. Six lessons. ☆☆☆☆☆

Drawing

I HAVE A couple of budding artists in my house. There's no need to teach them to draw. One son already loves drawing; another is completely obsessed. He carries a backpack stuffed with paper and pencils and notebooks every time he leaves the house, even if he's only going over to visit the neighbors. Inside the house, he carries around a clipboard with his latest project and can be found any time—day or night—crouched under a table or behind a door, tongue between his teeth, "fixing" his newest drawing.

Draw: From the Old Norse *draga (to draw or drag)*. To create a likeness or picture with lines.

Whether your little darlings are future Gary Larsons and Mort Druckers or have already made their artistic "mark," here are some resources they'll enjoy.

Art Lessons with Talent Teacher
www.talentteacher.com

An amazing site. Step-by-step illustrated instructions for projects in various media, including crayon scribbling, hand printing, Japanese paper sculpture, black-and-white landscape, seascape wash, cartoon strips, Japanese ink, Renaissance perspective, color pencil barn, Chinese wash, computer graphics, and more. This is an entire art course, and it's free. ☆☆☆☆☆

Basic Art Lessons   home.att.net/~tisone/lessonpg1.htm

A collection of drawing lessons, along with lessons in painting and art history. Aimed at older kids. ☆☆☆☆

Drawing Subjects
www.saumag.edu/art/studio/chalkboard/draw.html

Everything your budding artist must know about the theory of drawing—perspective, interiors, composition, shading, texture, and much more. Part of the Art Studio Chalkboard site. ☆☆☆☆☆

HomeSchoolArts   www.homeschoolarts.com

Drawing and online art lessons dedicated to teaching the visual arts. Pen and ink, pencil/graphite, pastels, colored pencils, and more. Beautifully illustrated. ☆☆☆☆☆

Perspective Drawing
forum.swarthmore.edu/sum95/math_and/perspective/perspect.html

A mathematical demonstration of perspective drawing, for elementary and intermediate ages. Well explained. ☆☆☆☆

Art Appreciation

Hotlinks

Art Lessons with Talent Teacher
www.talentteacher.com

HomeSchoolArts
www.homeschoolarts.com

Radicalman
www.radicalman.com

👪 *How We Homeschool*

"In art, my seven-year-old has moved past the usual scribbles and is producing drawings and artwork that is quite good. The five-year-old, unfortunately, has decided that the siding on the house makes a great canvas!"

—**Ann M. Glass**, homeschooling mother of two, Everson, Washington

---

Radicalman   **www.radicalman.com**

Illustrated examples of how to draw horses, prehistoric creatures, and in the best link of all, Hot Drawing Tips for drawing anything. ☆☆☆☆☆

Figure 7.5

HomeSchoolArts: Online drawing lessons for homeschoolers.

Refrigerator to Renoir

www.education-world.com/a_lesson/lesson106.shtml

Education World presents ten great art lessons on the Net, including a few in painting techniques. ☆☆☆☆

Painting

WE ONCE LIVED on the fourth floor of a cement building in Taipei. Out back was a long cement balcony that extended the length of the house.

In the center of the balcony was a small drain.

Guess how my children learned to paint?

I kept them supplied with all the essentials: watercolors, tempera paint, finger paint, and their favorite, colored chalk. Afternoons—winter or summer—would usually find my kids out on the back balcony dressed in "something washable," with their chalk and paint and big brushes, decorating the cement wall.

Paint: From the Latin *pingere (to tattoo)*. To depict an image using liquid pigments.

Whenever it became overcrowded, we'd go out back with a few buckets of water and a scrub brush, and they'd soon have a fresh new canvas.

They'll be well qualified when they graduate from the school of "try it and see how it works." I assume they're in good company. The Irish painter Francis Bacon was self-taught and became well respected for his artistic satire. My kids may not end up famous artists, but they've got a good start at knowing how it feels to paint. The following resources may inspire your kids to a lifetime of painting.

A.A. Art   www.1art.com
▤ Classical art gallery of oil paintings, digital illustration, and art education. Modern classical realism. Includes a free online lesson in classical painting. Beautiful. ☆☆☆☆☆

Artchive   www.artchive.com
▤ An amazing collection of artwork and commentary on famous artists. Although easily accessed, some of the picture files are huge and slow-loading—a necessary trade-off if you want to print a picture so your kids can examine the detail. ☆☆☆☆☆

Art Appreciation

ArtSchool OnLine   www.angelfire.com/ar/rogerart

The Web site's author writes: "It is my goal to make these lessons available to all who wish to learn more about the art of oil painting and general fine-art techniques. Each week I will present a new lesson or idea for you to examine." I've signed up and received my first lesson. It's fun, and you can't beat the price! ☆☆☆☆☆

Art to Zoo: Landscape Painting   educate.si.edu
/resources/lessons/art-to-zoo/landscape/cover.html

Artists Who Love the Land—a Smithsonian lesson plan. ☆☆☆☆

Explore Art
hometown.aol.com/powers8696/artindex.html

Lessons on various painters. Create projects that help your kids understand artists such as Rodin, Cezanne, and Chagall. ☆☆☆☆☆

Finger Painting   www.fingerpainter.com

This unusual artist explains her art and her method. ☆☆☆☆☆

Painting Subjects
www.saumag.edu/art/studio/chalkboard/paint.html

I found this site while looking for a way to explain complementary colors to my children. What a treasure trove! Not only does it explain colors and color matching in great depth, but it also explains the mechanics of stretching a canvas, the properties of various kinds of pigments and paints, and much more. Part of the Art Studio Chalkboard site. ☆☆☆☆☆

Painting in the Style of Georgia O'Keeffe
www.inficad.com/~arted/pages/okeeffe.html

A painting lesson for kids aged ten and younger, based on the huge flower paintings of artist Georgia O'Keeffe. ☆☆☆☆

Hotlinks

A.A. Art
www.1art.com

ArtSchool OnLine
www.angelfire.com/ar
/rogerart

Finger Painting
www.fingerpainter.com

Painting Subjects
www.saumag.edu/
art/studio/chalkboard
/paint.html

Art Appreciation

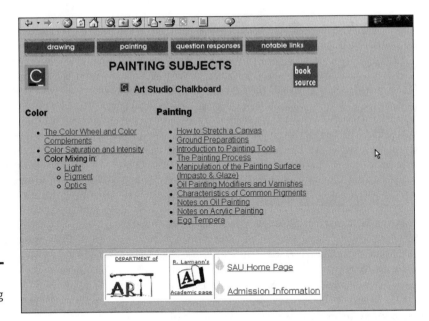

Figure 7.6

Painting Subjects:
Tricks of the painting
trade.

Telling a Painting's Story

educate.si.edu/resources/lessons/collect/telpai/telpai0a.htm

Writing about art—a Smithsonian lesson plan. ☆☆☆☆

Whalesongs and Action Painting

whales.ot.com/whales/resources/action_painting.html

A painting lesson based on whale songs. ☆☆☆☆

Sculpture and Ceramics

SCULPTURE INSPIRES. Whether carved marble or bronze casting or
gold-leafed monument, there's something "larger than life" about seeing
heroic historical figures and dramatic events carved out in three dimensions.

Sculpture also inspires children. Homeschooling mom Keithena
Kibbe from Goodyear, Arizona, explains how sculpture keeps her five
children interested in art. "Music and art have a real impact on my children," she says. "They all are very inspired. Right now, my six-year-old

really wants to sculpt like Michelangelo. A lot of working with clay and banging on rocks is going on. And my five-year-old daughter is sure she will grow up to be a singer!"

Keithena has made this foundation part of her combined art and music curriculum. "We always do art and music events as a unit study," she says. "This year we did a short four-day unit on Monet, and at the end of the week we visited his showing at the local art museum.

> **Sculpt:** From the Latin *sculpere (to carve)*. To shape or mold with artistry and precision.

"Because four of my children are very young, we haven't selected a music program yet, but our church has many, many resources and lessons. My 16-year-old son takes guitar and bass lessons twice a week, so I expect that most of the music will be taught there. Everything else we do will be in unit studies."

When your little clay benders need inspiration and direction, the following Internet resources will come in handy:

Artistic Heritage of Clay
www.artsednet.getty.edu/ArtsEdNet/Resources/Sampler/g.html
A sort of ceramics appreciation course, with interesting artifacts. ☆☆☆

CeramicsWeb   **art.sdsu.edu/ceramicsweb**
Click the education link for access to several interesting articles, photographs, and handouts on ceramics. ☆☆☆☆

DeAnza College Ceramics   **kilnman.fhda.edu**
The ceramics glossary is helpful, but the link I like best is basic throwing. Great information for beginning potters. ☆☆☆☆☆

Grafica Obscura   **www.sgi.com/grafica**
All sorts of unusual art information, but my favorite is the paper-folding project. Click the link, and you'll

Hotlinks

DeAnza College Ceramics
kilnman.fhda.edu

Grafica Obscura
www.sgi.com/grafica

Papier-Mâché Aliens
www.alienexplorer.com
/createalien/paper1.html

discover a step-by-step picture guide and directions for creating a paper sculpture. ☆☆☆☆☆

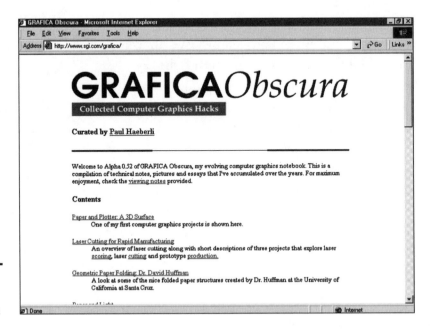

Figure 7.7

Grafica Obscura: Surprising paper sculptures and more.

Art Appreciation

Joseph Wu's Origami Page   www.origami.vancouver.bc.ca

Paper sculpture, Japanese style. Folding instructions for dozens of projects. ☆☆☆☆

Papier-Mâché Aliens   www.alienexplorer.com/createalien/paper1.html

Detailed step-by-step instructions for sculpting in papier mâché. ☆☆☆☆☆

Sculpture
www.awesomelibrary.org/Classroom/Arts/Sculpture/Sculpture.html

Links to materials, multimedia, and papers related to sculpture. ☆☆☆

Web Page for Ceramic Art Teachers/Potters
www.in-motion.net/~cgareri

Interesting photos, but the best things here are the links to dozens of ceramics sites of interest to art teachers. ☆☆☆

Visual Arts

PHOTOGRAPHY IS MY favorite visual art form. Not only is it one I can be good at without knowing how to make a recognizable ear, but it's also one that has the capacity to be the most poignant, the most memorable, for future generations of our family.

> **Visual art:** From the Latin *visus (sight)*. The production of images.

Homeschooler Cheryl Northrup, a Lamar, Colorado, mother of seven, explains how she schooled her son in the visual arts. "We bought the book *How to Draw.* We didn't do very much with it, unfortunately. Then we had a teacher come to our house and teach several kids from our homeschooling group. That was a fair experience. Art is like anything else; if they are really going to progress, there needs to be some regularity, and we had a hard time fitting it in.

"Now that we are in Lamar, my mother is here. She taught art in the public schools for 22 years, and comes over and tutors my kids twice a week. My son painted a full-sized mural on his bedroom wall of a tropical rainforest. That was his project for nearly a year. She has had them doing ceramics, life drawing, still life, and landscapes in pencil and watercolor, and now my 14-year-old-son is doing art merit badges (art, architecture, sculpture). For us, it's perfect. And homeschooling gives us the flexibility to stay with it all day if they still feel inspired. They have done some very nice work and have discovered an audience in the county fair, where they have even won some premiums.

"We have also done art appreciation à la Charlotte Mason. I have purchased several art books with great works in them, some with artist bios included. Those have been very good. The Art for Children series is particularly good. Because of my mother's influence, my children have been to many museum showings as well."

Visual arts is the catchall category for art that defies categorization. It is murals, photography, graphic arts, stained glass, collage, and more. The following resources will help your children learn more about the visual arts:

Ansel Adams

www.book.uci.edu/ePOS?form=/exhibitions/anseladams/index.html

Easily my favorite photographer of all time, except perhaps for Mathew Brady, the Civil War photographer. Ansel Adams is a Northwesterner who proves that photography is art. Click the Fiat Lux link for access to some of his work. ☆☆☆

Hotlinks

Apogee Photo Magazine
www.apogeephoto.com

How to Make and Use a Pinhole Camera
www.kodak.com/global/en
/consumer/education/lesson
Plans/pinholeCamera

Online Photo Course
www.agfaphoto.com
/library/photocourse

Apogee Photo Magazine   www.apogeephoto.com

A site that will inform and entertain photographers of all ages and levels. A tremendous collection of articles and advice for photography buffs, from rank amateur to professional. ☆☆☆☆☆

Art Education Jump Station

www.fms.k12.nm.us/mesaview/art

Contains both a photography section and a section on unusual visual art, including cave art and Stonehenge. Created by students; lots of links. ☆☆☆

Electric Origami Shop   www.ibm.com/stretch/EOS

Kaleidoscopes, fractals, puzzles, crystals, and high-tech art. Lots of visual stimulation. ☆☆☆☆

Enhancing Learning Through Imaging

www.kodak.com/US/en/digital/edu/education.shtml

An educational site sponsored by Kodak, with separate components for all age levels, science fairs, higher education, and more. Within the K–12 section are more than a dozen lesson plans and articles to help you teach the art of photography to your kids. ☆☆☆☆

How to Make and Use a Pinhole Camera   www.kodak.com/global/en
/consumer/education/lessonPlans/pinholeCamera

By using common household materials, you can make a camera that will produce pictures. Making and using a pinhole camera will acquaint you with the basic elements of photography while providing an inexpensive and interesting way to take pictures. ☆☆☆☆☆

Art Appreciation

Knowledge Hound: Photography
www.knowledgehound.com/topics/photogra.htm

Links to a handful of really great lesson plans. ☆☆☆

New York Institute of Photography   www.nyip.com

Photo tips of the month will keep you coming back. Analyze the photo of the month. Visit the reference shelf. Click, point, shoot . . . see what develops! ☆☆☆☆

Online Photo Course   www.agfaphoto.com/library/photocourse

Some of this may be appropriate only for mature children—the nude photography section comes immediately to mind—but the remainder will be useful to anyone studying photography. ☆☆☆☆☆

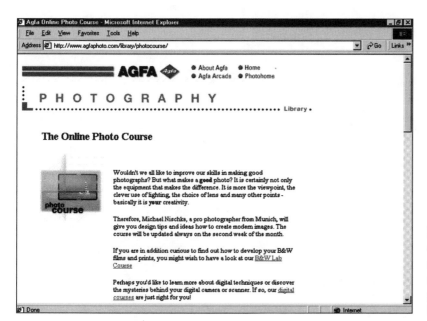

Figure 7.8

Online Photo Course: How to take pictures of anything, anywhere.

Chapter 8

History Highlights

© PHOTODISC

MY FAVORITE PART of homeschooling: teaching my young ones about history. Helping them find their place in their extended family, community, and world. To me, history is what makes us human. History is how we remember who we are, and why we matter. An appreciation of history creates in children a love for those who were heroic, and an aversion toward evil.

The more children understand of history, the better perspective they have for handling the present. A real understanding of history equips kids for living well in the real world. A historian from Missouri, who now works as a political consultant, answers the question "What is history?"

"I have studied history for as long as I remember, and the only answer I have ever come up with is that it is everything! I know that is vague, but let me expand for a moment.

"What are we if not history? Our lives are long and full of experience. We yearn for more and more experience, more knowledge, more joy, every moment that we live. But once it is lived, it is gone. What would we be if we could not remember, could not live, over and over, in a past moment? Why would we yearn for more if we could not remember anything before? We all wish to believe that we are living for today and looking toward the future, but in fact we spend most of our time in the past. The history of us, our personal history, our cultural or intellectual or geological history, is an integral part of why we live and hope and dream.

"To study history is to take the extra step from simply remembering and appreciating to trying to understand what came before. Perhaps we will make better choices. In any case, it is pure pleasure when it is felt as a precious personal memory. This is what I feel.

"When I find an old, turn-of-the-century book in which Bobby has written, 'I love Susie,' I believe I can feel what Bobby felt when he scrib-

History Freebie

"Learning Partners: Let's Do History" provides interesting ways to teach family and international history. Call 877-4-ED-PUBS and request order product number MIS 96-6516.

History Lesson

"'You all remember,' said the Controller, in his strong deep voice, 'you all remember, I suppose, that beautiful and inspired saying of Our Ford's: History is bunk. History,' he repeated slowly, 'is bunk.'

"He waved his hand; and it was as though, with an invisible feather whisk, he had brushed away a little dust, and the dust was Harappa, was Ur of the Chaldees; some spider-webs, and they were Thebes and Babylon and Cnossos and Mycenae. Whisk. Whisk—and where was Odysseus, where was Job, where were Jupiter and Gotama and Jesus? Whisk—and those specks of antique dirt called Athens and Rome, Jerusalem and the Middle Kingdom—all were gone. Whisk—the place where Italy had been was empty. Whisk, the cathedrals; whisk, whisk, King Lear and the Thoughts of Pascal. Whisk, Passion; whisk, Requiem; whisk, Symphony; whisk. . . ."

—**Aldous Huxley**, *Brave New World*

bled those words. When I walk along a battlefield or a historic way, or in one of those old houses, I half expect those who strode through, so long before, to turn the corner and offer to talk with me awhile. I believe I feel as they felt when they were there, and I am stronger and more comfortable with my being because of that feeling.

"We cannot study the future, and the present changes too fast to lend itself to anything more than criticism. The past is all we truly own and are capable of understanding. It is everything we are."

In this chapter, you'll be introduced to American history, the American West, ancient and medieval history, family history, modern American history, religious education, state history, and world history.

First, though, are some great tools for teaching history from multiple eras.

On History

"History is philosophy learned from examples."
—Thucydides,
Greek historian

Academic Subjects: History

www.wannalearn.com/Academic_Subjects/History

▤ Tutorials, instructional materials, and more from the WannaLearn site. ☆☆☆

History

Biographies   www.incwell.com/Biographies

A slow-loading site with great, illustrated biographies of people your kids should know. Includes a link to an interactive game that challenges you to match historical figures to the century in which they lived. Your kids will come away with a better perspective on how young *you* actually are! ☆☆☆☆

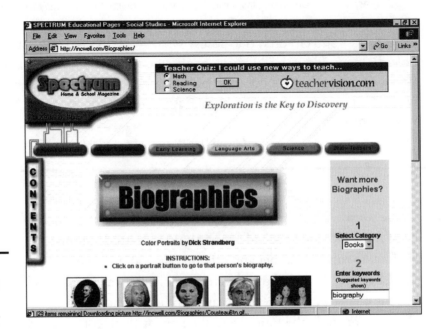

Figure 8.1

Biographies: Illustrated histories of people who changed the world.

Biography.com   www.biography.com

From cable's A&E channel, this database provides short biographies of more than 20,000 famous people. ☆☆☆☆☆

Digital History LTD   www.digitalhistory.org

A history of French, English, and American conflicts. ☆☆☆☆

Helping Your Child Learn History   www.ed.gov/pubs/parents/History

All the help you need to learn how to teach history to your children. This government-sponsored site is full of history hints for parents and teachers. ☆☆☆☆☆

History

History

db.bbc.co.uk/educationwebguide/pkg_main.p_results?in_cat=550

History information, categorized by age group, from the BBC's Education Web Guide. Sites are reviewed by subject specialists who explain how to integrate each site into the home or school classroom. ☆☆☆☆

History Center

www.education-world.com/history

The timeline is cross-referenced by grade level, which is only the beginning of the great stuff on this site. Everything's here: original articles, curriculum guides, site reviews, theme units, and much, much more. ☆☆☆☆☆

History Update   **www.eduplace.com/ss/history**

The latest discoveries in social studies in the form of news briefs from around the world. Appears to be updated about monthly, although one month's list was still posted when we checked back the following month. Still, it's a fine service. ☆☆☆☆

National Center for History in the Schools

www.sscnet.ucla.edu/nchs

The link to history standards is quite useful, and some of the links to history competitions and contests will be interesting. ☆☆☆

National Humanities Center

www.nhc.rtp.nc.us:8080/tserve/tserve.htm

The "Divining America" project at this site examines the role of religion in the historical development of the United States. It's part of the NHC's TeacherServe project, offering high school English and history teachers practical help in planning courses and presenting rigorous subject matter to students. ☆☆☆☆

Hotlinks

Biographies
www.incwell.com/Biographies

**Helping Your Child
Learn History**
www.ed.gov/pubs/parents
/History

History Center
www.education-world.com
/history

Telling Your Story
educate.si.edu/resources
/lessons/collect/telsto
/telsto0a.htm

History

Repositories of Primary Sources

www.uidaho.edu/special-collections/Other.Repositories.html

▉ Links to collections of original historical documents, sorted by geographic location. ☆☆☆

Telling Your Story

educate.si.edu/resources/lessons/collect/telsto/telsto0a.htm

▉ A site from the Smithsonian about writing history. ☆☆☆☆

American History

YOUR KIDS KNOW the Revolutionary War came before the Civil War, right? But do they understand the social and economic forces that brought about each conflict? The most important part of learning history is not dates and names; it's reasons and responses.

A New Jersey history teacher, John J. Leddy Jr., explains why it's important that your children learn history: "Knowing your history won't ensure a salary increase or win you a prize, but it will add a new dimension to your life. You are no longer trapped in the present. Both the past and what may be likely to happen in the future are open to you. Reading history gives wings to your mind. Dates and places take on new importance. Imagine for a moment that you have found yourself standing in a field. To the unaware, it is a field like any other. But this field is very different to people who know their history; to them it is known as Gettysburg."

> **America:** Named after the Italian explorer Americus Vespucius.

This section covers the history and institutions of the United States of America. These resources give your children access to information on everything from the first European contact with North America to the early part of the twentieth century.

You'll find related resources later in this chapter covering the American West, modern American history, and world history. You can also find information about American pre-history in the anthropology

History

Americus Vespucius

The man we know as Amerigo Vespucci was taught at his boyhood home in Florence by his uncle, who schooled him in the humanities. When he was only 25, the famous Italian family, the Medicis, hired him to be their spokesman to the king of France. In 1491 he went to Spain on Medici family business and became associated with the man who outfitted Columbus' ships. Five years later, Vespucci was managing the shipfitter's agency, and the following year he began making voyages of his own.

and multicultural education sections of chapter 10. Also in that chapter is an entire course on civic duty, which might well be taught concurrently with the American history lessons.

Ready to teach American history? Here are your best bets:

American History (up to 1877)
www.pinkmonkey.com/coreconcepts/subjects/amer-up-to-1877.htm
A list of research resources, arranged by subject. Register at the PinkMonkey Web site (www.pinkmonkey.com). ☆☆☆

American History Text   **www.pinkmonkey.com**
The full textbook, online. Register at the tremendous PinkMonkey site (it's free), then click on the Study Guides link to access the text. ☆☆☆☆☆

American Memory   **memory.loc.gov**
Historical collections from the National Digital Library. The Library of Congress has cataloged part of its collection for online viewing. You paid for it. Enjoy! ☆☆☆☆

America's Homepage   **www.pilgrims.net/plymouth**
History around the time of the pilgrims. Tour the plantation, learn about native whaling, discover the people who settled the area. ☆☆☆☆

Colonial Williamsburg Freebie

Call 888-223-5080 for a free scenic calendar and information packet on Colonial Williamsburg.

History

Hotlinks

American History Text
www.pinkmonkey.com

Crossroads
ericir.syr.edu/Virtual
/Lessons/crossroads

From Revolution to Reconstruction
odur.let.rug.nl/~usa

Thomas Historical Documents
lcweb2.loc.gov/const
/consthome.html

Crossroads   ericir.syr.edu/Virtual/Lessons/crossroads
American history essays and lesson plans, arranged by grade level from kindergarten through college. ☆☆☆☆☆

Founding the American Colonies
www.seanet.com/Users/pamur/13colony.html
History and resources for each of the thirteen colonies. ☆☆☆☆

From Revolution to Reconstruction   odur.let.rug.nl/~usa
There's so much here I hardly know where to start: historical outlines, documents, essays, presidents . . . oh, just go take a look. It's wonderful! ☆☆☆☆☆

Great Chicago Fire and the Web of Memory
www.chicagohistory.org/fire
An interesting bit of Americana that explains a significant moment in Chicago's—and America's—history. Oh, and if you're wondering: it was 1871. ☆☆☆☆

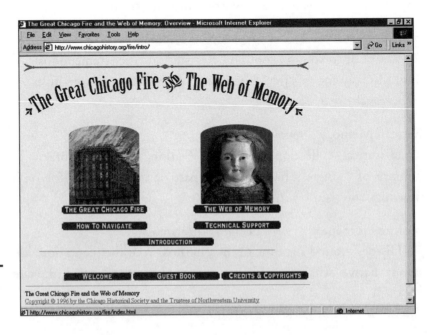

Figure 8.2

Great Chicago Fire: The legacy of a cow and a lantern.

Mr. Donn's U.S. History

members.aol.com/MrDonnHistory/American.html

This teacher's collection of lesson plans covers everything American from the pilgrims to the twentieth century. Includes information on Native Americans, the colonial period, the American Revolution, Western expansion, the Civil War, "modern America emerges" (immigration, invention, industry, imperialism), presidents, famous American women, wars and actions, and economics. ☆☆☆☆☆

PBS TeacherSource: U.S. History

www.pbs.org/teachersource/recommended/rec_links_social.shtm#4

A collection of social studies–related Web sites from PBS Teacher-Source. ☆☆☆

Presidents of the United States   www.ipl.org/ref/POTUS

Illustrations and biographies. ☆☆☆☆

Thomas Historical Documents

lcweb2.loc.gov/const/consthome.html

The four biggies: Continental Congress documents, the Declaration of Independence, the Federalist Papers, and the Constitution. Online. Searchable. There. ☆☆☆☆

American West

WHY IS THE American West a separate section in this book? Much of early American history focuses on the East Coast. From Plymouth Rock to the War Between the States, the bulk of the geographical United States was unexplored.

If that had been the end of it, the United States and Canada would both be bit players on the world stage. It was the opening of the West, and the transcontinental contact, that made the two North American countries so powerful. That, and the attitude that developed concurrently with the

West: From the Latin *vesper (evening)*. The direction in which the sun appears to set.

History

Westward expansion, combined to make the North American bloc of Canada and the United States the most potent political and military force in world history.

East Coasters, Midwesterners, Mountain Westers, or West Coasters, your children are affected by the Westward expansion. Are you prepared to help your children appreciate their great Western heritage? Use these excellent online resources to teach your kids about the opening of the West. Happy trails!

American West   www.theamericanwest.com
Exhibitions, events, archaeology, and everything you might need to study the American West. ☆☆☆☆

Discovering Lewis and Clark   www.lewis-clark.org
A bit tricky to access, but the information here is priceless. A thorough treatment of everything West. ☆☆☆☆☆

Lewis and Clark   www.pbs.org/lewisandclark
Fascinating information about Native Americans, Lewis and Clark's journals, an interactive story of the trek, and much more. An award-winning page. ☆☆☆☆☆

Little House in the Big Woods Activities
www.geocities.com/Heartland/Flats/2467
An affectionate page about Laura Ingalls Wilder, pioneers, and the Westward expansion. ☆☆☆☆

Little House on the Prairie
www.geocities.com/~perkinshome/littlehouse.html
A Christian-themed page for younger children on the subject of Laura Ingalls Wilder, pioneers, and the Westward expansion. ☆☆☆☆

Mormon Trail
www.esu3.k12.ne.us/districts/elkhorn/ms/curriculum/Mormon1.html
A Nebraska middle school put together this very well done site on the Mormon pioneer trail. ☆☆☆☆☆

Oregon Trail Freebie

Get a free educational resource guide from the National Historic Oregon Trail Interpretive Center. Call 541-523-1843, or order from www.or.blm.gov/NHOTIC/Education/teacher%20packets.htm.

History

Native American Indian Resources

indy4.fdl.cc.mn.us/~isk/mainmenu.html

A full course on Native American culture and history. ☆☆☆☆☆

Native American Resources

www.hanksville.org/NAresources

Culture, history, archaeology, languages. . . . There's an awful lot of information here. Your child's fascination with American Indian culture will be satisfied. ☆☆☆☆

New Perspectives on the West

www.pbs.org/weta/thewest

This may be one of the best educational sites on the Net. I promise that no matter how much you think you know about any aspect of America's Westward migration, you'll learn something new here. It's one of my personal areas of interest, and I found lots I'd never known. So will you. ☆☆☆☆☆

Hotlinks

Lewis and Clark
www.pbs.org/lewisandclark

New Perspectives on the West
www.pbs.org/weta/thewest

Oregon Trail
www.isu.edu/~trinmich
/Oregontrail.html

Trail of Hope
www.trailofhope.com

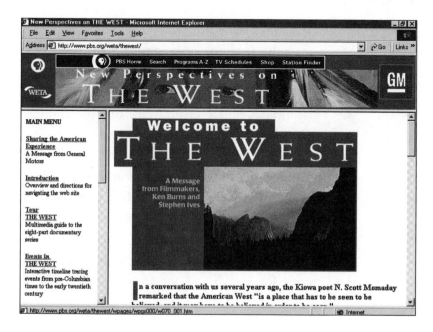

Figure 8.3

The West: A round-up from pre-Columbian history to the present.

History

Oregon Trail   www.isu.edu/~trinmich/Oregontrail.html

Facts, tutorial, and two dozen sites along the trail. An award-winning page. There's so much information here. . . . Your children will be well taught. ☆☆☆☆☆

Spanish Missions of California   library.thinkquest.org/3615

An explanation and analysis of the California missions. An award-winning page. ☆☆☆

Trail of Hope   www.trailofhope.com

A PBS special on the history of the Mormon trail. ☆☆☆☆

WestWeb   www.library.csi.cuny.edu/westweb

Women of the American West, Native Americans, cowboys, gold rush, expansionism—they all take an outing at this award-winning site. ☆☆☆☆☆

Ancient, Medieval, and Renaissance History

YOUR KIDS ARE sure to find something to love about ancient history. If it's not the heroic legends of Arthurian knights, it's the plays and romance of the Renaissance.

Medieval: From the New Latin *medium aevum (Middle Ages)*. The period from the collapse of the Roman Empire to the Renaissance.

This section covers world history, from 6,000-year-old Chinese civilization, through the Greeks and Romans, to the European Renaissance. You can find related resources in the anthropology section of chapter 10, which covers prehistory and archaeological findings, as well as in the world history section later in this chapter, which covers post-Renaissance world history.

Following are some of the best educational resources on the Internet for teaching about ancient, and less-ancient, history.

Ancient Egypt on the Web   **guardians.net/egypt**

I've never yet met a kid who didn't spend some time being fascinated by Egyptian history and culture. It's a part of growing up. There's plenty for kids to love at this site, which is full of great information on pyramids, hieroglyphics, and all things Egyptian. ☆☆☆☆☆

Byzantine and Medieval Links Index

www.fordham.edu/halsall/medweb

An awe-inspiring collection of sites. If Byzantine or Medieval is your area of historical interest, this is your site. ☆☆☆☆

Daily Life in Ancient Civilizations

members.aol.com/Donnclass/indexlife.html

Well-written, approachable information about the daily lives of people in ancient Egypt, Greece, Rome, China, India, and more. Includes links to lesson plans for teachers. ☆☆☆

Mr. Donn's Ancient History

members.aol.com/donnandlee

Ancient history lesson plans and activities. Use this site as a foundation for teaching about Mesopotamia, Egypt, Greece, Rome, China, India, and Africa. Discuss ethnic groups such as the Incas and Mayans. This site contains units, lesson plans, activities, and online resources. ☆☆☆

Open University Guide to the Renaissance

www.open.ac.uk/Arts/renaissance/guide.htm

Order a free printed copy, or simply peruse this beautifully done online guide. Open University is also worth considering for college courses. The school has an amazingly difficult curriculum, but enrollment is wide open. Some courses are available anywhere in the world. In any event, the guide is a treasure. ☆☆☆☆☆

Hotlinks

Ancient Egypt on the Web
guardians.net/egypt

Open University Guide to the Renaissance
www.open.ac.uk/Arts
/renaissance/guide.htm

Resources for the Study of World Civilizations
www.wsu.edu/~wldciv

History

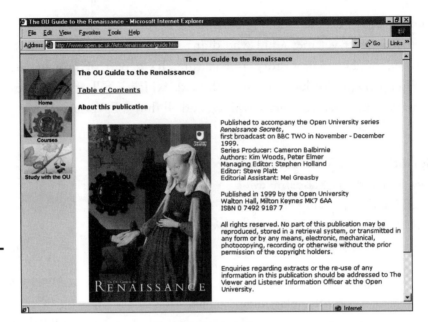

Figure 8.4

OU Guide:
Fascinating take
on the rebirth of
European culture.

Renaissance Faires and Information

webhackers.cygnus.com/~meissner/ren.html

Amazingly popular, Renaissance Faires are springing up all around North America. Here's how you can participate. ☆☆☆

Resources for the Study of World Civilizations   **www.wsu.edu/~wldciv**

Ever wonder what Confucius really said? Browse through the fascinating sampling in this anthology of readings from ancient civilizations. Learn about China, India, the agricultural revolution, human prehistory, and much more. ☆☆☆☆

Scrolls from the Dead Sea

sunsite.unc.edu/expo/deadsea.scrolls.exhibit/intro.html

This site, reorganized from Library of Congress resources, has an enormous amount of information on the scrolls and the artifacts found with them. ☆☆☆☆

Seven Wonders of the Ancient World

ce.eng.usf.edu/pharos/wonders

What they are, and why they're "wonder"ful. ☆☆☆☆

History

Family History

IS THERE A more important aspect of history than what your children can learn about their own family? Whether your ancestors were kings or paupers, there's a lesson there for your children.

Genealogical research has come into its own over the past two years. Not only have technological advances changed the nature of archiving documents; online resources have also made it possible for large extended families to work together to conduct research and share information.

> **Family:** From the Latin *familia (household)*. Those related to an individual by blood or marriage.

Our extended family gathers together one Sunday a month to work on genealogy, family histories, and scrapbooks. The younger kids play with their cousins and dads, and the women and older children sit around the table with scissors, rubber stamps, and adhesive to mount photos on scrapbook pages and compare genealogical research. Now that we have scanners and good-quality color printers, we even swap photos and print out copies on the spot.

This section on Family History includes resources for genealogy and personal history. If you are working across curricula, consider the possibility that genealogical research can teach technology, writing, reading, and foreign languages.

No matter how you view it—as an academic exercise or as a means for drawing families together—genealogy works.

CuteStuff Scrapbook Poetry   www.cutestuff.net

Part of keeping your family history is documenting your family present. Learn a bit about journaling and memory albums. ☆☆☆☆

Electronic Field Trips: Ellis Island

commtechlab.msu.edu/sites/letsnet/frames/bigideas/b1/b1u1.html

Lesson plan that helps students conduct primary and secondary research to learn more about their cultural and ethnic heritage. ☆☆☆

History

Family History Map   family.go.com/Features/family_1999_04/famf
/famf49histmap/famf49histmap.html

▦ A fun family project. Introduce your child to history with a map that traces the migration of your ancestors. ☆☆☆☆

Hotlinks

FamilySearch
www.familysearch.org

Genealogy Classes
www.genealogy.com
/genealogy/university.html

Mother Hubbard's Cupboard
www.rootsweb.com
/~genclass

Rememory
www.rememory.com

FamilySearch   www.familysearch.org

▦ In its first year, this site had more than 3 billion hits. FamilySearch houses more than 640 million genealogical records and is available free to the public. Download a free copy of Personal Ancestral File, a tremendous software tool for organizing your own genealogical records. Click the Browse Categories link for a view of all the tools on this site. There's a good chance you might even find information on one of your own ancestors. ☆☆☆☆☆

Genealogy   www.execpc.com/~dboals/geneo.html

▦ Lesson plans and links from the History/Social Studies Web Site. ☆☆

Genealogy Classes

www.genealogy.com/genealogy/university.html

▦ Genealogy Research Associates offers this well done online course, with more than 100 free lessons, covering beginning genealogy, tracing immigrant origins, and more. If your kids aren't already genealogy buffs, this will get them hooked! ☆☆☆☆☆

Mother Hubbard's Cupboard   www.rootsweb.com/~genclass

▦ The classes are free, online, and self-paced. The beginning genealogist will learn all the steps from "the bushel basket system" to computerized genealogy. Lessons discuss family records; local, state, and federal records; church records; census records; land and probates; school records; immigration and naturalization records; and miscellaneous records that are hard to find. RootsWeb is one of the premier genealogy sites on the Net. You can't go wrong with these lessons. ☆☆☆☆☆

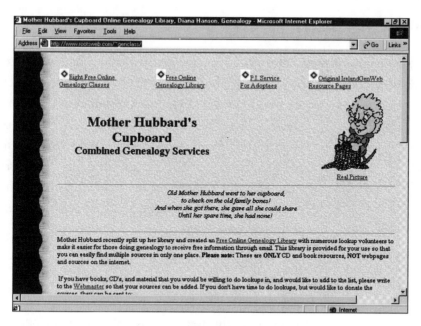

Figure 8.5

Mother Hubbard:
No more excuses.
Pull out the family
records.

Rememory   www.rememory.com

I love this site. Not only does it provide a safe place for personal histories; it also provides regular encouragement and reminders to update my own journal and scrapbook. Best of all: these people are willing to *pay* me for what I ought to be doing for nothing. But ssshhhh! Don't tell anyone: This is the sort of site I'd be willing to pay *them* for! ☆☆☆☆☆

StudyWeb Genealogy

http://www.studyweb.com/Family/genealtoc.htm

Education-oriented genealogy resources, from StudyWeb. ☆☆☆

Who We Are   www.eduplace.com/hac/who.html

Activities for younger children that will help build family ties. Create a memory box, a family totem pole, and more. ☆☆☆

Zing   www.zing.com

Another of those perplexing free Web sites that cause one to wonder how it is these people make a living. Zing! allows free, unlimited storage of your family photos. You can organize your graphics by album, customize your albums, and share with family members. ☆☆☆☆☆

Modern American History

THE VIETNAM WAR before your time? Watergate just a shadowy memory? What can you tell your kids about the Gulf War? If those subjects are tough, how will you teach them about the New Deal? The Depression? Prohibition? Monroe Doctrine? Expansionism? From World War I to the present, these are the forces that shape modern American life. Check out the following sites to improve your own knowledge and find teaching ideas and materials.

Modern: From the Latin *modo (just now).* Of contemporary or recent origin.

Hotlinks

Abridged History of the United States
www.us-history.com
/nonf/chap_1_1.html

History of the World Timeline
www.historychannel.com
/Centurytime

Twentieth Century
library.hilton.kzn.school.za
/History/c20th.htm

Abridged History of the United States
www.us-history.com/nonf/chap_1_1.html
The twentieth century in American history is covered, in depth, in this tremendous online text. ☆☆☆☆☆

Age of Imperialism
www.smplanet.com/imperialism/toc.html
Thoughtful collection of information on U.S. foreign policy during the eighteenth and nineteenth centuries. This history unit covers U.S. expansionism around the turn of the eighteenth century, with many links to related sites on the Net. There's also a lesson plan available. ☆☆☆☆☆

American History (After 1877)   www.pinkmonkey.com/coreconcepts/subjects/amer-after-1877.htm
A list of research resources, arranged by subject. Register at PinkMonkey (www.pinkmonkey.com). ☆☆☆

American Leaders Speak   lcweb2.loc.gov/nfhome.html
The Nation's Forum collection gathers fifty-nine sound recordings of speeches by American leaders at the turn of the eighteenth century. ☆☆☆☆

Celebrate the Century   encarta.msn.com/ctc/explore.asp

Less cool than it could be, but there's still some well-done information on this site. Dig around to find lesson plans and a curriculum
grid. ☆☆

History of the World Timeline   www.historychannel.com/Centurytime

Extremely well compiled collection of information on modern history, primarily from an American perspective. ☆☆☆☆☆

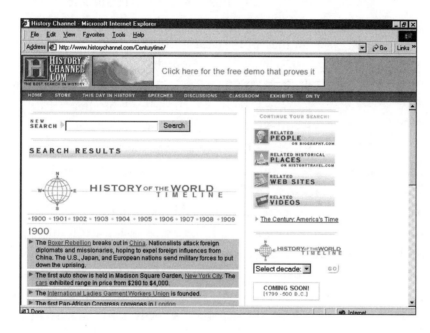

Figure 8.6

History of the
World: An ambitious
undertaking.

New Deal Network   newdeal.feri.org/classrm

Lesson plans, projects, and resources relating to Franklin Delano
Roosevelt and the New Deal. Middle and secondary students will
benefit most. ☆☆☆☆☆

Twentieth Century   library.hilton.kzn.school.za/History/c20th.htm

Tremendous resources for studying the past century of American history. A decade-by-decade breakdown of information.
☆☆☆☆☆

History

Religious Education

THIS MAY BE the single most significant factor in most people's decision to homeschool: The desire to make a spiritual education part of their children's academic experience. In fact, well over half of all homeschoolers describe themselves as "biblically based Christians."[1] Add to that mix the large numbers of other faithful who are homeschooling—members of other Christian denominations, Jews, Bahá'ís, Muslims, and even Wiccans and Pagans—and it's clear that spirituality is a big factor in most families' home education.

> **Religion:**
> Associated with the Latin *religre (to tie fast, rely)*. Reliance on a supreme being or supernatural influence.

Religion is indisputably a major influence on the homeschooling movement. That's a good thing, say people who have considered the alternatives. Dr. Henry Simmons, head of the Presbyterian School in Richmond, Virginia, explained in a recent radio broadcast the effect of ignoring or downplaying the teaching of religious philosophies and doctrines: "What happens when religion is cut out? What happens when we try to create a world that is perfectly secular, that has no religion, has no place for God, has no place for a community of faith? First of all, we're creating a strange world in terms of humankind."

Simmons worries that the practice of teaching secular lessons—lessons without a religious foundation—undermines the well-being of individuals and the health of our society: "What is going to sustain you when the things that society prized and rewarded you with or for, fall away? When you no longer are handsome or beautiful, when you don't have physical strength? When you, perhaps, don't have the same quickness of wit or whatever, and don't dress as well? Can't do all the things society does? Can't play a good game of golf? What's going to sustain you? What's going to sustain you as an individual? And what's going to sustain you and me together? That thing is the knowledge that there is some-

1. Nanette Asimov, "Teaching the Kids at Home: Internet Swamped with Homeschool Resources," *San Francisco Chronicle,* January 29, 1999, www.sfgate.com/cgi-bin/article.cgi?file=/chronicle/archive/1999/01/29/MN87634.DTL.

Comparative Religions

"Our studies of Africa brought up both Islam and the native animism, and we spent time learning about both. My son attends Sunday school, and as his questions come up I answer them and explain my beliefs. We actually found so much similarity between our faith and Islam—more than I thought we would."

—**Leanne Dohy**, homeschooling mother of three, Calgary, Canada

thing that is deeper than us or that transcends us, that we are related to in some real and powerful way."[2]

For Dr. Anthony Davis, assistant professor of economics and finance at Pittsburgh's Duquesne University, education that neglects morality is without substance. The economist calls himself a strong supporter of homeschooling and explains why:

"I support homeschooling because I believe that young minds cannot be taught without the background of moral context. Knowledge, no matter how we might wish otherwise, is not independent of morality. It is an incomplete and hollow education that speaks of truth without addressing how one should respond to that truth.

"What good does it do for our children to learn of history without learning that this or that person behaved well or poorly, and so should or should not be emulated? What good does it do for our children to learn of science without learning that the ability to act is not, of itself, license to act? What good does it do for our children to learn if they are not taught that it is truth that is absolute and opinion that is relative? It is precisely the moral context that homeschooling can and does bring to education. It is this context that, in its fruition, marks the difference between knowledge and wisdom."

Kimberley Daly is a homeschooling mother of three in Washington State. She began homeschooling last summer and credits her church associations for giving her the courage to start. "We have always been

2. Quoted with permission from *The Faith and Families Report*, radio broadcast for March 11–17, 2000, produced by the Church of Jesus Christ of Latter-day Saints.

History

👪 How We Homeschool

"Alexander is a bit young for formal religious training, but I plan to do with him much as my parents did with me. My parents encouraged me to study a variety of religious faiths in order to know which resonated within me. We do plan to raise him following our path, but the ultimate decision as to how he will relate to the Divine will have to be his own.

"I think how we live our everyday lives *is* our spiritual practice. For us, we cannot separate what we believe from what we do. When we treat others with respect and dignity, when we recycle, when we pick up garbage, when we eat healthy foods, when we honor the Earth and all Her inhabitants, we are acting in a spiritual way. My goal is to teach my son that all these things are a part of spirit as well as a part of physical life. Is it formal? Not in the sense of dogma, but it is in the sense that it is what our spiritual path teaches is right."

—vanessa ronsse, homeschooling mother of one, Seattle area

around homeschooling families. Every church we've been in has been full of homeschoolers. While I don't mean to make this a religious issue, we did feel like God was telling us something.

"We finally decided to homeschool because we felt that not only were our children not learning what they should, but they were learning things they shouldn't. We were looking for a safer environment without the peer pressure problems. So I guess for us it was everything put into one, not just one big thing that led us to homeschool."

Kimberley has made it part of her homeschooling program to teach her children about religion. "I don't teach my children about other faiths, but they do know that there are other faiths out there (my family is a different faith than we are) and that they are not to be the judges of others. Not only do our children do a Bible study every day, but we also read Bible stories to them and they are active in our church as well."

Susan D. Clawson homeschools five children in Clearfield, Utah. She says her religious faith sustained the family during their years in the military, and the variety of religious associations her children have made has been beneficial to their own spiritual development. This is what she says about how she has educated her own children about religious faiths other than her own: "We have friends from various religions and some who don't claim any religion at all. Having been moved around with the military in their early years, my two older boys had a wide variety of playmates: all different religions, ethnic backgrounds, and cultures.

"When we look up something on a map as we're reading the newspaper or *National Geographic* or listening to the news, we'll talk about the people who live there. Their religion, their food, their manner of dress, and other aspects of their lives are discussed, all informally. I wouldn't say that we've ever undertaken a formal survey of world religions, but it sounds like a fascinating area of study!"

In her own homeschooling, Susie has developed her own curriculum based strictly on the religious works of her family's faith. "I don't use any religious materials in our homeschooling, other than the scriptures. I dislike the slant that many religious publishers put on their works. I prefer to discuss how a particular theory stacks up against what *we* believe to be true. While we don't believe in evolution in the Darwinian sense, I have no fear of my children being exposed to the theory, because we have discussed it at home.

"As for faith and values, we live our religion twenty-four hours a day. Our conduct is based on what we believe, if that makes any sense. We're active participants in worship services in our church, in its youth programs, men's and women's groups, et cetera. We use this as a springboard of sorts. We help our children understand that what we learn at church is to be used in our lives, to serve and love others, and not to judge. Our faith is big on building bridges with other faiths and cultures. Instead of dwelling on our differences, we find links between our similarities, still holding on to our beliefs. We're helping our kids to learn to live this way by doing it ourselves."

The history of religion is stormy—but virtually everyone agrees that better understanding of unfamiliar religious faiths can't help but improve your children's own level of spirituality. Where it reinforces their faith, they benefit, and where it causes them to ask questions, you're there to respond.

History

New Views

"Moses led the Hebrew slaves to the Red Sea, where they made unleavened bread, which is bread made without any ingredients. Moses went up on Mount Cyanide to get the Ten Commandments. He died before he ever reached Canada."

—Alleged response given by a sixth grader to a history exam question

The following resources are of two types: comparative and explanatory. The comparative religion links avoid the name-calling and controversy that is so easily found on the Internet. They focus instead on the facts about various religious movements and faiths, and compare them in a matter-of-fact manner you're sure to find refreshing.

The explanatory sites represent the doctrine, history, or theology of the world's major religious movements. For the most part, they are scholarly in nature and avoid material of a proselytizing nature. If you're inclined to teach your children how the rest of the world lives its beliefs, here's a start:

Hotlinks

Adherents.com
www.adherents.com

BBC Education: Religion
www.bbc.co.uk/plsql
/education/webguide
/pkg_main.p_results?
in_cat=557

Religious Studies
www.clas.ufl.edu/users
/gthursby/rel

Academic Info: Religion Gateway
www.academicinfo.net/religindex.html
A gateway to religious movements around the world.
☆☆☆☆

Adherents.com   **www.adherents.com**
An amazing site. A compilation of nearly 40,000 records documenting the membership of some 4,000 religious faiths. ☆☆☆☆☆

American Prophet   **www.pbs.org/americanprophet/prologue.html**
A documentary PBS special on the founding of Mormonism.
☆☆☆☆☆

History

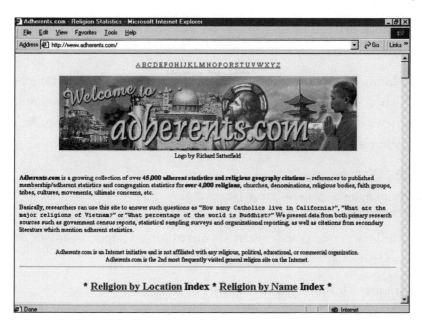

Figure 8.7

Adherents.com: Endless collection documenting the existence, and size, of all known religious denominations.

Antiquity Online   fsmitha.com/h1/

Comparative developments in religion, rule, and philosophy, from 8000 B.C. to the Middle Ages. ☆☆☆☆

Bahá'í World   www.bahai.org

This growing worldwide religious movement now has some 7 million members. Its roots are akin to Islam, although the organization itself was founded less than 200 years ago. This is the faith's official Web site, so as might be expected, it lacks academic rigor. ☆☆☆

Beliefnet   www.beliefnet.org

A wide-ranging collection of articles and news relating to various belief systems. Very thoughtful. And the columnists are tremendously interesting. ☆☆☆☆☆

BBC Education: Religion

db.bbc.co.uk/education-webguide/pkg_main.p_results?in_cat=557

The BBC examines various religious faiths and presents information by age level. From the BBC's Education Web Guide. Subject

History

specialists have written reviews on how to integrate each site into learning, both in the classroom and at home. ☆☆☆☆☆

Bible Links Page   www.geocities.com/Athens/Aegean/3446/bible.html

▤ These Biblical links were collected specifically for homeschoolers. Reviews suggest ways to use the sites in your homeschooling. An excellent resource. ☆☆☆☆

Buddhism, Confucianism, and Taoism
www.human.toyogakuen-u.ac.jp/~acmuller

▤ The five Confucian and Taoist classics are particularly interesting, but this is a good place to start if you're doing a paper on any of these three religious faiths. ☆☆☆

Christianity Online   www.christianity.net

▤ A very well done collection of articles and advice for the Protestant/Evangelical Christian community. ☆☆☆☆

Christian School Resource   www.csrnet.org

▤ "A huge site for educators seeking resources: lesson plans, Web-based lessons, distance education, homeschool resources, Christian resources (Biblical studies, software, missions), and educational articles, just to mention a few. This site will keep you busy for a while. I tend to go through and bookmark what looks good and then come back to those bookmarks at a later time. Otherwise . . . lots of rabbit trails!" —A.G. ☆☆☆☆☆

Hindu Universe   www.hindunet.org

▤ What Hindus believe. ☆☆☆

IslamiCity   www.islam.org

▤ Not the least bit scholarly, but you'll learn something about this growing religious movement, from a Muslim perspective. ☆☆

Jehovah's Witnesses   witnesses.miningco.com/culture/witnesses

▤ There is very little credible scholarly information on the Net about this religious movement. Although this is probably the largest unofficial site, it suffers from a real lack of academic weight. ☆☆

Judaism 101   www.jewfaq.org
Online encyclopedia of Judaism. ☆☆☆☆

New Advent Catholic Website   www.newadvent.org
A well-done site explaining Catholicism, although it mostly ignores the Orthodox faiths. ☆☆☆

Religious Studies   www.clas.ufl.edu/users/gthursby/rel
Considers numerous new religious movements and traditions from an academic perspective. ☆☆☆☆

State History

I GREW UP in the Seattle area and every year, on my birthday, my father took me out for a day to do anything I wanted to do. Nearly all of my birthday trips involved a visit to downtown Seattle, where we would visit the farmers' market, walk to the piers on the waterfront, and, best of all, take the tour of Seattle's historic underground, the first floor of the city that existed before fire consumed most of the wooden buildings in town.

> **State:** From the Latin *status (condition).* Political subdivision of a nation.

Today you can ask me anything about Seattle history. Those childhood trips made me an expert, and as a result, I learned to love my hometown.

Perhaps your state requires you to teach your children local history. Or you may simply be fond of the place you live, and believe your kids are better off knowing about those who made it what it is today.

In either case, the Internet is ready to help. The following resources do a great job explaining the history, and in some cases the law and other information, for every state in the United States.

Social Studies: State History
ericir.syr.edu/Virtual/Lessons/Social_St/State_history
State history lesson plans from the U.S. Department of Education's AskERIC project. ☆☆

History

Stonewall Jackson

Orphaned at a young age, Thomas Jonathan "Stonewall" Jackson had little formal education. He grew up in the homes of relatives and, in 1842, received his appointment to West Point. He did poorly at first, but he eventually graduated and gained his commission as a second lieutenant in the Army. It was during the Mexican War that he first met General Robert E. Lee, the future commander of the Confederate armies, and his noteworthy military future was set. Prior to his orders to return to the military, the future Civil War hero taught natural philosophy at Virginia Military Institute.

Social Studies: State History

thegateway.syr.edu/index2/socialstudiesstatehistory.html

A substantial collection of lesson plans on the histories of various states. Not nearly comprehensive enough, but what's there is good. Some lessons are applicable to any state. ☆☆☆☆

State and Local Government on the Net

www.piperinfo.com/state/states.html

Government-sponsored sites for every state, and for lots of counties and cities. ☆☆☆☆

Stately Knowledge   www.ipl.org/youth/stateknow

Basic facts about every state in the Union, as well as Washington, D.C. Includes comparative data. ☆☆☆

States and Capitals   www.50states.com

Great information about each of the fifty American states. ☆☆☆☆☆

StudyWeb: States

www.studyweb.com/History__Social_Studies/tocUSstud.htm

State-by-state listing of local information, including history. ☆☆☆

Hotlinks

The Graham Family Hits the Road!
www.usatrip.org

States and Capitals
www.50states.com

The US50
www.theus50.com

History

The Graham Family Hits the Road!   www.usatrip.org

Our nomination for top homeschooling family in America—somewhere in America! This family sold their home and set out to visit every state. This is their account of their adventures. ☆☆☆☆☆

Figure 8.8

The Graham Family: Get your kicks on route America.

The U.S. 50   www.theus50.com

Extensive history and other information about every state. ☆☆☆☆☆

WashLaw Web   www.washlaw.edu

Legal information for each state. ☆☆☆☆

World History

HOW DID I teach my kids about the history of the world?

I packed them up and moved them to China.

You may want to pursue a different route.

Whatever you teach them of world history, you will make them better, and better-educated, people.

Scott Schickram is an avocational historian in Houston, Texas. He believes an understanding of world history is critical to becoming an educated, contributing member of society. "My understanding of history helps me understand current events," he says. "But the most important benefit is the appreciation of what a great nation we live in here in the United States."

He suggests that one of the most interesting ways to learn history is to get to know great historical figures. "In preparation for the future, I think high school students should study biographies of famous people. History is really a history of people, not just dates. By reading the biographies of Washington or Franklin, I've learned to appreciate the events they helped shape. It also made me realize they were human beings like myself. Often their problems were far worse than any I face."

The following resources introduce the history and institutions of world civilizations. (See also the related sections on social issues, minority education, and anthropology in chapter 10.)

> **World:** From the Old English *woruld* (*human existence*). All matters related to earthly life.

Hotlinks

Amazing Ancient World of Western Civilization
www.omnibusol.com/ancient.html

Rulers
www.geocities.com/Athens/1058/rulers.html

World History Links
www.grossmont.k12.ca.us westhills/staff/dmcdowell/class/worldhistory.html

World History Text
www.pinkmonkey.com

Amazing Ancient World of Western Civilization
www.omnibusol.com/ancient.html
Primarily covers ancient history, but continues all the way to modernity. Weaves together the peoples of those lands and civilizations and the way they lived.
☆☆☆☆☆

Breaking the Seal   www.open2.net/breakingtheseal
Scripts, documents, and other excellent resources from a television program affiliated with London's Open University. The program explores documentary evidence of important English historical events.
☆☆☆☆

History of the World   www.hyperhistory.com

▤ Includes a massive, graphically hyperlinked timeline covering 3,000 years of world history. Also includes more than 1,800 files. It's real world history and comes highly recommended. ☆☆☆☆☆

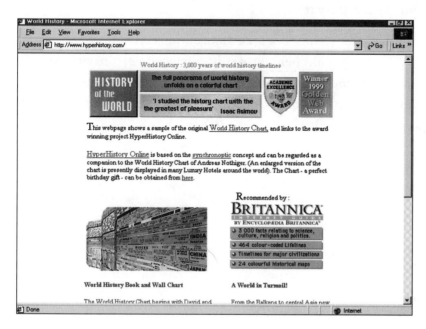

Figure 8.9

History of the World: History at the click of your mouse.

Non-Western History   www.execpc.com/~dboals/hist.html

▤ A huge collection of lesson plans about nations around the world. Hundreds and hundreds of resources. ☆☆☆☆

Rulers   www.geocities.com/Athens/1058/rulers.html

▤ When they ruled, and who ruled whom. Excellent research resource. ☆☆☆☆

World History Links

www.grossmont.k12.ca.us/westhills/staff/dmcdowell/class/worldhistory.html

▤ Greece and Rome, the Renaissance, the Middle Ages, slavery, Columbus, the Enlightenment, the French Revolution, and more— right up to modern times. ☆☆☆☆☆

History

World History Text   www.pinkmonkey.com

▨ The full textbook, online. Register at the tremendous PinkMonkey Web site (it's free), then click on the study guides link to access the text. While you're on the page, see the related link to Pink Monkey's European history text. ☆☆☆☆

World Resource Center   www.education-world.com/regional

▨ "There are links here for nearly every country imaginable, as well as links to other subjects and news items. An awesome place simply to explore—an education in and of itself. Marvelous help for researching a particular country." —A.G. ☆☆☆

Music Marathon

I SPENT TEN years in piano lessons.

And practiced for half an hour a week.

During my lesson. I don't know why my mother paid for this exercise in futility.

It wasn't until I became an adult and had to play the piano for Sunday school that I actually learned to play. I'll never get an invitation to play Carnegie Hall, but I can manage to get through the sheet music without too much trouble. I hope that modest ability—and the fact that my husband is a musical genius—qualifies us to teach music.

Well, OK. . . . And also the fact that we have access to so many good resources for teaching music, including musicians in our community and on the Internet who are unfailingly generous with advice and suggestions.

Shelly and Ryan Simmons are among them. Shelly is the music cataloger at the University of California at San Diego and a student in music psychology. Ryan plays associate principal bassoon in the San Diego Symphony. They offer some good advice to parents who are looking for ways to teach their children to appreciate music: "Our best recommendation is for parents to realize that everyone can be a musician, and everyone can sing. The reason people think they can't do these things is because they feel there is a level of education or expertise needed to even try.

"Start young children off with simple rhythm exercises: clapping to the beat on the radio or CDs, using different hands for different beats, learning to count with the rhythms. Anyone can do this. There are great rhythm instruments to be had at any local music store: blocks, fish, sanding blocks, and so on. Every local guitar and drum music shop has these rhythm instruments, and for under $30, a parent can get one lesson in their use if absolutely necessary. Children through elementary school can use these as accessories to the radio, piano, CDs, or other music.

Music

🏃 How We Homeschool

"We have many classical CDs in our home. I use a combination of those and resource materials to round out their study of music. We include the great classics as well as classic rock, show tunes, and gospel music. Because so much modern rock and country music is filled with immoral themes, we leave those off.

"For both art and music, I will occasionally assign my children an artist and have them work up a biography, do a timeline, assess how his or her environment or the times affected what that artist produced, and find notable events around the world that occurred during that artist's lifetime. To me, it is not enough to look at pictures or listen to music. It is more important to find out why people painted certain ways or particular subjects, why they wrote particular pieces of music, and how things in their lives affected what they produced. It is important to learn about the real person behind it all. In doing this, my children have often learned how great men and women have overcome all sorts of odds to do what they loved—how they had victories, and sometimes how they had defeats."

—**Ann Crum**, homeschooling mother of two, central Arkansas

"Another extremely easy but effective (and fun) exercise is for the parent or teacher to either play piano or put on a classical, jazz, or other music recording and have the children dance to the music. A great example is choosing ballet music and having the kids pretend they are butterflies emerging from cocoons, or trees in the wind.

"These simple yet effective exercises are both fun and imaginative, and allow the participants to feel that they are interpreting and making music. This then should be followed by age-appropriate music lessons with a local professional, if desired—piano lessons being the most beneficial."

Ryan and Shelly endorse the resources at the Music Educators National Conference (www.menc.org) for parents and other educators of children. They also recommend a site called Music Games (www.bobchilds.co.uk/mtrs/games.htm) as a helpful resource for music teachers.

Hotlinks

**Chinese Music Society of
North America**
www.chinesemusic.net

Curriculum
www2.potsdam.edu/crane
/campbemr/curriculum

**Mr. E's Virtual Music
Classroom**
cnet.unb.ca/achn/kodaly
/koteach/resources/toc.html

Those are only the beginning of the dozens of great resources available for free to parents who are teaching music.

In this chapter, you'll be introduced to composition, music appreciation, musicianship, and vocal music:

We start, though, with some general tools for teaching music.

Art and Music Education   www.emtech.net/arts.htm

Dozens of very well chosen resources. ☆☆

Chinese Music Society of North America
www.chinesemusic.net

I used to think the words "Chinese" and "music" were oxymoronic. It took more than a decade of Chinese opera blaring outside my window at nights, but I've almost started to like it. This site isn't so informative as a Taiwanese puppet show, but it'll do. ☆☆☆☆

Figure 9.1

Chinese Music Society: It's not all drums and dragon boats.

Curriculum   www2.potsdam.edu/crane/campbemr/curriculum

Of particular interest is the link called From Theory Into the Classroom, which explains theories of teaching music. Very complex, very useful. ☆☆☆☆

Music   www.knowledgehound.com/topics/music.htm

How to write, play, and perform music. Links to numerous really great lesson plans. ☆☆☆

Mr. E's Virtual Music Classroom   cnet.unb.ca/achn/kodaly/koteach /resources/toc.html

I love this site! Composer of the month, lessons, songs, recipes, and more. ☆☆☆☆

Music   www.pbs.org/teachersource/recommended/rec_links_art&lit .shtm#6

A collection of recommended Web sites from PBS TeacherSource. ☆☆☆☆

Music Links   www.geocities.com/Athens/Aegean/3446/music.html

These reviews describe how to use music resources in your home-schooling. An excellent resource. ☆☆☆☆

Teachers.Net: Music   www.teachers.net/cgi-bin/lessons/sort .cgi?searchterm=Music

Dozens of music lesson plans submitted by teachers. ☆☆☆

Composition

I WAS ASTOUNDED to discover that when he was a Beatle, Paul McCartney couldn't read music. I suppose good looks, attitude, innate talent, and luck must compensate for other failings!

For the rest of us—those who'll never find work as "the cute one"— the musical world is more approachable when we're better educated.

To call themselves educated, your kids really do need to know at least the basics of musical notation. They should know what an octave is. They should understand the difference between a treble and a bass clef. They should recognize a quarter note, and know how many beats in a measure. They should be able to find middle C on a sheet of music and on a piano. And they should be able to conduct a simple song in 4/4 time.

If their aspirations are somewhat higher, they'll certainly be better off if they learn to read, compose, and improvise music.

This section presents resources for teaching your children the basics of improvising, composing, reading, and notating music. Your children might not compose the next "Hey, Jude," but they might—at least—be able to read it when someone else does!

> **Compose:** From the Old French *composer* (*to alter*). To create a musical work.

Children's Music Web www.childrensmusic.org

Children learn about composers and composing music, among other things. An award-winning site. ☆☆☆☆☆

Figure 9.2

Children's Music Web: Fun music resources for parents and kids.

Wolfgang Amadeus Mozart

Perhaps the most famously homeschooled student in all the world is Mozart, the remarkable child prodigy who was taught by his father. When he was just four years old, Mozart was picking out chords and playing short pieces on the harpsichord. By the age of five, he was composing concertos and playing at the Bavarian court in Munich. Shortly after that, he was performing in Vienna and enjoying the beginnings of his worldwide fame as a composer and musician.

Music

Classical Music Composers   www.hnh.com/qcomp.htm
Bach, yes. Bacharach, no. An impressive list of classical composers and their work. Get your little ones hooked early! ☆☆☆

Classical Net   www.classical.net
While your kids learn about composers and musicians, you can study classical CD recommendations. ☆☆☆☆

Music Composition
www.mcrel.org/resources/plus/compose.asp
Music composition in the classroom and composers in electronic residence are both fascinating. ☆☆☆☆

Online Course in Songwriting
www.euronet.nl/users/menke/songs.html
A songwriter's handbook. Very helpful. ☆☆☆☆☆

Practical Guide to Musical Composition   esi24.esi.umontreal.ca
/~belkina/bk
Fundamental principles of musical composition, in concise, practical terms. Also provides guidance for young composers. ☆☆☆☆

Hotlinks

Children's Music Web
www.childrensmusic.org

Online Course in Songwriting
www.euronet.nl/users/menke
/songs.html

Music

Standard Notation Tutorials   www.netmusicschool.com/tutorials /notationsplash.html

▤ Both guitar and piano notation, from the great Net Music School site. ☆☆☆

Techniques of Musical Composition   portoweb.com.br/compor /defaultt.htm

▤ It's not updated often, but this guide to techniques of composition does a good job of covering harmony, harmonic movement, melody, counterpoint, techniques of motive variation, and more. ☆☆☆☆

Yahoo! Classical Composers   www.yahoo.com/entertainment/music /genres/classical/composers

▤ Introduces students to composers such as Bach and Mozart. Click on a period to find biographical information, pictures, and descriptions of various composers. ☆☆☆☆

Music Appreciation

IN OUR HOME, Dad is the music nut. There's nothing he doesn't know and few instruments he doesn't play, so the kids get much of their musical education just through osmosis.

Appreciate: From the Latin *appretiare* (*to appraise*). To understand the value or worth of a thing.

Cheryl Northrup is a bit more focused. "The arts have a high priority in our homeschool," says the homeschooling mother of seven from Lamar, Colorado. "When we lived in Denver, we could get tickets from the public schools to go to ballets, symphonies, plays, and opera, all for six dollars or less.

"Now that we're in a small town, we have taken our children, from a very young age, to community concerts and high school performances. The quality of these programs can be outstanding, especially in the larger schools.

I found, though, that in the cities you had to be more careful that you knew the play being produced—the public schools there are much less conservative than here.

"To prepare for these experiences, we read the stories of the opera or ballet, and sometimes listen to some of the music ahead of time.

"We don't forbid any kind of music in our home except that with explicit lyrics; however, the children are very aware of what we approve of and don't. They all have personal copies of good classical music, so there is always an option. One son in particular fell in love with Gilbert and Sullivan, so I buy those for him whenever I find one I can afford. In addition, all six living children have had lessons in various instruments, including piano, violin, and bassoon."

Homeschooler Ann M. Glass from Everson, Washington, has found that music has a soothing effect on her two children. She keeps her home filled with the sounds of music: "We play classical quietly in the background during school, and everything else—gospel, jazz, children's, band, and more—is played at all other times."

Ann sometimes takes her sons to concerts as well. To prepare them for the experience, they spend time in advance of the event discussing and listening to the type of music they'll hear at the concert. She is also teaching them concert etiquette and has five rules for behavior during concerts:

1. Sit quietly with hands and feet to yourself. Listen and learn.
2. Stay in one place without standing up.
3. Follow the action with your eyes.
4. Help others by setting a good example.
5. Show appreciation with applause—not yelling or shouting.

Has this experience had any impact on her boys' artistic or musical ability? "Yes!" she says. "My five-year-old tends to be a bull in a china shop, a one-man demolition squad. But he is extremely gentle with musical instruments. He handles them with reverence and awe! He has developed good timing and has a good

Musically Appreciated

Q: An unfortunate man went to work in a mine and, on his first day, fell down a mine shaft. When he finally hit the bottom, what musical note was he singing?
A: A-flat minor, of course!

sense of rhythm. When he can read and write, he is looking forward to beginning piano lessons."

All the education has paid off with her older son as well. "My seven-year-old was at the dentist listening to the music and exclaimed that it was Mozart. I'm still trying to convince the dentist that the child is not a prodigy! Both boys can listen to a piece of music and tell you something about it: the composer, the style of music, and the instruments used."

With the following helpful online resources, your children can be musical "prodigies" as well. Here's a short course on music appreciation that will soon have them listening to and analyzing music and understanding music history:

Hotlinks

CultureFinder Guide to Classical and Opera: Dictionary
www.culturefinder.com /artsresources/music /cfguide/dictionary

Gary Ewer's Easy Music Theory
www.musictheory.halifax .ns.ca

Music Arrangers
www.musicarrangers.com

Classroom   **www2.potsdam.edu/crane/campbemr/lessons**
Tremendously thorough lessons on analyzing music. ☆☆☆☆☆

Computer Music   **www.csse.monash.edu.au/~acb/music**
There's a lot to like about this collection of music information, but the greatest thing about it is the free music theory tutorials. Teach your kids about constructing and sequencing chords, inversions, and smooth voice-leading. ☆☆☆☆

CultureFinder Guide to Classical and Opera:
Dictionary   **www.culturefinder.com/artsresources /music/cfguide/dictionary**
From adagio to vivace: definitions of music terminology, with links to information on opera and classical music. Toss around these musical terms at the dinner table, and watch your little ones grow up brilliant. ☆☆☆☆☆

Gary Ewer's Easy Music Theory   **www.musictheory.halifax.ns.ca**
Just about anything anyone would ever want to know about music. Although it's a complete online musical theory course, there's stuff here for your younger kids, too. The definitions and transposition chart are worthwhile, but more than anything, you'll be interested in the MIDI files and illustrations covering the grand staff, notes, the

keyboard, note durations, measures, tones and semitones, major scales, key signatures, intervals, double sharps and double flats, harmonic and melodic minor scales, time signatures, tonic and dominant triads, key identification, triads and Roman numerals, octave transposition, triplets, key transposition, triad inversions, cadences, modes, other clefs, score formats, and more. ☆☆☆☆☆

How to Read Music   www.flash.net/~whitco/readmusicpreface.html
A self-contained online textbook on reading music, by composer Richard White. A bit lecture-y, but your older children will find the information interesting. ☆☆☆

Music Arrangers   www.musicarrangers.com
Want to understand music? This is your spot. Pages of lessons in music theory, notation, and other information that any musically educated person ought to know. ☆☆☆☆☆

Music Perception   www.ucpress.edu/journals/mp
For your brilliant musicians, here are research papers on how music is perceived. They're beyond most people, but if you have musicians in the house, they'll be intrigued. ☆☆☆

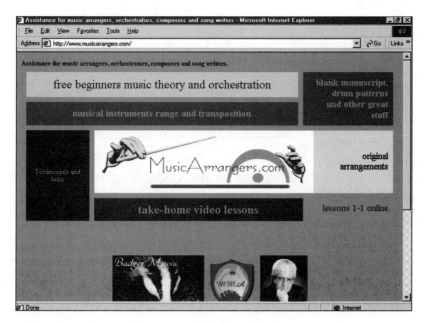

Figure 9.3

Music Arrangers: A musical smorgasbord, with online lessons.

Musical Fundamentals   www.guitarland.com/Music10/MusFund/toc.htm

A fourteen-module online course in pitch, major scales, note values and rhythms, meter, beaming, major key signatures, minor scales, major/minor relationships, intervals, triads, and modes, with guitar- and piano-specific applications. ☆☆☆

Sharon's "Tiny Hands" Music Tutorials   www.nspace.com.au /~mvisser/musictut

Music worksheets for children. The Australian author of the site writes: "We attend a music education class with our two oldest, but because of their spurning interest, [we] needed something to push them along a bit." ☆☆☆☆

Theory on the Web   www.smu.edu/~theory/toc.htm

This online course moves rapidly from the basics to fairly advanced theory. By the eighteenth lesson, your kids will already understand how to write inverted chords, parts, and nonchord tones. Whew. The site is illustrated with images and MIDI files. ☆☆☆☆☆

Musicianship

ALL CHILDREN ARE natural musicians.

Many mothers swear that their children respond to music even before they're born.

> **Instrument:** From the Latin *instrumentum* (*tool, implement*). A device for creating or performing music.

Shortly after her birth, my youngest daughter would sometimes be weeping with all the usual frustrations of babyhood, but when someone would begin playing soft piano music, she'd immediately stop and listen, rapt, to every note.

The moment children gain control over their little hands and feet, they begin to use floors, pans, tables, and cabinets as percussion instruments. And eventually every instrument in the house gets played—no matter how badly—by any child who has access.

On Creativity

"Creativity is more than just being different. Anybody can play weird—that's easy. What's hard is to be as simple as Bach. Making the simple complicated is commonplace—making the complicated simple, awesomely simple—that's creativity."

—Charles Mingus, American jazz composer and pianist

Teaching children to play music is mostly a matter of allowing their natural fascination to find a disciplined course. The following resources will go far in helping you direct that course. Here are some of the best Internet sites for teaching children to play musical instruments.

Allegro   www.talentz.com/MusicEd/Allegro.mv

The Music Education Search Site. Everything musical, sorted by instrument, grade level, theory and more. It ain't pretty, but there's a full musical education contained in these pages. ☆☆☆

Classical Guitar Home Page
www.guitarist.com/cg/cg.htm

Interesting commentary on guitar music of all different sorts. ☆☆☆☆

Danman's Music Library   www.danmansmusic.com

More than 160 free online video music lessons! Guitar, bass, harmonica, flute. ☆☆☆☆☆

Dansm's Guitar Chord Theory
www.dreamscape.com/esmith/dansm/chords/chords.htm

Beginner's guide to guitar and guitar theory. ☆☆☆☆

Net Music School   www.netmusicschool.com

Wow! This is the future of the Internet. OK, they're selling something (music lessons), but there's so much here that's free, and the free stuff is so well done, and even the commercial stuff is so cheap, that it's a can't-miss site. My guitar-playing husband bookmarked the guitar chord database. ☆☆☆☆☆

Hotlinks

Danman's Music Library
www.danmansmusic.com

Net Music School
www.netmusicschool.com

Piano on the Net
www.artdsm.com/piano

PlayMusic
www.playmusic.org

Music

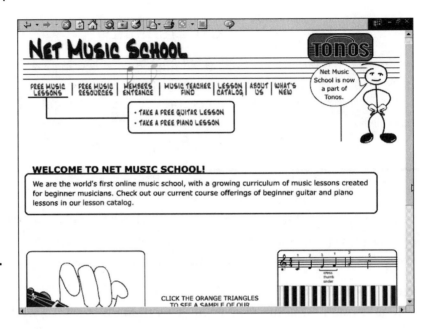

Figure 9.4

Net Music School:
Free lessons, find a
teacher and more.

Piano Answer Wizard   www.culturefinder.com/artsresources/music/answerwiz/piano

Answers to hundreds of questions related to piano. The site isn't taking any new questions, but the archive alone is an education in music. ☆☆☆☆

Piano on the Net   www.artdsm.com/piano

"I have accomplished only one lesson so far with my six-year-old girl, but I have previewed a couple others. The lessons are short and easy for kids to learn (and their moms too). The site starts with very basic information of notes and how to read music. My daughter enjoyed her lesson and has asked for more. The site layout is easy to navigate; you need only remember which lesson you completed last, then click on the next lesson. Once in, there are Next and Previous buttons to help you maneuver." —R.T. ☆☆☆☆☆

PlayMusic   www.playmusic.org

An online tour of all the instruments in the orchestra. ☆☆☆☆☆

Vocal Music

IS THERE ANY need to *teach* children to sing?

Heaven knows, I spend enough energy trying to get some of my kids to *stop* singing!

Despite my ongoing struggle for some peace and quiet in my noisy house, I recognize that there are plenty of times when disciplined singing not only benefits an individual voice, but also teaches the entire group of children to listen to one another's voices in order to harmonize and modulate their singing.

The only thing I haven't been able to teach effectively is the long *rest!*

The following resources will help you teach vocal music, and turn your little angels into a heavenly choir.

Sing: Akin to Dutch *zingen*, German *singen*, Icelandic *syngja*, Gothic *siggwan*, Danish *synge*. To create music with the voice.

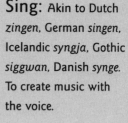

Music

Alexander Technique   www.alexandertechnique.com

This is in large part a commercial site, but it has a substantial body of free information that will have a positive influence on your and your children's singing. ☆☆☆☆

Choosing Songs for the Classroom

www2.potsdam.edu/crane/campbemr/curriculum/repertoire/song-select-1.html

There are some generally agreed-upon criteria that elementary general music teachers use to guide them in teaching singing and selecting songs. This site guides music selection. ☆☆☆☆

Folk Song Database   www.mudcat.org/threads.cfm

Database with words and music for thousands of folk songs. The bulk of this site is a discussion board about folk and blues. Search by title, full text, or keywords. ☆☆☆

Hotlinks

Frequently Asked Questions
members.aol.com/casawa/faq1.html

How to Sing: Posture and Breathing
www.geocities.com/Vienna/9423/sing.htm

How We Homeschool

"We like music and try to attend concerts and listen to a variety of music, from the Three Tenors to bagpipes to Gregorian chants. Taking lessons with our kids is a choice. My eight- and nine-year-olds are taking piano. I don't play the piano, so they have a teacher.

"I'm learning flute and my husband is playing the banjo. The others aren't interested right now, but the two youngest (3 and 5) play with the electronic keyboard when they want."

—**Susan D. Clawson**, homeschooling mother of five, Clearfield, Utah

Frequently Asked Questions   members.aol.com/casawa/faq1.html

Is Boyz II Men an a cappella group? You decide. This site has answers to pages of questions about vocal music. ☆☆☆☆☆

How to Sing   stjoes.iosys.net/Howtosing.html

A 1761 treatise on vocal music from John Wesley's selected hymns. Good advice, even now. ☆☆☆

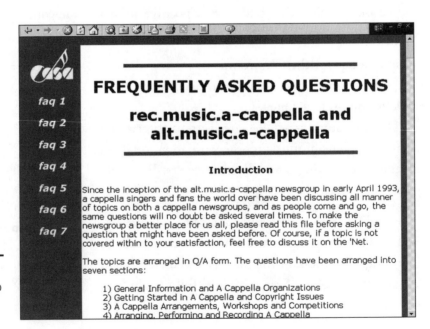

Figure 9.5

Frequently Asked Questions: What do you want to know about vocal music?

How to Sing the Blues   www.computrek-mn.com/hartke/blues.htm

A silly page about singing. Your children will smile. ☆☆

How to Sing: Posture and Breathing   www.geocities.com/Vienna/9423

When you finish the Posture and Breathing page, click the Tone Production link to learn everything there is to know about creating vocal music. ☆☆☆☆☆

Name That Tune   family.go.com/Categories/Education/Features /family_1998_10/dony/dony108songs/dony108songs.html

Why singing to your children is so important. Includes links to the lyrics of fifty classic songs for children. ☆☆☆☆

Social Studies Skills

I REMEMBER, WHEN I was in the sixth grade, spending half the school year studying Central and South America.

But we didn't study Central and South America, exactly. Our teacher decided, instead, to have each student pick an individual country and study it. At the end of the school year—the plan went—we would each do a presentation on our country, and somehow, magically, we'd all be educated about Central and South America.

So for several months I spent every waking moment worrying about "my" assigned country. I read every encyclopedia article, copied out all the entries in every book I could find, and searched every available magazine for the tiniest mention. I drew topographical maps and political maps. I traced the native costumes and photocopied pictures of local pottery. Then I wrote a turgid, boring report about my assigned country.

When it was all over, I couldn't have told you the name of any other country in all the rest of the Western Hemisphere. But I was the world's leading sixth-grade expert on a forgettable little place called French Guyana.

Somehow, I don't think my experience was the best possible way to learn about another culture.

The real goal of a social studies education is, in the words of the National Council for the Social Studies (www.ncss .org), to teach students "the content knowledge, intellectual skills, and civic values necessary for fulfilling the duties of citizenship in a participatory democracy."

What I learned from that experience was simply that I absolutely, unequivocally, completely *loathed* French Guyana.

When it came time to teach my own kids about our southern neighbors, I took an entirely different tack. Listening to the *Evita* CD piqued their interest. Silly competitions ("Want this jelly bean? Name the biggest country in South America") got them searching the globe. Earnest discussions about Cuban politics got them thinking.

Social Studies Freebie

"Learning Partners: A Guide to Educational Activities for Families" has reproducible activities, such as Let's Do Geography! and Let's Use TV! Call 877-4-ED-PUBS and request product number MIS 97-6518.

🏃🏃🏃 How We Homeschool

"Our school year starts in January, and we school year round. We have a structured curriculum but an unstructured day. We start our days with devotionals, as
school always goes better when we have a formal devotional.

"We start in the late morning or early afternoon, and go sometimes until ten at
night. The kids do a lot of work on the computer with educational programs. They
read without compulsion from the time their eyes open until they fall shut at night.

"We have a schoolroom, but many times they like to work on the sofa. We also
occasionally use the dining room table. I am in the process of adding some new
curriculum, and my goal is to have all the assignments determined in advance for
each subject. Then the children will know exactly what is expected next for each
subject. If they have to take extra time for some topic, the schedule is not messed
up. They just do the next assignment when they are ready for it.

"I don't keep track of grades. We do standard achievement tests each year, in
compliance with state law. If they can progress to the next grade level in a subject, they are allowed to do so. If they are behind a grade level in a subject, they
just continue to work on that."

—**Marji Meyer**, homeschooling mother of six, Renton, Washington

And guess what? All my kids know how to find French Guyana.

In this chapter, you'll be introduced to resources for teaching about
anthropology and sociology, civics, current events, economics, geography, minority groups, psychology, and social issues.

We begin, though, with resources that cover the entire spectrum of
social studies.

Adventure Online   **www3.adventureonline.com/home_portnew.asp**

⬛ Scuba diving, Alaskan Inuit dogsled racing, a kayak expedition, a
Pacific Crest Trail trek, and more: These Adventures Online deliver core
learning materials in math, reading and writing, social studies, and
science. Each subject or activity comes alive through a real-world
adventure. ☆☆☆☆

Brennan Family Study Center: History Resources

members.tripod.com/~JBrennan/academic/history.html

One homeschooling family's database of information. ☆☆

Hotlinks

Castles on the Web
www.castlesontheweb.com

Lonely Planet Destinations
www.lonelyplanet.com/dest

Social Studies
commtechlab.msu.edu/sites
/letsnet/frames/subjects/ss

Brookings Institution   www.brook.edu

Brookings produces research and publications in economics, government, foreign policy, and the social sciences. The information is good college-prep material. ☆☆☆☆

Castles on the Web   www.castlesontheweb.com

"Wonderful site to build a unit study around. Take your pick of topics: English history, medieval times, King Arthur, and more. This site has links, photos, Web pages, free greeting cards, tours, book lists, information on medieval studies heraldry, and more—all to do with castles. It even has a question-and-answer section and a list of contacts for vacationing in castles. One can only dream!" —A.G. ☆☆☆☆☆

Social Studies

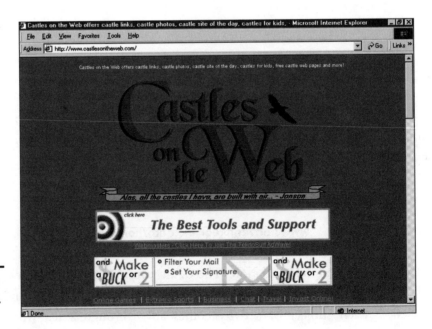

Figure 10.1

Castles in the Air: A medieval experience, on line.

Classroom Connect   www.classroom.com

▦ Each week, a new social studies topic with activities, lesson plans and projects. Recent topics included healthy habits and the Great Depression. ☆☆☆☆

Educational Web Adventures   www.eduweb.com/adventure.html

▦ Links to really well done Web learning adventures in history, geography, science, and art. These interactive educational Web sites include several social studies adventures. ☆☆☆☆

Internet Field Trip Library: Social Studies

teacher.scholastic.com/fieldtrp/index.htm#social

▦ Internet Field Trips are guided tours to the best of classroom-appropriate Web sites. Each field trip provides quick suggestions for using targeted Web sites to teach a specific topic. ☆☆☆

Kerameikos   home.earthlink.net/~dboals1/keram1.html

▦ Resources on Ancient Greece, including museums and archaeology. See related site at matrix.crosswinds.net/~dboals/keram2.html. ☆☆☆

Lonely Planet Destinations   www.lonelyplanet.com/dest

▦ Lonely Planet travel guides got me around much of Asia. This Web site is more of a very good thing. Get the scoop on what happens in most countries around the world, in a much more enjoyable format than any encyclopedia. An interactive, clickable world map allows students to "travel" to countries around the world. Click the slide shows for odd facts and information about environment, history, economy, culture, and events, along with beautiful photos of the people who live there. ☆☆☆☆☆

Ms. Hos-McGrane's Class Web   www.xs4all.nl/~swanson/origins

▦ Interesting social studies projects by several classes of fifth and sixth graders. Topics include Geotopia Projects (creating an imaginary country), Grandparents' Stories, Family Timelines, A Day in the Life at Terra Amata (a unit on human origins), Cro-Magnon Caves,

Creation Stories, Puppets, Folk Tales, and Ancient Civilizations. Links to related projects and resources are also included. ☆☆☆☆

Social Studies
www.pbs.org/teachersource/recommended/rec_links_social.shtm#pdr
A collection of social studies-related Web sites from PBS Teacher Source. ☆☆☆

Social Studies   **commtechlab.msu.edu/sites/letsnet/frames/subjects/ss**
A dozen or more lesson plans on a range of social studies topics. ☆☆☆☆

Social Studies   **www.csun.edu/~vceed009/socialstudies.html**
A great collection of resources, including lesson plans, strategies, geography, resources, multimedia, ancient worlds, museums, and organizations. ☆☆☆

Social Studies Lesson Plans
educate.si.edu/resources/lessons/sslist2.html
Lesson plans by the Smithsonian. ☆☆☆☆

Social Studies Lesson Plans   **www.col-ed.org/cur/social.html**
Very large collection of social studies lesson plans sorted by grade level. Not a very attractive page, but the information is useful. ☆☆☆

Anthropology and Sociology

THE STUDY OF us! What's more fascinating than all the history, culture, and language of human beings?

Anthropology and sociology are similar disciplines. Whereas sociologists study contemporary societies, anthropologists examine societies that existed in the ancient past and societies that are less technologically advanced than their own.

This is how Ann M. Glass, a homeschooling mother of two in Everson, Washington, introduces anthropology and other research-worthy topics into her homeschooling: "My sons are five and seven, and this is the third year that we've done research-type learning," she says.

"At first we used books. The boys chose the topic, and I broke it down into manageable chunks. Our resources were the library, our own personal library, interviews, and the Internet. My oldest would read the information aloud. The boys would dictate to me what they wanted written. As my older son became more proficient in writing, he began to do some of the writing for himself.

> ### Anthropology:
> From the Greek *anthrop (man)* and *logia (study)*. Study of the cultural and physical history of humankind.

"Our first topic was snakes. (Ugh!) We tacked white construction paper with headings on it all over the house. As we came across information, we wrote it on the paper under the correct heading using various colors of Sharpie pens. In addition to the research, we also read stories, watched videos, and happened upon a snake in our garden who was shedding his skin right in front of us!

"After we completed our book, I pasted the pages back to back. (If you write on both sides of one sheet, the ink leaks through.) Then I hole-punched the pages and hooked them all together with metal rings.

"The second year the boys chose the whole continent of Africa. Like a foolish, enthusiastic mom, I agreed. (Do you have any idea just how big Africa is?!)We pretty much did the same thing with Africa that we did with snakes. We divided the continent into its regions and compared the regions. We also tried new foods, played African games, and learned some Swahili. It was very much like a unit study, except we did a lot of reading and writing, as well as map work. This too was laminated into a book.

"This year we chose the Philippines. Instead of a book, we bought a large three-ring binder and divided it into sections: geography (maps, climate, land, provinces), missions and beliefs (Protestantism, Catholicism, Islam, and animism), history (heroes, World War II, presidents, symbols), culture (people, way of life, festivals, work, leisure pastimes), fauna (mammals, reptiles, sea life, insects, birds), and flora (edible and nonedible)."

Social Studies

Your own approach to anthropology and sociology may not be as wide-ranging, but no matter how you address it, the subject is immense, and it's well worth the effort to make it interesting.

In this section, we consider resources for anthropology and sociology, including ancient and modern cultures and social groups. You'll find related sections on minority education and social issues later in this chapter, and a section on world history in chapter 8.

Hotlinks

Anthropology Biography Web
kroeber.anthro.mankato
.msus.edu/information
/biography/index.shtml

Anthropology Tutorials
daphne.palomar.edu
/anthro/tutorial.htm

Fieldwork: The Anthropologist in the Field
www.truman.edu/academics
/ss/faculty/tamakoshil

Sociology/Anthropology
staff.uwsuper.edu/hps/mball
/soc_home.htm

Social Studies

Anthropology Biography Web

kroeber.anthro.mankato.msus.edu /information/biography/index.shtml

Biographies of more than 300 influential anthropologists. ☆☆☆☆☆

Anthropology Tutorials

daphne.palomar.edu/anthro/tutorial.htm

A collection of rigorous tutorials on physical anthropology (evolution and genetics) and social and cultural evolution. ☆☆☆☆☆

Art to Zoo: Japan   educate.si.edu/resources /lessons/art-to-zoo/japan/cover.html

Images of a People: a lesson plan from the Smithsonian. ☆☆☆☆

China   www.lee.k12.fl.us/schools/oak/Day1.htm

A series of lessons on China that integrates social studies, reading, language arts, and math. ☆☆☆☆☆

Fieldwork: The Anthropologist in the Field

www.truman.edu/academics/ss/faculty/tamakoshil

Learn how anthropologists work in the field. This site describes the many complicated steps of fieldwork while detailing the research of Dr. Laura Zimmer Tamakoshi in Papua, New Guinea. If you've considered doing some anthropological fieldwork with your own kids, you'll find this site most enlightening. ☆☆☆☆☆

How We Homeschool

"I will begin homeschooling my nine-year-old daughter in one month. I think one of the most interesting results that has come from my research into homeschooling has been my paradigm shift concerning education. Previously, I was content to leave education to the schools. When my daughter asked me to homeschool her, I told her I would look into it. Even at this point, while I'm still in preparation, I have realized that her education is my responsibility, whether she goes to a private school or is homeschooled. Now I have a strong desire to teach her so many things. Before, I didn't have that. So I guess I'm the one who has learned the most here, not her!"

—Jeanne Vellingas, homeschooling mother of one, Bowling Green, Ohio

Fossil Hominids   **www.talkorigins.org/faqs/homs**

This site is openly argumentative against creationism. Whether you're a Creationist or an anti-Creationist, you should be familiar with these arguments in order to defend your position. This site, part of the Talk.Origins Archive, discusses the evidence of human evolution, as well as the theory of creationism. The additional Web site and resource listings are also helpful. ☆☆☆☆

Gathering of the Clans   **www.tartans.com**

Devoted to all things Scottish. Includes information on Scottish folklore, history, and culture, and images of Scottish heraldry. ☆☆☆

History and Social Studies: Anthropology
www.studyweb.com/links/2046.html

Educational resources covering anthropological projects, studies, theories, and more. A large collection. ☆☆☆

Kinship and Social Organization
www.umanitoba.ca/faculties/arts/anthropology/kintitle.html

An interactive tutorial involving studies of various cultures and their social and familial taboos. This interesting tutorial on the ways

Social Studies

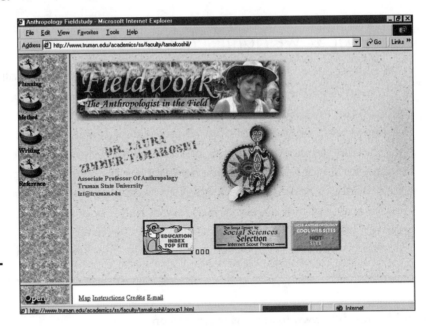

Figure 10.2

Fieldwork: Let a pro teach you how to dig.

various societies govern family structure is part of the University of Manitoba's excellent anthropology page. Your older children will be very interested. ☆☆☆☆☆

Social Studies: Anthropology

thegateway.syr.edu/index2/socialstudiesanthropology.html

Funeral customs, bound feet, and much more in this collection of lesson plans from the U.S. Department of Education's Gateway to Educational Materials projects. ☆☆☆☆

Social Studies: Sociology

ericir.syr.edu/Virtual/Lessons/Social_St/Sociology

Covers multicultural sensitivity and other sociological issues. Lesson plans from the U.S. Department of Education's AskERIC project. ☆☆☆

Sociology/Anthropology   staff.uwsuper.edu/hps/mball/soc_home.htm

Have questions about sociology? Here you'll find answers to the most frequently asked questions about sociology, with many links to various research, statistics, and archives. ☆☆☆☆

Teaching from Objects and Stories

educate.si.edu/resources/lessons/siyc/eskimo/start.html

Learning About the Bering Sea Eskimo People: a lesson plan from the Smithsonian. ☆☆☆☆

Civics

Social Studies

I'VE ALWAYS BEEN fascinated by government and the law, but it wasn't until I was in law school at a British university that I actually learned to appreciate the American political system.

As I studied English legal systems and began to understand the roots of much of American law, I became increasingly aware of the brilliance of the U.S. Constitution and the system of government it empowers.

I appreciated the Constitution even more when I learned, during my English Constitutional Law course, that England doesn't even *have* a document called a constitution. You can imagine how tough that made things at test time!

Unfortunately, the subject of civics—government, law, politics, citizenship—is given short shrift in many school curricula. As a homeschooler, you have the freedom to be sure your own children are well schooled in the workings of government and in their duties as citizens.

Gilbert Scott Wolfe, a senior planner for the City of Westlake Village, California, worries that too many teachers aren't teaching children what they need to know about civics. "I'm very happy to hear that education in government and civics is taken seriously by educators in the homeschool arena," he said. "I have seen that in many schools, the subject is glossed over or taught more as history than as a subject that has meaning for every citizen today. There is yet hope for our future!"

> **Civics:** From the Latin *civicus (citizen)*. Study of the rights and duties of citizenship, and the function of government.

I asked how his civics education affects his daily life. "As an urban planner," he responded, "the basic education I acquired in civics classes is actually used on a day-to-day basis. Knowledge of the relationships among federal, state, and local levels of government is very important in determining which programs and policies we can implement at the city level and which we might be precluded from enacting by state or federal law.

"A general knowledge of the Constitution is also important. Because planners write many local laws, we need to know how the Constitution serves as the basis for all of our laws at every level of government, as well as how various constitutional amendments protect the rights of citizens."

Parents who want to educate their children about civic duties, citizenship, the legal system, and American government can get plenty of help. This section describes the complex political institutions, laws, and customs through which the function of government is carried out. These resources will get your kids on track for political and civic involvement.

You'll find related sections on legal issues related specifically to homeschooling, in the section on legal issues in chapter 2. Sections on American history, the American West, and modern American history are located in chapter 8.

American Government Text   www.pinkmonkey.com

The full textbook, online. Register at the tremendous PinkMonkey Web site (it's free), then click on the Study Guides link to access the text. ☆☆☆☆

American Perspectives   www1.mightywords.com/freedom

Essays on each of the first ten amendments to the U.S. Constitution, free for download in PDF format. These essays, written by well-known authors such as Peggy Noonan and Coretta Scott King, provide fascinating insights on the history and application of the Bill of Rights. ☆☆☆☆

Civics Freebie

See a town meeting of renowned experts, local educators, and community leaders in *Creating Community: Engaging Students in Civic and Character Education.* Call 877-4-ED-PUBS and request Satellite Town Meeting #65, product number EK 0183V.

Social Studies

 *Patrick Henry*

Fiery orator and Bill of Rights campaigner Patrick Henry was a home scholar. He was tutored at home by his well-educated Scottish father, who was trained in the classics. Henry did attend a local school for a short time, but the future lawyer and governor of Virginia was mostly self-taught. Henry's memorable words "If this be treason, make the most of it" and "Give me liberty or give me death" were a catalyst to the American Revolution.

America Rock

genxtvland.simplenet.com/SchoolHouseRock/america.hts?hi

Remember that song about how a bill gets made? Here it is, along with great songs about the Declaration of Independence, the Constitution, great American inventors, the three branches of government, and more. This stuff is great! ☆☆☆☆☆

Art to Zoo: Winning the Vote   educate.si.edu

/resources/lessons/art-to-zoo/elections/cover.html

How Americans Elect Their President: a lesson plan from the Smithsonian. ☆☆☆☆

Center for Civic Education   www.civiced.org

Sample lessons, free instructional materials, and more. ☆☆☆☆

Government and Civics   tlc.ai.org/thistory.htm#GOV

Lesson plans, fact book, documents, and more. ☆☆☆

Government and Civics Links

www.geocities.com/Athens/Aegean/3446/government.html

This page from Coyle's Where in the Web, reviews civics resources and describes how to use them in your homeschooling. An excellent—albeit very conservative—resource if you want your kids to get politically involved. ☆☆☆☆

Hotlinks

American Perspectives
www1.mightywords.com
/freedom

America Rock
genxtvland.simplenet.com
/SchoolHouseRock
/america.hts?hi

**Justice for Kids
and Youth**
www.usdoj.gov/kidspage

Thomas Documents
lcweb2.loc.gov/const
/consthome.html

Social Studies

Government Resources
members.tripod.com/~JBrennan/academic/government.html

One homeschooling family's database of information. ☆☆

Justice for Kids and Youth   www.usdoj.gov/kidspage

Topics such as crime prevention, hate crimes, and inside the court-room. The U.S. Department of Justice and the attorney general's explanation of how to prevent prejudice is sure to cause controversy, but there's plenty of uncontroversial information here as well. Information for older kids covers crime, drugs, safe Internet use, and civic duty. ☆☆☆☆☆

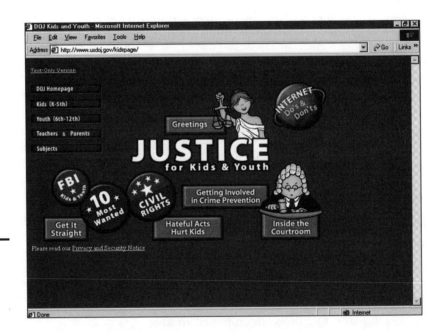

Figure 10.3

Justice for Kids: What the Department of Justice wants your kids to know.

Thomas Documents   lcweb2.loc.gov/const/consthome.html

The four biggies—Continental Congress documents, the Declaration of Independence, the Federalist Papers, and the Constitution—online and searchable. ☆☆☆☆

You Will Be a Tax Expert   www.progress.org/banneker/cintro.html

It's never too soon to start teaching kids who want money about the principle of taxation. This course is more about the philosophy of taxation than about the mechanisms of filling out a form. You'll probably want to discuss your personal philosophy of taxation with your kids before setting them loose. ☆☆☆☆

Current Events

DO YOUR KIDS know what's going on in the world?

Naturally, nobody knows *everything* that's going on. Newspaper and television news editors struggle all the time with trying to decide which of all the world's events most deserve space or time in their medium.

In the same way, homeschooling parents get the privilege of deciding which of all the thousands of issues being discussed around the world, which of the millions of events going on every day, deserve time and space in their homeschooling curricula.

Popular music? Movie stars? Substance abuse? The extramarital intimacies of celebrities?

Naaahhh . . . you've got more discernment than that! When *your* kids study current events, they can do so in a framework that encourages them to understand the reasons wars happen, the real issues behind the political "sound bites," the "correct" side of the abortion issue . . . in short, anything you decide to expose them to.

Current: From the Old French *courre (to run, course)*. Events in progress at the present moment.

A knowledge of current events is more than simply being able to recite the events of the day. When children thoroughly understand current events, they understand how those events affect the way people live.

Here's how we do it in our house: Every day, each kid is expected to read one nonfiction article and prepare to report on it orally. From time to time we have "speech" class, during which each child gives an impromptu talk on any subject we assign. The only ground rules: You have to speak for the entire time period (which varies according to the age of the child), and you have to tell us something we didn't know. The assignments are sometimes very specific, but lately we've gone to vague

Media and Homeschooling

"We use TV news, the Internet (a nearly unlimited learning tool), and periodicals to fill in the gaps in our homeschool."

—**Ann Crum**, homeschooling mother of two, central Arkansas

assignments, on topics such as "circles" or "light." For two minutes or so, the child speaks on the assigned subject, usually with hilarious results. They've all become quite adept at drawing analogies between the assigned topic and serious subjects about which they actually know something.

The resources in this section suggest fun ways to teach current events. They also provide sources for the news stories that explain the events that children need to be aware of in order to converse intelligently around *anybody's* dinner table! (See related sections on social issues later in this chapter and on modern American history in chapter 8.)

Awesome News   **www.awesomelibrary.org/news.html**
Current events and news by location or by topic. ☆☆☆

Current Events
www.weeklyreader.com/features/ce.html
For your young children, this site is the best: It's *Weekly Reader's* Current Events page! ☆☆☆☆

Current Events
www.eduplace.com/links/gen/current_events.html
NPR, CNN, and the rest of the alphabet. Links to lots of news providers. ☆☆☆

Current Events in the Social Studies Classroom
www.eduplace.com/ss/current
Every month, the Social Studies Center at Education Place highlights an issue currently in the news. The Current Events page is written at approximately a third-

Hotlinks

Current Events
www.weeklyreader.com
/features/ce.html

Learning Resources
www.literacynet.org/cnnsf

**New York Times
Learning Network**
www.nytimes.com/learning

**Newsweek Education
Program**
school.newsweek.com

Social Studies

grade level, but the issues are usually complex and will appeal even to older readers. ☆☆☆☆

Detroit Newspapers in Education   www.dnie.com

▦ Several dozen lessons, heavily oriented toward current events. This site will be useful, whether or not you're a Michigan resident. ☆☆☆

History, Social Studies and Current Events

www.geocities.com/Athens/Aegean/3446/history.html#CURRENT EVENTS

▦ Coyle's Where in the World site reviews these topical links and describes how to use them in your homeschooling. An excellent resource. ☆☆☆☆

Learning Resources   www.literacynet.org/cnnsf

▦ Web-based literacy instruction using current and past news stories from the San Francisco bureau of CNN. ☆☆☆☆☆

Newsweek Education Program   school.newsweek.com

▦ Every week, *Newsweek* puts a current events page on the Web. ☆☆☆☆☆

New York Times Learning Network   www.nytimes.com/learning

▦ The Gray Lady is online and designed just for kids. The *NYT* Learning Network has two areas of interest to homeschoolers: Teacher Connections and Parent Connections. Click the link to the Newspaper in Education program for curriculum guides, a calendar, a newsletter, and more. ☆☆☆☆☆

Legal News   legalnews.findlaw.com

▦ Brief news items, with links, about the civil rights, tort law, decisions before the Supreme Court, and much more. This is a great foundation for discussions about current political controversies. ☆☆☆☆☆

Twenty Ideas for Teaching Science Using the Newspaper

ericir.syr.edu/Virtual/Lessons/Science/Instruct_issues/ISS0001.html

▦ Use the newspaper to teach science. How's that for double duty? ☆☆☆

Social Studies

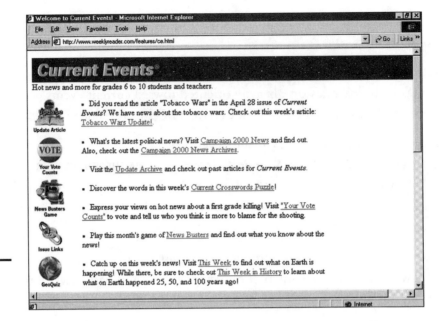

Figure 10.4

Current Events:
Up-to-date info
for your kids.

Economics

MY EDUCATION CAME pretty easily to me. Other than the lousy college semester when I had a cancer scare with my oldest son, I pretty much pulled easy A's and B's.

Until I took economics.

My college professors provided the demand. I had a tough time finding the supply. This was a *tough* subject!

Over the course of the semester, I read and sweated and agonized over economics, struggling to incorporate the philosophical "social" part of the science with the quantitative mathematical part. Eventually, one of my study buddies came to my rescue by explaining that the philosophical part meant that economics was a squishy science that really *couldn't* be quantified. All the math was just more philosophy; there *is* no real, measurable way to define the relationship between supply and demand.

Economics: From the Latin *oeconomicus* (orderly, methodical). Study of the production, consumption, and distribution of goods and services.

👪 *How We Homeschool*

"I have a notebook with records and plans. All my children have their own calendar-style accordion folders. They place all their daily work and a list of what they have read in the proper day. I empty it at the end of the month and make sure their records are complete.

"A schedule is important for me to keep on task, but we are very flexible. Everything starts out on the calendar and planner in pencil.

"A typical day looks like this: Breakfast. Math with Daddy if he has late hours that day (or math in late afternoon or early evening if he has early hours). Then run like crazy outside with the dog. Come in the house and read aloud several chapters (we are into unit studies). Discuss what was read, and ask and answer questions. Get on the computer for a spelling or keyboarding program. Play outside some more, exploring with nature kits. Come in and do science or history/social studies. Make lunch and eat while watching *Little House on the Prairie* or a video (*Anne of Green Gables* or *Veggie Tales*). After lunch is free exploring time—usually reading, games, imaginative play, or science experiments. Chores are done before dinner."

—Kathleen Thomas, homeschooling mother of four, Orange County, California

Oooohhhhhh . . .

Once I understood the principle, the nature of my study changed. I stopped worrying about formulae and definitions and began considering the philosophy. If I couldn't *measure* the effects of the "invisible hand," I could certainly *observe* it in commerce and politics and even my own personal finances. Once I understood what it was I was looking at, I saw it in everything around me. When George Bush described Ronald Reagan's economic plan as "voodoo economics," I had the grounding to form my own opinion. When the air traffic controllers struck, I had an opinion about how they should be confronted. None of it required math. It was all about the principle.

Dr. Anthony Davies is an assistant professor of economics and finance at Pittsburgh's Duquesne University and a strong supporter of homeschooling. He explains why it's important for children to

John Quincy Adams

The sixth president of the United States was schooled on the run. The son of President John Adams, John Quincy spent much of his childhood traveling on diplomatic missions with his father. At the young age of fourteen, he became private secretary to the American envoy in St. Petersburg, Russia.

understand the principles behind economics: "Economics is not a discipline that teaches one *what* to think," he says. "Rather, economics teaches one *how* to think.

"To master economics is to look at the world through eyes that are fundamentally altered. The economic thinker sees human actions as the results of motivations tempered by constraints. To the economist, all actions—no matter how irrational they appear—have a rational explanation if one simply takes the time to understand the motivation of and constraints placed on the actor.

"For example, the economist is not surprised when an increase in the minimum wage leads to lower earnings among minimum-wage workers. The economist knows that firms will respond to the increased cost of labor by—where possible—replacing workers with machines."

Dr. Davies clarifies the reason for my own frustration in economics class, and explains how you can prepare your middle- and high school–aged children for their first college-level encounter with economics: "The best preparation for studying economics," he says, "is at least one course in practical calculus. By 'practical' I mean that the student need not spend overly much time on learning *why* calculus works the way it does, but rather that the student be able to wield calculus like a tool—to be able to 'speak' in equations as one might speak in English. Easily 80 percent of economics students get caught up in the vagaries of graphing and mathematical manipulation such that they rarely get to delve into the more meaty issues of economics."

When it comes to practicality, says Scott Schickram, director of product development at Ranger Insurance in Houston, Texas, a solid economics education beats all. "Every day we are faced with decisions concerning what to buy, where to live, and who to work for. These are important decisions.

"In studying economics, I've learned that it's important to find the right information, consider different options, and not make decisions without considering all the choices. Fortunately, information can be found to help make good decisions about purchases or job choices.

"Economics has also made me realize how important it is to save and invest for the future. Seeing how different countries have grown their economies and become prosperous reminds me that 'compound interest' works and is one of the greatest miracles in the world."

Whether you're teaching younger kids about being wise consumers, educating your middle school-aged children about supply and demand, or introducing older kids to stock market analyses and economic indicators, these great resources will be useful. (You'll find related resources on our companion Web site www.hsfree.com, under the Business and Commerce heading in the Vocational Education section, and under the Financial Planning and Investing heading in the Home Management section.)

Hotlinks

EconomicsAmerica
www.economicsamerica.org

The Economist
www.economist.com

KidsBank
www.kidsbank.com

Secrets of Making Money
www.pbs.org/wgbh/nova
/moolah

Social Studies

CoreConcepts: Economics

www.pinkmonkey.com/coreconcepts/subjects/economics.htm

 A list of economics resources, arranged by subject. Register at the PinkMonkey Web site (www.pinkmonkey.com). ☆☆☆

Economic Education   www.emtech.net/economic_education.html

 Scores of very well chosen resources. ☆☆

Economic Resources

members.tripod.com/~JBrennan/academic/economics.html

 One homeschooling family's database of information. ☆☆

Economics

www.pbs.org/teachersource/recommended/rec_links_social.shtm#1

A collection of economics-related Web sites from PBS Teacher-Source. ☆☆☆

EconomicsAmerica   **www.economicsamerica.org**

A serious site, but the very well prepared lesson plans are written specifically for different grade levels—so you've got everyone covered. ☆☆☆☆

Economics in the Elementary Classroom

www.richmond.edu/~ed344/webunits/economics/econhomepage.html

This curriculum is tied to Virginia standards and teaches economic concepts throughout the elementary years. Interesting lesson plans. ☆☆☆☆

Economics Text   **www.pinkmonkey.com**

The full textbook, online. Register at the tremendous Pink Monkey site (it's free), then click on the Study Guides link to access the text. ☆☆☆☆

The Economist   **www.economist.com**

My absolute, undisputed, incontrovertibly favorite magazine in all of publishing-dom. And a good-sized chunk of it is now available on-line. This is journalism at its finest. ☆☆☆☆☆

Experts in Economics   **www.askme.com/cat/showcategory_888_xp_1.htm**

Want to talk directly with an expert who has volunteered to answer questions about this subject? AskMe.com is one of several expert sites on the Internet. ☆☆☆☆

KidsBank   **www.kidsbank.com**

Your children will love learning about money, banking, and economics with these cartoon characters. Easy to read, lots of fun. ☆☆☆☆☆

Secrets of Making Money   **www.pbs.org/wgbh/nova/moolah**

How to make a buck. A PBS special on the history and manufacture of currency. Really fun, very educational. ☆☆☆☆

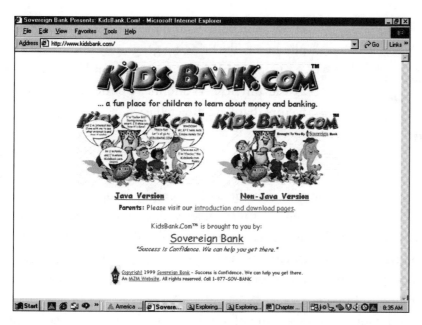

Figure 10.6

KidsBank: All about money.

Stock Talk   www.sia.com/publications/html/stock_talk.html

Irregular newsletters full of fascinating information on the markets. Worth the read. ☆☆☆☆

Teacher Guide to Economics and Business   tlc.ai.org/teconidx.htm

The Access Indiana Teaching & Learning Center contains lessons, resources, and more. A good foundation. ☆☆☆

What Is Currency?

educate.si.edu/resources/lessons/siyc/currency/start.html

Lessons from Historic Africa: a lesson plan from the Smithsonian. ☆☆☆☆

Geography

IF YOU WERE to name a country or a state, most of my kids could find it on the globe.

It's not because they're particularly smart (although I like to think they are). It is, frankly, because they've *been* there. Or if they haven't, they

Geography: From the Greek *geographia (earth + map)*. Study of the earth and its physical features.

know somebody who has. Nothing brings geography home like bringing geography home!

Geographers study the earth and its life, as well as the physical, economic, political, and cultural factors that have affected each.

Why is it important to study geography? T. Ulysse, a professor of geography in Brantford, Ontario, Canada, answers: "It is essential that citizens be well educated in the field of geography in order to participate fully in the improvement of their society. There are many important issues upon which the ordinary person must make choices every day. A good education, particularly in the field of geography, will go a long way toward providing future citizens with the tools to find their way in the vast jungle of modern society.

"Of course, I am speaking of a well balanced program of geography in which each student is given ample opportunities to:

On Finding One's Path

"Do not go where the path may lead; go instead where there is no path, and leave a trail."
—Ralph Waldo Emerson, poet

- develop his or her independent and critical thinking
- develop an appreciation for the multicultural nature of the society in which he or she lives
- understand the interaction and the interdependence that exist between human beings and the rest of the natural world
- understand that each of our actions affects our physical as well as our social environment

A basic understanding of geography is a critical component of your children's education. Not only will it earn them a spot on *Jeopardy!,* it'll also help them find their way across the country or around the world, knowing where they're going and why it's worth the trip.

The following geography resources look at the world up close and from far, far away. (You'll find related sections on Earth science in chapter 12 and on state history in chapter 8.)

Academic Subjects: Geography

www.wannalearn.com/Academic_Subjects/Geography

▤ Tutorials, instructional materials, and more from the WannaLearn site. ☆☆☆

Art to Zoo: Contrasts in Blue   educate.si.edu/resources
/lessons/art-to-zoo/contrast/cover.html

▤ Life on the Caribbean Coral Reef and the Rocky Coast of Maine: a lesson plan from the Smithsonian. ☆☆☆☆

Experts in Geography

www.askme.com/cat/showcategory_817_xp_1.htm

▤ Want to talk directly with an expert who has volunteered to answer questions about this subject? AskMe.com is one of several expert sites on the Internet. ☆☆☆☆

Flags of the World   fotw.digibel.be/flags

▤ An almost unbelievably large collection of flag images, flag history, flag rules, and other flag information. Read more than 4,300 pages of information and view more than 8,600 images of flags. The site is fed with news and images posted to the FOTW mailing list and with other contributions. ☆☆☆☆☆

Geography

www.pbs.org/teachersource/recommended/rec_links_social.shtm#2

▤ A collection of geography-related Web sites from PBS Teacher-Source. ☆☆☆

Geography Links

www.geocities.com/Athens/Aegean/3446/geography.html

▤ This Coyle's Where in the World site reviews these geography links and describes how to use them in your homeschooling. An excellent resource. ☆☆☆

Geography Resources

members.tripod.com/~JBrennan/academic/geography.html

▤ One homeschooling family's database of information. ☆☆

Hotlinks

Flags of the World
fotw.digibel.be/flags

JASON Project
www.jasonproject.org

Outline Maps
www.eduplace.com
/ss/ssmaps

Social Studies

GeoZone Quiz Center   www.maps.com/NEWSITE/DOCS/geozone.html

▊ Geography links, games, terminology, and much more at this site sponsored by maps.com. ☆☆☆

National Geographic Bee

Write National Geographic Bee, National Geographic Society, 1145 17th St. NW, Washington, D.C. 20036-4688. Annual registration deadline is mid-October.

JASON Project   www.jasonproject.org

▊ After discovering the wreck of the RMS *Titanic,* world-famous explorer and oceanographer Dr. Robert Ballard received thousands of letters from students around the world wanting to go with him on his next expedition. To bring the thrill of discovery to millions of students worldwide, Dr. Ballard founded the JASON Project, a year-round scientific expedition designed to excite and engage students in science and technology. An award-winning page. ☆☆☆☆☆

Maps and Charts   www.emtech.net/maps.htm

▊ Scores of very well chosen resources. ☆☆

National Geographic   www.nationalgeographic.com

▊ My kids' favorite magazine, and one of my very favorite Web sites. Click the Education link to access information on, among other things, the National Geographic Bee, hosted by Alex Trebek. Lesson plans, a teachers' store (hey, they've got to cover expenses, right?), and more. ☆☆☆☆

Outline Maps   www.eduplace.com/ss/ssmaps

▊ A wide collection of outline maps, including physical, political, and others from a variety of areas around the world. Print or download any of these maps for your personal use in activities, reports, or stories. ☆☆☆☆☆

Teacher Guide to Geography   tlc.ai.org/tgeogidx.htm

▊ The Access Indiana Teaching & Learning Center contains lessons, resources, and more. A good foundation. ☆☆☆

Three-D Atlas Online   www.3datlas.com

▊ Geography stuff and then some. Includes world news, research links for every country, free downloads, and the Geographic Glossary. This one is definitely worth the visit! ☆☆☆☆☆

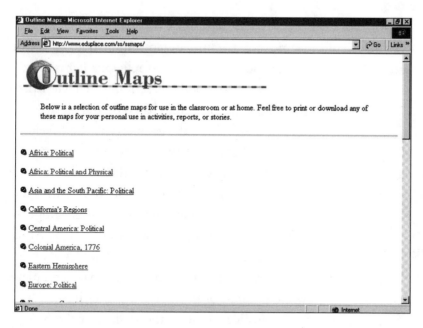

Figure 10.7

Outline Maps: Borders around the world.

WorldMap   **daniel.aero.calpoly.edu/~dfrc/World**

A downloadable map of the world, along with lesson plans for incorporating it in the classroom. ☆☆☆

Minority Education

BOOKER T. WASHINGTON is one of my heroes. He once said something that, when I read it, changed the way I thought about the world. The former slave and founder of Alabama's Tuskegee University said of his racist critics, "I will permit no man to narrow and degrade my soul by making me hate him."

Racism is an ugly, hurtful condition present in too much of the world. My blond sons experienced it while living overseas, when local kids would sometimes mock them with shouts of *gweilo* (*white ghost* is the kindly translation). And my beautiful daughter, who is Chinese, has experienced it in the United States from neighborhood children who pulled their eyes into a slant and repeated ugly, hurtful words about her ethnicity.

Social Studies

I fight racism, in part, by refusing to use the word "race." We are, it seems to me, all of the same race, the human race. And while our cultures and ethnic backgrounds and social systems and religious faiths vary, we do ourselves no good by ascribing characteristics to our fellow human beings based on the melanin content of their skin or the geometry of their eyelids.

> **Minority:** From the Middle Latin *minoritas* *(smaller)*. Segment of the population that differs from the rest because of cultural, religious, ethnic, or other characteristics.

I also fight it by trying to educate my own children about what is right. It's education that will, in the end, put an end to the cruelty of racism and the unhealthy divisions among us. Reformer Robert C. Winthrop once said of the condition of African Americans in the United States: "Slavery is but half abolished, emancipation is but half completed, while millions of freemen with votes in their hands are left without education. Justice to them, the welfare of the States in which they live, the safety of the whole Republic, the dignity of the elective franchise—all alike demand that the still remaining bonds of ignorance shall be unloosed and broken, and the minds as well as the bodies of the emancipated go free."

When each child understands the assumptions and practices and beliefs that make us different, the ugly notion of "racism" will die. In its place will rise an appreciation for and celebration of ethnic differences. You see it already in the St. Patrick's Day observations that have everyone, of any color, Irish for a day; and in the Mardi Gras and Fat Tuesday observations that make all the world Catholic for a day. More and more, I see intelligent people show respect for observations of Easter, or Rosh Hashanah, or Kwanza, or Lent, or Chinese New Year, or Cinco de Mayo.

Our cultural differences and religious faiths make us interesting, and they're worth studying. My Polish, Swedish, and English heritage influences my perceptions, just as my husband's French, Italian, and Jewish heritage influences his. Learning about our ethnic backgrounds, and recognizing how they affect our interactions and understanding of the world, makes it easier for us to communicate and helps us to appreciate the struggles of our ancestors.

Booker T. Washington

It was intense poverty that kept emancipated slave Booker T. Washington from gaining a formal education . . . but that didn't stop him from wanting to learn. The ambitious young man was born into slavery. At the age of nine, after his emancipation, he began working in a salt furnace, and later toiled in a coal mine. At sixteen, he enrolled himself in an agricultural institute and worked as a janitor to pay his expenses. Perhaps the most visible and influential African American of the nineteenth and early twentieth centuries, Washington founded what is now Tuskegee University.

No matter which minority you are a part of (for surely, there *is* no group that makes up a majority in a multicultural society) or which minority groups your friends and neighbors represent, the following resources will be useful in teaching your children to understand and appreciate ethnic and religious differences. (Related resources on genealogy, religious history, and world history are located in chapter 8; the anthropology and sociology section is found earlier in this chapter; the social issues section appears below; and you'll find a section on languages in chapter 11.)

African American Odyssey

memory.loc.gov/ammem/aaohtml/exhibit/aointro.html

A Library of Congress exhibit documenting the history of the U.S. civil rights movement. ☆☆☆☆☆

African American Perspectives

lcweb2.loc.gov/ammem/aap/aaphome.html

Panoramic, eclectic review of African American history and culture, spanning almost one hundred years, from the early nineteenth through the early twentieth centuries, with the bulk of the

Hotlinks

African American Odyssey
memory.loc.gov/ammem/
aaohtml/exhibit
/aointro.html

African American Perspectives
lcweb2.loc.gov/ammem
/aap/aaphome.html

Chinese New Year
harmony.wit.com
/chinascape/china
/culture/holidays/hyuan
/newyear.html

Social Studies

material published between 1875 and 1900. Fascinating historical documents, and lots of good links to related resources. ☆☆☆☆☆

Chinese New Year harmony.wit.com/chinascape/china/culture /holidays/hyuan/newyear.html

The most-observed holiday in the world: Chinese New Year. Teach your kids what the celebration's all about. ☆☆☆☆

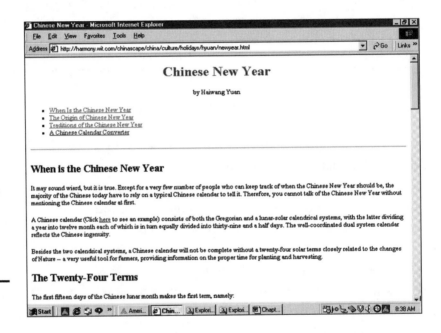

Figure 10.8

Chinese New Year: *Gung Syi Fa Tsai!*

Ethnic/Cultural Studies www.educationindex.com/culture

Everybody gets a mention here: Croats, Maya, Czechs, Estonians, Hispanics, Greeks, Russians, Native Americans, and, well, everybody! Lots of links. ☆☆☆

Foreign Language: Cultural Awareness

thegateway.syr.edu/index2/foreignlanguageculturalawareness.html

Discusses the immigration and integration experiences of many U.S. cultural groups. Lesson plans from the U.S. Department of Education's Gateway to Educational Materials projects. ☆☆☆☆

Languages and Culture   www.emtech.net/lang.htm
A collection of language and culture resources. Good links. ☆☆☆

Multicultural

www.awesomelibrary.org/Library/Materials_Search/Lesson_Plans /Multicultural.html
Lesson plans from Awesome Library. A very thorough collection. ☆☆☆

Multicultural Education   www.emtech.net/multicultural_education.html
Scores of very well chosen resources. ☆☆

Multicultural Topics

www.pbs.org/teachersource/recommended/rec_links_social.shtm#3
A collection of Web sites related to multicultural studies from PBS TeacherSource. ☆☆☆

Native American Indian Resources

indy4.fdl.cc.mn.us/~lsk/mainmenu.html
Impressive site with very good information about Native American observations, folklore, and society. ☆☆☆☆

Native Americans   www.emtech.net/native.htm
Carefully chosen Native American resources. ☆☆

Writing Black   www.keele.ac.uk/depts/as/Literature/amlit.black.html
Literature by and about African Americans. The works of Maya Angelou, Saul Bellow, Marcus Garvey, Mark Twain, and many more are introduced here. Unfortunately, a few links are broken. ☆☆

Psychology

ONE OF MY dearest friends and I spent a semester of high school researching the psychology of children's drawings.

We visited preschool and kindergarten classes, and asked children to draw pictures of their families.

Then we compared their drawings with some information we found in a book, and wasted about an hour of class time psychoanalyzing their artwork. "This child is abused," we proclaimed, "because the mommy in his drawing has no arms." "This child feels divided from her family because she drew herself in the bottom corner."

Oh, we were a dangerous pair.

If you want to raise children who are less arrogant than we were, closely supervise their access to the following resources. (Related information is located in chapter 13, under mental health.)

Psychology: From the Greek *psukhikos* (soul) and *logia (study)*. The study of an individual's behavioral characteristics.

General Psychology Online
astro.fccj.cc.fl.us/~jwisner/syllabus.html

An entire online course. Midway through the syllabus are links to class notes and homework assignments. This site—plus all the other resources available to you on the Internet— make up a complete course in psychology. ☆☆☆☆☆

K–12 Sociology and Psychology
members.aol.com/Donnpages/Sociology.html#Psychology

Lesson plans on general psychology, Freud, Jung, Skinner, IQ tests, personality tests, dreams, and more. Interesting links. ☆☆☆

Psychology Resources   www.educationindex.com/psych

More than a dozen reviews of psychology resources for educators. ☆☆☆

Psych Web   www.psywww.com

Lots of well-organized, interesting psychology resources. Includes two psychology textbooks and various psychology brochures. ☆☆☆☆☆

Self-Help Magazine   www.shpm.com

Articles, discussion forums, news, and much more. ☆☆☆☆☆

Social Studies: Psychology
ericir.syr.edu/Virtual/Lessons/Social_St/Psychology

A small collection of psychology-oriented lesson plans from the U.S. Department of Education's AskERIC project. ☆☆

Hotlinks

General Psychology Online
astro.fccj.cc.fl.us/~jwisner /syllabus.html

Psych Web
www.psywww.com

Self-Help Magazine
www.shpm.com

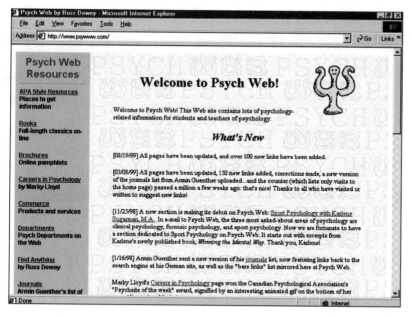

Figure 10.9

Psych Web: The mind, online.

Social Studies: Psychology

thegateway.syr.edu/index2/socialstudiespsychology.html

Several dozen lesson plans from the U.S. Department of Education's Gateway to Educational Materials projects. See a related link for Human Behavior at thegateway.syr.edu/index2 /socialstudieshumanbehavior.html. ☆☆☆☆

Social Issues

THERE ARE PERSISTENT social problems and controversies in the world.

How will you teach your children about feminism and abortion and poverty? What about world hunger? Human rights abuses? Response to natural disasters?

How will the next generation solve problems that our generation continues to struggle over?

They'll be able to do it because we'll teach them how. We'll give them a social conscience, and train them to think about solutions.

When our children take over, they'll be well equipped to make the world a better place. The following resources are a great start for their social education. (See related sections on community service, and values and standards, in chapter 4; and the section on minority education earlier in this chapter.)

Social: From the Latin *socius (companionship)*. That which arises from living in communities and groups.

Brookings Institution   www.brook.edu

A research and public policy organization that publishes papers in support of school choice, the Brookings Institution also takes a strong stand on many other social issues. Your children will definitely come away from this site with an opinion! ☆☆☆☆

The Foundation for Individual Responsibility and Social Trust
www.libertynet.org/first

A nonprofit organization dedicated to inspiring young adults to resolve political and social issues. Very interesting articles appear on this site. ☆☆☆☆☆

Food for the Hungry   www.fh.org

This site by a Christian hunger-relief organization will educate your kids about hunger issues. ☆☆☆☆

Literary Censorship
www.mnsfld.edu/~jgertzma/litcens.html

Banned books, and information about taboos, contemporary incidents of censorship, including school and library censorship, subversive doctrine; pornography and obscenity, and offensiveness to minorities and women. This is the syllabus for a college course; it's worth looking at if you want to teach your own children about the arguments for—and against—censorship. ☆☆☆☆

Mackinac Center   www.mackinac.org

Cultural advancement through policy research. This Michigan organization backs school choice and takes

Hotlinks

FIRST: The Foundation for Individual Responsibility and Social Trust
www.libertynet.org/first

Mackinac Center
www.mackinac.org

Social Studies

Figure 10.10

Food for the Hungry: What your kids should know about world hunger.

strong stands on a number of social issues. It's a completely biased, intelligent look at current controversies. ☆☆☆☆

News and Current Events   www.historyserver.org/HSSWeb/news.html
Lesson plans for current events–related issues such as the right to die, school violence, and child labor. ☆☆☆☆

Social Issues   www.wsu.edu/~brians/serious/social.html
Looking for controversy? Here it is. Find links to information about Greenpeace, Cambodian genocide, human rights, land mines, population issues, and much more. ☆☆☆

Women and History   www.emtech.net/women_history.html
Scores of very well chosen resources on women's history and feminism. ☆☆

Women's Studies
www.pbs.org/teachersource/recommended/rec_links_social.shtm#5
A small collection of women's studies–related Web sites from PBS TeacherSource. ☆☆

Chapter 11

Humanities Home

© PHOTODISC

I WAS CONTEMPLATING the other day the notion of senses. You'll agree, I think, that most of us experience the world with five physical senses. Many have suggested that intuition is a sixth sense. But how, I wonder, do you account for some other "senses"?

How do you explain rhythm? I watch my youngest child at 21 months dance and skip and twirl every time she hears music with a beat. She stomps her little feet and bounces her shoulders and pumps her arms in time to the music. How does she know how to do that?

And how is it that we can discern beauty? What gives some people a sense of harmony or balance or aesthetics? Why do even young children know the difference between young and old, clean and dirty, pretty and ugly?

Why do people cry or smile or feel joy? How do we know whether or not a thing is funny? What makes a sense of humor? What causes sensitivity?

And why can't dogs dance?

The humanities. It's what makes us human. It's everything and anything to do with the arts. It's language. It's poetry. It's literature and music and painting and sculpture.

In other chapters of this book, we look specifically at certain segments of the discipline called humanities: Chapter 5 introduces language arts, chapter 7 examines the visual arts, and chapter 9 covers music. In this chapter we look at the other arts: dance, drama, foreign language, journalism, and philosophy.

This chapter begins, though, with great resources that cover the entire spectrum of humanities education:

Arts Journal   www.artsjournal.com

I love this site. Very, very readable news digest for all the arts. *Arts Journal* says it combs through more than 180 English-language newspapers, magazines, and other publications featuring writing about arts

Hotlinks

Arts Journal
www.artsjournal.com

Humanities Net
www.h-net.msu.edu

PBS Online Arts
www.pbs.org/arts

Humanities

and culture. Includes direct links to many stories. Worth book-marking! ☆☆☆☆☆

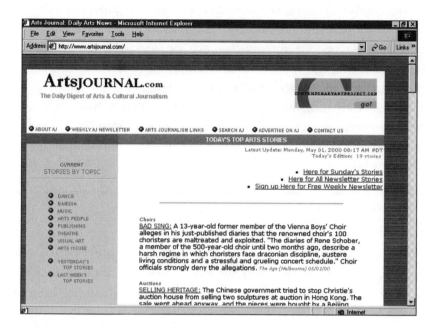

Figure 11.1

Arts Journal: News about the persons, places, and things that define culture.

EDSITEment   edsitement.neh.gov

Lesson plans and links to top humanities Web sites. Constantly growing collection of valuable online resources for teaching English, history, art history, and foreign languages. ☆☆☆

General Humanities   www.wsu.edu/~brians/serious/genhum.html

Another collection of humanities links. This one is not nearly as thoughtful or up to date as the others, but it's still worth considering. ☆☆

Humanities/Art   www.historyserver.org/hssweb/human.html

Several hundred lesson plans and links for poetry, literature, art, museums, music, dance, theatre, and the ubiquitous "general" re-sources—links to other people's links. If you ever run out of ideas, this is a great place to shop for more. ☆☆☆

Humanities

How We Homeschool

"I may not have started homeschooling because of deep-seated convictions or religious beliefs, or a desire to protect my kids, but I do have those things now. I believe that I am the best person to teach my children. The reason I know this is that teaching academics, although very important, is only *one* of a variety of necessary factors in preparing a child for adulthood. Why remove a child from a loving, nurturing home for the majority of the day, for the entirety of his or her childhood (the formative years in particular), to be taught and guided by strangers? It makes *no sense* to me."

—**Mary Batchelor**, homeschooling mother of six, Sandy, Utah

Humanities Net   www.h-net.msu.edu

News, articles, reviews, and other humanities-oriented information. H-Net is an interdisciplinary organization of scholars dedicated to developing the enormous educational potential of the Internet.
☆☆☆☆

PBS Online Arts   www.pbs.org/arts

If pop and folk art interest you, you'll enjoy this site. An eclectic collection of humanities resources from PBS, it includes resources on architecture, drama, dance, film, fine arts, literature, and music.
☆☆☆☆☆

Dance and Performance Art

MY MOTHER DREAMED of turning her daughters into ballerinas, so at the age of three, I was enrolled in ballet class.

I loved it. I'd skip and turn and whirl in the basement of the local Anglican church until, finally, it came time to practice for our annual recital.

Eagerly I'd drag my mommy to my dance classes, and we'd wait outside the "studio" door for the previous class to be dismissed. It was a

🎭 Serge Lifar

The famous Russian dancer was a self-taught success. Born in 1905, Lifar taught himself the intricacies of the ballet and grew up to become a teacher, choreographer, director, and dance historian. In 1929 he created the title role in George Balanchine's *The Prodigal Son*. Lifar was the principal dancer and ballet-master of the Paris Opéra in the thirties, forties, and fifties. He is known for his own works, the 1950 ballet *Phèdre* and his 1969 oeuvre, *Le Grand Cirque*.

dark, dingy place, that basement hallway, with low ceilings and bare light bulbs, but I didn't care! I was going to be in a recital, with my four-year-old ballet partner—a partner who was always late to class.

On the day of our dress rehearsal, my mommy took me early to dance class, and I stood there in that basement hallway, dancing circles around my mother, waiting for my partner to show up so that I could go practice my little dance.

As we stood there in the basement that day, a noisy delivery truck drove around the side of the church to the holding area near the top of the stairs to deliver some metal chairs.

It seems they were somewhat less graceful than the dainty little girls who arrived at ballet class early and stood around the basement hallway waiting for their partners.

Crash! Bang! Slam! The drivers dropped an entire pallet of metal chairs on the bare cement floor, and several of them came crashing down the stairs.

My mother says I didn't miss a beat.

Hearing the horrendous crash of metal chairs falling down a flight of cement stairs, I turned to her and asked: "Is that my partner?"

Clumsy children or graceful dancers, your children will get—at the very least—some cultural literacy out of these free resources. With any

> **Perform:** From the Old French *perfournir (to finish)*. To present entertainment before an audience.

luck, they'll also be inspired to dance. These sites discuss dance, as well as resources for the performing arts in general. You'll find related information in the drama section later in this chapter and in chapter 9.

ABT: Online Ballet Dictionary   www.abt.org/dictionary

The American Ballet Theatre has created this extraordinary dictionary of terminology that includes videos of various steps as they are performed professionally. ☆☆☆☆☆

Hotlinks

ABT: Online Ballet Dictionary
www.abt.org/dictionary

Dance Answer Wizard
www.culturefinder.com
/artsresources/dance
/answerwiz

Argentine Tango Dancing
home.att.net/~larrydla/basics_0.html

Online half-hour lessons that help you learn the Argentine tango. Covers simple tango step patterns, how to lead and follow, how to navigate around the dance floor, and more. ☆☆☆☆

Ballet Web   www.novia.net/~jlw

The Electric Ballerina link illustrates and animates complicated dance steps. ☆☆☆☆

Ballroom Dance I   cs.beloit.edu/Ballroom

An illustrated guide to the basics of ballroom dance. Covers leading and following, styling, dance positions, terminology such as *walking step* and *quick step,* waltz basics, cha-cha basics and moves, rumba moves, jive moves, tango basics, and more. ☆☆☆☆

Dance Answer Wizard   www.culturefinder.com/artsresources/dance

Attention balletomanes! Get answers to those nagging dance questions. This site responds to hundreds of questions relating to ballet and the dance. ☆☆☆☆☆

How to Dance   www.knowledgehound.com/topics/dance.htm

Links to a handful of really great lesson plans. ☆☆☆

Online Ballroom Dance Tutorial   www.dancetv.com/tutorial

Online tutorial and lots of dance tips for ballroom basics, waltz, foxtrot, East Coast swing, and more. ☆☆☆☆

Humanities

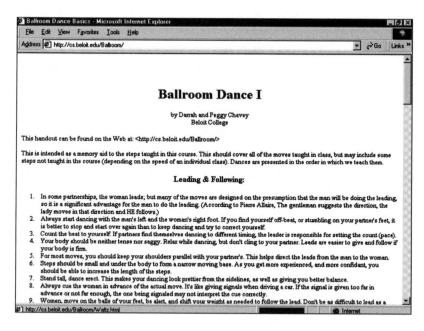

Figure 11.2

Ballroom Dance I:
Update your style
from Fred Flintstone
to Fred Astaire.

Performance Art

www.pbs.org/teachersource/recommended/rec_links_art&lit.shtm#7

A collection of recommended Web sites from PBS TeacherSource.
☆☆☆☆

Performing Arts Resources   www.educationindex.com/theater

A nice collection of links to dance, film, drama, and miscellaneous
forms of performance art. ☆☆☆

Drama

ONE OF THE best things we ever did with our children was take them
to see a live performance of *A Christmas Carol*. The performance was
part musical, part drama, and part slapstick. The kids loved it!

There's no better way to get your children really involved in a work
of literature than to let them see it live.

If you have a house full of children, you've got a great opportunity to
act out some of the dramatic fiction and historical work you've read in
other parts of your curriculum.

Joshywa Schrader, cofounder of the Colorado Art Theatre in Denver, Colorado, has some suggestions for getting your children involved in the dramatic arts. "The way I motivate people with little or no theatre experience is by using one simple word. I use the same word for adults and children. The word is 'play.'

> **Drama:** From the Greek *dran (to act)*. The portrayal of life or situations on the stage or in film.

"Children love to play, and adults are normally too self-conscious about trying something new, so all we do for a while is play.

"I understand it sounds strange. The reason I use this approach is because what a lot of people do not realize is that when they are playing . . . they are acting! Think of when children play Doctor, or House, or Cowboys and Indians. They are at the first stages of developing characters. They are, in fact, already practicing the art of theatre.

"So I first assign them a scene in which they will play. Literally, play. Once they have developed their own characters through their playtime, we only have to develop those characters, and then they are on their way. They feel comfortable because in a lot of aspects, they are not performing."

The following resources will inspire you and your family in teaching film and theatre in your homeschool curriculum. (Related resources on literature and public speaking are in chapter 5.)

Discovery Theater Learning Guides and Teacher Resources
www.si.edu/tsa/disctheater/disctech.htm

Use these Smithsonian resources as examples for preparing your children for theatrical performances. ☆☆☆

Film, Television, and Video
www.knowledgehound.com/topics/film.htm

Links to a handful of really great lesson plans. ☆☆☆

Internet Movie Database   **www.imdb.com**

I use this site all the time. All the world's knowledge about film, compiled in one giant, free database. A related link is Hollywood

Humanities

👪 How We Homeschool

"I worked from my son's special interests. For example, he loved wires, cables, stereos, speakers, and creating and building. I looked for ways to build on these in a learning experience.

"Volunteer work also proved very valuable. He volunteered at a local theater as a set builder, then as a set designer, then as the sound engineer (playing the music), then as the sound designer (picking the right music), and finally as the sound manager (putting it all together). I had friends come and watch him. He came down at intermission to meet them and was so proud."

—Joyce Dumire, homeschooling mother of one, Akron, Ohio

.com (www.hollywood.com), but IMDB is focused more on film lore and less on show times. ☆☆☆☆☆

Lesson Plan Exchange   artemis.austinc.edu/acad
/educ/atpweb/lessonplan/lesson.htm
For teachers of the theatre, this is a wonderful place to share ideas and learn new techniques. A terrific database of lesson plans. ☆☆☆☆☆

Mr. William Shakespeare and the Internet
daphne.palomar.edu/shakespeare
Complete annotated guide to the scholarly Shakespeare resources available on the Internet. Includes Charles and Mary Lamb's wonderful *Tales from Shakespeare,* indisputably the premier work for introducing Shakespeare to children. ☆☆☆☆☆

National Children's Film Festival
www.childrensfilmfest.org
Children aged nine to eighteen are invited to contribute their own films to this international festival dedicated to young people creating films and videos, expressing what is of interest and significance to

Hotlinks

Internet Movie Database
www.imdb.com

Lesson Plan Exchange
artemis.austinc.edu/acad
/educ/atpweb/lessonplan
/lesson.htm

Mr. William Shakespeare and the Internet
daphne.palomar.edu
/shakespeare

Teach with Movies
www.teachwithmovies.org

Humanities

them. Download an entry form from the Web site, and read up on how to create your own movies. ☆☆☆☆

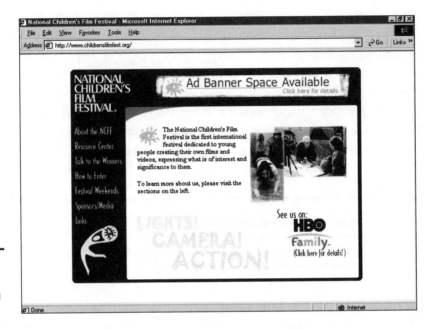

Figure 11.3

National Children's Film Festival: Find the next Spielberg in your household.

Teach with Movies   www.teachwithmovies.org

If you're raising film buffs, you'll enjoy this site. Use film to entertain and educate about history, noteworthy people, ethical issues, and other cultures. ☆☆☆☆☆

Theatre Lesson Plan Exchange   www.geocities.com/Shalyndria13

Blindingly bad graphics, but the lesson plans, warm-ups, inputs, and other resources are worth the eye damage. ☆☆☆☆

Foreign Language

WHEN MY OLDEST child was 18 months old, we moved to Taiwan. I'd had a few weeks of intensive Chinese instruction before we arrived, so I was able to at least buy groceries and find the correct bus.

To maintain my visa, I had to enroll in a Chinese-language class—something I was actually looking forward to. After all, I'd studied French for four years and assumed I'd have no trouble picking up a third language. So off I went to my daily Chinese class, while my baby spent the better part of his days playing with the Chinese children in our little neighborhood. I worked and worked. He played and played. Within two months, guess who was the fluent Chinese speaker in the family?

Eventually, my baby became so fluent at Chinese that he refused to speak English at home. As a consequence, my Chinese had to improve if I wanted to speak to my own son.

> **Foreign:** From the Latin *foranus (outside)*. That which is unfamiliar or nonnative.

Mark Thorne is a fourth-year Latin student at Southwest Missouri State University. He has at least a passable ability in seven languages. Upon graduation, he hopes to become a professor of Latin and ancient history. A strong supporter of homeschooling, Mark offers this encouragement to parents teaching their children another language. "Having come this far, I can truly attest to how good it feels to know something of another language. It's a very liberating feeling, because you no longer feel mentally confined to this continent."

As you might expect, he believes Latin is particularly useful for people who are getting started in language studies. "Even the most basic knowledge of history and languages of the past is incredibly useful," he says. "For starters, a study of Latin forces students to look carefully at their own language, both at its structure and at how it works. They communicate more clearly and effectively when they are more sensitive to how languages function.

"It has been said that just under half of English vocabulary comes from Latin (albeit largely through French); knowledge of Latin, therefore, can sometimes help you figure out what words mean, even if you have never heard or read them before. This has obvious benefits for someone taking such tests as the SAT, ACT, or GRE.

"Latin comes in really handy when traveling. It allows you to read what's written on medieval paintings, on tombstones, beneath statues of famous heroes, on cornerstones of buildings, and even on the backs of paper money!

Humanities

"Latin is the foundation of all Romance languages. If you speak or come into contact with anything related to French, Italian, Spanish, Portuguese, or Romanian (and if you speak English, that includes you), Latin matters to you whether you realize it or not. *Valete!*"

When your baby is ready to speak—or sign—another language, these resources are here to help:

AltaVista Translations   babelfish.altavista.digital.com/cgi-bin/translate

"This page will translate text or an entire Web site from English to French, German, Italian, Portuguese, or Spanish, or from any of those to English. It's very literal, so it's not of much use for anything too complicated, but it's fun to play with." —L.H. ☆☆☆☆

Hotlinks

AltaVista Translations
babelfish.altavista.digital
.com/cgi-bin/translate

**American Sign Language
Browser**
commtechlab.msu.edu/sites
/aslweb/browser.htm

Berlitz
www.berlitz.com

**Free Online Language
Courses**
rivendel.com/~ric
/resources/course.html

American Sign Language Browser
commtechlab.msu.edu/sites/aslweb/browser.htm

"Our favorite. Has little video clips of a person actually doing the signs. A very easy site to navigate and understand." —S.C. ☆☆☆☆☆

ASL Fingerspelling   some.where.com/scott.net/asl

"Fingerspelling dictionary, converter, and quiz, along with a stand-alone software program for Macintosh users." —R.T. ☆☆☆☆

Basic Dictionary of ASL Terms
www.masterstech-home.com/ASLDict.html

"Here are a few American Sign Language terms to help you communicate with a person who signs but does not hear. Included is the basic alphabet and numbers one through ten. Includes animated and text versions of the dictionary entries as well as animated and photographed finger spelling." —R.T. ☆☆☆☆

Berlitz   www.berlitz.com

The famous international language school offers lots of fun cultural tips, and occasionally free language lessons, on its site. ☆☆☆☆

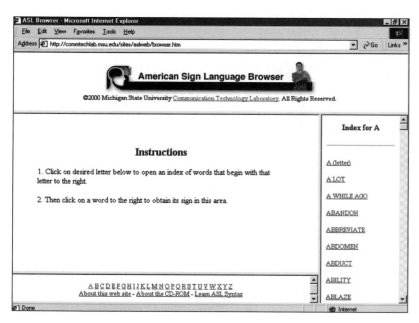

Figure 11.4

American Sign Language Browser: Words and phrases are never more than a link away.

English Page   www.englishpage.com

Online lessons for intermediate and advanced ESL students. Weekly lessons on conjugations, tenses, irregular verbs, and all the other things non-native speakers find so puzzling about English. ☆☆☆☆

Foreign Languages for Travelers   www.travlang.com/languages

An award-winning page containing mini language lessons in more than seventy different languages. ☆☆☆☆☆

Free Online Language Courses
rivendel.com/~ric/resources/course.html

"This site provides links to online courses and tutorials in languages from Ainu to Xhosa, including the more usual French, German, and Spanish. Icelandic, anyone?" —L.H. ☆☆☆☆☆

French Revision   www.canonave.ndirect.co.uk/gcse

This is how the Brits study French, in preparation for the national GCSE examination (comparable to the American GED). Speech, grammar, writing, and more. It's all detailed on this extensive, well-written site. ☆☆☆☆

Humanities

♟♟♟ *How We Homeschool*

"I have taught, and plan to teach, all my children at home. I have a supportive and talented husband, who speaks three foreign languages and plays the piano, so when the time comes, I plan to lean on him for help in instructing the children in a foreign language (or more!) and music. We both sing, and the children love to sing with us."

—**Mary Batchelor**, homeschooling mother of six, Sandy, Utah

Language Trade   www.languagetrade.com
"Connect with native speakers of a language you are studying who wish to learn your native tongue. You can be listed under more than one language if you like. I signed up as a native speaker of English hoping to learn Spanish, and received a list of 32 potential chat partners." —M.B. ☆☆☆☆

Learn Spanish   www.studyspanish.com/tutorial.htm
A great site. Your kids can learn Spanish at home with this free on-line tutorial. ☆☆☆☆☆

Sign Language Dictionary   www.handspeak.com
"Animated photographs of finger spelling and words. Includes the numbers one through ten. Pretty cool." —R.T. ☆☆☆☆

Sign Language Teacher   home.att.net/~aslslant
My kids have known how to fingerspell since they were young. It comes in handy during church when I have to tell someone to stop elbowing a sibling. Download this piece of software to get your own kids started on American Sign Language. ☆☆☆☆☆

Journalism

I BECAME A journalist because I thought I could change the world. At the beginning of my career, I was full of optimism and hope. I expected

Humanities

that my deep sense of right and wrong—and my sharp-tipped pen—would somehow right all the injustices in the world and make humankind happier and better.

Over the years I've grown a thick layer of cynicism about my profession. I've found that few reporters are willing to admit to having biases—worshiping, as they do, at the altar of "objectivity." Yet they filter their news choices through a net that screens out or mocks any point of view that doesn't adhere to their own worldview—all the while protesting that they're simply being objective.

> **Journalism:** From the Middle French *journal (daily)*. The collection, writing, and presentation of news and opinion.

It was an argument I engaged in frequently while in J-school. My professors didn't see it the same way. Journalism has to be objective, they'd insist. "Why?" I'd ask. The only answer I ever got: Because Sears won't advertise in controversial newspapers, and Sears pays the bills.

So American journalism limps along, pretending objectivity while being completely unable to avoid taking a stance.

Case in point: Because journalists tend to be low paid, many are the second earner in a two-income household. This situation often means that their children end up in low-level day care facilities. Even so, I was a little surprised to see a major news story in a very conservative newspaper decrying the evils of a government that doesn't provide free day care for two-income families.

The author of the story, who found a multitude of sources supporting what was clearly her personal concern, gave just a cursory, derisive nod to the idea that many working families are just as passionate about wanting a *break* from their tax burden so they can stay home and raise their *own* children.

That's why I appreciate the British view of journalism. Objectivity is rarely the goal. Publications are openly biased. They make no pretense of being able to adequately represent the argument against whatever issues they support. Readers know what they're reading and choose their publications accordingly.

Humanities

🚶 How We Homeschool

"I began scheduling after reading a book called *Managers of Their Homes*. I started by doing some simple things, such as posting our breakfast and lunch menu. We have the same thing for these two meals each week. This cut down on arguments because the menu runs Monday through Saturday, so my children each got three days on the list to pick what they wanted. We eat breakfast whenever they both wake up; lunch is always at 12:30.

"Then we moved up to scheduling room cleaning. Cleaning is done after breakfast and before any 'fun stuff' (outdoor play, games, or computer time). We are working toward a schedule for the entire day, but it is a long process. I can measure the success of scheduling by the lack of fighting. When my kids are bored, they pick at each other. But when I actually follow my schedule, we have wonderful, productive days.

"These little accomplishments mean the world to me because they show the people I care about that I can handle homeschooling and that the children will learn from me. But I have to put effort into it as well."

—**Shea Wilkinson**, homeschooling mother of two, Huntington, West Virginia

Humanities

Fortunately, for *my* vision of how journalism ought to operate, the Internet is making it possible to economically produce any kind of publication: opinionated, outrageous, intelligent, investigative, heterodox, orthodox, devout . . . all of it espousing a particular worldview, and all of it causing readers to actually *think* about their beliefs and perspectives.

Journalist Linda Sherwood believes there are other good reasons for exposing your children to the craft of journalism. Linda, who works for two northern Michigan weekly newspapers, is the editor of Small Town Press (smalltownpress.homestead.com), a Web site for community journalists. She explains how the study of journalism and mass media teach life skills: "Journalism helps you understand the way an article or a six-second TV clip becomes news," she says. "It helps you evaluate and understand a situation more than the average person can.

"I work from home and often take my children with me on assignment. Often the assignment is something I would be doing with my family anyway. Maybe we will go to a parade where I take a few photos for the paper or to a community event where I scribble a few notes and snap some pictures while enjoying the event with my family.

"Sometimes my articles change what happens just because the public becomes aware of it. It's amazing the change in atmosphere when a board or council realizes there is a reporter in the room. Things aren't done in secrecy."

Alex Johnson, an editor and producer for MSNBC.com, makes use of his journalism training every day. The Redmond, Washington–based journalist says that although he can't answer for other people, "I can tell you how I use my journalism background in daily life.

"I'm essentially a shy, quiet person. But that won't fly if you're a reporter, whose job—when you break it down—is to confront and ask people questions they don't want to be asked. Learning how to do this has made it a lot easier for me to deal one on one with people in general.

"Since journalists are trained to find ways to keep people talking, you become more adept at conversation because you know how to listen. If you can't listen attentively, you'll never be a good reporter. If nothing else, being a journalist means you can always find someone to talk to!"

If your children are ready to gain a journalism education of their own, here's help. Related resources for developing research skills are found in chapter 4. You'll also find links to writing and reading materials in chapter 5. The following resources cover print, broadcast, and electronic journalism.

E-ZineUniversity   www.ezineuniversity.com/courses

Electronic magazines are the most fascinating new developments in journalism. Turn your kids into the Matt Drudge of your neighborhood with this free online course in writing and marketing e-zines. They'll learn marketing, preparation and research, planning and development, content development and writing, publishing and mailing list management, marketing and promotion, developing advertising copy, and creating profits with an e-zine.
★★★★☆

Free Press Releases

www.netgain.co.nz/press_minicourse.htm

One of the most unfortunate elements of journalism is the ubiquitous press release. Whether you write them or read them, they're part of the business. Here's a free online course in writing effective press releases—the kind that make it beyond the first wastebasket of the newsroom. ☆☆☆☆☆

Jobs Page   www.freep.com/jobspage/high

This is a home for high school journalists who are too savvy (or too impatient) to wait until they get out of college to start taking lessons with the professionals. A great, useful site for anyone learning the business. ☆☆☆☆☆

Journalism   www.pbs.org/teachersource/recomended

/rec_links_art&lit.shtm#3

A collection of recommended Web sites from PBS TeacherSource. ☆☆☆☆

Journalism Lesson Plans

pierce.gp.k12.mi.us/~taylora/journalism

Lesson plans for journalism students, written by a middle school journalism teacher. ☆☆☆☆☆

Language Arts: Journalism

ericir.syr.edu/Virtual/Lessons/Lang_arts/Journalism

These lesson plans will appeal to younger children interested in journalism. ☆☆

Media History Project   www.mediahistory.com

Learn the history of media, from petroglyphs to pixels. OK, it's not quite that ambitious. But almost. The Time Line link is especially interesting. The site appears to be infrequently maintained. ☆☆☆☆

Hotlinks

E-ZineUniversity
www.ezineuniversity.com
/courses

Journalism Lesson Plans
pierce.gp.k12.mi.us
/~taylora/journalism

Only a Matter of Opinion?
library.thinkquest.org/50084

Project for Excellence in Journalism
www.journalism.org

Television Production
www.cybercollege.com
/tvp_ind.htm

Humanities

Only a Matter of Opinion?   library.thinkquest.org/50084

All about writing editorials and opinion pieces. This site is slow to load, but it contains an excellent discussion of editorials, commentary and columns, and editorial cartoons. ☆☆☆☆☆

Project for Excellence in Journalism   www.journalism.org

An initiative by journalists concerned about the purpose and standards of the American press. This is a project of the Columbia University Graduate School of Journalism—arguably the second-best J-school in the world. Click the daily briefing link for access to the most important journalism publications around, as well as news and commentary by and about the media.
☆☆☆☆☆

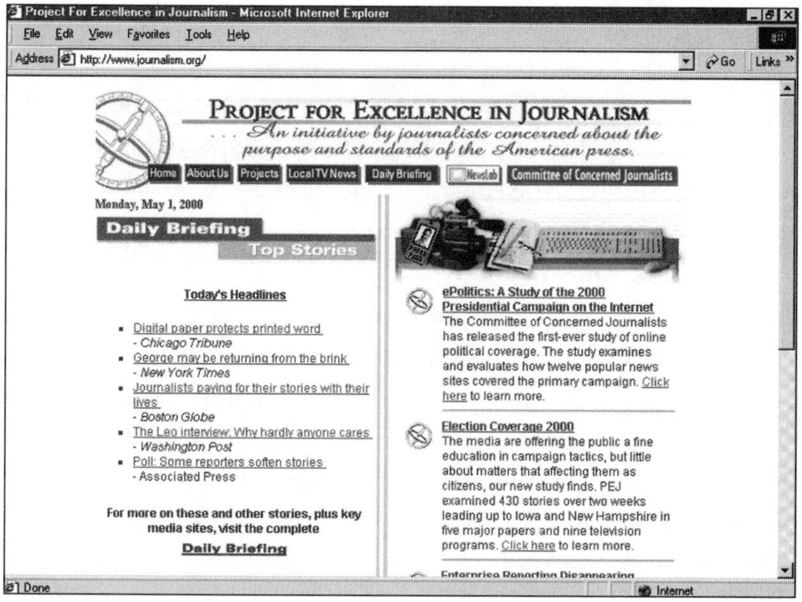

Figure 11.5

Project for Excellence in Journalism: Write on!

Humanities

Television Production   www.cybercollege.com/tvp_ind.htm

A comprehensive online course in studio and field production. If your kids are fascinated by the tube, they'll appreciate this free class. ☆☆☆☆☆

Philosophy

THE DISCIPLINE called philosophy crosses several curriculum areas. From Greek beliefs about logical thought to Heidegger's and Sartre's existentialist revolt, philosophy covers logic, reason, art, communication, reading, writing, critical thought, and theology.

Steve Naragon is an associate professor of philosophy at Manchester College North in Manchester, Indiana. He has a theory about how philosophy is useful in everyday life: "Studying philosophy brings with it a great many advantages," he says. "Studying philosophy sharpens your ability to understand and evaluate arguments, to make fine conceptual distinctions, and to clear up any number of misunderstandings that result from a misuse of language or logic. In this regard, philosophers can be quite handy to have around.

> **Philosophy:** From the Greek *philosophos (lover of wisdom)*. The discipline that considers core logic, aesthetics, and ethics.

"The study of philosophy is most valuable, however, in the course of one's own life. Philosophy helps us think through the really hard questions—What is the meaning of life? Is there one? What does it mean to be human? What is the good life? What can be known, and what lies beyond human reason? It helps us do this with a clarity and precision that lets us get much closer to something resembling an answer. (With some of these questions, of course, studying philosophy is a bit like buying a four-wheel drive truck: Instead of getting stuck as soon as you leave the road for the backcountry, it lets you first get a good twenty miles into the middle of nowhere, and then it leaves you stranded. . . .)

"Philosophy helps instill us with humility, both moral and intellectual; ever since Socrates, it has been demonstrating to us how little we actually know about a great many things (with the lesson that we ought not to be too self-satisfied, nor push our views on others too vigorously). Philosophy helps us debunk much of the nonsense offered up to us by the wider culture. Philosophy can help us find some ground or center for our beliefs and our sense of self, and it can help us articulate and act upon our particular conception of the good. If the Socratic claim that

Humanities

𝕏𝕏𝕏𝕏 *How We Homeschool*

"We have two notebooks. One has ideas and plans; the other is full of activities for the girls to do. It includes wipe-off pages and pages from workbooks. We also have flash cards in little rings. We have two shelves just for the girls' homeschooling stuff. We are trying to do some unschooling while they are still young, so I don't push regular times to do all this. We do it whenever and only if the girls are willing. I wish schedules were better for my family, but they aren't, so we don't do them! Every day is so full of new ideas and different things. Maybe that is why my house looks so lived in!"

—**Marrenzy Brown**, homeschooling mother of two preschoolers, Indiana

'The unexamined life is not worth living' rings true for you, then philosophy is indispensable."

The following resources will help you get a handle on philosophy:

Academic Subjects: Philosophy
www.wannalearn.com/Academic_Subjects/Philosophy
▤ Tutorials, instructional materials, and more from the WannaLearn site. ☆☆☆

Experts in Philosophy
www.askme.com/cat/showcategory_887_xp_1.htm
▤ Want to talk directly with an expert who has volunteered to answer questions about this subject? AskMe.com is one of several expert sites on the Internet. ☆☆☆☆

Internet Encyclopedia of Philosophy   **www.utm.edu/research/iep**
▤ This site has a way to go before it's "encyclopedic," but the articles available are worth reading. ☆☆☆☆

Philosophy   **philosophy.about.com/education/philosophy**
▤ Lots of information about well-known philosophers, schools of philosophical thought, ethics, existentialism, and much more. Resources collected at About.com. ☆☆☆☆

Humanities

Philosophy   **www.educationindex.com/phil**

Lots of reviewed links on philosophy; really well done. ☆☆☆

Hotlinks

The Republic
classics.mit.edu/Plato
/republic.html

**Stanford Encyclopedia of
Philosophy**
plato.stanford.edu

Philosophy

www.studyweb.com/History__Social_Studies/philos_toc.htm

Information categorized by philosophical system: aesthetics, ancient philosophy, critical thinking, empiricism, epistemology, ethics, existentialism, general philosophy, humanism, logic, medieval philosophy, nihilism, objectivism, organizations and associations, phenomenology, philosophy of mind, philosophy schools, rationalism. As you might imagine, tons of links. ☆☆☆☆

The Republic   **classics.mit.edu/Plato/republic.html**

If you haven't tackled Plato, you haven't experienced philosophy. Here it is, online. ☆☆☆☆

Stanford Encyclopedia of Philosophy   **plato.stanford.edu**

This one actually is encyclopedic. Articles on everything philosophical. ☆☆☆☆☆

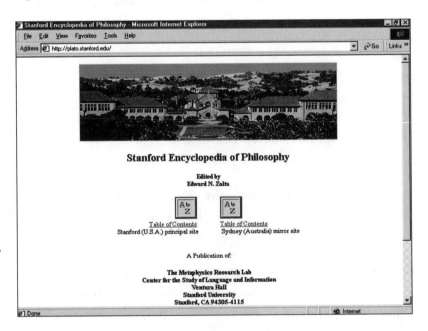

Figure 11.6

Stanford
Encyclopedia of
Philosophy: It loads,
therefore we learn.

Science

Science Scholarship

When my siblings and I were children, we got all our best science lessons hands-on. Our parents had a family membership to the local science center, and the four of us used it as the family playground whenever our parents had business downtown.

Homeschooling families find lots of ways to make science fun and educational for their children. Joyce Dumire, a homeschooling mom in Akron, Ohio, has found dozens of science activities for her teenage son. Among their projects: kite flying; rocket building and launching; visiting a city water works; city park activities; visiting state parks as they traveled; ripping out and changing a flower bed, replanting it, and redesigning it for plants, sun, and water flow; taking apart a computer and rebuilding it; talking with a landscape architect; doing lots of home experiments based on a book she picked up from a homeschool fair; and checking the local county extension office for activities, letting her son pick things he enjoyed, and finding a way to make them into a lesson. That's not all, she says. "We also found volunteer activities that covered many subjects. We live near the National Inventors Hall of Fame, so he has even been a teen volunteer there."

Joyce's extended family took up spelunking (cave exploration) as well. "We camped out (preparing was part of home economics) and learned about the rocks, formations, animal and plant life, and history of the area. This was more as conversation and planning than as straight studying. It also included physical education because for some of the caves, you get quite a workout."

Ann Crum homeschools two children in central Arkansas. Living out in the country, with goats, chickens, and a garden makes for some great laboratory experiences, she says. "The kids have learned so much about

Free Smithsonian Publication

Smithsonian in Your Classroom explores a single topic through an interdisciplinary, multicultural approach. Contact Smithsonian Office of Education, Arts and Industries Building, Room 1163, MRC 402, Washington, DC 20560, or order via fax: 202-357-2117.

👪 *How We Homeschool*

"I have not been homeschooling very long and find each day a learning experience. I work full-time, but at a job with flexible hours, which allows me to homeschool my son. We use a very flexible system, which seems to work well for us. Some days we improvise, and other days we stick to traditional schoolwork. My son seems to enjoy both. He is a little short on focus some days, and it is good to take those days and let him lead me in a new direction. Have you ever noticed that children seem to have a really good attention span for something they really want to do?"

—**Colleen Lee**, homeschooling mother of one, Maine

reproductive biology, conservation, animal husbandry, ecology, agriculture, nutrition, diseases, parasites, and good stewardship from our animals and garden. Last spring their project was a section of our vegetable garden. They had to plot the area, estimate the crop production, choose vegetables and flowers that would grow well here, and keep a journal of their activities. They even had to figure the cost of seeds and soil amendments and weigh that against their projected harvest. We also included a small course on composting, which is a scientific adventure as well!"

Ann and her kids have recently started making soap, which has, she says, "become a sort of chemistry course for us. There is quite a bit of math involved in the soap-making process, as there is with any science-related enterprise. My kids are quickly learning that math is something you simply must learn to get along in any area of your life. We operate with some basic ratios and use the percentage charts for figuring the amount of lye in each batch.

"Basically, what I strive for is not necessarily for my children to learn a lot about a particular scientific or math discipline, but to learn how to use the scientific method in all areas of their lives. To learn to explore and be curious. Along the way, they learn to apply science to real life."

Real life is what science is all about. The resources in this chapter will help you teach your children all the hard sciences: anatomy, archaeology, astronomy, biology, botany, chemistry, Earth science, ecology, physical science, scientists, technology, and zoology.

We start this chapter with general tools for teaching all different kinds of science:

On Intelligence

"Intellectual growth should commence at birth and cease only at death."

—Albert Einstein, 1879–1955

Internet Field Trip Library

teacher.scholastic.com/fieldtrp/index.htm#science

Unit lessons on a range of science topics. Internet Field Trips are guided tours to the best classroom-appropriate Web sites. Each field trip provides quick suggestions for using targeted Web sites to teach a specific topic. ☆☆☆

Let's Find Out   www.letsfindout.com

"Lots of information on bugs, aviation, and more." —T.F. ☆☆☆☆

McRel's Accessible Science Series   www.mcrel.org/whelmers

"Quite a few science experiments listed that you can do with your kids. Instructions for all grade levels are included." —A.C. ☆☆☆☆☆

Practical Hints for Science Fair Projects

www.scri.fsu.edu/~dennisl/CMS/special/sf_hints.html

Great advice for young students on how to approach a science fair project. Among the very good suggestions: Start early! ☆☆☆☆

Science Forum for Home Educators   www.kaleidoscapes.com/science

The Kaleidoscape message boards are wonderful—very popular, very helpful. The message boards are where the science discussions are usually held. Experiments, science studies, and links can also be found here. ☆☆☆☆☆

Science and Health   metalab.unc.edu/collection/scihealth.html

A funky collection of online databases and exhibitions: herbal home page, gardening, beekeeping, planetariums, patents, DNA mutations, hurricanes, and more. Strange. ☆☆☆

Science Center   www.education-world.com/science

▤ A full science curriculum, with everything you need to make it great: standards, resources, lesson plans, teaching themes, great scientists, and more. ☆☆☆☆☆

Science Curriculum Units

www.uen.org/cgi-bin/websql/lessons/query_lp.hts?corearea=3&area=2

▤ Well-prepared science lesson plans for all ages. A very complete science education. ☆☆☆☆☆

Science Lesson Plans   www.col-ed.org/cur/science.html

▤ Lesson plans sorted by grade level. Not a very attractive page, but the information is useful. ☆☆☆☆

Science News

www.sciam.com/bookmarks/editselect.html#a

▤ From the editors of *Scientific American,* a list of favorite resources, along with evaluations. See also the Amateur Scientist site at www.sciam.com/bookmarks /editselect.html#b. ☆☆☆

Science Unit Themes

users.massed.net/~wphillip/unitthem.htm

▤ An eclectic collection of lessons covering the entire spectrum of science. ☆☆☆☆☆

Thinking Fountain

www.sci.mus.mn.us/sln/tf/nav/thinkingfountain.html

▤ "This site has a variety of science activities and projects—all organized alphabetically, by topics, or by themes. Each listing also has a book corresponding to the subject matter, which can be purchased or borrowed from the library. This is a fun site for kids to explore and learn from on their own. I also find it very useful in developing hands-on lessons for my kinesthetic learner." —A.G. ☆☆☆☆☆

Hotlinks

Science Center
www.education-
world.com/science

**Science
Curriculum Units**
www.uen.org/cgi-bin
/websql/lessons/query
_lp.hts?corearea=3&area=2

**Science Forum for
Home Educators**
www.kaleidoscapes.com
/science

Thinking Fountain
www.sci.mus.mn.us/sln/tf
/nav/thinkingfountain.html

Science

Science

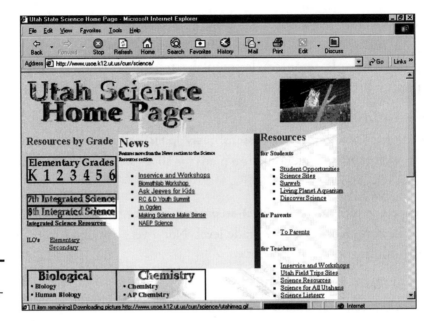

Figure 12.1

Utah Science Home Page: Educational re-sources for all.

Utah Science Home Page   www.usoe.k12.ut.us/curr/science
A science education for every grade, in every subject—and then some. This is a really, really great site. ☆☆☆☆☆

Anatomy

THE KNEE BONE'S connected to the . . . leg bone . . . or something like that.

From the time they first start talking, kids get a thrill out of naming parts of their own bodies.

Now it's time to take it to the next level. Anatomy teaches children to appreciate not just the names of body parts, but also the complexity of their own bodies. Through anatomy, kids learn how their bodies are structured while discovering the fascinating qualities of eyeballs, hair, toenails, and all the other things that make them, physically, who they are.

These Internet resources provide a better anatomical foundation than anything your kids would ever hear in a classroom, because they let kids examine real photos of real bodies. The Visible Human Project, for example, may be the single most amazing science project in the world.

So here they are, the resources for an online anatomy class. (For related resources, see the human development section in chapter 13 and the biology section, which includes genetics, later in this chapter.)

Anatomy: From the Greek *anatome (dissection)*. The study of the structure of the body.

Anatomy and Physiology   tlc.ai.org/anatomy.htm

Lots of strange resources here on hair transplants, dermatology, knee operations, head injuries, and stinky feet—as well as links to the usual fare. Lesson plans, sponsored by Access Indiana. ☆☆☆

Body Quest   library.thinkquest.org/10348

"The introduction says it's for ages eleven to sixteen, but my seven-year-old loves this site! Here you can tour the human body and discover how each of its systems works. You can also search for specific information, perform experiments, or take a quiz." —A.G ☆☆☆☆☆

CardioDoc Play Doctor
www.medfacts.com/crdiodoc/preappnt.htm

"No, this is not what you think! Kids can check the appointment sheet, choose a patient, click through a list of symptoms, and then consult reference materials to reach a diagnosis. Lots of fun!" —A.G. ☆☆☆☆

Explore the Brain and Spinal Cord
faculty.washington.edu/chudler/introb.html

"Learn about the brain, the spinal cord, the effects of different drugs on brain function, and other topics related to the nervous system. Lots of information." —A.C. ☆☆☆☆☆

Hotlinks

Body Quest
library.thinkquest.org
/10348

Explore the Brain and Spinal Cord
faculty.washington.edu
/chudler/introb.html

Guided Tour of the Visible Human
www.madsci.org/~lynn/VH

My Body
kidshealth.org/misc_pages
/mybody_LP.html

†††† How We Homeschool

"We don't get organized, we don't have my son sit to do work, we don't monitor his work, and our days are all different. My son plays with Legos, reads, plays on the computer, practices his flute, plays with friends, plays in the mud, cooks, runs errands with me, plays with his brother, goes to various activities—you get the point. Every day is different, and I wouldn't change it for the world.

"In regard to academic progress: We don't worry about it. He's obviously learning so many things that are way beyond 'grade level' that I'm not concerned about whether he's covering every little point of someone else's second-grade curriculum. He uses math all the time (it always amazes people when he figures out the tip when we're at a restaurant), he's interested in many types of science (he enjoys devising his own experiments), he reads constantly, and he just soaks up the world like a sponge. We're not worried."

—**Lillian Haas**, unschooling mother of two, Audubon, New Jersey

Guided Tour of the Visible Human   www.madsci.org/~lynn/VH
View digitized images from the Visible Human Project. Includes animations and "interactively annotated" images. ☆☆☆☆☆

Human Anatomy and Physiology
www.pbs.org/teachersource/recommended/rec_links_science.shtm#6
A collection of anatomy-related Web sites from PBS Teacher-Source.

The Heart: An Online Exploration   www.fi.edu/biosci/heart.html
"Thoroughly explore the heart and the history of heart science. Great information for the homeschooler or any student, for that matter." —A.C. ☆☆☆☆

My Body   www.kidshealth.org/misc_pages/mybody_LP.html
"Anyone planning on studying the body? We are, and here's an awesome site that's just perfect for younger kids. It divides the body into its various systems (circulation, muscles, respiration, and more). Kids can hear a heart beat, go inside a human ear, listen to hiccups

Science

Figure 12.2

The Heart: Travel
the heart, inside
and out.

and learn what causes them, and a whole lot more! You will need the
Shockwave plug-in, but it can be downloaded for free." —A.G.
☆☆☆☆

Archaeology and Paleontology

I ONCE HEARD of a kid who didn't care about dinosaurs.

Naaah. Just joking.

Paleontology and archaeology are fundamentally related. They involve the two things kids—especially kids of the male variety—love best:
dinosaurs and digging in the dirt.

Danish Geologist Susie Mathia describes the many kinds of scientists
who examine the Earth and the things in it. Generally speaking, geologists study the bedrock to determine the location of certain attractive raw
materials (such as sand, water, minerals, and coal) and to estimate their
quality. "As you can imagine," she says, "geologists work in many fields.
As a professional, I examine rocks with respect to structure, mineral

Science

composition, and chemistry. The result of such an examination aids in ore exploration.

"Other scientists examine the underground for petroleum, and they have the title *petrologist*. Scientists looking for water have the title *hydrogeologist*. Geologists working with soft materials such as sand, gravel, and clay are called *sedimentologists*. Geologists also work with earthquake predictions *(seismologists)* and volcanic activities and the building of our planet *(volcanists)*.

> **Archaeology:**
>
> From the Greek *arkhaiologia (antiquities + study)*. The systematic study of material remains.

"A certain type of geologist examines the development of life on Earth—everything from human beings to bluefish, dinosaurs, trilobites, insects, and mammals. This sort of geologist has the title *paleontologist*. Some consider paleontologists more related to biologists than to geologists. A paleontologist knows about the ecosystem and environment of a certain group of now-extinct animals/living forms."

If you want to give your favorite dirt diggers some purpose, the following resources will be helpful. See the related section on anthropology in chapter 10, and another related section, earth science, later in this chapter.

Hotlinks

Archaeology Magazine
www.archaeology.org

Dinosaurs and Us
commtechlab.msu.edu
/sites/letsnet/frames
/bigideas/b1/b1u4.html

Kids Dig Reed
www.kidsdigreed.com

Archaeology

ericir.syr.edu/Virtual/Lessons/Social_St/Anthropology
This page is actually misnamed Anthropology, but it contains a smallish collection of lesson plans on archaeology, from the U.S. Department of Education's AskERIC project. ☆☆

Archaeology   www.studyweb.com/links/1760.html
A great collection of educational materials related to ancient sites, digs, rock art, and more. ☆☆☆

Archaeology
www.ukans.edu/history/VL/methods/archaeology.html
A list of archaeology-related links from the World Wide Web Virtual Library. ☆☆

👪 *How We Homeschool*

"I started out by asking my nine-year-old son how he wanted to begin studying our province's history: with the natives or the dinosaurs? (The 'official' curriculum seemed to imply that history began with the settlers.) We spent a couple of months on our area's natives and incorporated all of our subjects into the study. We read like crazy and pursue topics that interest him. I find that he absorbs so much, and takes a wonderful ownership of his learning, because they're his topics."

—**Leanne Dohy,** homeschooling mother of three, Calgary, Alberta, Canada

Science

Archaeology Magazine   www.archaeology.org

▦ The Archaeological Institute of America publishes a fascinating magazine, chock-full of fascinating studies, many of which are available online at this site. ☆☆☆☆☆

Archaeology and Paleontology

www.sciam.com/bookmarks/editselect.html#c

▦ From the editors of *Scientific American,* a list of favorite resources, along with evaluations. ☆☆☆

Art to Zoo: Decoding the Past

educate.si.edu/resources/lessons/art-to-zoo/arch/cover.html

▦ The Work of Archaeologists: a lesson plan from the Smithsonian. ☆☆☆☆

Dinosaurs and Us

commtechlab.msu.edu/sites/letsnet/frames/bigideas/b1/b1u4.html

▦ Kids too old for Barney? Then they're old enough to appreciate some real dinosaurs. Here's how to teach them. ☆☆☆☆

Experts in Archaeology

www.askme.com/cat/showcategory_502_xp_1.htm

▦ Want to communicate directly with an expert who has volunteered to answer questions about this subject? AskMe.com is one of several expert sites on the Internet. ☆☆☆☆

Kids Dig Reed   www.kidsdigreed.com

▤ Archaeology for the little ones. Your youngest child will laugh at this talking-cow tour guide that takes them on an actual archaeological site. They learn about how archaeologists work, and reconstruct how people lived over 150 years ago, with games, puzzles, and a virtual site tour. ☆☆☆☆☆

Figure 12.3

Kids Dig Reed: A virtual archeological dig at an actual site.

Mesoamerican Archaeology   copan.bioz.unibas.ch/meso.html

▥ A collection of information on Mayan, Olmec, and other Mesoamerican and pre-Colombian cultures. ☆☆☆

Midwest 16,000 Years Ago

commtechlab.msu.edu/sites/letsnet/frames/bigideas/b1/b1pop3.html

▤ Great elementary-aged lesson on ancient, ancient America. ☆☆☆

Astronomy

TWINKLE, TWINKLE, LITTLE star . . . Here I am with seven kids and a busy life . . . and I *still* wonder what you are!

The science of astronomy has many facets: planetary and solar systems, black holes, rocketry, aviation . . . in short, the whole universe. It can all be a little mind-boggling.

Fortunately, there are a lot of resources available to you to help get your children thinking about things beyond the tops of the trees.

One way to get kids interested in astronomy is simply to get them out looking, says Brad Kirshenbaum Sr. Brad is the head of the astronomy department at St. Robert Bellarmine in Omaha, Nebraska. He says his goal as a teacher is to get people interested in astronomy, but he worries that astronomy intimidates some people into thinking that it is a very difficult job, profession, or hobby. "So many times each year," he says, "I will be outside with my eight-inch LX200 telescope (which attracts a lot of attention), and people walking by will stop and ask what I am looking at and if they can have a look. I always say yes, and take them to some very eye-pleasing objects such as Saturn, Jupiter, the Orion Nebula, or Sagittarius to grab their attention. When they ask questions, I try to keep them interested with 'down to earth' responses. When I see their excitement, it is a very exhilarating feeling."

A real education in astronomy can open doors—space shuttle doors, even—for people who pursue it. Mike, a Houston-based instructor for the International Space Station and a NASA employee, says he uses his astronomy education every day. "Both the space shuttle and the space station use instruments for navigation that require sightings of specific stars. We have to be able to recognize those stars and where they are in the sky to do star sightings.

"A great deal of my job also involves understanding orbital mechanics, since this governs how objects orbit the Earth. A basic understanding of astronomy is a must for me to determine that our training simulators are 'traveling' correctly in simulated space."

> **Astronomy:** From the Greek *aster (star)* and *nomas (wander)*. The study of matter outside of the Earth's atmosphere.

Ben Fillmore is a postgrad student in astronomy at University College, London. He says a working knowledge of astronomy also has a lot of practical applications. "It is used for everything from predicting the financial growth of various markets to catching today's speeders. The programs used in data extraction in astronomy are essentially the ones used in predicting the NASDAQ and the Financial Times Index. The theory of special relativity leads to the programs used to operate police speed guns and calculate the criminal's speed. "Public knowledge on the subject is not too hot. Although movies and documentaries make people aware of the dangers our planet faces, many take a comical view of what astronomers do. But if anyone discovers an asteroid that could hit the Earth or observes a coronal mass ejection (from the sun) heading right toward us, we could some day save the human race."

If you want to get your kids looking skyward, the following great resources can help. Related resources on weather and atmosphere are in the earth science section, later in this chapter.

Astronomy   www.awesomelibrary.org/Library/Materials_Search/Lesson_Plans/Astronomy.html

Lesson plans from Awesome Library. A very thorough collection. ☆☆☆

Astronomy and Astrophysics
www.sciam.com/bookmarks/editselect.html#d

From the editors of *Scientific American,* a list of favorite resources, along with evaluations. ☆☆☆

Astronomy Course for Students Using the Internet
www.cnde.iastate.edu/staff/jtroeger/astronomy.html

This online course is fantastic! Includes sections on STARGZR; observing the night sky; dark skies versus light pollution; finding your way around the sky; messages from the cosmos; binoculars and telescopes; the moon, the sun, the solar system; stars, nebulae, and star clusters; galaxies and quasars; cosmology; and other really cool astrostuff. Doesn't that about cover everything? ☆☆☆☆☆

Astronomy Freebie

The *Teachers' Guide to Windows on Mars* kit shows how educators can use the Mars Millennium Project Participation Guide with the *Window on Mars* video. Call 877-4-ED-PUBS and request product number EK 0229P.

Science

Exploration in Education   www.stsci.edu/exined/exined-home.html

"This site features resources produced by a subsidiary of NASA, using astronomical data. The main page is very simple, and all the downloadables may be obtained directly. All the software required to run the products is also free and available for downloading." —M.B. ☆☆☆☆

FirstFlight   www.firstflight.com

My husband, the flying buff, wants desperately to get a pilot's license. This free online flying course offers help. The first lesson covers taxiing, takeoff, straight and level flight, turns, climbs, descent, landing, and post-flight procedures. It gets tougher from there. If your kids are enamored of flying, this course might keep them happy until they're old enough to buy their own plane. ☆☆☆☆☆

How Things Fly
educate.si.edu/resources/lessons/siyc/flight/start.html

Activities for Teaching Flight: a lesson plan from the Smithsonian. ☆☆☆☆

Jet Propulsion Laboratory   www.jpl.nasa.gov

NASA's rocket site presents the Mars report—all about the solar system, Earth, the universe, and technology. You'll also find a link to NASA, of course. ☆☆☆☆☆

Life Beyond Earth   www.pbs.org/lifebeyondearth

Materials to accompany a PBS special on extraterrestrial life. Video demonstrations are sold separately, but the abundant educational material will address the subject thoroughly, even if you don't have access to the video. ☆☆☆☆☆

Space and Astronomy   www.emtech.net/space.htm

Scores of very well chosen resources. ☆☆

Hotlinks

Astronomy Course for Students Using the Internet
www.cnde.iastate.edu/staff
/jtroeger/astronomy.html

FirstFlight
www.firstflight.com

Jet Propulsion Laboratory
www.jpl.nasa.gov

Life Beyond Earth
www.pbs.org
/lifebeyondearth

Science

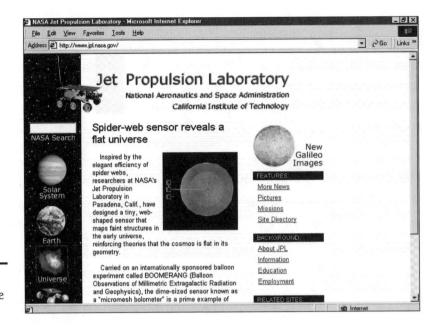

Figure 12.4

Jet Propulsion
Laboratory: Visit the
stars, for a start.

Space and the Planets

www.pbs.org/teachersource/recommended/rec_links_science.shtm#12

A collection of astronomy-related Web sites from PBS Teacher-Source. ☆☆☆

Biology

FROM ASTRONOMY—WHICH deals with some of the biggest things in the universe—to biology—which deals with some of the smallest: microscopes, DNA, RNA, cellular material, and everything else required for the study of living systems.

Peggy Klass, a high school science teacher in southwest Missouri, says studying biology teaches kids much more than simple facts about the structure of cells or frogs. "Through the study of biology and the scientific method, kids can internalize a way of questioning and examining facts that readily transfers to everyday life.

"We want to become informed, well-rounded citizens, capable of asking relevant questions. A population that blindly accepts the majority of information given on network news programs and mainstream newspapers will become a society without freedom. We have a responsibility to question information and seek the facts. The structure of biological inquiry facilitates the expansion of the mind and appreciation for the magnificent beauty and continuity of life around us."

Jessa Jones, a predoctoral graduate student in human genetics in Baltimore, Maryland, agrees. "I use my knowledge of biology all the time! In fact, I can remember first becoming interested in biology when my high school teacher explained how it is biologically impossible for any shampoo to repair split ends, despite what they may claim.

"Here are some biology-related questions that might be of interest in the real world: Does that Atkins low-carbohydrate diet really work? Why are all calico cats female? How do the trees know that it is autumn and therefore lose their leaves? How is this antibiotic going to make me better, and why do I have to take *all* of it? Why is it that ultraviolet radiation causes cancer, but microwaves do not? Why am I lactose intolerant? Why does a woman's chance of having a baby with Down syndrome go up as she ages, while her husband's does not? Why do my legs get really sore after I run? How do nerves really work? Is it true that I should wait thirty minutes after eating before I swim?

"I can use the general principles of biology to answer each and every one of these questions. Studying biology is studying how life works, how people work, what makes you *you*! What could be more interesting than that?"

Biology: From the Greek *bio (life)* and *logia (study)*. The science of living organisms.

The following resources on biology, genetics, and the life sciences will teach your children how life works. Related resources on human anatomy are in the anatomy section earlier in this chapter; links to anthropology are in chapter 10, and information on human development is found in chapter 13.

Biological/Health   www.minnetonka.k12.mn.us/science/curric.html#bio
Links to good educational resources, sponsored by a Minnesota school district. ☆☆

Science

Biology and Medicine   www.sciam.com/bookmarks/editselect.html#e

From the editors of *Scientific American,* a list of favorite resources, along with evaluations. ☆☆☆

Hotlinks

Microscopic Adventures
www.greatscopes.com /activity.htm

Morgan: A Genetics Tutorial
morgan.rutgers.edu /MorganWebFrames /How_to_use /HTU_Frameset.html

Online Frog Dissection
curry.edschool.virginia.edu /go/frog/menu.html

Virtual Microscope
www.dccc.edu /virtualmicroscope /VMPage /very1st.htm

Biology Text   www.pinkmonkey.com

The full textbook, online. Register at the tremendous Pink Monkey site (it's free), then click on the Study Guides link to access the text. ☆☆☆☆

CoreConcepts: Biology
ww.pinkmonkey.com/coreconcepts/subjects/biology.htm

A list of research resources, arranged by subject. Register at the pinkmonkey.com Web site. ☆☆☆

Genetic Lesson Plan Ideas
www.kumc.edu/gec/lessons.html

Wondering how to clone a sheep or extract some DNA? This site offers some answers among its several dozen lesson plans for teaching genetics. ☆☆☆

Microscopic Adventures
www.greatscopes.com/activity.htm

"Lots of great, fun microscope activities, many written by homeschoolers, all of which can be easily done using common items found around your own home." —A.C. ☆☆☆☆☆

Life Sciences   www.eduplace.com/science /bestofthenet/life_sciences.html

From Houghton Mifflin, an anthology of sites that provide tons of information on interesting wildlife. The sites were selected for their outstanding science content. ☆☆☆

Morgan: A Genetics Tutorial
morgan.rutgers.edu/MorganWebFrames/How_to_use/HTU_Frameset.html

Rutgers University sponsors this free multimedia tutorial covering the basic principles of genetics. Your older high school students will learn the most from this course, but intelligent younger kids will also gain much. ☆☆☆☆☆

Online Biology Book

gened.emc.maricopa.edu/bio/bio181/BIOBK/BioBookTOC.html

A regularly revised text for a college entry-level biology course. There are fifty (count 'em) illustrated, diagrammed, and hyperlinked chapters. Are you sure this is enough biology? ☆☆☆☆☆

Online Frog Dissection   curry.edschool.virginia.edu/go/frog/menu.html

"For those of us who, for whatever reason, do not have, or desire to have, a live frog to dissect, this site is great. It takes you through the dissection step by step. Then you can answer questions about each step to see if you have learned anything." —A.C. ☆☆☆☆☆

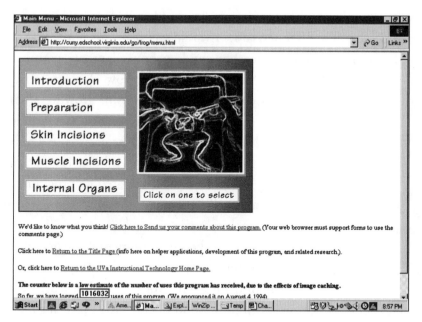

Figure 12.5

The Curry School of Education: For those with the stomach to do frog dissections at home.

SMILE Program Biology Index   www.iit.edu/~smile/biolinde.html

Want to teach memorable lessons about anatomy and physiology, zoology, botany, microbiology, genetics, environmental studies and ecology, biochemistry, general biology, and more? Choose from

this collection of almost 200 single-concept lessons. Very well done.
☆☆☆☆

Virtual Microscope
www.dccc.edu/virtualmicroscope/VMPage/very1st.htm

"View online photos of slides of a variety of tissues. Select the magnification and whether or not you want your selections to be labeled. When finished, use the online reviews to test your knowledge." —A.C.
☆☆☆☆

Botany

"EVEN IF I knew that tomorrow the world would go to pieces," Dr. Martin Luther King Jr. once said, "I would still plant my apple tree."

The science of botany teaches children how plant life germinates and grows, how plants are differentiated, and how they are related. Agricultural science teaches children everything from growing a small window garden to managing the family farm. Richard Marcley is a research scientist and a homeschooling dad living on Vashon Island, near Seattle. His teenagers participate in a program that encourages self-study and that uses parents and professional resources to teach.

> **Botany:** From the French *botanique* (herb). The study of the life and structure of plants.

Richard studied environmental science in college and now does research for Weyerhaeuser, the paper company. "The work I do is hardcore fundamental science concerned with how wood fibers made up of sugars and lignin (a material similar to crab shells) react in and to water, and how the chemicals we put in that fiber soup affect the many kinds of paper we make. To do this work, I must understand the scientific method and must have learned the basic skills of chemistry, biology, statistics, engineering, and the like.

"Science is an art," he says, "and it really helps if you are creative and can think out of the box. I believe the best people in any field have broad interests, a characteristic that helps them see relationships and draw conclusions that those too close to a subject just might be blind to. That's what all the geniuses say!"

Richard finds that he uses very few of the facts he learned while studying environmental science. But he doesn't regret his studies. On the contrary, he believes any of the sciences can teach the same basic principle: "The beauty of environmental science, like all of the hard sciences—chemistry, biology, physics, and the like—is that it teaches you the scientific method.

"Science is linked by some fundamental rules known as the scientific method, honed skills of observation and an honest search (corny but true) for the truth. Science enables many folks to communicate regardless of language because we all speak the same fundamental language of science."

Your little farmers and scientists will have fun finding out about flora with the following resources. Related resources on weather and atmosphere are in the earth science section, later in this chapter.

Back to Nature   family.go.com/Features /family_1998_07/famf/famf78nature/famf78nature.html

A nicely illustrated site on learning how to keep a nature journal. See Grow Something, a related site, at family.go.com/Features/family_1999_07/famp /famp79easygreen/famp79easygreen2.html.
☆☆☆☆☆

Botany
cc.owu.edu/~mggrote/pp/botany/f_botany.html

Lots of hands-on activities. Project Primary is a collaboration of professors from the departments of botany, chemistry, education, geology, physics, and

---

On Science

"The important thing is to not stop questioning."
—Albert Einstein

Science

Hotlinks

Back to Nature
family.go.com/Features /family_1998_07/famf /famf78nature/famf78nature .html

Botany
cc.owu.edu/~mggrote/pp /botany/f_botany.html

KinderGARDEN
aggie-horticulture.tamu .edu/kindergarden /kinder.htm

zoology at Ohio Wesleyan University, along with several Ohio school-teachers. ☆☆☆☆

Experts in Agriculture
www.askme.com/cat/showcategory_772_xp_1.htm

▤ Want to talk directly with an expert who has volunteered to answer questions about this subject? AskMe.com is one of several expert sites on the Internet. ☆☆☆☆

KinderGARDEN   aggie-horticulture.tamu.edu/kindergarden/kinder.htm

▤ An introduction to the many ways children can interact with plants and the outdoors. Tips, research, and much more about gardening with kids. An award-winning page. ☆☆☆☆

Figure 12.6

KinderGarden: Discover the green thumb hiding within your child.

Life Science   www.sbgschool.com/teacher_activities/science/life

▤ Lots of plant and life science lesson plans so children can learn how things grow. ☆☆☆☆

Plants and Animals
educate.si.edu/resources/lessons/siyc/pollen/start.html

▤ Partners in Pollination: a lesson plan from the Smithsonian. ☆☆☆☆

Science: Agriculture   ericir.syr.edu/Virtual/Lessons/Science/Agriculture

A small collection of lesson plans from the U.S. Department of Education's AskERIC project. See related lessons at ericir.syr.edu /Virtual/Lessons/Voc_Ed/Agriculture. ☆☆☆

Telegarden   www.usc.edu/dept/garden

At this award-winning site, your kids can help tend a living garden using a remote industrial robot to perform simple requested tasks such as watering, planting, and viewing the garden. The garden can be viewed by clicking on Guest Entrance. ☆☆☆☆

Chemistry

CHEMISTRY IS THE study of the basic physical elements that make up everything around us. A good working knowledge of chemistry principles helps not only professional chemists, but also people who cook and clean and paint.

Kari Farrell Matthews is a math and chemistry teacher in Rossville, Illinois. She's married to a farmer, and she explains how a good knowledge of chemistry affects their lives. "Chemistry is an amazing thing. It is a science that describes everything around us. Why do we sand wood, cook hamburgers, put bleach in our white laundry loads? Why does soap work? What causes sickle cell anemia? Why does bread smell so good while it is baking? How do batteries work? Chemistry answers these questions.

"My husband uses chemistry on the farm all the time. When he is trying to determine the best kind of fertilizer to buy, or when he is looking at analysis reports of soil samples from his fields, he must use his understanding of chemistry to make the best choices for the farm.

> **Chemistry:** From the Middle Latin *alchymista (alchemist)*. Scientific study of the composition, structure, and properties of an organism or substance.

"Not many people are farmers, of course, but most people do basic household chores, like cooking and cleaning. Understanding chemistry

Carl Wilhelm Scheele

Like so many other successful people, German chemist Carl Scheele was entirely self-taught. Scheele was apprenticed to a druggist, but in his spare time he conducted his own experiments. Although he's not well known—mostly because he was slow to publish his findings—he made some of the most significant discoveries in human history. In 1772 he discovered the existence of oxygen (he called it "fire air"), and later he discovered chlorine, glycerine, hydrogen sulfide, and several types of acid.

helps us make good decisions when we are unsure about what to do next. For instance, chemistry explains how to get a grass stain out of pants. My knowledge of the chemical makeup of the things in my home and on the farm comes into play every day."

Chemistry is a career choice for Doron Wolf, a chemical engineer who lives in Israel. He explains how his knowledge of chemistry affects his work each day. "Chemistry and biology are the main issues when talking about environmental engineering," he says. "I can't design waste treatment without involving chemical or biological considerations.

"Let's say wastewater from a plant contains caustic soda ($NaOH$) from cleaning and some organic solvents (such as MEK and acetone). How do you treat them?

"If you don't know chemistry and biology, you can't give the right answer. The correct answer is: First you remove the caustic soda with an acid like chlorine, to get salt with water. Then you treat the solvents with microorganisms or activated carbon that removes them.

"I also use my chemistry at home. Let's say you are cleaning your kitchen. There are many cleaning chemicals used in the process. On a product label, you might find, 'Contains caustic soda, ammonia, citric acid, hydrochloric acid, organic solvents, and more.' If you don't know some chemistry, you don't understand the meaning of those words, and your lack of knowledge can make your cleaning less efficient or can even cause an accident.

"This is not the main problem, however. The main problem begins when people try to combine chemicals to get better results—or so they think. If you mix an acid-based chemical like common chlorine bleach with ammonia, you cause a reaction that releases toxic vapors of ammonia gas. A little knowledge of chemistry might help."

Ready to try your hand at chemistry? The following resources will help.

Bizarre Stuff   **freeweb.pdq.net/headstrong**
Start fires, make clouds in bottles, get electricity from a lemon . . . these are the kinds of experiments that turn kids into mad scientists for life! ☆☆☆☆☆

Chemical Elements   **www.chemicalelements.com**
When the party's over, your serious students can come to this site to memorize the periodic table of the elements. Click an element from the chart and learn all its properties. Very easy to use. ☆☆☆☆☆

Chemistry   **cc.owu.edu/~mggrote/pp/chemistry/f_chemistry.html**
Baby chemistry. Your children will love watching you make ice cream from liquid nitrogen, or working together on any of these other great projects. Now your only problem is finding some liquid nitrogen. Author's contact information is included. ☆☆☆☆

Chemistry
www.sciam.com/bookmarks/editselect.html#g
From the editors of *Scientific American,* a list of favorite resources, along with evaluations. ☆☆☆

Chemistry Text   **www.pinkmonkey.com**
The full textbook, online. Register at the tremendous Pink Monkey site (it's free), then click on the Study Guides link to access the text. Also visit the related chemistry resources at www.pinkmonkey.com/coreconcepts/subjects/chem.htm: a full list of research resources, arranged by subject. ☆☆☆☆☆

Hotlinks

Bizarre Stuff
freeweb.pdq.net/headstrong

Chemical Elements
www.chemicalelements.com

Chemistry Text
www.pinkmonkey.com

Food and Science
www.uen.org/cgi-bin
/websql/utahlink
/lessonbook.hts?book_id=111

Elements   **www.ultisoft.demon.co.uk/elements.html**

From H to Pu, short essays about each of the chemical elements.
☆☆☆☆

Food and Science

www.uen.org/cgi-bin/websql/utahlink/lessonbook.hts?book_id=111

Cook-and-eat chemistry: lesson plans, supplemental materials, and more. Very scientific discussion of food handling and food management. ☆☆☆☆☆

Ooey, Gooey Recipes for the Classroom

www.minnetonka.k12.mn.us/science/tools/ooey.html

All sorts of fun science experiments in your kitchen! ☆☆☆

Figure 12.7

Ooey, Gooey: Recipes for disaster and other sorts of household fun.

Quick and Easy

www.eecs.umich.edu/mathscience/funexperiments/quickdirty/quick.html

"My kids love this one. Hands-on science for all ages, listed by grade level—very dirty play. Long but worth it." —A.D. ☆☆☆

Robert Krampf's Science Education Company

members.aol.com/krampf/news.html

A free mailing list that provides a weekly science experiment, along with explanations of the related scientific principles. Unfortunately, the back issues are not available online. ☆☆☆

SMILE Program Chemistry Index   www.iit.edu/~smile/cheminde.html

Want to teach memorable lessons about basic tools and principles, atomic and molecular structure (including moles), states of matter, types and control of chemical reactions, and chemistry of elements, compounds, and materials? Choose from this collection of almost 200 single-concept lessons. Very well done. ☆☆☆☆

Earth Science

GEOLOGY ROCKS. JUST ask the kid who's found her first agate. Or the one who pounds a rock on the sidewalk and observes it break apart in layers.

This section considers resources for the study of earth processes, earth science and geology.

Jenn Sides, who lives in southeastern Pennsylvania, is nearly ready to graduate from college with her degree in environmental geoscience. Although she's not yet a professional scientist, she finds many opportunities in daily life to use her knowledge of geology. "I just look around me and see the wonder of it all," she says. "It sounds silly, but I like the fact that I can look at an outcrop of rock and know its history.

"I also like knowing what mechanisms are at work around me. For instance, just recently I had a friend who wanted to buy a new house. She was looking at a nice new development near where I live, but I warned her that the property was smack in the middle of a floodplain for a little

Earth: Related to the Hebrew 'erets (world) and the Aramaic 'araq (world). The geographic formation of the planet.

Science

stream that ran through the area. I also knew that the soil would hold the water for a while. Lucky for her, she listened and bought elsewhere. Hurricane Floyd nailed us not too long after, and had she bought that house, she would have been floating in the middle of the little stream because it flooded its entire floodplain!"

Geology has other important practical applications. Sharon D. Pérez-Suárez is a graduate student at the University of Florida investigating a mid-ocean volcanic ridge in the Caribbean plate. The ridge is spreading, and Sharon is studying its magma chamber, part of her research into the effects of volcanic eruptions on the environment.

During her internship she studied sulfur dioxide clouds in the ozone formed by volcanic eruptions. Because gases play an important role in eruptions, she says, it's important to know the amount and composition of gases in magma chambers before an eruption occurs. When volcanoes erupt, they spew sulfur dioxide into the stratosphere, where it gets converted to aerosols, which absorb ultraviolet light and cause global climate change. In her research, she found a mathematical relationship between the total mass of erupted sulfur dioxide and the occurrence of volcanic activity.

On Scientific Inquiry

"Some people see things as they are and say why; I dream things that never were and say why not?"
—Robert F. Kennedy, quoting George Bernard Shaw

Thomas Ferrero, a consulting engineering geologist in Ashland, Oregon, explains how his work makes the world a better place for many people. Every day, he says, he shows mining companies, government agencies, engineers, architects, construction contractors, homeowners, and others how to solve large and small problems having to do with the earth. He teaches people how to do everything from drain a basement to stabilize a foundation on an unstable slope or prevent soil erosion.

"I have located valuable mineral deposits," he says. "I have found groundwater where others failed. I have stopped landslides. My work is always varied and interesting. I love what I do for a living."

The school of hard rocks—er, knocks—is now online. The following resources cover the study of earth processes, earth science, and geology. (Related resources are in the archaeology section, earlier in this chapter.)

Athena: Earth and Space Science for K–12   athena.wednet.edu

Oceans, Earth, weather, space, and more. Lessons include topics such as the Mount St. Helen's blast, wetlands science, the Kobe earthquake, El Niño, and more. ☆☆☆☆☆

Earth and Environment

www.sciam.com/bookmarks/editselect.html#f

From the editors of *Scientific American,* a list of favorite resources, along with evaluations. ☆☆☆

Earth and the Environment

www.pbs.org/teachersource/recommended/rec_links_science.shtm#4

A collection of science-related Web sites from PBS TeacherSource. ☆☆☆

Earth Science   www.minnetonka.k12.mn.us/science/curric.html#ea

Links to good educational resources, sponsored by a Minnesota school district. ☆☆

Earth Science Resources

iceage.umeqs.maine.edu/geology/k12.htm

"Information to help teach earth sciences to all grade levels. All the links offer serious scientific information; these aren't the fun 'bells and whistles' type of Web pages. Science is not my forte, so I really appreciated these sites: They're straightforward and easy to understand and implement." —A.G. ☆☆☆☆

Earth Sciences

www.eduplace.com/science/bestofthenet
/earth_sciences.html

From Houghton Mifflin, an anthology of Internet sites on glaciers, meteorology, and more. The sites were selected for their outstanding science content. ☆☆☆

Hotlinks

Athena
athena.wednet.edu

Natural Sciences Curriculum
explorer.scrtec.org/explorer

Ride the Wind
family.go.com/Features
/family_1999_07/famp
/famp79easygreen
/famp79easygreen3.html

Weather Unit
faldo.atmos.uiuc.edu/w_unit
/weather.html

U.S. Geological Survey Earth Science Corps

Be part of the federal volunteer network with The Earth Science Corps. Write to Earth Science Corps, MS 513, U.S. Geological Survey, Reston, VA 20192, or call 800-254-8040.

Minerals, Crystals, and Gems

educate.si.edu/resources/lessons/siyc/gems/start.html

Stepping Stones to Inquiry: a lesson plan from the Smithsonian. ☆☆☆☆

Natural Sciences Curriculum

explorer.scrtec.org/explorer

Click the Natural Sciences link to find plans for life, physical, and earth sciences. Learn about erosion, earthquakes, and much more from this large collection of resources. ☆☆☆☆☆

Ride the Wind   family.go.com/Features/family_1999_07/famp/famp79easygreen/famp79easygreen3.html

If you've wondered, as I do, how wind works, here's the answer. ☆☆☆☆

Figure 12.8

Ride the Wind: Features more than just a lot of hot air.

Weather Unit   faldo.atmos.uiuc.edu/w_unit/weather.html

This complex unit integrates the study of weather into all curriculum areas. Includes fourteen science lessons for weather. ☆☆☆☆☆

Ecology

ECOLOGICAL STUDIES COVER lots of subject matter, including plant and animal ecologies, environmental education, and, for our porpoises—er, purposes—oceanography.

How does the ocean affect the environment? Maria Therese Greenfield, a graduate student doing volunteer work in England's oceans, explains: "The marine environment is undoubtedly one of the most hostile and productive environments on this Earth," she says. "It's also one of the least understood."

Maria believes that any person who deals with the sea in any form should have a basic understanding, "to learn to respect its power and life-giving attributes. The world would be a lot colder place without the oceans, as heat is stored in them during the summer months and released during the winter!"

> **Ecology:** From the Greek *oikia* (dwelling) and *logia* (study). Relationship between organisms and their environments.

This is how she teaches schoolchildren about the sea and its power: "Initially, I start with local oceanographic phenomena, such as tides, waves, pollution, currents, storms, temperature, and survival techniques. Then I go on to the global, such as tsunamis, hurrcanes, El Niño, seawater, hydrothermal vents, and information on the oceans themselves.

"With the activities taking place out of school hours, it can be difficult to keep the children's interest. Field trips, where kids can see what they are being taught, also help. One of the children I taught told me, 'I thought the ocean was wet, salty, and dead; now I think it's dangerous but cool!' It made me realize that I've been doing some good, without scaring anyone away from the ocean."

Your children can have the same appreciation for the world around them. Get started teaching with the following resources. (Related resources are in the biology section, earlier in this chapter.)

On Failure

"I haven't failed—
I've found
10,000 ways that
don't work."
—Thomas Edison

CD-ROMs, Posters, and Slides

topex-www.jpl.nasa.gov/education/poster.html

▤ "Free CD-ROMS, posters, and slides on such topics as El Niño, Visit to an Ocean Planet, and Perspectives on an Ocean Planet. Teacher packets available; one free per teacher per topic. I ordered my packet, but have not yet received it." —D.A. ☆☆☆☆

Hotlinks

Environmental Education for Kids!
www.dnr.state.wi.us/org
/caer/ce/eek

Marine Biology Learning Center
www.marinebiology.org

National Wildlife Federation
www.nwf.org/nwf
/wildlifeweek

Ounce of Prevention
www.cygnus-group
.com/NSTA.html

Ecology

www.minnetonka.k12.mn.us/science/curric.html#ec

▤ Links to good educational resources, sponsored by a Minnesota school district. ☆☆

Environmental Education for Kids!

www.dnr.state.wi.us/org/caer/ce/eek

▤ "This is an awesome e-zine for kids. There's information and activities about plants, animals, and the environment. Kids can find out about careers in natural resources, send in letters and artwork, and answer the riddle of the day. There are also teacher pages with extra stories, information, and activities. It says it's for fourth through eighth grade, but I thought it was more suited for younger kids who can read well." —A.G. ☆☆☆☆☆

Experts in Ecology and Environment

www.askme.com/cat/showcategory_801_xp_1.htm

▤ Want to communicate directly with an expert who has volunteered to answer questions about this subject? AskMe.com is one of several expert sites on the Internet. ☆☆☆☆

Green and Growing   **www.gatewest.net/green**

▤ From the Ground Up. A teacher's guide containing detailed lesson plans on food, agriculture, electricity and sustainable development. Teach your children about renewable, sustainable agriculture and energy. ☆☆☆☆

Marine Biology Learning Center   www.marinebiology.org

▤ The Marine Biology Learning Center offers several free online lessons about ocean biology. Visit the site to find courses in ichthyology; sharks, rays, and bony fish; coral reef fish ecology; coral reef bleaching; dolphins; and much more. ☆☆☆☆☆

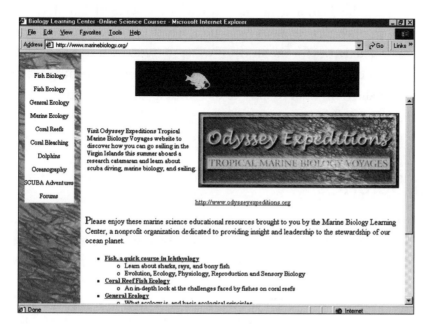

Figure 12.9

Odyssey Expeditions: Real voyages for real adventures.

National Wildlife Federation   www.nwf.org/nwf/wildlifeweek

▤ "The NWF is the organization that publishes *Ranger Rick* and *Big Backyard.* Every April the NWF sponsors National Wildlife Week. At this site, you can request a free poster and check out their educator's guide, which is available in both Spanish and English. The site also lists additional resources and interactive games, and offers the previous year's educator's guide." —A.G. ☆☆☆☆☆

Natural Wonders   family.go.com/Features/family_1999_07/famp/famp79easygreen/famp79easygreen.html

▤ Great suggestions for using computers to teach kids to love the great outdoors. ☆☆☆☆

Free Stuff

Call the Soil and
Water Conservation
Society at 800-843-
7645 to obtain a free
conservation kit.

Ocean Planet

educate.si.edu/resources/lessons/currkits/ocean/main.html

▌ Interdisciplinary Marine Science Activities: a lesson plan from the Smithsonian. ☆☆☆☆

Ounce of Prevention   **www.cygnus-group.com/NSTA.html**

▌ The National Science Teachers Association has developed this booklet on waste reduction, which provides fifteen curricular activities for the study of waste prevention and management. Students learn that it is better not to create something (source reduction) than to have to deal with its disposal later.

☆☆☆☆☆

Physical Science

THE PHYSICAL SCIENCES are all the processes you had to learn formulas for when you studied science. In this section we cover physics and the properties of physical objects, including the study of matter, energy, force, and motion.

> **Physics:** From the Greek *phusikos (nature)*. Study of the interactions between energy and matter.

There's no need, of course, to teach your young children the mathematics of physics. They're born scientists who, given the space, will spend their entire childhoods investigating gravity and motion and that unmovable object called parents.

Susie Clawson, a homeschooling mother of five in Clearfield, Utah, has found ways to teach the physical sciences without having to rescue the good china before it gets tossed from the deck. "Science is something that often gets pushed aside at our house," she says. "We love doing experiments, but it is usually something that gets put on the back burner and then forgotten.

"We recently started a science group with a couple of other homeschooling moms and their kids. We decided to keep it in our local area so that it wouldn't get to be a burden to drive great distances.

"Once a month we meet at one of our homes, and the hostess leads the day. We really have no rules for which topics we're doing, but usually it is something that our children have expressed an interest in pursuing in great detail.

"This week is my turn, and we're starting with some basic physics. We're also going to do some weather. My daughter is a Girl Scout, and she wanted to work on some experiments for a badge. Also, one of the other kids in the group just finished a weather study, and he's going to share his stuff with us."

You'll enjoy getting physical with the helpful resources below!

CoreConcepts: Physics   www.pinkmonkey.com /coreconcepts/subjects/physics.htm

A list of research resources, arranged by subject. Register at PinkMonkey (www.pinkmonkey.com). ☆☆☆

Girls Ask Why   www.girlscouts.org/girls/Why/why.htm

This Girl Scouting page is for girls who like to explore the world around them and find out how things work. Lots of science-related content written to appeal to girls. ☆☆☆☆

How Stuff Works   www.howstuffworks.com

One of the coolest sites on the Web. Learn how absolutely everything works. The site covers automotive, technical, health, food, electronics, and all other scientific matters. Subscribe to the newsletter, or just revisit this frequently updated site. ☆☆☆☆☆

Newton's Apple   ericir.syr.edu/Projects/Newton

"This site has lots of science lessons, complete with activities. Most experiments can be done with things you find around your home or things you can easily purchase. Although the activities are not extremely long, they are packed with ways of learning the information on which they focus. Even though the lessons are

Hotlinks

How Stuff Works
www.howstuffworks.com

Newton's Apple
ericir.syr.edu/Projects/Newton

Physics 2000
www.colorado.edu/physics /2000/index.pl

School of the Web
www.mcasco.com /school.html

Science Rock
genxtvland.simplenet.com /SchoolHouseRock /science.hts?hi

Science

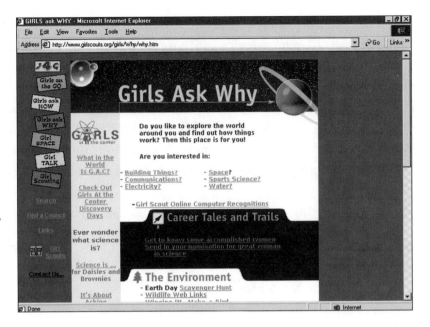

Figure 12.10

Girl Scouts of America: More valuable than all cookie sales are answers for the inquisitive minds.

geared toward particular episodes of the TV show Newton's Apple, we have found that we can use them even if we haven't viewed the programs." —A.C. ☆☆☆☆☆

Physical Sciences
www.eduplace.com/science/bestofthenet/physical_sciences.html
From Houghton Mifflin, an anthology of Internet sites that discuss energy, lasers, and more. The sites were selected for their outstanding science content. ☆☆☆

Physics Tutorials   www.physics.uoguelph.ca/tutorials/tutorials.html
Getting started in physics? Here are physics tutorials and modules for entry-level physics courses, providing everything you need to know to get yourself up to speed on physics. ☆☆☆☆☆

Physics 2000   www.colorado.edu/physics/2000/index.pl
An interactive journey through modern physics with the University of Colorado at Boulder. Have fun learning visually and conceptually about twentieth-century science and high-tech devices.

Pierre Curie

French scientist Pierre Curie was homeschooled. His doctor father taught him at home, and by the time young Pierre was 14 he was passionate about mathematics, particularly spatial geometry. A few years later he finished college and began working as a laboratory assistant at the Sorbonne, where he met his future wife, Marie. The two of them were awarded the Nobel Prize for physics in 1903.

Explains Einstein, basic principles of waves, quantum mechanics, polarization, the periodic table, and more in an easy-to-read format that will make a scientist out of your most truculent child. ☆☆☆☆☆

School of the Web   www.mcasco.com/school.html

Two online courses—Introduction to Order: A Closer Look at Chaos and Introduction to Physics 1: Mechanics. The topics include classical mechanics, Newton's laws, chaos, fractals, Mandelbrot and Julia sets, complex numbers, dynamical systems, strange attractors, chaotic attractors, Feigenbaum's number, gravity, phase space, and ballistics. There is no charge at this time for the courses, but you are required to register online. The material, written in a breezy conversational tone, is very readable. ☆☆☆☆

Science Rock

genxtvland.simplenet.com/SchoolHouseRock/science.hts?hi

Musical gravity, weather, anatomy, energy, and much more. Schoolhouse Rock is online! ☆☆☆☆☆

SMILE Program Physics Index   www.iit.edu/~smile/physinde.html

Want to teach memorable lessons about matter, mechanics, fluids, electricity and magnetism, waves, sound and optics, and more? Choose from this collection of almost 200 single-concept lessons. Very well done. ☆☆☆☆

Scientists

FROM THE MOST quantitative to the most qualitative: We move now from hard science to fun scientists. In this section we discover scientists and inventors, the history of science, and science careers.

Homeschooling and science are a natural fit. Little Alexander Bell (the "Graham" was added later) was schooled at home for most of his youth. He spent two years in high school, graduated at 14, and became a music and elocution teacher. Later he became a resident master at Weston House Academy, where he began studying sound. His great invention changed the way the world communicates. After he invented the technology that is still used in modern telephone communications, he continued working as a teacher and a scientist for the rest of his life.

> **Scientist:** Related to the Latin *scientia (to know)*. One who is trained in the study of a particular field of inquiry.

And he's just one of dozens of well-known scientists and inventors who were schooled at home.

Do your budding scientists need inspiration? The following resources will help.

Careers in Science
outcast.gene.com/ae/AE/AEPC/WWC/1991/careers_in_science.html
  Is your child interested in becoming a scientist? This lesson plan will provide guidance. ☆☆☆☆

Classroom Materials Pages   www.aande.com/class/teach
  From A&E, inventors, scientists, and many other significant people. ☆☆☆

Dictionary of Scientific Quotations
www.naturalscience.com/dsqhome.html
  It's short. It's interesting. And it's quotable. What famous scientists have said. ☆☆☆☆

Exploratorium   www.exploratorium.edu
  An online collection of 650 science, art, and human perception exhibits. ☆☆☆☆

Five Most Influential Scientists in History
tlc.ai.org/lessons/scntstlp.htm

   A lesson plan for learning about scientists. ☆☆☆

Inventions   **www.pbs.org/teachersource/recommended /rec_links_science.shtm#8**

   A collection of Web sites related to scientists, provided by PBS TeacherSource. ☆☆☆

Inventors and Inventions   **tlc.ai.org/invent.htm**

   Offering everything from a photo of Thomas Edison to hundreds of lesson plans, quotations, and other resources, this site, sponsored by Access Indiana, is a treasure. ☆☆☆☆

Museum of the History of Science   **www.mhs.ox.ac.uk**

   How things became what they are. Fascinating online exhibitions from Oxford's Museum of the History of Science. The real thing is housed in the world's oldest surviving purpose-built museum building, the Old Ashmolean Building. ☆☆☆☆☆

Hotlinks

Exploratorium
www.exploratorium.edu

Museum of the History of Science
www.mhs.ox.ac.uk/

National Inventors Hall of Fame
www.invent.org/book

Science

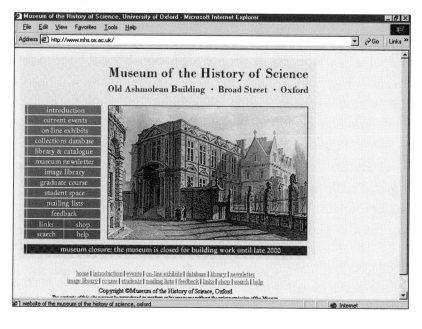

Figure 12.11

Museum of the History of Science: The museum may be closed, but, thanks to the Internet, the exhibits remain open.

National Inventors Hall of Fame   **www.invent.org/book**

This Akron, Ohio, institution honors inventors who have contributed to the technological advancements of the United States.
☆☆☆☆☆

Technology

IF YOUR CHILDREN are to be competitive in the world they grow into, technology and computer science may be the most critical areas of all for them to understand. But it's not just for their future that kids should understand technology. Research has demonstrated that kids who are adept Internet users get less caught up in television and talk shows than those who aren't. And they hear and see more science and news programming than those who don't use the Internet.[1]

Technology: From the Greek *tekhnologia* *(craft + study)*. The practical application of scientific knowledge.

Being Internet savvy has plenty of practical applications, as well. Lillian Haas, who homeschools two children in Audubon, New Jersey, says the Internet is turning her kids into better learners. "My son uses both the library and the Internet to do research. If he needs help focusing his search, either my husband or I will help. He generally doesn't write down his results, and I don't ask him to, because when he is researching something, it's for his own purposes. He does what he wants to with his information."

Homeschooler Joyce Dumire has enrolled her teenage son in two Internet-based classes, algebra and geometry. Technology helped her son be better educated in other ways, too. "I found older friends and relatives with special skills who shared time with my homeschooled son. One is a computer specialist who keeps the systems running for a large company; my son now is very good with computers. Another loves music and

---

1. Kenneth Klemmer, "Media Cannibalization: Myth and Reality," December 28, 1998, www.forrester.com/ER/Research/Brief/0,1317,5156,FF.html.

showed him how to work sound boards, which taught him science, math, and music."

In Susie Clawson's home, the technology-oriented learning has been a little more casual. "I had wonderful visions of my kids using all these interactive sites I'd find," says the Clearfield, Utah, mother of five. "But the reality in our house is that they each use the Internet for their own personal pursuits and rarely for homeschool. Usually their use has something to do with their favorite books or cartoons. They use the Internet when they do art. Both of my older boys are into cartooning, especially Japanese-style cartoons. They copy pictures from different sites as practice."

These are some of my favorite sites *on* the Net for learning *about* the Net—as well as the rest of the technological revolution your kids are a part of.

From Carbons to Computers

educate.si.edu/scitech/carbons/start.html

The Changing American Office: a lesson plan from the Smithsonian. ☆☆☆☆

How To   **www.emtech.net/how_too.htm**

Dozens of answers to "How Do I?" questions about technology and the Internet. Scores of very well chosen resources. ☆☆

Internet Guide for Teachers of Core Knowledge

www.lee.k12.fl.us/schools/oak/Internet_Guide.htm

A detailed guide for teaching (and learning) about the Internet. ☆☆☆☆

Online Games and Activities

www.4kids.com/playroom/konline.html

A hundred or more enjoyable things for kids to do online. Let them have fun while improving their computer skills. ☆☆☆☆

Hotlinks

Scooter Computer and Mr. Chips
genxtvland.simplenet.com /SchoolHouseRock /computer.hts?hi

Technology Center
www.education-world.com /technology

Texas Information Literacy Tutorial
tilt.lib.utsystem.edu

Typing
www.wannalearn.com /Business_and_Careers /Office_Skills/Typing

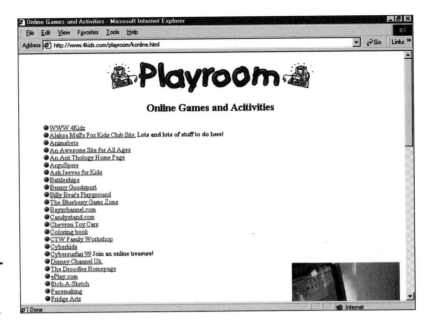

Figure 12.12

4kids Playroom: Features online games and activities.

Internet Freebie

"Parents' Guide to the Internet" provides parents with strategies for navigating the Internet and for maximizing its use as an educational tool. Call 877-4-ED-PUBS and request product number ERL 0105P.

Science and Technology
www.pbs.org/teachersource/recommended/rec_links_science.shtm

See the sections on computer technology and the Internet in this collection of computer science-related Web sites from PBS TeacherSource. ☆☆☆

Scooter Computer and Mr. Chips
genxtvland.simplenet.com/SchoolHouseRock/computer.hts?hi

Schoolhouse Rock gets technical. Memorable songs about technology, software, hardware, and data processing. What a great way to learn! ☆☆☆☆☆

Technical Courses   www.innovast.com/courses.html

These online technology courses teach HTML, DOS, and FTP basics. There are also quizzes to test kids' understanding. ☆☆☆☆

Technology Center   www.education-world.com/technology

Your kids need to understand technology, and here's a set of standards for teaching them about it. The Center is chock

full of tools for teachers. Lesson plans, curriculum standards, tutorials, and much, much more. ☆☆☆☆

Texas Information Literacy Tutorial   **tilt.lib.utsystem.edu**
Know everything you should about the Internet? This
tremendous online tutorial explains all the basics of technology and the Internet. You and your kids will be pros
by the time you finish. ☆☆☆☆☆

Tutorials on the Net   **www.emtech.net/tutorials_on_net.htm**
Tutorials on how to use various kinds of popular computer software and the Internet. Scores of very well chosen resources. ☆☆

Typing   **www.wannalearn.com/Business_and_Careers/**
Office_Skills/Typing
Three free courses on keyboarding. ☆☆☆☆

Technology Freebie

Free video: *Preparing
Classrooms for the
Future: Ensuring Access
to the Internet.* Focuses
on preparing classrooms
for the future by ensuring
access to the Internet.
Call 877-4-ED-PUBS and
request Satellite Town
Meeting #46.

Zoology

WHICH OF YOUR children intends to grow up to become a veterinar-
ian? Any kid who ever fell in love with a dog or a gerbil has entertained
the thought.

That's why the study of zoology has the potential to be so much fun. Zoology is the science of animal life and includes a sub-branch called
entomology. It's a bug's life.

It can also be your kids' life. Larissa Nituch, a
zookeeper and zoology student in Montreal,
Canada, explains how: "The best way to prepare
for a career in zoology is to volunteer, volunteer,
volunteer! Anyone over the age of sixteen can volunteer his or her time at
most animal shelters, wildlife rehabilitation centers, veterinary offices,
and zoos. This is the best way to get valuable experience with animals

> **Zoology:** From
> the Greek *zôion (living
> being).* The study of
> animal life.

and will greatly increase your chances of getting a job later on. You should also take any animal- and science-related classes available at your school, and read all the books you can get your hands on. It is sometimes difficult to get into this field, but if you are dedicated and work hard, there is no doubt that you will succeed!"

Not sure you can teach science? Jim Sherrard, an environmental coordinator in Plano, Texas, has some inspiration for you: "I am most passionate in my belief that teaching is one of the highest callings to which we can aspire; certainly it is one of the most rewarding. It is the one profession where one person can contribute and make a quantum change in society." About his job as a zoologist, he says, "I have been fortunate as a zoological professional to have traveled the Earth. I have seen firsthand the degradation of the rain forest in South America; man's inhumanity to man in dealing with the indigenous inhabitants; and the staggering, awesome, humbling vastness of the Amazon River. Being a zoologist in the corporate environment, I have had the unique opportunity to teach and bring man closer to his environment—even if only for a fleeting second."

Whether it's antelope or ants, beetles or bears, houseflies or horses, your child will find something of interest in these whinny-ing resources:

Animals   www.pbs.org/teachersource/recommended/rec_links_science.shtm#1

A collection of animal-related Web sites from PBS TeacherSource. ☆☆☆

Animals and Plants
www.cincyzoo.org/mainhtm/2index.htm

"The Cincinnati Zoo's site. We love zoos, especially when they're available online. This one is a favorite with my seven-year-old son. It has photos and information on both animals and plants, as well as online exhibits." —A.G. ☆☆☆☆

Hotlinks

Cleveland Metroparks Zoo
www.clemetzoo.com

Detroit Zoological Institute
www.detroitzoo.org
/site_map.htm

Dr. Frog's Recipe Page
frog.simplenet.com/froggy
/recipes.shtml

**Katerpillars
(and Mystery Bugs)**
www.uky.edu/Agriculture
/Entomology/ythfacts
/entyouth.htm

Cleveland Metroparks Zoo   www.clemetzoo.com

"Some zoo sites are better than others. This is one of the best I've seen so far. It features a virtual tour of the zoo itself and an in-depth virtual tour of the zoo's rain forest. It also contains information on more than 100 animals and offers online zoo quizzes and coloring pages." —A.G. ☆☆☆☆☆

Detroit Zoological Institute   www.detroitzoo.org/site_map.htm

"Another zoo. This one is unique in that it has a behind the scenes section where you learn about the jobs of a zookeeper and a vet. You also get to tour a zoo hospital. The online zoo includes an aviary, a giraffe house, a river otter building, a snow monkey area, an elephant barn, and many more." —A.G. ☆☆☆☆

Dr. Frog's Recipe Page   frog.simplenet.com/froggy/recipes.shtml

"A fun page, provided you are a five-year-old boy! Of course, there are girls, too, who will probably appreciate this site. It includes a wonderful list of recipes for insects suitable for human consumption. If you can forget about the fact that you are eating bugs, the recipes are quite tasty. I used this site when we studied the rain forest, and am now using it as we study the Philippines (some of these dishes are similar to ones I actually ate while living there)." —A.G. ☆☆☆☆☆

Katerpillars (and Mystery Bugs)

www.uky.edu/Agriculture/Entomology/ythfacts/entyouth.htm

Keep your youngster's interest with an afternoon of bug hunting. This University of Kentucky site introduces entomology in all its buggy glory. My daughter likes this kind of thing probably more than my sons do. Lots of icky stuff, but her hands stay clean. ☆☆☆☆☆

King Cobra

www.nationalgeographic.com/kingcobra/index-n.html

"This excellent interactive site from *National Geographic* is good for beginning or ending a study on reptiles or snakes, in particular.

Free Video Insect Zoo

With *Planet Insect,* you can tour the O. Orkin Insect Zoo at the Smithsonian Institution's Museum of Natural History. Call 800-563-4687.

Science

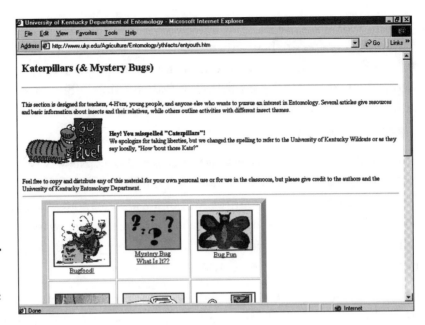

Figure 12.13

Katerpillers: A great site for anybody itching to learn more about entomology.

My son first began using this site when he was five; he is now seven and still loves it. It's very informative and gives a nice feeling of low-key suspense." —A.G. ☆☆☆☆

Reviled and Revered
educate.si.edu/resources/lessons/siyc/herps/start.html
Toads, Turtles, Snakes, Salamanders, and Other Creepers and Crawlers: a lesson plan from the Smithsonian. ☆☆☆☆

Zoology   cc.owu.edu/~mggrote/pp/zoology/f_zoology.html
A small collection of lessons, such as Breakfast for the Birds, designed for the youngest grades. ☆☆☆☆

Health Handbook

I SUPPOSE WE'RE a typical family when it comes to health. One son is a vegetarian. My older daughter is an athlete. Another son works at McDonald's. And so it goes.

Health education ain't what it used to be. As mankind's knowledge about health issues has grown, so too has the complexity of living a fit and healthy life.

Where your childhood was spent learning about jumping jacks and cigarettes and eating your apple a day, your children face a world with food pyramids and aerobics and DARE programs and HIV. Substance abuse, gerontology, untreatable viruses and infections, abortion—they're all part of the new face of health education, which today comprises physical fitness, personal hygiene, and the development of lifestyle practices that improve the quality of life.

Jody O'Donnell, from Columbus, Ohio, is a nurse who home-schools two of her seven kids. She explains how she incorporates health lessons as a natural part of her complete homeschooling program: "A lot of our homeschooling comes from doing chores," she says. "When the oldest cooks, she's learning math and home economics. When we shop, there's math again, and socialization. By participating in church activities, she learns socialization, church history, music (she sings solos at times), and art (she recently designed and made bracelets with her youth group). For science, we have gone to a space museum and my husband builds and flies model rockets with the kids.

"My daughter was with me through my last pregnancy and delivery and wrote a paper on it. This pregnancy was different from the others; I was diagnosed with gestational diabetes, so that was a little more to research.

"If my daughter reads a book, she writes a report. Right now she is reading a series of books and will write summaries of what she reads. We place everything in a file for her end-of-the-year evaluation.

"My oldest is a good kid, and I feel blessed to be spending this time with her. The house is cluttered, but the kids have fun!"

👪 How We Homeschool

"My kiddies have never gone to public school. When my oldest, now 11, was just barely two and in the church's nursery, he couldn't sit still. He would finish with the little cut-and-paste activity very quickly and would then want to move on to other things. Usually he'd be running around because all the other kids were sitting still, trying to figure out where to paste the circle and where to paste the triangle. I got very tired of him being treated as if he were a behavior problem.

"I had heard of homeschooling only on a sitcom. The mom started homeschooling her son because he was getting mixed up with the wrong kids at school. I didn't think that this kind of thing really existed, until I learned that there was a homeschool family just down the street! I picked their brains, and learned that there were homeschool families at my church. So I picked their brains, too.

"At that time my husband was in Saudi Arabia with the Air Force. He called one day, and I told him I had decided to homeschool. He said we should think about it, and I told him, 'No. You don't understand; I've already decided.' I've never looked back.

"To sum it up, we started because I couldn't bear the thought of my sweet active child being forced to sit in one seat all day long. How unnatural! We do it now because we love it."

—**Susan D. Clawson**, homeschooling mother of five, Clearfield, Utah

In this chapter, you'll be introduced to resources on community health, drug abuse education, human development, mental health, nutrition, personal health, physical education, and safety and first aid.

First, though, we visit some resources that address a wide variety of health topics:

Complete Home Medical Guide   cpmcnet.columbia.edu/texts/guide
An online health textbook covering most major health-related issues. This one's very comprehensive, but the writing sometimes lapses into medicalese. ☆☆☆☆

Health Education Curriculum   Unitswww.uen.org/cgi-bin/websql
/lessons/query_lp.hts?corearea=7&area=2
Very thorough lesson plans for all ages. A complete health education. ☆☆☆☆☆

HealthWorld   www.healthy.net

▤ Pick the Library! Your kids will enjoy this graphic page that lets them click on a building in a health complex to find almost anything related to healthy living. ☆☆☆☆☆

Hotlinks

HealthWorld
www.healthy.net

KidsHealth
www.kidshealth.org

**Virtual Office of the
Surgeon General**
www.surgeongeneral.gov

World Health Organization
www.who.int

iVillage allHealth   www.allhealth.com

▤ An interesting health site covering everything from attention deficit disorder to vaginal infections. Learn about dozens of kinds of tests, and choose from dozens and dozens of prescription drugs. News, boards, chats . . . a doctor could get lost in here and not come out for weeks. Imagine what you'll find! ☆☆☆☆☆

KidsHealth   www.kidshealth.org

▤ Separate sections for kids, teens, and parents. All about growing up, staying healthy, illnesses, and more. Be aware of the section on contraceptives; the remainder of the site is uncontroversial. ☆☆☆☆☆

Prevention Online   www.health.org

▤ Your preadolescent daughter will enjoy the Girl Power! link; your younger children will learn from the Kids Only link. ☆☆☆☆

Spring 4 Health   www.directcon.net/spring4/index.html

▤ A school nurse authored this site that integrates health education and fitness strategies. ☆☆☆

Teacher Guide to Health Education   tlc.ai.org/thealth.htm

▤ Organized lesson plans on diseases, fitness, nutrition, aging, and much more. Access Indiana provides this Teacher's Guide. Interesting. ☆☆☆☆

Virtual Encyclopedia Health and Medicine
www.refdesk.com/health.html

▤ Health news and several hundred alphabetized links to health resources on the Internet. ☆☆☆☆

Virtual Office of the U.S. Surgeon General   www.surgeongeneral.gov

The For Kids link contains sections for parents and teachers, as well as a Learn More About link to lots of important health information. The articles here are written with clarity and are easy to read. ☆☆☆☆☆

World Health Organization   www.who.int

Click the Health Topics link for tons of well-organized information on worldwide health topics. The WHO coordinates health initiatives worldwide. ☆☆☆☆☆

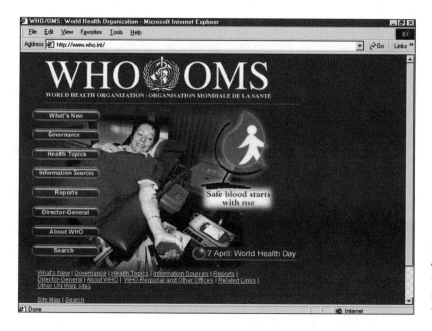

Figure 13.1

World Health Organization: WHO wants to help?

Community Health

THERE WAS A time, just a few years ago, when the medical and scientific community was optimistic about someday finding cures to all the world's ills.

That's all changed now. Not only are all-new diseases—including new and quickly mutating strains of hepatitis—making an appearance, but also some of the old standbys are proving intractable. Resistant strains of certain viruses and other microbes have developed in recent years, and physicians are observing that some diseases that once seemed imminently treatable are, in fact, incurable.

Health: From the Old English *hal (hale, whole)*. The condition of being sound of mind and body.

Moreover, behavior-associated diseases and conditions—heart disease, AIDS, lung cancer, fetal alcohol syndrome, and many others—are simply beyond the reach of the medical community as long as people continue the behaviors that enable the conditions.

Dr. Jens Query, a doctor of internal medicine at a university in Münster, Germany, says there are many reasons for teenagers and children to take an interest in health and in disease prevention: "First, the best therapy for a disease is to prevent the disease. One of the best examples is the incidence of lung cancer. Since the 1980s, the United States and other countries have spent millions of dollars for cancer research. The results might

Personal Health Freebie

"Rosalie's Neighborhood" combines interesting story lines and concepts with basic preventive health information. Call 877-4-ED-PUBS.

have been better if the government had closed down cigarette production and supported the workers. It's clear that the best way to prevent lung cancer is by not smoking; the epidemiological data demonstrate this effect. Yet what has happened? Whereas in the 1950s it was primarily men who smoked, now both men and women smoke, so the incidence of lung cancer is equal. This will be an important time for children and teenagers who smoke, because they are in the beginning stages of smoking. Unfortunately, it's very difficult to convince them of the danger posed by smoking, because they will not see the risk, and the cancer does not appear until years later.

"Another point of prevention will be adipositas (obesity). It's a very important issue because young people tend to eat only fast food and sweets. Adipositas is an important risk factor for several diseases, including diabetes and heart failure. Yet the number of obese people is growing, so it is very important to teach young people the problems associated with this condition.

"The worst thing for a doctor is a patient with a chronic disease, because in this stage we can often only reduce pain or give a symptomatical therapy."

When you're looking for ways to teach your children the fundamentals of health, the following resources will come in handy. They deal with medical issues, epidemiology, disease control, and prevention; some offer specific information on AIDS, HIV, and STD education.

Your children may not be ready to cure cancer, but with these resources at hand, they'll certainly be able to keep themselves healthy.

Better Homes & Gardens Guide to Colds, Flu, and Allergies
www.bhglive.com/health/coldflu.html

Just the facts about colds, flus, and allergies. Lots of fun stuff to keep you and your kids entertained while you battle a cold. ☆☆☆☆

Cancer Facts for Kids   **www.newsnet5.com/news/cancer/kids.html**

What kids should know about cancer. Includes a special area for elementary-age kids that explains the basics of cancer, answers frequently asked questions, and provides suggestions for things kids can do to help people they know with cancer or to raise cancer awareness/support in their community. For older kids, the site also includes updated news about cancer treatment, a quiz, a discussion area, and in-depth features on certain kinds of cancer. ☆☆☆☆☆

Cancer Treatments
ericir.syr.edu/Projects/Newton/9/cncrtrts.html

A well-done, illustrated lesson on cancer prevention and treatment. It's part of the *Newton's Apple* science program on PBS. ☆☆☆☆

Centers for Disease Control and Prevention
www.cdc.gov

The online presence of the U.S. government's Centers for Disease Control in Atlanta. (Aren't these the guys who tried to operate on E.T.?) Contains a

Hotlinks

Cancer Facts for Kids
www.newsnet5.com/news
/cancer/kids.html

Epidemic!
www.pbs.org/fredfriendly
/epidemic/home

Mediconsult
www.mediconsult.com

OncoLink
oncolink.upenn.edu

Health

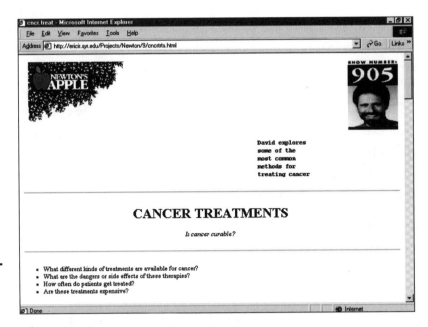

Figure 13.2

Cancer Treatments:
Preventions and
cures.

huge collection of data on everything the CDC is responsible for.
☆☆☆☆☆

Children with Diabetes   www.childrenwithdiabetes.com

Juvenile diabetes is a terrible disease. This fantastic site includes a
huge database of the most up-to-date information on diabetes. Ask a
panel of experts a question, or enter an age group-specific chat room
and find others dealing with similar issues. Very impressive collection
of information, and very child-friendly. ☆☆☆☆☆

Epidemic!   www.pbs.org/fredfriendly/epidemic/home

How today's medicine may be making tomorrow's bacteria
stronger. Resources, lesson plans, and more. A PBS-sponsored site.
☆☆☆☆☆

The Future of Medicine   library.advanced.org/28281

Is there hope for a cure? This slick site is packed with information and articles about where the field of medicine is headed. Geared
toward advanced students, it's a bit abstract. Your kids will find plenty

to think about in sections on designer drugs, robosurgery, genetic engineering, and other controversial topics. ☆☆☆☆

Hepatitis Central   www.hepatitis-central.com

Four times as common as AIDS, hepatitis C is an increasingly common disease. C, along with the alphabet soup of other strains of hepatitis, is explained here, together with information about research and treatments. ☆☆☆☆☆

HIV InSite   hivinsite.ucsf.edu

The University of California at San Francisco sponsors this huge site about HIV and AIDS, which is cosponsored by an impressive array of pharmaceutical companies and the National Institute of Mental Heath. ☆☆☆☆☆

Mediconsult   www.mediconsult.com

A compilation of information from eight major medical sites. Pick a medical condition, and get advice and information to make it better. ☆☆☆☆☆

Merck Manual   www.merck.com/pubs/mmanual

People used to pay for this stuff! The centennial edition of *The Merck Manual of Diagnosis and Therapy* is online and free. ☆☆☆☆

OncoLink   oncolink.upenn.edu

Support for cancer patients, and good information about various therapies and treatments. New research, answers to frequently asked questions, and much more. Your kids will consider this University of Pennsylvania resource one of the best references for up-to-date cancer information. So will you. ☆☆☆☆

University of Washington Online Continuing Medical Education
www.uwcme.org/courses/courseindx.html

These are online continuing education courses for doctors, who have to pay for them, but they're available absolutely free to the public. Of course, much of the information here will go right over the heads of us mere mortals. Still, it *is* free. ☆☆☆☆

Drug Education

ALCOHOL ADDICTION CAUSED Russ Taylor to lose his job, his children, his home, and, for a time, even his freedom. For a time, he even gave serious consideration to suicide.

Russ now lives in upstate New York and is battling Hodgkin's disease.

Drug: Related to the Middle English *drogge* (from *dry,* as in dried plants). Chemical substance affecting central nervous system, resulting in changes in behavior.

This is part of his very long, chilling tale of the effects of alcoholism: "My story," he says, "is one of alcohol abuse. I didn't know it at the time; being a product of the 1950s, when alcohol was a part of life, I thought the drinking was normal. It was the way I grew up. Drinking and driving were a part of tolerant society . . . and condoned."

When Russ was a teenager, his father was a heavy drinker. "The attitude he conveyed to my friends and me," says Russ, "was 'if you need to party, you do it in front of me.' I understand his thought process, though I don't condone it now."

Russ says that in his teen years, drinking made him feel competent, as though he "fit in," and was "cool." The truth, he says, was different. "What it really did was lead to my feelings of isolation, being unaccepted, having a small circle of friends, and becoming a dropout my senior year."

He pulled his life together enough to attend college and marry. In the beginning, the drinking was mostly under control. When his oldest child was three, however, his marriage began to crumble, and after his wife left home with his two children, he began drinking more heavily. Intermittent attempts to overcome the addiction were unsuccessful, and over the course of nearly two decades his condition deteriorated to homelessness and a period of incarceration, with his sons bouncing between foster homes and sometimes living on the streets or in shelters.

There's no happy ending to this story. Russ's life is beginning to come together now, despite crushing debt and continuing worry about being able to support himself. He's trying to rebuild a relationship with his sons, even as he faces a disease that is often fatal.

Health

👪 How We Homeschool

"We do what is called controlled chaos. We have a schedule that is not set in stone, except where the children have to be at the Catholic schools for their band.

"We start the day with devotional (prayer, hymn, scripture). Then they are on their own to do their work. They can work anywhere in the house they want, as long as they get the work done. They aim to finish by noon. The afternoon is for what they want to do, but no television. The television is on only at certain times, for certain things.

"Our kids go at their own pace. It is their education, so they need to have a feeling of ownership. Since we don't really have goals to have a certain thing done at a certain time, we are never 'behind' or 'ahead.'

"The schedule is not so rigid that if something interesting comes up, we can't change it. The only given is the morning devotional."

—Trent and Anita Joblin, homeschooling six of their nine children, Wisconsin

Russ is now a strong supporter of homeschooling and urges parents to teach their children the dangers of addictions: "Abuse of any substance—be it alcohol, illicit drugs, or nicotine—has a profound effect on your physical, emotional, and spiritual well being," he says. "Alcohol is a depressant, stripping away self-esteem, damaging brain cells, and killing vital organs such as the liver. Society has become less tolerant of drunks, and the legal consequences of a drinking and driving offense can exceed $2,500 or more, plus the risk of incarceration.

"Use of illicit drugs, even marijuana, exacts a heavy financial and legal toll too. In most states, simple possession of an illegal substance can warrant incarceration for two years or more. On the physical side, illicit drugs physically affect all organs of the body in varying degrees, and in some individuals, the small effects of one drug lead to cravings for more powerful ones.

"Nicotine is one of the hardest drugs to get away from. In most cases, addiction is instantaneous. Smoking-related conditions are among the top three killers, and include consequences such as cancer, heart and vascular problems, and fires. Health costs for the care and treatment of smokers are extremely high; most insurance companies triple your premium for coverage. And if you smoke in your home and then try to sell your home, a lot of people will not buy it.

Drug Prevention Freebie

"Murals Reflecting Prevention" has ideas for creating and collaborating on murals that engage young people in alcohol, tobacco, and other drug prevention activities through the arts. Call 877-4-ED-PUBS and request product number ESN0010K.

"Today's teens are under constant pressure to conform to the desires of their peers, and substance abuse is one of the negatives that the youth of today cannot escape. You can turn on television and see alcohol and drugs being used, and alcohol advertised on sports events, all giving the concept that it is *cool* to use. What is not shown is the grief, the pain, and the sickness that these substances cause with prolonged use . . . nicotine included."

Kathy Bohon was trained as a certified drug and alcohol counselor. She is now a stay-at-home mother of three living in Georgia. She explains the critical need for teaching children about substance abuse, even if they're homeschooled: "Homeschooled kids may face less risk of peer-induced substance abuse than other children, but they will one day enter college and be exposed to the high-pressure alcohol and drug culture common among young adults. Entry-level jobs are also a high-risk environment. Children should understand the health risks and techniques for avoiding pressure.

"Kids should receive accurate information that lets them evaluate what some people see in various drugs, while contrasting this information with the negative potentials."

The following online resources are the best around for teaching your children the truth of substance abuse.

Addiction

www.pbs.org/teachersource/recommended/rec_links_health.shtm#a
  A collection of recommended Web sites from PBS TeacherSource. ☆☆☆

Betty Ford Center   **www.bettyfordcenter.com**
  You don't have to be a celebrity to benefit from the alcohol and drug dependency information on this site. The Resource Room link has good educational materials. ☆☆☆☆

Health

Common Sense   www.pta.org/commonsense

Strategies for raising alcohol- and drug-free children, from the National Parent-Teacher Association and GTE. You'll find information about drug and alcohol prevention, family activities, support boards, and more. ☆☆☆☆

Drug Abuse Resistance Education
www.dare.com/index2.htm

The nationally acclaimed DARE program is online with drug-resistance educational materials for parents and other teachers. Read news and research as well. The parents' page discusses warning signs, the dangers of inhalants, and more. The pop-up ad from the sponsor is an irritant. ☆☆☆☆

Drug and Drug Abuse Information
www.schoolwork.org/drugs.html

Lots of categorized and reviewed educational links from Schoolwork, Ugh! ☆☆☆

National Institute on Drug Abuse   www.nida.nih.gov

This may be the premier drug abuse education resource in the world. Not only will you find information on every illegal substance; there's also good material on government policy initiatives, advice for students and teachers, research on treatment for addictions, and much, much more. ☆☆☆☆☆

Overcoming Addictions
www.knowledgehound.com/topics/overcome.htm

A whole collection of sites on recovery from addiction. Addresses smoking, sobriety, and drug addictions. ☆☆☆☆

Partnership for a Drug-Free America   www.drugfreeamerica.org

Get to know your children's friends, advises this site. PDFA lists tips for teaching your children to stay away from drugs. It's primarily a parent-oriented site. ☆☆☆☆☆

Hotlinks

National Institute on Drug Abuse
www.nida.nih.gov

Partnership for a Drug-Free America
www.drugfreeamerica.org

Prevention Dimensions
www.uen.org/cgi-bin /websql/utahlink /lessonbook.hts?book_id=114

Stop Drugs
www.stopdrugs.org

Health

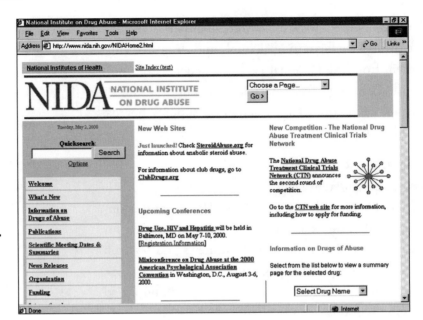

Figure 13.3

National Institute
on Drug Abuse:
Everything there is
to know about drug
education.

Health

*Drug Education
Freebie*

"How to Raise Drug-
Free Kids" presents
information from the
popular "Growing
Up Drug-Free: A
Parent's Guide to
Prevention." Call
877-4-ED-PUBS and
request product
number ED406640.

Pharmacy   www.utexas.edu/world/lecture/phar

A collection of college-level tutorials and primers, with lesson plans, syllabi, and resources ☆☆☆.

Prevention Dimensions   www.uen.org/cgi-bin/websql/utahlink /lessonbook.hts?book_id=114

Dozens of drug abuse prevention lesson plans, with text documents to support the lessons. Sponsored by UtahLink. ☆☆☆☆

Stop Drugs   www.stopdrugs.org

The usual collection of information about drugs, including steroids and inhalants, plus good information about identifying drug use and staying safe when approaching someone under the influence. ☆☆☆☆☆

Substance Abuse Prevention

thegateway.syr.edu/index2/healthsubstanceabuseprevention.html

Lesson plans from the U.S. Department of Education's Gateway to Educational Materials projects. ☆☆☆

Human Development

THIS MAY BE the section of the book that engenders the strongest reactions from parents. How do you effectively teach something as intimate and important as human growth and development, reproduction, and aging?

Many homeschoolers say they've found practical ways to broach the subject of human intimacy with their children.

Ann Crum homeschools a 12-year-old daughter and a 14-year-old son in central Arkansas. Living in a rural area, she says, has made things easier for her. "Over the course of time, sex ed has come into play not as a specific course, but as a part of everyday life. Through the years, we have had pets who have bred and had babies. We have talked openly about reproduction and gestation in those animals.

> **Development:** From the Old French *des (un)* and *veloper (wrap)*. Growth and change in an organism.

"My kids have witnessed breeding and birth and all the processes that occur in the mother animal during the gestation period. We have made it a point not to shelter them from these basic facts of life. We have also made it a strong point that we are humans, not animals, and that we have a commitment to our spouse before we have babies. Although the physical processes are similar, the moral aspects are quite different.

"My children were interested to learn, however, that geese mate for life. So they know that not all animals breed just with any old mate. They have witnessed the loyalty of a gander toward his mate when she is setting eggs or raising goslings and the fact that he will step up and block you from getting near by hissing and spreading his wings.

"We also raise goats, so they became yet another opportunity for hands-on sex ed. We have witnessed the breeding, the birthing, and the nursing of the kids. My children were impressed at how strong a bond exists between a doe and her kid."

Jody O'Donnell of Columbus, Ohio, is a nurse, and homeschools two of her seven kids. She advises parents to teach kids at their own level.

Health

"I would never tell my 6-year-old what I could tell my 16-year-old," she says. "When my daughter Hollie was asking these questions, I was in nursing school. She would sit there and look over my shoulder when I was studying and learned a lot."

Gerontology Freebie

"Teaching About Aging: Enriching Lives Across the Life Span" instructs parents and other educators about how to explain the aging process. Call 940-565-3450 or send an e-mail request to <natla@scs.unt.edu>.

Jody has advice for parents who feel squeamish about the subject: "Be honest with them. Use the correct terms, even if they repeat it to Great-Grandma. I would rather hear the correct terms than the slang words that society seems OK with.

"My oldest daughter went through Lamaze with me for my six-year-old and has witnessed two of her brothers' births. She even cut the cord on the youngest. Her best friend was there for this last birth, and Hollie explained to her what was going on.

"Kids need to know that their bodies are theirs and that if anyone touches them, it's OK to tell you about it. Be sure they know that no matter what, *you* will be there and will listen."

Another component of human growth and development is the aging process. Dr. Howard Dombrower is associated with a geriatric care center in Toronto, Canada. He believes it's important to teach children about the aging process for several reasons: "Aging affects all of us, and for this reason alone it is important to learn about aging," he says. "It helps us to better understand ourselves."

Another reason? We have some influence over how aging affects us. "Our grandparents and some of our parents are now experiencing age-related changes that affect memory, hearing, vision, skin, the joints in their bodies, their reflexes—even how their heart, lungs, liver, and kidney function. If we are to better understand our parents and grandparents, then it is important to increase our awareness and understanding about these changes."

Dr. Dombrower reminds children that some of the worst effects of aging are not inevitable: "Many of these age-related changes should not be confused with diseases. For example, although it is normal for short-term memory to decline in the elderly, it is not normal for the elderly to lose judgment, long-term memories, perceptual abilities, or abstract thinking."

Virginia Porter, a nurse practitioner in the Tampa area, has a great idea for teaching your children sensitivity for the aged: "A good educational experience for children is to rent or borrow a wheelchair for a day. Put a sling on one of their arms, make them wear sunglasses, and plug their ears with cotton. This sensitizes them to the way some elderly live; otherwise children's good health may prevent them from empathizing.

"Once the children have been sensitized with a wheelchair, spend the day at a nursing home. Listen to the residents' stories of what happened and how they got there. This would be the greatest learning experience in disease prevention."

With the following resources, your own children will be well prepared for the physical changes they experience throughout life:

Adolescence: Change and Continuity
www.personal.psu.edu/faculty/n/x/nxd10/adolesce.htm
Lots of information about physical and emotional changes particular to the teenage years. Covers social, emotional, and physical development. Case studies of three teenagers include sexual situations that many parents will consider inappropriate; controversial information also appears on the sexuality link. The remainder of the site is informative. ☆☆☆☆

Basic Anatomy and Human Reproduction
www.campuslife.utoronto.ca/services/sec/phy.html
"This site may not be appropriate for young children, but preteens and teenagers will like it. It is informative and has a FAQ section. It discusses sexual readiness and has pretty good descriptions of male and female reproductive organs." —R.B. ☆☆☆

Body Matters   www.bodymatters.com
Tampax sponsors this educational site that explains reproductive and menstrual health issues for girls. Warning: The site is nonjudgmental about unmarried sex and birth control, and uses the word

Health

Hotlinks

First Nine Months
www.pregnancycalendar
.com/first9months

**National Academy for
Teaching and Learning
About Aging**
www.unt.edu/natla

Straight Talk
www.straight-talk.com

Visible Embryo
www.visembryo.com

Health

"partner" rather than "husband" when discussing pregnancy. In addition, the site is liberal with self-promotion. Despite those two caveats, it's likely your intelligent daughter will find useful information here about reproductive issues. ☆☆☆

Developing Relationships with Older People
**ericir.syr.edu/Virtual/Lessons/Social_St/Sociology
/SOC0002.html**
Lots of good resources for teaching children empathy for people of older generations. ☆☆☆

First Nine Months
www.pregnancycalendar.com/first9months
A hypertext pregnancy calendar. Watch this show with your kids. View text and photographs that follow the development of a child in the womb. If this site doesn't leave you with a lump in your throat, you just don't have enough kids yet! ☆☆☆☆☆

Figure 13.4

First Nine Months:
See the baby grow.

Friends First   www.friendsfirst.org

Learn how to teach teens how to have the best sex . . . by waiting until marriage. Frequently asked questions, links, and research. ☆☆☆☆

National Academy for Teaching and Learning About Aging
www.unt.edu/natla

Research, curriculum, lesson plans, and more. ☆☆☆☆☆

Reproductive System and How It Works   www.stclement.pvt.k12.il.us
/StudentWeb/science/reproductionc/scienceindex.htm

"This site is more appropriate for younger children. Although it doesn't deal with sexual response, it does give explanations of fertilization. It also discusses development from infancy through adulthood. A great resource for my kids." —R.B. ☆☆☆☆

Social Studies: Gerontology

thegateway.syr.edu/index2/socialstudiesgerontology.html

Lesson plans for teaching about aging. From the U.S. Department of Education's Gateway to Educational Materials project. ☆☆☆

Straight Talk   www.straight-talk.com

Trying to teach your kids about abstinence? This site will be a big help. Includes dating strategies, 99 ways to enjoy intimacy without sexual involvement, reasons for abstaining, and more. ☆☆☆☆☆

Visible Embryo   www.visembryo.com

An online guide to the first forty weeks of human development, with text and Shockwave animations. Watch and read as a child develops from conception to birth. ☆☆☆☆

Mental Health

GOOD MENTAL HEALTH makes for a good life. Understanding mental health issues such as depression and an alphabet soup of other disorders makes healthy children more sympathetic, and helps children and adults

Health

who are afflicted with these disorders know when and how to seek treatment. In this section, we cover knowledge of self and others, self-esteem, and other mental health issues.

Dr. Basil Johnson, a retired forensic psychologist in Roseburg, Oregon, has spent 35 years in the mental health field, 22 of them as a doctoral-level psychologist with a specialty in forensic psychology. He describes the reasons it's important to teach your children about good mental health:

Mental: From the Latin *mens (mind)*. Relating to the order of the mind and brain.

"Perhaps other professionals would respond somewhat differently, but I believe that all of us have had or will have contact with one or more individuals during our lives who have experienced or are experiencing a major mental disorder. Some knowledge of mental health and mental illness is important so that we may recognize the symptoms and be able to respond in an appropriate manner.

"It often surprises people to know that 10 percent of the human population will experience a disabling mental disorder at one time during their lives. However, the extent to which that disorder impairs the victim is often dependent on the severity of the disorder, how willing the victim is to seek and receive treatment, and how the significant others (friends and relatives of the victim) respond to the disorder.

On Esteem

"He who knows others is wise; He who knows himself is enlightened."
—*Tao Te Ching*

"Without attempting to describe the symptoms of the 200-plus mental disorders, it's simplest to subdivide mental disorders into two distinct categories: thought disorders and depressive disorders. Generally speaking, thought disorders are characterized by illogical thinking and speech, bizarre behavior (well beyond what one would consider 'normal' behavior), erroneous beliefs (for example, that TV is controlling one's thoughts), and/or hallucinations (for example, a sincere belief that one can communicate with an entity that is incapable of communication, such as a rock).

"Depressive disorders are characterized by 'feeling blue,' easy irritability, outbursts of irrational anger, too much or too little sleep, eating too much or too little, self-isolation, feelings of despair, occasional feelings of hopelessness and helplessness, and, ultimately, self-harming or suicidal thoughts.

"Fortunately, all mental disorders are amenable to treatment, and treatment is available throughout the United States. The easiest way to find such services is typically in your local telephone directory, under the headings of 'mental health' or 'psychologists,' 'psychiatrists,' 'counselors,' and 'social workers.' You can also find help in the offices of your family doctor or local mental health centers."

Although she's now been "converted" to homeschooling as a principle, Shari Setter, a Peyton, Colorado, mother of five, started teaching her children at home simply to protect their self-esteem. When her second child was in kindergarten, his teacher informed her that her son had attention deficit/hyperactivity disorder. But her doctor disagreed. "The doctor said he was just a boy! The teacher wanted to hold him back in the half-day kindergarten program. I said *no way.* We lived on a street with five other kids who went to kindergarten with him. If that wouldn't have been a self-esteem killer, what would have?

"Then my daughter was suspended on her birthday for eating a piece of candy! (Her attitude had changed tremendously that year, and that had a lot to do with the suspension.)

"We decided to start homeschooling, and it has since become a personal conviction. I can't bear the thought of putting my kids into public school again. We live sixty miles from Columbine High School—too close to home!"

Your homeschooled children are probably more secure, more healthy, and more capable than many of their peers. But if they ever have to deal with their own or someone else's depression or bipolar, attention deficit, or other disorder, familiarity with the information in these resources will be a big help. You'll find related information on psychology in chapter 10 and on marriage and family relationships in the home management section of our companion Web site, www.hsfree.com.

Mental Health Freebie

"Warning Signs: A Violence Prevention Guide" aims to help youth avoid violent situations and even stop violence before it happens. Call 800-268-0078.

Health

American Psychological Association Help Center   helping.apa.org

Advice from the APA on coping with common problems at work or in your family. Some of the information here is a self-serving attempt to get you and your family into psychotherapy, but there's other good, practical information on improving family relationships. The material has an adult orientation, but it will prepare you well to teach it to your children. ☆☆☆☆

Counseling Center   www.couns.uiuc.edu/brochure.htm

Full text of numerous self-help brochures on various mental health topics. ☆☆☆☆☆

Health Education: The Medical Basis of Stress, Depression, Anxiety, Sleep Problems, and Drug Use
www.teachhealth.com

Stress, brain chemistry, sleep, and related health issues of particular interest to teens. ☆☆☆☆☆

Health Center   www.health-center.com

There's a lot of information here about mental health disorders, but you'll also find material on children's health care, seniors, strokes, smoking, and more. ☆☆☆☆☆

How Can We Strengthen Children's Self-Esteem?
www.accesseric.org/resources/parent/selfest.html

This online brochure from the U.S. government offers good advice for coping with esteem issues. ☆☆☆

Keirsey Temperament Sorter II
www.keirsey.com/cgi-bin/keirsey/newkts.cgi

The Myers-Briggs Personality Type Indicator. This self-test, and the interpretations you'll find on the site, are very popular for understanding personality types. Of course, some people think it's comparable to fortune cookies. You decide. ☆☆☆☆

Mental Health Info Source   www.mhsource.com

Information on dozens of mental health disorders and their treatment. ☆☆☆☆☆

Hotlinks

Counseling Center
www.couns.uiuc.edu
/brochure.htm

Health-Center
www.health-center.com

Mental Health Info Source
www.mhsource.com

Health

Figure 13.5

Health Center:
Mental health,
and more.

Health

Mental Health Net   www.cmhc.com

If you're teaching about mental health, mental illness and various treatments, this is your place. There's an extensive self-help section available here, too. ☆☆☆☆

Self-Worth   www.self-worth.com

Kids struggling with a poor self-image might enjoy this site. The author has been through some difficult times, and motivates people to be optimistic and happy about the future. ☆☆☆☆

Nutrition

I DON'T KNOW about you, but I've always found it a little off-putting to be told I am what I eat.

From a macular, cellular perspective, though, it's true. Every single cell in the human body is a product of the food, liquid, air, and other products that get processed by that body. If you consume nothing but crayons and bleach, your body will, in very short order, prove that it's a

Health

product of what it eats, and cease to function. When kids live off Twinkies and Pepsi, they have to consume an awful lot of pastry to try to suck out enough nutrients to sustain life.

Ryan Rupp is a baseball player in Leo, Indiana, who did course work in biology. He says being careful about nutrition changed his ability to compete athletically. "From my own experience I have noticed a huge difference with my gains in the weight room after beginning to take nutritional supplements. I feel that it is nearly impossible to get all necessary nutrients from food that I eat, so I usually take several dietary supplements each day."

> **Nutrition:** From the Latin *nutritus (to give suck, nurture)*. Substances that sustain life and promote growth.

He suggests a good way to motivate children to practice good nutrition: "Parents of a homeschooled child will want to find a topic that interests their child and that also relates to nutrition. For example, a child might look up to professional athletes. A professional athlete must maintain proper nutrition at all times or risk losing his or her competitive edge.

"Proper nutrition can prevent illness and help the body ward off disease. Not too many children like being sick, so they might be motivated to not repeat previous experiences with illness. Just like in the old milk commercials, the best way to motivate children to learn about nutrition is to explain how this knowledge will help them to grow taller and stronger, and how proper nutrition allows children to grow into healthy adults."

Nutrition Freebie

"Boning Up on Calcium" is available from Kellogg's. Call 877-644-5437.

Nurse and certified childbirth educator Danielle Leopold has been teaching about human growth and development for 14 years. She reminds parents and adolescents that temporary unattractive physical changes are a natural part of growing up. "Many preteens will go through a rapid time of weight gain before a time of sudden growth (getting thick in the waist and then tall). Let them know this is a normal change, so they do not get caught up in worrying about being 'fat' when they are really just metamorphosing."

🚶🚶🚶 How We Homeschool

"This is my first year, and we are fortunate to be experimenting on a kindergartner. I didn't use to see much value in unschooling, but I seem to be doing just that.

"He uses computer programs a lot, such as Reader Rabbit. (By the way, we got those at Sam's Club when they had a rebate equal to the purchase price—making them free, of course!) He began reading and spelling and sounding things out the week after we started the Learn to Read program. I suppose that means that we just lucked out in the reading category.

"For math we play games. He adds very well and subtracts a little. We play probability games such as "$3 of gas out of a $5 bill leaves how much change?" He helps with purchases a lot.

"I have a home-based business, so he is with me frequently while I work, and he learns constantly. He works on much of his busywork in the car, because we travel back and forth from Texas to New Orleans quite a bit.

"I know we would do better if we had a more formal schedule, and it is a goal of mine to schedule myself time to sit down and write out a schedule."

—Gina Zuiderduin, homeschooling the youngest of her three children, New Orleans, Louisiana

Danielle, too, has a suggestion for parents who want to motivate their children to learn about good nutrition. "Plan a menu for a healthful diet together. Meal planning is an effective way to teach. Adolescent girls need 2,400 to 2,700 calories a day; boys need 3,100 to 3,600 a day. Use balanced diet information and good nutritional guidelines. Have the child plan a week's worth of family menus to understand what goes into making a healthy life."

Joel Drakes, a personal trainer and nutritionist in New York, has been training for more than 15 years and is certified in fitness and nutrition. Joel says he has seen for himself the benefits of eating nutritiously. "I began exercising and eating properly around 17 years old and have never regretted it. I have never been sick, other than the regular cold (if you call that being sick), and have had no need of doctors.

"I watch people destroying their health trying to be wealthy, wolfing down their foods, and as they get older, their health wanes, then the same hard-earned cash has to be spent trying to get health back. Take a close look at the food the average person eats: It consists primarily of fat. Why do junk foods taste so great? Because of the fat content. It is no secret that fats makes food taste better.

"My son, who is eight, is very active in karate, swimming, and inline skating. All this activity makes him very lean and muscular. I recommend that parents get their children involved in some kind of activity, and that they lead by example. Forget the pizzas, french fries, and burgers for now. Consume wholesome foods."

To teach your own kids the importance of consuming whole foods, consider the following resources. (Related resources are in the physical education section later in this chapter and in the home management heading the in the Home Economics section of our companion Web site at www.hsfree.com.

Food and Fitness
www.uen.org/cgi-bin/websql/utahlink/lessonbook.hts?book_id=110

Sixteen thorough lesson plans on nutrition and food science for older students. Includes supplemental materials. Fifteen related lesson plans are available at www.uen.org/cgi-bin/websql/utahlink /lessonbook.hts?book_id=113. A very complete nutrition curriculum. ☆☆☆☆

Food Science and Nutrition Supplemental Resources
www.uen.org/cgi-bin/websql/utahlink/lessonbook.hts?book_id=3105

Well-done food science/home management lesson plans for older students. ☆☆☆☆

Food Timeline   www.gti.net/mocolib1/kid/food.html

It's an actual timeline for food. Ever wonder what the Vikings ate when they set off to explore the New World? How Dolly Madison made her ice cream? What the pioneers cooked along the Oregon Trail? Check out the Morris County Library's food timeline, jam-packed with recipes and historical information. Also available are historical recipe collections and lesson plans. ☆☆☆☆☆

Healthy Choices for Kids Online

www.healthychoices.org/ch1/ch1-index.html

Great unit study on nutrition. There are lesson plans and worksheets on nutrition for children at five levels. ☆☆☆☆

Introduction to Food and Nutrition

www.uen.org/utahlink/lp_res/nutri100.html

A nutrition and food curriculum guide. Teaching strategies, lesson plans, and more good information than you could use in a very long time. This curriculum guide is intended for use as a semester course in basic nutrition and foods. Discusses essential nutrients, vitamins, fats, fiber, energy, and more. Best for middle school and older students. ☆☆☆☆☆

Kids Food Cyber Club   **www.kidsfood.org**

Here's some fun: a site for kids, teachers, and parents that raises awareness about nutrition, healthy habits, hunger, meal planning, food preparation, and more. Kids will find games, recipes, and quizzes; you will enjoy the lesson plans, resource information, and at-home activities. ☆☆☆☆☆

Munch a Lunch

enternet.lth1.k12.il.us/w-cook/ricka/teacher.html

Participate in creating a multimedia cookbook. This multidisciplinary unit lets kids plan, prepare, and evaluate healthy meals. Database and spreadsheet activities will be used for gathering and tabulating information. A multimedia cookbook filled with student recipes will be shared with those who participate. ☆☆☆☆

Nutrition

www.pbs.org/teachersource/recommended/rec_links_health.shtm#4

A collection of recommended Web sites from PBS TeacherSource. ☆☆☆

Hotlinks

Food Timeline
www.gti.net/mocolib1/kid/food.html

Introduction to Food and Nutrition
www.uen.org/utahlink/lp_res/nutri100.html

Kids Food Cyber Club
www.kidsfood.org

Nutrition Café
www.exhibits.pacsci.org/nutrition

Nutrition Expedition
www.fsci.umn.edu/nutrexp/signpost.htm

Health

Nutrition Café   www.exhibits.pacsci.org/nutrition

My kids' favorite brick-and-mortar science place, Seattle's Pacific Science Center, presents this interactive site that introduces kids to essential nutrients and proper meal planning. Visitors may play Nutrition Jeopardy, volunteer to be detectives in nutrition case studies, or plan a meal and get instant nutritional information. The Science Center practices what it preaches. If you're ever in the Pacific Northwest, stop by the real cafe in the Science Center for the best, and most nutritious, sandwiches in Seattle. And a hint for fellow cheapskates: If you purchase an inexpensive annual membership, admission is free and you get a discount on food and other merchandise. ☆☆☆☆☆

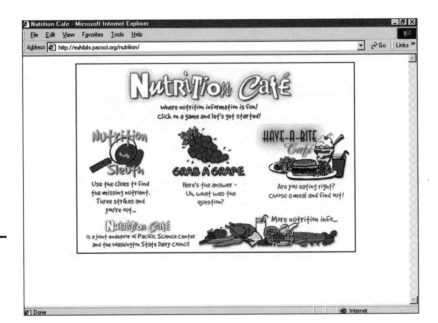

Figure 13.5

Nutrition Café: Yummy, healthy food, with nutritional information online.

Nutrition Center   www.healthy.net/nutrit

HealthWorld Online's nutrition section features, among other things, a chart describing all known vitamins and their function. There's lots of good information. ☆☆☆☆

Nutrition Expedition   www.fsci.umn.edu/nutrexp/signpost.htm

The University of Minnesota's Department of Food Science and Nutrition sponsors this Trail Guide for Educators, for middle school kids. It contains thorough lesson plans, ideas for extension, handouts, and links to related Web sites. Best of all: a parallel set of pages, written specifically for student use in the classroom, which includes fun assignments related to calcium, vegetarianism, and fast food. Includes nutrition-related links with suggested learning objectives and activities that can be used with each site. ☆☆☆☆☆

Personal Health

THE OLD SAW about snips, snails, and puppy dog tails certainly holds true in our family. With five boys, only some of whom are full-fledged teenagers, there's hardly an hour in our day where Dad and I aren't asking, "And did you wash those grimy hands?"

Fortunately, puberty seems to have a positive effect on personal hygiene. Whenever there's a dance or some other social event that involves *girls,* our older boys are found steaming up the bathroom, hanging over sinks brushing their teeth, searching for a new container of deodorant, or carefully pressing their shirts and pants.

Too bad their mother doesn't count as a *girl*!

That's little comfort, though, to parents whose children aren't yet to the point of obsessing over their own personal hygiene or other personal health considerations. If your children are younger, you may find yourself struggling to teach these principles effectively.

Laurie Welton is a hospital- and clinic-based infectious disease specialist and a professor of medicine in Michigan. She describes the importance of personal hygiene on the health and well being of your entire family: "A lot of common infections are

> **Hygiene:** From the Greek *hugieine (the art of health).* The habits and practices that promote good health.

transmitted from one child to another and then to the whole family by hands. A child sneezes into his hand; then, by not washing his hands, he can spread it to all the other kids and the rest of the family in the same household. The most common infections transmitted are colds, viral gastroenteritis, and even hepatitis A, which is often transmitted by a fecal/oral route if good hand-washing is not done around small children."

For parents, she offers this advice: "You might try some games to show kids how easy it is to transfer germs. Try using something that washes out but is easily passed to another by shaking hands or touching something. You could even make a game of it. Take something sticky (jelly or jam?) in different colors, name a different infection for each color, and let them enjoy themselves in a place away from your good furniture. Let them also brush their teeth with water-soluble black food coloring to let them see what their teeth would look like if they did not brush them."

This section looks at resources for teaching hygiene, personal care, and dental health.

Hygiene Freebie

Want to give your kids a graphic demonstration of the effects of dirty hands? Call 304-367-7137 or send an e-mail request to <alvra@fghi.com> for the agar plates, swabs, and gloves for the experiment.

Dental Zone   http://www.betterwebbuilders.com:80/dznewsletter.html
Hasn't been updated in a while, but the tips on dental care are worth reading. ☆☆☆

Health and Body   www.noahsays.com/cat.asp?cid=21
Stop nosebleeds. Drink more water. How to do a breast self-exam. Dozens of helpful articles on personal health. ☆☆☆☆

Hot Tooth   www.hottooth.com
Teeth hurt? Here's how to know whether you need a root canal. This illustrated site lists pain symptoms commonly experienced with teeth and gums, and suggests possible causes for each. ☆☆☆☆

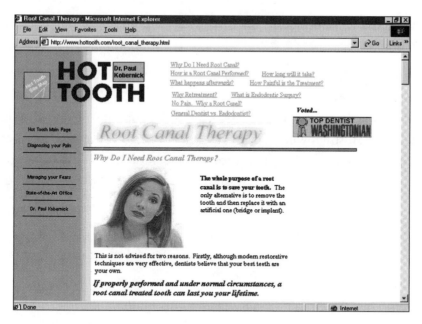

Figure 13.7

Hot Tooth: Oowie!
Read this *before* you
need a root canal.

Knowledge Hound: Personal Care

www.knowledgehound.com/topics/personal.htm

Hair, makeup, and grooming advice. ☆☆☆

Obesity   **www.obesity.com**

Eat for health: This site examines the nutritional component of obesity and suggests plenty of ways to combat it. News, information, and online community support for people concerned with health, fitness, and weight issues and weight loss. ☆☆☆☆

Oral-B Teaching Tools

www.oralb.com/teaching/index1.htm

Toothbrush makers have a vested interest in getting your kids to brush their teeth. Since you have the same goal, the educational materials here will prove helpful. Teach your kids the basics of oral health care with Oral-B's primary school lesson plans. The lessons are presented in five-day modules. You'll also find

Hotlinks

Hot Tooth
www.hottooth.com

**Preventing the Lion's Share
of Disease**
www.labs.net/schools
/marion/mms/health.htm

background information on oral diseases, proper oral hygiene, and tooth anatomy. ☆☆☆☆

Preventing the Lion's Share of Disease
www.labs.net/schools/marion/mms/health.htm

▤ Personal hygiene is the message, and the good people at Fairmont General Hospital will even provide the materials for teaching the lesson. Drive home the importance of hand washing with these experiments that demonstrate how germs are spread by unwashed hands. ☆☆☆☆☆

Sleep: From A to Zzzz   **library.advanced.org/26459**

▤ This project addresses basic sleep issues, including sleep disorders, dreams, and recent research. ☆☆☆☆

Yo, It's Time for Braces   **tqjunior.thinkquest.org/5029/**

▤ All sorts of great information on different types of braces and appliances. Explains what happens at the orthodontist's office, and what's involved in living with braces. Great advice about what foods to avoid and how to help with soreness. ☆☆☆☆

Physical Education

WHEN MY GRANDMOTHER was young, she went with a few friends to Washington, D.C., to work for the 1930 U.S. Census. While she was there, she played basketball and became a member of the national women's basketball team. I still have pictures of her in her bloomers and prim basketball blouse.

Unfortunately, I didn't inherit the family jock genes. Those went to my siblings, and, in particular, to my youngest sister, who, at 6'2", is a mean competitor on the basketball court.

But women's basketball has become a bit more competitive since 1930. Despite my sister's im-

Athlete: From the Greek *athlon (contend for a prize)*. One who possesses or acquires strength, agility, or endurance.

🚶🚶 How We Homeschool

"The best part about homeschooling is that you really *know* your kids inside and out, and the family becomes very close and respectful of one another as people. There is no peer dependency to speak of, no sexualizing of your children by the schools and by other kids, and your kids look to *you*, the *parent*, as the role model, not to a pack of prepubescents who are just as immature as they are."
—Gita Schmitz

mense athletic skill, she makes her living as an accountant and spends her weekends and evenings being a jock. She'll outlive me by forty years.

Lisa Williams teaches physical education and coaches softball in Eureka Springs, Arkansas. She has some great ideas for helping kids get enthusiastic about improving their fitness. "To motivate them, I tell them how much healthier P.E. can make them and how much fun they can have by getting and staying healthy," she says. "All kids are different, so you have to treat them differently when teaching them. Some give up easily; some won't give up trying until they are exhausted. I tell them not to give up and just do the best they can. Nobody is perfect. Keep trying!

"Reward them with something different and fun once in a while. Go hiking, swimming, or fishing as a reward. Kids can have physical education and not even know it! If you're teaching at home, try to have your child get some form of cardiovascular exercise at least three days a week for 45 minutes. Running, jump rope, cycling, and swimming are a few good examples. Make sure they warm up and stretch before any strenuous exercise. If you have access to a computer, check out the PE Central Web site (pe.central.vt.edu). It has all of the info you will need to get started."

Howard Martin is a certified fitness instructor and the founder and owner of a fitness consulting firm located in Victorville, California, and operates a commercial Web site that promotes exercise. He shares some thoughts about the importance of fitness for youngsters today. "We are meant to move, walk, run, jump, and be active," he says. "Not only does the body want to move, but it actually needs to move. It responds in a positive way when we do. The body becomes stronger and more flexible through exercise, and the mind gets a big benefit as well. When we exercise and use proper nutrition, we actually feel better mentally and perform better in such things as memory.

On Principles

"On matters of style, swim with the current; on matters of principle, stand like a rock."
—Thomas Jefferson

"We have invented all sorts of games that involve movement of the body, yet we as a collective society are becoming more sedentary. One of the best gifts we can pass along to our children is good health. By training young people to make better choices in their diets and teaching them the importance of regular exercise, we will be giving them a lifetime of better health. So become active with your kids. Get them involved in an activity with others. Get them jogging, rollerskating, and participating in sports. This can and will make a huge difference in their lives. Being fit and healthy is not an accident; it is achieved just like anything else, through becoming educated. Fitness is not looking like someone on the cover of a fashion magazine, either. Fitness is about a lifetime of exercise and proper nutrition."

If you're not yet motivated to "hit the road," these resources will give you plenty of helpful information about physical education, fitness, sports, and athletics.

Character Counts! Sports   www.charactercounts.org/sports/sports.htm
Pursuing victory with honor is the goal of this organization. While the site is not specifically directed at homeschoolers, the initiatives here will give parents a good foundation for teaching their children about sportsmanship. At the bottom of the page are numerous links to organizations (such as Citizenship Through Sports Alliance, www.sportsmanship.org/main.html) that promote good sportsmanship. ☆☆☆☆

Fitness Files   fyiowa.webpoint.com/fitness
I love this site. It's full of fitness tips for the self-taught. Included here are activities designed to determine target heart rate, ideal calorie and fat intake, the right sports or activities, and the Culinary Conscience Cafe, an interactive menu planner that explains the fat and

Health

calories in food. Other features include information about home gym equipment, sports first aid, the food pyramid, and basic stretches and exercises. ☆☆☆☆☆

Health and Sports Outline   commtechlab

.msu.edu/sites/letsnet/noframes/subjects/health

A unit study on fitness and sports from Michigan State University and Ameritech. Good lesson plans and activities. ☆☆☆☆

Learn and Share

www.rei.com/reihtml/LEARN_SHARE

/camptop.html

Camping is the first of eight subject areas on this site. Learn everything there is to know about practical fitness. In addition to the dozens of educational articles on camping, find information on climbing, cycling, paddling, snow sports, general fitness, fishing, and travel. ☆☆☆☆☆

Hotlinks

Character Counts! Sports
www.charactercounts.org
/sports/sports.htm

Fitness Files
fyiowa.webpoint.com/fitness

Learn and Share
www.rei.com/reihtml
/LEARN_SHARE/camptop.html

PE Central
pe.central.vt.edu

Health

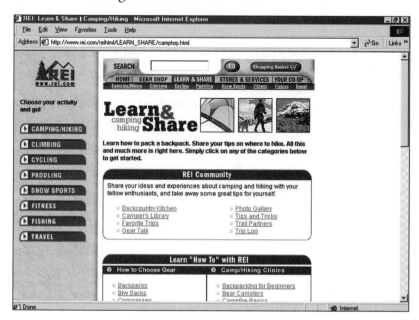

Figure 13.8

Learn and Share: Camping and more, from REI.

Nitrox Online Courses

www.coralspringsscuba.com/tdi_tech/tek_n2o2_door.htm

This is a little beyond my own experience—I only aspire to dive—but for a free course, it strikes me that there's an awful lot of information here. By completing the online portion of this course, your kids will learn all about safe diving. Then the next time you're in Florida, they can follow a few simple procedures, hand over some cash, and instantly become certified Nitrox divers, allowing them to dive Nitrox the world over. ☆☆☆☆☆

PE Central   pe.central.vt.edu

The ultimate site for health and physical education teachers, parents, and students. Lesson plans, adaptations for disabilities, top Web sites, and ideas for teaching preschoolers. ☆☆☆☆☆

Physical Education   www.sasked.gov.sk.ca/docs/physed.html

A Canadian curriculum for teaching P.E. to all ages. Lots of ideas, schedules, and more. ☆☆☆

Physical Education Curriculum Units

www.uen.org/cgi-bin/websql/lessons/query_lp.hts?corearea=16&area=2

Well-done P.E. lesson plans for elementary and intermediate-level students, with a handful of lessons for secondary students. A very complete P.E. curriculum for young children. ☆☆☆☆

Recreation   www.knowledgehound.com/topics/recreati.htm

It's all here: resources for baseball and softball, basketball, board games, boating, chess, computer games, cycling, football, golf, hiking and camping, line dancing, pool, running, jogging and walking, skiing and snowboarding, surfing and wakeboarding, other board and party games, and other sports. This is primarily a list of links, but they're well organized and regularly maintained. ☆☆☆☆

Weighty Matters   staff.washington.edu/griffin/weights.html

A fun place for people who lift weights. Selective archive of power-lifting and bodybuilding posts from the old misc.fitness and the newer misc.fitness.weights and other chat groups, plus bits and pieces from the "weights," "strength," and "weights-plus" electronic discussion groups. ☆☆☆

Safety and First Aid

OUR HOME SAFETY program is pretty simple: We all chase the toddler around and make sure she stays out of the Drano. It's sort of a combination fitness and safety curriculum.

There are almost certainly better, more disciplined, ways to approach this subject. Paramedic Barbara Kartchner has some suggestions for teaching first aid and emergency preparedness. She says the strategies for teaching these subjects are age-dependent and should include hands-on training as well as explanation. For several years Barbara was an instructor for both the American Heart Association and the Red Cross, and taught adult first-aid classes for a community college district in southeastern Arizona. She addresses her advice specifically to kids. Here is what she says:

"If any of you are Boy or Girl Scouts, you probably know the motto 'Be prepared.' What does that really mean to you? I think sometimes young people believe that because they are young, they can't handle emergency situations as well as adults do. First of all, let me tell you that some of the best students I had when I taught CPR were the younger people in class, such as in grade school. I think you are not as afraid to try new things, or as embarrassed when you make a mistake learning something, as adults are.

"I would also like you to think about a family member or a good friend being in an emergency situation right in front of you. Let's say they are burned by a pot of boiling water, or fall and break a bone, or become ill enough to need a doctor. How would you feel if you couldn't help them?"

> **Aid:** From the Old French *ade (help)*. To provide assistance or relief.

Health

Health

"All of the things I described, you could handle and get help for with the proper training. Give yourself credit for the ability to learn new things.

"My daughter Karen worked at our town's swimming pool in the summer as a lifeguard. One day a small boy dove into the pool awkwardly and hit his head. Because Karen had taken first-aid training, she and the other lifeguards were able to rescue the child and help him properly until the ambulance arrived. Karen said she didn't have time to be scared but almost automatically remembered what to do. She also said she was really glad to be able to do a good job in helping. I hope you will think about being prepared and be confident in learning to do so."

The following resources will get you started teaching your kids what they need to know about home safety, highway safety, and emergency first aid:

BoatSafe Kids www.boatsafe.com/kids

Are your kids fortunate enough to have access to a boat? If so, you'll appreciate this site, which promotes boating and water safety. Learn about life jackets, distress signals, and required boating safety equipment. In addition to safety topics, there are questions and answers about boating, a word puzzle, and nautical flags. And spell out your name in semaphore! ☆☆☆☆☆

California Poison Control System Answer Book
wellness.ucdavis.edu/safety_info/poison_prevention/poison_book

Download the booklet and print it out for emergencies. This site has information about common poisons and poison-related conditions including insect bites, Lyme disease, snakebites, mushrooms, pesticides, and food poisoning. It also includes a babysitters' guide, poisoning prevention tips, emergency first-aid information, and a section on pet poisoning. ☆☆☆☆☆

Buckle Up

Buckle-Up Safety Kit from the National Safe Kids Campaign. To order, call 800-441-1888.

Hotlinks

BoatSafe Kids
www.boatsafe.com/kids

Further Adventures of Kidd Safety
www.cpsc.gov/kids/kidsafety

Learn CPR
www.learncpr.org

University of Texas Trauma Home Page
rmstewart.uthscsa.edu

Dental Emergencies

www.healthy.net/library/books/healthyself/firstaid/dental.htm

Emergency first aid for teeth. Teach this material *before* the emergency; you won't want to go hunting for it with a broken tooth in hand. ☆☆☆☆

FEMA for Kids   www.fema.gov/kids/icons.htm

Get your kids involved in emergency management. The Federal Emergency Management Agency helps people survive disasters such as hurricanes, tornadoes, floods, and earthquakes. On this site are some games and stories for the younger kids, and serious information about establishing a family disaster plan. There's a checklist of emergency supplies and a section about how you might feel during and after a disaster. Maps, photos, videos, and lots more are part of this site. ☆☆☆☆☆

First Aid: Skill for Life   firstaid.ie.eu.org

Dozens and dozens of first-aid situations, with treatment and advice. Very thorough. ☆☆☆☆

Further Adventures of Kidd Safety

www.cpsc.gov/kids/kidsafety

The U.S. Consumer Product Safety Commission developed this site to prevent injuries associated with consumer products. Take the Kidd Safety Challenge (a hangman-style spelling game), visit Cranium Canyon's three games on helmet safety, join the Kidd Safety Club (a skateboard, inline skate, and mountain-bike safety game), study up on fireworks safety, and much more. ☆☆☆☆☆

Learn CPR   www.learncpr.org

This is what your kids need to know about CPR. It's online, illustrated instruction for saving lives. ☆☆☆☆☆

Louisiana State University Trauma Center   www.trauma.lsumc.edu

Click the Prevention link to find good information on auto and firearm safety, burn prevention, and home safety. ☆☆☆☆

Safety Tips

Free Child Safety Kit, including "My Eight Rules to Safety," child safety tips, and the McGruff Safe Kids Identification Kit. Call 800-373-1284.

Health

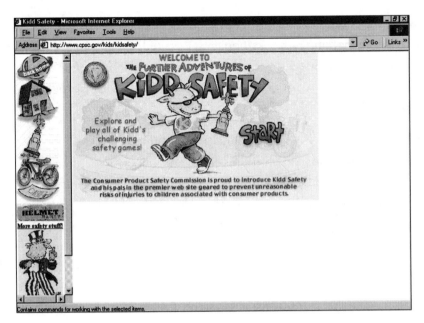

Figure 13.9

Kidd Safety: Your children's safety superhero.

Operation Lifesaver www.oli.org/oli

A train collides with a person or a vehicle every 115 minutes. Have a young driver in your home? A potential driver? You will want to introduce her to this tremendous site that aims to prevent deaths and injuries at highway-rail crossings and along railroad right-of-ways. Includes statistics and driving tips for young drivers, and a section with coloring pages, games, and safety tips for younger kids. ☆☆☆☆

University of Texas Trauma Home Page rmstewart.uthscsa.edu

Your kids need to check out this site, and so do you. It's an online visit to the emergency room—very educational, with lots of information about what causes injuries and death. ☆☆☆☆☆

Chapter 14

Graduation Guidance

© PHOTODISC

Graduation

Y OU'VE RAISED THEM, taught them well, and turned them into good people. Your parenting is never done, but at some point, your hands-on role as their primary educator will be. What's next?

In this final chapter, we look at what it takes to launch your kids into adulthood.

What do homeschoolers do when they finish their secondary education? Recent research suggests that homeschoolers don't differ greatly from the population at large. In two studies of 232 students homeschooled for an average of seven years, who had completed a high school course of study, 69 percent went on to post-secondary education and 31 percent found jobs. In the general population, those figures differed by only two percentage points.[1]

Other studies suggest that homeschoolers enter college at an even higher rate than the general population. A Department of Education study[2] found that just under two-thirds of public high school graduates enroll in college by age thirty. Interestingly, only a quarter of all high school graduates earn bachelor's degrees by the age of thirty.

A different study, this one of 20,000 homeschooled children, found that 88 percent of homeschooled children continue their education beyond high school, a figure the report compared with the 50 percent of the general population that do so.[3]

In this chapter, you'll find information on college aid, including resources for Advanced Placement, university and college search, college

1. National Home Education Research Institute, 1990 and 1996 studies, as quoted in Nanette Asimov, Teaching the Kids at Home, *San Francisco Chronicle,* January 29, 1999, www.sfgate.com /cgi-bin/article.cgi?file=/chronicle/archive/1999/01/29/MN87634.DTL.

2. Lynn Olson, Study Links High School Courses with College Success, *Education Week,* June 2, 1999, www.edweek.org/ew/1999/38grad.h18.

3. Stephan Archer, New Evidence Supports Homeschooling, *WorldNetDaily,* March 24, 1999, www.worldnetdaily.com/bluesky_exnews/19990324_xex_new_evidence.shtml, based on information available from the HSLDA site at www.hslda.org.

👪 How We Homeschool

"My daughter homeschooled during her senior year and a couple of months during her junior year. During her senior year, she primarily read a lot, concentrated on her music writing and singing, and worked.

"Before she started homeschooling, her public school experience had turned her off to traditional education, and she didn't see college in her future, though she had no particular goal. After working to help a friend by caring for her grandmother, she found she liked working with the elderly. She got a job at a nursing home, but the only job she could get was in housekeeping with a promise for training to become an aide, which never materialized. It was during her work there that she decided she wanted to become a physical therapist.

"She didn't have to take a GED, because she was enrolled in an umbrella group that had a graduation ceremony and offered transcripts and a high school diploma (The Learning Community, Columbia, Maryland, www.tlcn.org). She went on to community college, where she is currently in her second year. She plans to go on to university with a major in psychology. It's an adventure; who knows where it will lead? I believe her unschooling experience helped her renew her interest in education and believe in her ability to achieve whatever she wants."

—Joyce Dowling, graduated homeschooling mother of two, Prince George's County, Maryland

---

testing, financial aid, and admissions. Visit our Web site at www.hsfree .com for lots of additional resources on business and vocational education, and home management.

We begin with general resources for college preparation.

About College Topic List www.aboutcollege.com/topiclist.htm
▤ Questions and answers about virtually any topic having to do with college and campus life. Includes questions on topics such as adjusting to college, time management, and roommate issues. ☆☆☆☆

College www.powerstudents.com/college
▤ A whole new site every week, with dozens of articles on a whole new topic. Recent subjects included technology on campus, study abroad, and more. Very useful and very well done. ☆☆☆☆

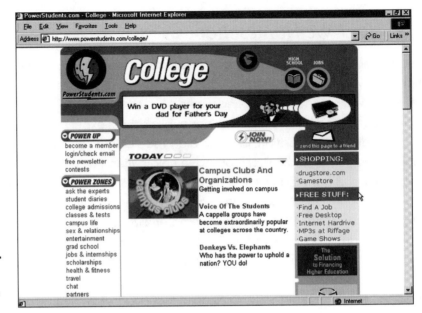

Figure 14.1

College: Survival guides, college buzz, and lots more.

High School and College Tips for Home Educators
www.kaleidoscapes.com/colleges

The Kaleidoscape message boards are wonderful: very popular, very helpful. Find answers to your burning questions about homeschooling high schoolers, and read great advice about getting homeschooled students into college, whether college is even right for your homeschooler, which tests and courses to aim for while schooling your child through high school, and much, much more! ☆☆☆☆☆

High School, College, and Beyond
www.nhen.org/emfiles
/High%20School,%20College%20and%20Beyond.txt

Good background information from the National Home Education Network for students nearing adulthood. Includes assorted articles and e-mail on the topic of high school, college, and apprenticeships. ☆☆☆☆

Hotlinks

Higher Education Center
www.education-world
.com/higher_ed

**High School and College Tips
for Home Educators**
www.kaleidoscapes.com
/colleges

**Preparing Your Child for
College**
www.ed.gov/pubs/Prepare

Graduation

Higher Education Center
www.education-world.com/higher_ed

A diverse collection of resources for your future graduate. Not specifically homeschool oriented, but there's so much here, it's a can't miss. Explore careers; find the right school, college, or university; find the right financial package or scholarship; choose a graduate school; or advance your professional career. It's all available here. ☆☆☆☆

LearningWare   **www.internet2.edu/html/learningware.html#**

Describes progress on the Internet2 initiative, which seeks to jump-start distance learning with new technologies. ☆☆☆☆

PowerStudents   **www.powerstudents.com**

Includes a discussion on "Will Homeschooling Hurt My Chances?" Warning: In general, you'll want to steer your kids away from the high school site, where so-called experts use foul language, tell a pregnant 14-year-old to obtain an abortion without telling her parents, explain to teenagers how to have oral and anal sex, and call a student who wavers over a decision to abstain from sex "schizophrenic." Consider having a word with the many commercial sponsors of the site about this "expert" advice. Other than that, it's an excellent site. ☆☆☆☆

Preparing Your Child for College: A Resource Book for Parents
www.ed.gov/pubs/Prepare

General questions, preparing for college, choosing a college, financing a college education, long-range planning, important terms, career planning. ☆☆☆☆☆

Princeton Review Home Page   **www.review.com**

A really great college database, with information on financial aid, career planning, and lots more. Princeton is a commercial site, but the free information here is worth reading. ☆☆☆☆

College Prep Freebie

"Parents: Your Children Can Go to College! Start Planning in Middle School" encourages parents to plan early for college. Call 877-4-ED-PUBS and request product number EAT0015P.

Graduation

Getting Ahead

FUNNY THING ABOUT homeschoolers is that they're so uniformly precocious. Every time I meet homeschooled children, I am struck again by their maturity, their civility, and their ability to hold forth intelligently.

Perhaps it's the company of adults that engenders such quality.

No matter what the cause, the result is that homeschooled children are often in a position to take college classes at an earlier age than average.

The goal here isn't getting them out of the house earlier. The goal is getting them through college economically—meaning securing the best possible education at the lowest possible cost.

> **Advanced placement:**
> College-level courses and exams for high school students.

If you've prepared your children to participate in academically rigorous coursework, it's a good beginning. Research suggests that the strongest indicator of whether or not your child completes a four-year degree is the quality of his academic preparation.[4] But you might also consider a couple of programs that can further ease your children's transition to college.

The first is called Advanced Placement (AP). The AP program offers college credit for college-level courses and examinations given to high school–aged children. The program covers 18 subject areas with 32 courses. If the local school district is cooperative, your kids may want to consider supplementing their home education with an AP class through the local high school, or they may wish simply to take the AP test for college credit.

The second program, offered in several states, is called Running Start. One educator I talked to called it Running Scared, because too many public school children use the program as nothing more than an excuse to get out of school. Basically, pre-college students take an examination, called the COMPASS, that tests their ability to perform at col-

4. Lynn Olson, Study Links High School Courses with College Success, *Education Week,* June 2, 1999, www.edweek.org/ew/1999/38grad.h18.

Graduation

👪 How We Homeschool

"I have lots of homeschool friends who get comments concerning their kids' educations and prospects of college, but most of the comments I get from people concern my sanity or how I can stand to be with my children all day. I smile and tell them that I love my kids. I think it is human nature to slip into the comfort zone of thinking that other people are better at teaching your child than you are: Sunday school, academics, domestic skills, et cetera."

—**Susan D. Clawson**, homeschooling mother of five, Clearfield, Utah

lege level. The three-part exam covers reading, math, and writing, and in the three states I'm familiar with, a high score on two of the three parts makes the child eligible to take classes at a local college for free.

Can't beat the price!

If you're interested in getting your children started early on the college path, these resources will be useful.

Advanced Placement Program
www.collegeboard.org/ap

📄 Basic AP info for parents and students. Read about the history of the program, view a calendar, and learn what your kids need to do to take the exams. ☆☆☆☆☆

AP Prep   **www.collegeboard.org/ap/students/prep**

📄 This is a commercial site, but it's chockablock with free stuff: sample essays, practice questions, essay-taking advice, and more. Worth visiting. ☆☆☆☆

AP Statistics   **www.bbns.org/us/math/ap_stats**

📄 An Advanced Placement statistics course, most of it online. ☆☆☆☆

Apex Learning   **www.apexlearning.com**

📄 A commercial site, but the demos are instructive if you're designing your own AP curriculum . . . and they're free. Apex uses Internet technology for its AP curriculum. ☆☆☆

Hotlinks

Advanced Placement Program
www.collegeboard.org/ap

Mr. Kelley's AP Calculus Home Page
www.geocities.com/Athens/Oracle/2613

AP Statistics
www.bbns.org/us/math/ap_stats

Graduation

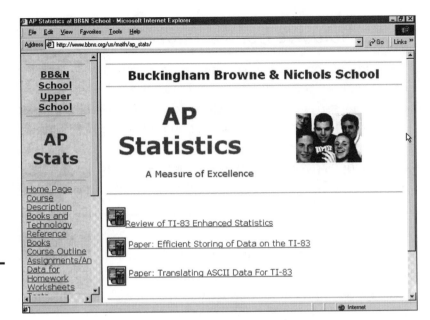

Figure 14.2

AP Statistics: Measuring excellence, for credit.

College Prep Freebie

"Think College? Me? Now? A Handbook for Students in Middle School and Junior High School" encourages middle and junior high school students to begin planning for their college education now. Call FSAIC at 800-4-FED-AID and request product number 820192.

COMPASS　**www.csi.edu/ip/ADC/testing/compass.htm**
Sample items designed to illustrate the form of the items in the COMPASS battery of tests. Includes pre-algebra, algebra, trigonometry, reading skills, and writing skills. ☆☆☆

International Baccalaureate　**www.emtech.net/ib.htm**
Scores of very well chosen resources. ☆☆

Is Your Teen Saying "Maybe" About AP?
www.familyeducation.com
/article/1,1120,21-13774-1,00.html
How the AP program can save your kids time and money in college. ☆☆☆☆

Mr. Kelley's AP Calculus Home Page
www.geocities.com/Athens/Oracle/2613
Good prep materials from teacher Michael Kelley. Among other features, this site offers answers to middle and high school math questions. ☆☆☆☆

Social Studies School Service: Advanced Placement   www.socialstudies
.com/c/@T0liJCvTaPG4w/Pages/advancedplacement.html

▤ Free sample AP-oriented lesson plans, covering U.S. history, U.S. government and politics, European history, economics, and psychology. Sure, they're trying to sell you something. But the free stuff is pretty good all on its own. ☆☆☆☆

College Search

YOU MAY OR may not do much "searching" for a college. The community college down the street might suit your children perfectly. If not that, then the nearest state school probably offers a rigorous course of study that will appeal.

> **College search:**
> Which college is best for the homeschooled child?

But as a homeschooling family, you may well want to do a *very* thorough search of colleges. Not only will you have to deal with the inevitable questions about your child's real level of educational attainment, but you'll also have to persuade red tape–bound admissions committees that your child's education has provided sufficient preparation for college, without benefit of official transcripts, which all too often substitute for thought among people without authority to change policies and rules.

Times are changing, though. Some prestigious schools not only accept homeschoolers; they actually actively seek them out, having seen the evidence that homeschoolers have more self-discipline, more maturity, and a better ability to "think outside the box" than their peers.

You'll find among the following resources a large number of home-school-friendly tertiary institutions—some private, some public. Happy hunting!

CollegeLink College Search   www.collegelink.com/cs

▤ The College Board's database holds more than 3,200 two- and four-year colleges. You can search by name if you have a specific school in mind or search by criteria (location, type of school, financial

Graduation

Hotlinks

Colleges That Admit Homeschoolers

www.learninfreedom.org
/colleges_4_hmsc.html

Homeschool-Friendly Colleges and Universities

www.rsts.net/colleges

How to Choose a Community College

www.accesseric.org
/resources/parent/commun.html

aid, sports, and so on) to find schools that match your preferences. ☆☆☆☆

Colleges That Admit Homeschoolers

www.learninfreedom.org/colleges_4_hmsc.html

Hundreds of colleges that admit home-schoolers, rated and ranked. ☆☆☆☆☆

Get Educated   www.geteducated.com

The homeschool of colleges and universities. Accredited college programs that offer degrees on-line or via distance learning. A growing list. ☆☆☆☆

Homeschool-Friendly Colleges and Universities

www.rsts.net/colleges

Most of the hundreds of colleges and universities on this page are linked directly to the school's Web site. Prospective students can even request information directly from the

Figure 14.3

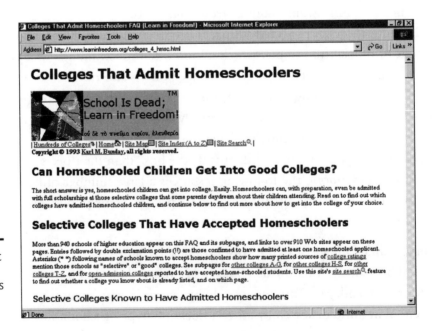

Colleges That Admit Homeschoolers: Select a school that's simpatico with home education.

Graduation

various colleges. Several dozen institutions actually advertise for homeschooled students from this site. ☆☆☆☆

How to Choose a Community College
www.accesseric.org/resources/parent/commun.html

A well-written brochure for parents seeking information about community colleges for their children. ☆☆☆☆

International Travel and Study Center
www.istc.umn.edu/study/search.html

Here's another way to go: This tool searches hundreds of study-abroad programs for one that suits your child's interests. As I'm a parent who lived overseas for many, many years, you won't be surprised to learn that I'm in favor of study abroad! ☆☆☆☆

Peterson's College Quest   www.collegequest.com

Search for the perfect college at this site. Includes financial aid and other useful information. ☆☆☆☆

U.S. Universities, by State   www.utexas.edu/world/univ/state

Links to nearly every major college and university in the United States and its territories. Not very thorough when it comes to community colleges, though. ☆☆☆

More Freebies

"Getting Ready for College Early: A Handbook for Parents of Students in the Middle and Junior High School Years" outlines the steps that students and their parents can take to prepare for college. Call 877-4-ED-PUBS and request product number EE 0083B.

College Testing

HOW WILL YOUR child do on college entrance examinations? If she's typical of other homeschoolers, the answer is: Very well, thank you. A study sponsored by the Home School Legal Defense Association (HSLDA) demonstrated that homeschooled children do at least as well on standardized tests as their public-schooled counterparts. The HSLDA study found homeschoolers scoring, on average, in the 75th to 85th percentiles on the Iowa Test of Basic Skills.[5]

5. Stephan Archer, New Evidence Supports Homeschooling, *WorldNetDaily*, March 24, 1999, www.worldnetdaily.com/bluesky_news/19990324_xex_new_evidence.shtml

Graduation

> **College testing:**
>
> Which examinations does your child need to get into college?

In our own home, my toughest academic challenge recently took his GED test, with very little preparation, and came away with scores in the high 80s and 90s.

With these resources, your own children will be able to blast their way through college entrance exams, and the GED if they wish, without any problem at all.

College Board   www.collegeboard.org
Register for SATs, find test dates, and more. ☆☆☆☆

College Power Prep   www.powerprep.com
Tip of the day, free downloadable software, strategies for acing the ACT and SAT exams. Not bad for a site that's trying to sell you something! ☆☆☆☆

4Tests   www.4tests.com
Free, online practice exams. You'll find a variety of standardized exams including the PSAT, SAT, ACT, CLEP, LSAT, and several others. Why is this stuff free? ☆☆☆☆☆

Free Online GMAT Course   www.testtutor.com/gmat
This could be a bit beyond your high school students, but it may be just what they need to be well prepared for college entrance exams. The business school–oriented tutorials cover everything your kids will need to beat the GMAT. It also covers basic mathematics (fractions, algebra, and the like) that they may have forgotten. Test-taking tips and practice questions too. Wow. ☆☆☆☆☆

Free Online GRE Course   www.testtutor.com/gre
Covers the information required to do well on the Graduate Records Exam. Again, your high school stu-

Hotlinks

4Tests
www.4tests.com

GED Preparation
www.free-ed.net
/fr10/index.html

SAT Prep
www.pinkmonkey.com

Study Hall: Serial Vocabulary
rampages.onramp.net
/~studyhal/novela.htm

dent should be very challenged by the material, but it's worth study-
ing for all the tips. Anyone who does well on the GRE would ace the
SAT or ACT. In general, the tutorial has the same format as the
GMAT course (see above). ☆☆☆☆☆

Figure 14.4

Free Online GRE
Course: Can't beat
the price—and this
is just one of several
similar resources.

GED Preparation   www.free-ed.net/fr10/index.html

Amazing—you've just got to go visit this one! The whole thing is
absolutely free: with online GED prep courses, tutorials, and activities. ☆☆☆☆☆

General Education Development   www.amby.com/GED

Links to several dozen useful resources for preparing for the GED.
Includes resources arranged by subject area. ☆☆☆

Opinion on ETS Report on "Cut Scores"   www.heir.org/etsopini.htm

A critical opinion on new scoring that discriminates against homeschoolers. ☆☆

SAT English Level 1

www.familyeducation.com/software/0,1745,21-7966-1,00.html

▤ Downloadable software that prepares your child for SAT English Level 1. (The Level 2 package is at www.familyeducation.com /software/0,1745,21-7968-1,00.html.) Help your child improve her verbal section scores. ☆☆☆☆

SAT Prep   www.pinkmonkey.com

▤ This site's SAT Exam Study Guide contains more than 300 pages of study tips, resources, practice drills, and tests. This sort of stuff is supposed to cost money! After you register at PinkMonkey (it's free), click the Study Guides link to see the guide. ☆☆☆☆☆

Study Hall: Serial Vocabulary

rampages.onramp.net/~studyhal/novela.htm

▤ What a great idea for learning vocabulary! SAT words are incorporated into a mystery novella; definitions appear in a separate frame. ☆☆☆☆☆

Vocab Builder   www.number2.com/gre/free/vocabulary-builder/

▤ A sampling of words often included on the GRE. Having taken the GRE, SAT, PSAT, and ACT, I can say with some assurance that these vocabulary words will be useful for any college entrance exam. ☆☆☆☆

Financial Aid

I PAID MY own way through college, and until the last term of my senior year, I did it without taking out a long-term loan. At times it was tough coming up with tuition, and books, and materials. I remember once telling my father that I didn't know how I'd pay for an upcoming term and still keep a roof over my head or food in my tummy.

"Just pay it," he told me. Some advice. But somehow, I did. (And the double-digit size of my pants bears witness to the fact that I didn't starve, either.)

Between Pell Grants, scholarships, long- and short-term loans, and, of course, a job, I'm persuaded there's no reason any intelligent, healthy person, with or without spouse and children, can't go to college. It's not always pretty. I spent a lot of years without health insurance, living in basement apartments, and riding a bicycle. I persuaded an employer to pay my way through law school. Through grad school (where I finally succumbed to the lure of student loans), I managed to keep all my children healthy and happy, even if we did spend an inordinate amount of time in thrift stores.

Now that two of my children are trying to manage college and work, I've become aware of some other possibilities for getting through. If you're of a mind to help your children through college financially, there are a number of financial aid packages available to you.

And the option nobody ever told me about is plenty appealing to my sons: the military. Depending on what programs they consider, there's a possibility of obtaining $40,000 or more in free college money—plus their salary, health insurance, and room and board while they're in the service.

Here's what you and your children need to know about college loans, grants, scholarships, and work programs.

And just one more piece of advice, no matter who's footing the bill: When everything seems bleak, and you can't figure out how to cover tuition and books and all your other expenses . . . sometimes, you just have to buckle down and pay it.

> **Financial aid:**
> How will you and your child pay for college?

Financial Aid Freebie

Request a copy of the Student Guide for the next award year from the Federal Student Aid Information Center. Call 800-4-FED-AID.

Graduation

American Express Education Loans

home3.americanexpress.com/edloans

🖥 American Express wants your educational loan business, and they go out of their way to get it. Great information here for parents, students, and others. Includes answers to frequently asked questions.
☆☆☆☆

Hotlinks

American Express Education Loans
home3.americanexpress.com /edloans

FinAid! The Smart Guide to Financial Aid
www.finaid.org

Meeting College Costs
www.collegeboard.org /finaid/fastud/html /proform.html

Scholarship Page
www.scholarship-page.com

AmericaReads   www.ed.gov/inits/americareads

Information on a work-study program that pays college students to teach reading. ☆☆☆☆

Compare Your Aid Awards
nextstopcollege.cbreston.org/adms/tools/home.htm

This College Board-affiliated site explains what the government expects your family to pay toward the college tuition bill. ☆☆☆☆

FAFSA on ther Web!   fafsa.ed.gov

The government's Free Application for Federal Student Aid online. Check the status of your application, find answers to FAQs, check deadlines and more. ☆☆☆☆

FinAid! The Smart Guide to Financial Aid
www.finaid.org

An online guide to financial aid. Covers military benefits, loans, scholarships, grants, grad school funding, and much more. ☆☆☆☆☆

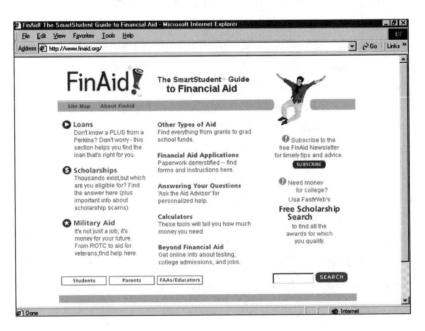

Figure 14.5

FinAid! It's pretty smart stuff.

Graduation

Free Scholarships and Financial Aid

www.collegefunds.net/examples.htm

A small sample from a large commercial database of scholarships. ☆☆☆

Graduate Assistantship Directory   www.acm.org/gad

Financial aid for graduate students in computing, organized geographically. ☆☆☆

Meeting College Costs

www.collegeboard.org/finaid/fastud/html/proform.html

Apply for financial aid, online. ☆☆☆☆☆

National Gifted Children's Fund   www.ngcfcharity.org

A nonprofit charity, created for the sole purpose of assisting profoundly gifted children with their education. The organization provides direct assistance in the form of tuition, tutorial fees, computers, software, musical instruments, books, science equipment, curriculum, testing, and other individual educational needs specific to each applicant. ☆☆☆☆

Scholarship Page   www.scholarship-page.com

Links, search tool, and much more. Lots and lots of good, free scholarship information. ☆☆☆☆☆

Services for Financial Aid Staff

www.collegeboard.org/toc/html/tocfinancialaid000.html

Dozens of articles about financial aid, and links to financing resources. ☆☆☆☆

Financial Aid Freebie

Going to College: Financial Aid Night presents an interactive teleconference where renowned national experts, local educators, and community leaders share ideas on financial aid for college. Call 877-4-ED-PUBS and order Satellite Town Meeting #56.

College Admissions

UNTIL I CAME straight up against it, I didn't put much thought into getting admitted to college. I think my little teenaged mind assumed some sort of fairy princess would come along and take care of all the paperwork for me.

That's how I ended up attending the local community college. It had very nearly an open admissions policy, meaning that I didn't have to do much of anything to be admitted.

> **Admissions:** How to wend your way through the red tape.

But it was a very quick trip from my first day of class to the realization that I really, really wanted to enroll in a "real" school—the big university that several of my favorite adults had attended. And I came face to face with the fact that I was utterly clueless about how to get into college. I had to go begging for help. Fortunately, one of those adults knew where to go to get the admissions application and was willing to walk me through the process.

Your kids needn't be as dumb as I once was. All the applications information they could ever want is available online, and most of it is free. In this section we consider general college and university admissions information, including vocabulary and definitions, and an introduction to college. Here you and your kids will learn how to complete written applications and essays, as well as find information about applications deadlines, planning, resources and more.

Prepare for College

"Preparing Your Child for College: A Resource Book for Parents" helps parents work with their children, teachers, and guidance counselors to ensure that their kids have the option of going to college. Call 877-4-ED-PUBS and request product number ED/OUS94-35R.

ApplyWeb   www.applyweb.com
⊟ Use this handy search form to locate official online applications. Search by location and degree level. ☆☆☆☆

Admission Secrets   www.powerstudents.com
/highschool/hs_prep/hs_admissionsecrets.shtml
⊟ Lots of articles about college admissions, plus the column "Ask the Admissions Gods"—questions from students on how to get into that ideal school. ☆☆☆☆

College Admissions Resources
connect.familyeducation .com/webx/webx.dll?230@@.ee6c97e
⊟ A message board for college admissions questions.
☆☆☆☆

♟♟♟♟ *How We Homeschool*

"I left public school after grade nine to go to university full-time. I had been taking classes part time (one per semester since grade five), but they wouldn't let me sign up full time until I had a diploma or a GED. So I jumped through the hoops, got my GED, and registered for classes. Since then I have never had anyone say anything about my not graduating high school, neither universities nor employers. I have never taken the SAT or the ACT tests, so I can't say what their influence might have been, as I had so many credits from my part-time classes I was considered a transfer student and not a new student. Depending on your child you might consider having them take a class or two at the local community college (not as matriculating students, just as drop-in students) to give them that padding on the their transcripts when it is time for them to apply to University."

—vanessa ronsse, homeschooling mother of one, Seattle area

Embark   www.embark.com
Apply online, or get recruited, through this useful service. ☆☆☆☆☆

High School and College Planning
www.familyeducation.com/subchannel/0,2794,21-110,00.html
The whole planning and admissions process, explained. Includes tips (writing a winning college admission essay), resources, and timelines for parents and teens. ☆☆☆☆☆

Homeschool Teens and College   www.homeschoolteenscollege.net
College application for homeschoolers, educating older children, and more. Good starting point for getting kids into college. Includes "How Homeschooling Leads to Admissions to the Best Colleges and Universities," a sample chapter of a book that describes how a family of homeschoolers were admitted to their first-choice colleges with substantial scholarships. ☆☆☆☆☆

Talbot's Articles   www.talbotsbook.com
Click the Articles link for instructional articles on topics such as "What Next After High School?" "Start Your Career Planning Now,"

Graduation

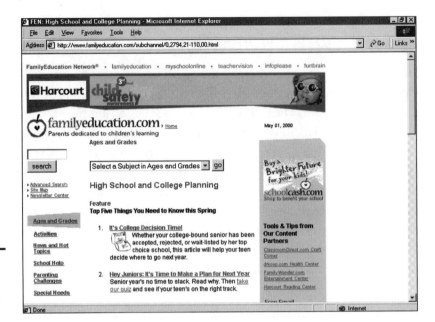

Figure 14.6

High School and
College Planning:
Good advice for the
college bound.

Hotlinks

**High School and College
Planning**
www.familyeducation.com
/subchannel/0,2794
,21-110,00.html

**Homeschool Teens
and College**
www.homeschoolteenscollege
.net

Talbot's Articles
www.talbotsbook.com

TheAdmissionsOffice
www.theadmissionsoffice.com

"Special Benefits of Small Colleges," "Is College Worth the Cost?" "Why Study the Liberal Arts?" "Your College Major," "Selecting the Right College," "Advantages of a Large University," "On Postponing College," "Coping with College," "Getting the Most out of College," and more. ☆☆☆☆

TheAdmissionsOffice
www.theadmissionsoffice.com
Lots of helpful admissions advice under the Ask Lisa heading, commingled with information about financial aid and everything else a potential college student needs to know. ☆☆☆☆☆

Writing the College Application Essay
www.collegeview.com/bookstore/collegegate.html
A three-part excerpt from CollegeGate's professional editing service covers brainstorming ideas, choosing a topic, and how to write an effective and powerful essay. ☆☆☆☆

Appendix

Curriculum:
Scope and Sequence
Recommendations

| Subject/Age | FAMILY YEARS | | | | | COMMUNITY |
	Preschool	5	6	7	8	9
Basic Education (service, library and media, listening, logic and thinking, reference materials, research writing, study skills, values and decision making. See Ch. 4)	Family service, library story time, basic family values	Basic listening and study skills	Children's section of the library	Overview of thinking skills and library reference materials	Community service, library card catalog, decision making	Community service, basic reference materials, intermediate study skills
Language Arts (etymology, grammar, literature, reading, speech, spelling, vocabulary, writing. See ch. 5)	Oral language, reading alphabet with sounds and first words	Oral language, recognition of written words, speech etiquette, writing alphabet	Homophones, basic grammatical tenses, reading sentences, basic spelling and vocabulary, writing words	Antonyms, basic punctuation, reading plotted stories, basic spelling and vocabulary, writing sentences	Synonyms, reading short books, speaking in small groups, intermediate spelling and vocabulary, writing paragraphs	Reading books with chapters, intermediate spelling and vocabulary, keeping a journal
Mathematics (basic math, pre-algebra, algebra, geometry, computer math, calculus, trig, statistics. See ch. 6)	Counting	Basic math	Basic math	Basic math	Basic math, keyboarding	Basic math, keyboarding
Art (art history, crafts, design, drawing, graphic, painting, sculpture, visual. See ch. 7)	Crafts, finger painting	Crafts, clay modeling	Crafts, poster paint	Art history, crafts	Design, basic photography	Drawing
History (American, American West, ancient, genealogy, modern American, religion, state, world. See ch. 8)	Family stories, fundamental religious principals	American history, family stories	American West, family stories	Ancient history, oral family history	Family albums, state history	Journals, world history
Music (composition, analysis, instrumental, vocal. See ch. 9)	Singing	Rhythm	Basic music appreciation, scales	Basic notation, instrumental lessons	Basic vocal skills	Basic music appreciation

AWARENESS	WORLD AWARENESS					LIFE SKILLS	
10	**11**	**12**	**13**	**14**	**15**	**16**	**17**
Juvenile section of the library, note taking, basic research skills	Service to children, nonfiction section of library, listening comprehension, basic research writing, values/ethics	Geriatric service, library periodicals, intro to logic, intermediate research skills	Advanced logic, review of reference materials, intermediate research writing	Adult fiction, outlining, intermediate research writing, decision making	Career-oriented volunteerism, critical analysis, intermediate research skills	Academic periodical section of library, review of reference materials, advanced research skills, advanced study skills	Advanced research writing, college-prep study skills
Word origins, intermediate grammatical tenses, reading and writing poetry, advanced spelling and vocabulary	More word origins, intermediate punctuation, American literature, non-fiction reading, advanced spelling and vocabulary, writing fiction	Grammatical word choice, American literature, reading periodicals, review of spelling and vocabulary	Foreign origins of English words, advanced grammatical punctuation, English literature, independent reading, interpretative speech	Modern usage, English literature, reading adult fiction, improvisational speech	Advanced grammatical tenses, world literature, reading adult non-fiction, expository speech	Style guides, world literature, reading academic journals, extemporaneous speech	Archaic usage, ancient/ Elizabethan/ Jamesian literature, independent reading, debate, college prep spelling and vocabulary
Pre-algebra	Pre-algebra, calculator skills	Pre-algebra, statistical principles	Algebra, spreadsheets	Geometry, computer research skills	Calculus	Trig, programming	Stats, advanced computer programming
Art history, watercolors	Soap and soft media sculpture	Advanced photography	Art history	Design	Drawing, pottery	Acrylics, ceramics	Oils, hard media sculpture
Basic genealogical research, modern American history	Genealogy, basic history of religious faith	American history	Ancient history	American West, religious doctrine	Religious history, state history	Comparative religions, world history	Modern history, comparative religions
Basic composition	Intermediate instrument	Intermediate vocal	Advanced music appreciation	Group vocal	Intermediate composition	Advanced vocal	Advanced instrument

Subject/Age	FAMILY YEARS					COMMUNITY
	Preschool	5	6	7	8	9
Social Studies (anthropology/ sociology, civics, current events/news, economics, geography, minority education, psychology, social issues. See ch. 10)	Basic etiquette, neighbor-hood geography, integrated playgroups	Problem solving	Basic economics	Children's periodicals	Sociology, local civics, city geography, community involvement, local issues	Reading the news, state geography, state issues
Humanities (dance, drama, languages (including ESL and American Sign Language), journalism, philosophy. See ch. 11)	Free dance, bilingualism in the home	Short skits	Radio news	Folk dancing	Community theatre	Broadcast news
Science (See ch. 12)	Experimen-tation	Earth science	Botany	Astronomy	Ecology	Zoology
Health (community health/disease preven-tion, drugs, human growth/ development/ aging, mental health/ self-esteem, nutrition, personal health, PE/ fitness, safety. See ch. 13)	Free play	Human develop-ment	Personal health	Nutrition	Mental, non-competitive sports	Drug education, personal fitness
Graduation (college preparation [advanced placement, college search, college testing, financial aid, admis-sions], vocational education [careers, resumes, business management], home economics [personal finance, home manage-ment, parenting, mar-riage and relationships]. See ch. 14)	Basic home manage-ment					

AWARENESS		WORLD AWARENESS				LIFE SKILLS	
10	11	12	13	14	15	16	17
Regional geography, regional issues	National geography, minority education, national issues	American government, reading adult periodicals, continental geography, issues in the Western world	Anthropology, responsibilities of citizens, world geography, world issues	American government, micro-economics	State government, macro-economics, minority education	World political systems, behavioral psychology	Civil rights, intermediate economics, abnormal psychology
Intro to drama	Familiar foreign words	Journalistic style	Dance appreciation, professional theatre, intro level language	Foreign language speech, editorials	Foreign language reading, newsletter publishing	Foreign language writing, philosophy	Shakespeare, language fluency
Archaeology	Anatomy	Scientists	Technology	Scientific method	Biology	Chemistry	Physics
Community health	Human development, competitive sports	Aging, personal health	Drug education, nutrition	Mental health, first aid	Community health	Fitness	Fitness
Relationships	Parenting	Intermediate home management	Personal finance	Advanced home management	Life skills	Vocational skills	College prep

Index

About the Authors

LAURAMAERY GOLD is the homeschooling mother of seven, ranging in age from babyhood to adulthood. She operates one of the largest homeschooling lists on the Internet and writes a weekly Internet column on homeschooling. She is also the author of a number of books on technology, religion, and business. She and her husband, Dan Post, teach their children through an eclectic curriculum of free educational resources, the scope of which grows as the children's interests develop. The former managing editor of several overseas editions of *PC World* and other technology publications, LauraMaery earned her law degree from London's Wolverhampton University. She did her graduate work in journalism at the University of Missouri at Columbia. Her undergraduate studies were in family financial planning and counseling. While living in Taiwan and Hong Kong, she studied Chinese. She and her family now live in Kent, Washington, where the children are finally getting to spend time with their grandparents, aunts, uncles, and cousins.

JOAN M. ZIELINSKI is the mother of four—one of whom is LauraMaery. Joan, a professional educator for nearly thirty years, recently retired to undertake volunteer work in literacy education. She is a former Teacher of the Year for the Kent School District, one of the largest districts in Washington State. She earned her bachelor's degree in Arts Education from the University of Washington, and her associate's degree in Art from Green River Community College. She and her husband, Stan, are also licensed dog show judges and raise champion St. Bernards.

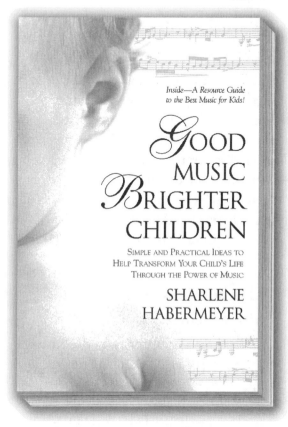

In a Class of Their Own

Pro football player, bestselling author, entrepreneurial millionaire . . . these successful people all have one thing in common: They were all homeschooled as children. In *Homeschoolers' Success Stories,* you'll discover their inspiring stories, along with those of a dozen other homeschooling "graduates" who have achieved success on many levels. In addition, you'll meet 12 younger people already well on their way to personal success.

"This beautiful book resonates with a feeling for how things really happen. It will make you smile, stimulate your spirit, chase away your fears. Read it today!"

—JOHN TAYLOR GATTO,
author of *The Underground History of American Education*

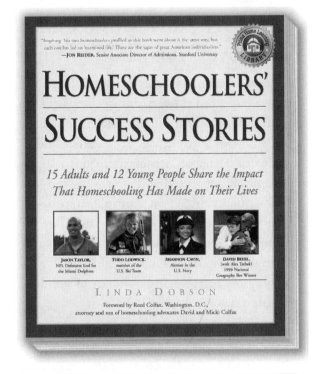

ISBN 0-7615-2255-7 / Paperback
304 pages / U.S. $16.95 / Can. $25.95

PRIMA

To order, call (800) 632-8676 ext. 4444 or visit us online at www.primalifestyles.com

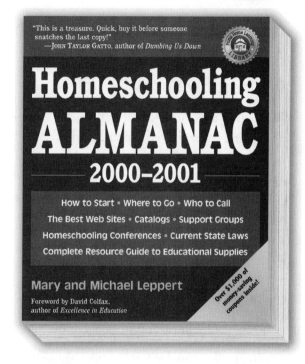

To Order Books

Please send me the following items:

Quantity	Title	Unit Price	Total
_____	**Good Music, Brighter Children**	$ _____	$ _____
_____	**Homeschoolers' Success Stories**	$ _____	$ _____
_____	**Homeschooling Almanac, 2000–2001**	$ _____	$ _____
_____	**Raising Self-Reliant Children in a Self-Indulgent World**	$ _____	$ _____
_____	_____	$ _____	$ _____
_____	_____	$ _____	$ _____
_____	_____	$ _____	$ _____
_____	_____	$ _____	$ _____

Subtotal	$ _____
7.25% Sales Tax (CA only)	$ _____
7% Sales Tax (PA only)	$ _____
5% Sales Tax (IN only)	$ _____
7% G.S.T. Tax (Canada only)	$ _____
Priority Shipping	$ _____
Total Order	$ _____

FREE
Ground Freight
in U.S. and Canada

Foreign and all Priority Request orders:
Call Customer Service
for price quote at 916-787-7000

By Telephone: With American Express, MC, or Visa,
call 800-632-8676, Monday–Friday, 8:30–4:30
www.primapublishing.com

By E-mail: sales@primapub.com

By Mail: Just fill out the information below and send with your remittance to:
Prima Publishing ▪ P.O. Box 1260BK ▪ Rocklin, CA 95677

Name —————————————————————————————

Address ———————————————————————————————

City——————————————————— State ——— ZIP ————

MC/Visa/American Express# ————————————— Exp.————

Check/money order enclosed for $ ——————— Payable to Prima Publishing

Daytime telephone ————————————————————————

Signature ———————————————————————————